MIDDLE CYPRIOT WHITE PAINTED POTTERY

AN ANALYTICAL STUDY OF THE DECORATION

BY

DAVID FRANKEL

STUDIES IN MEDITERRANEAN ARCHAEOLOGY

published by Professor Paul Åström, Södra Vägen 61, S-412 54 Gothenburg, Sweden

Suggested abbreviation for this series: *SIMA*

STUDIES IN MEDITERRANEAN ARCHAEOLOGY
VOL. XLII

MIDDLE CYPRIOT WHITE PAINTED POTTERY

An Analytical Study of the Decoration

BY

DAVID FRANKEL

GÖTEBORG 1974
STUDIES IN MEDITERRANEAN ARCHAEOLOGY
SÖDRA VÄGEN 61, S-412 54 GOTHENBURG, SWEDEN

Printed in Sweden

ISBN 91 85058 60 2

STOCKHOLM 1974
TRYCKSAKSSERVICE AB

CONTENTS

PREFACE

This study is a revised version of an M.A. thesis submitted to the University of Sydney in January 1973. It is based largely on my examination of some 1500 White Painted vessels in Cyprus, England, and Australia, although only those with known provenance have been included in the analyses. Various people have made it possible for me to examine collections, and to include much unpublished material. Most important in this regard are Dr V. Karageorghis, Director of the Department of Antiquities, Cyprus, and Mr K. Nicolaou, Curator of the Cyprus Museum, who gave me access to the large collections in Cyprus. The late Mrs A.G. Pieridou and the staff of the Cyprus Museum who assisted me in locating and extracting the pottery greatly facilitated my research. Mr M. Loulloupis and Mr A. Christodoulou allowed me to use the collection of the Archaeological Survey of Cyprus, which, as with that of the Ashmolean Museum, owes much to the work of Dr H.W. Catling.

Dr Ann Birchall of the Department of Greek and Roman Antiquities in the British Museum, and Dr M. Vickers and Mrs A. Brown of the Ashmolean Museum assisted me in the examination of the collections in their care.

Mrs J.R. Stewart and Dr Basil Hennessy permitted me to use material from the late Professor J.R. Stewart's excavations in Cyprus, at present being prepared for publication.

Professor Alexander Cambitoglou gave me access to the material in the Nicholson Museum, and also made it possible for me to travel to Cyprus and England in 1971 to examine collections there.

The computer programs to calculate percentages and the Jaccard coefficients of similarity were written and run by Mrs Jan Bubb of the Commonwealth Scientific and Industrial Research Organisation, Australia. Dr Doug Jeffrey of the Department of Geography, University of New South Wales. assisted me with the principal components analyses.

This study has benefited from my discussions with staff and students of the Departments of Archaeology and Anthropology, Sydney University, and of the Institute for Classical Studies, Gothenburg University. Miss Judy Birmingham supervised the initial stage of my research; Dr Basil Hennessy the latter stages. Professor Paul Åström has not only undertaken the publication of this work in Studies in Mediterranean Archaeology, but has given me the benefit of his detailed knowledge of Cypriot archaeology by making it possible for me to revise the text in Gothenburg. His personal, as well as his academic, assistance has been very much appreciated.

Finally I would like to thank my wife, Lena, without whose forbearance and support this study could not have been made.

Gothenburg
November 1973

David Frankel

ABBREVIATIONS

Publications:

CCM	Myres, J.L. and Ohnefalsch–Richter, M. *A Catalogue of the Cyprus Museum*, Oxford, 1899.
CVA BM	Smith, A.H. *Corpus Vasorum Antiquorum*, Great Britain 1, British Museum 1, IICa, London, 1925.
CVA Cambridge	Lamb, W. *Corpus Vasorum Antiquorum*, Great Britain 11, Cambridge 2, IICa, Oxford, 1936.
GCM	Dikaios, P. *A Guide to the Cyprus Museum*, 3rd (revised) edition, Nicosia, 1961.
HCC	Myres, J.L. *Handbook of the Cesnola Collection of Antiquities from Cyprus*, New York, 1914.
HNM	*Handbook to the Nicholson Museum*, 2nd edition, Sydney, 1948. (A.D. Trendall and J.R. Stewart).
Kypros	Ohnefalsch–Richter, M. *Kypros, Die Bibel und Homer* London, 1893.
MCBA	Åström, P. *The Middle Cypriote Bronze Age* Lund 1957. (reprinted as *The Swedish Cyprus Expedition* Vol. IV 1 B, Lund, 1972).
Patterns	Catling, H.W. "Patterns of Settlement in Bronze Age Cyprus" *Opuscula Atheniensia* IV: 129–169, 1963.
SCE	Gjerstad, E. *et al. The Swedish Cyprus Expedition. Finds and Results of the Excavations in Cyprus 1927–31*, Vols. I – IV, Stockholm and Lund, 1934–72.
SPC	Gjerstad, E. *Studies on Prehistoric Cyprus*, Uppsala, 1926.

Other publications are referred to by author and date. For a list of these see the bibliography.

Museums:

AM	Ashmolean Museum, Oxford.
BM	British Museum, London.
CM	Cyprus Museum, Nicosia.
CMF	Famagusta District Museum, Cyprus.
CML	Larnaca District Museum, Cyprus.
NM	Nicholson Museum, Sydney.

Names of Sites and Groups

Sites are referred to by the village or locality name. The full names are given in Appendix I, with a preliminary list which indicates the short names of the groups used in the analyses and general discussion (see also Chapter 2.1 and figure 2).

In some of the lists and figures these names are often further abbreviated, but are readily recognisable, and may also be identified by the group number.

Some of the most commonly used abbreviations are:

Ay. Iak.	Ayios Iakovos	(group 23)
Ay. P.	Ayia Paraskevi	(group 24)
Gal.	Galinoporni	(group 30)
Kalops.	Kalopsidha	(group 31)
L.	Lapithos	(groups 1–20)
Palaeal.	Palaealona	(group 41)
Pol.	Politico	(groups 42 and 43)
T.	Tomb number	

LIST OF TABLES

LIST OF FIGURES

CHAPTER 1

INTRODUCTION TO THE STUDY

1.1.The Historical and Theoretical Background

This study is an attempt to gain insights into the relationships between different regions in Cyprus during the Middle Bronze Age, using the decorative patterns on White Painted Pottery. Although largely independent of previous classifications of the material the earlier studies and conclusions provide the broad background for this specific analysis. In this chapter the theoretical and methodological bases of the present study are discussed in relation to the general pattern of Cypriot prehistoric studies, and several problems of more general interest are considered.

Despite the large scale but unorganised activities of di Cesnola and others earlier in the nineteenth century,[1] the first real contribution toward a prehistory of Cyprus was the work of Sandwith,[2] who in 1871 separated out the major pottery types, and arranged the cemeteries into five classes on the basis of the different wares found in each. The first two of these classes of cemetery were defined by the presence of Red Polished or of Base-Ring and White-Slip Wares, and which are therefore equivalent to earlier and later Bronze Age periods. At this time the different pottery styles were associated with ethnic or racial groups rather than interpreted in terms of a general technological scheme.[3]

Although adoption of this basic classification was slow at first,[4] with the larger body of well documented material from the various excavations carried out by the Cyprus Exploration Fund,[5] by Ohnefalsch-Richter,[6] and by Myres[7] in the last decade of the nineteenth century, the general pattern of development of what was now being referred to as the "Bronze Age" was becoming more clearly recognised.

The general paradigm of Stone, Bronze, and Iron Ages had been developed in Denmark earlier in the century,[8] and had become generally accepted in other areas as a universal evolutionary scheme. Before the end of the century Myres and Ohnefalsch-Richter had begun the subdivision of the Cypriot Bronze Age,[9] at least with a recognition of earlier and later tombs, using techniques which are clear from Myres' analysis of his 1894 excavations[10] (fig. 1a). This analysis was based on the identification of the major types of pottery - a general technological grouping - and the presence or absence of these *wares* in the tombs. A simple seriation of the tombs on this basis is presented in tabular form by Myres, refining both the types and the methods outlined by Sandwith, and allowing the closer subdivision of the material, as well as setting an important precedent for later work on Cypriot prehistory. Other attempts at subdividing the material more formally were made,[11] but the scheme developed by Myres and published in more detail in 1914,[12] remained unchanged until Gjerstad began his work on the island in 1923.[13]

During the first twenty years of the twentieth century many developments had taken place in archaeological method. Stratigraphic excavation was now a more refined technique, and interest was being taken in the changing proportions of the different pottery types from stratified sequences. Flinders Petrie had developed his method of Sequence Dating in terms of proportional occurrence of the different types in tomb groups,[14] and the use of seriation and comparative stratigraphy was becoming more common all over the archaeological world.[15] Concepts of cultural evolution were now influenced by the ninefold division of the Minoan Bronze Age made by Arthur Evans in 1905, and which formed the basis of his later full publication of the Knossos excavations.[16] This scheme was soon adopted on the Greek mainland,[17] and quickly came into general use.

It is against this background that the work of Einar Gjerstad, a student from an analytical Scandinavian school still influenced by the work of Montelius, should be understood.

Gjerstad continued and developed all the aspects of Cypriot prehistory that Myres had worked on, with topographical and analytical studies.[18] The major new contribution was the stratigraphic excavation of three Bronze Age sites, (Alambra, Kalopsidha, Nikolidhes) which gave him overlapping series of stratified deposits. The pottery from these sites and from the larger number of tomb-groups now available was analysed more closely than had been possible before, and divisions within the basic *wares* were recognised, and generally taken to have some chronological meaning. The proportional occurrence of these newly defined *wares* enabled not only a comparative stratigraphy of the settlement sites to be drawn up, but also supplied Gjerstad with a basis for the better seriation of the tomb groups[19] (fig. 1b, 1d; cf. fig. 1c). Although the shapes and decoration of the pottery were described, emphasis was placed on the technological developments, as a chronological factor permitting the grouping of the tomb material made this aspect more attractive.

Instead of following the example set by Petrie in his original Sequence Dating, Gjerstad chose rather to continue the trend toward following the Minoan-based subdivisions, a practice of which Myres was critical,[20] especially as the material did not fit the scheme well. This adoption of the 3x3 subdivision of periods has remained the basis for Cypriot chronological studies, although the criteria for the periods have changed.[21]

Although Myres was essentially in favour of the methods and general conclusions reached by Gjerstad, he does enter an important plea for caution regarding the use of material improperly excavated or published for such statistical analyses.[22]

Following the basis work of Gjerstad, the Swedish Cyprus Expedition (1927-31)[23] enlarged and developed the systems outlined earlier. Although the compartmentalised archaeology had begun to break down with the development of the "culture" concept by V.G. Childe,[24] the Swedish Cyprus Expedition continued with the older tradition, refining the subdivisions using more sophisticated seriations of their new tomb material still based on the same stratified sequences as Gjerstad's earlier work.[25] The statistics for each tomb are clearly presented as the basis for its dating and some summary tables were presented.[26] The classification of the pottery continued in the chronologically interpreted ware-series, although this too, was further refined.[27]

More attention to shape and decoration of the pottery was a development of the work in the 1930s by Dikaios and Stewart, mainly based on their excavations at Vounous.[28] While Dikaios applied his energies to the earlier periods[29] Stewart continued to develop a more detailed typology of the Early Bronze Age Material,[30] with an intricate system of classification by shape now separated from the technological *ware* classification which had been the base of the previous systems. This new classification began to treat the material in terms of the individual pot rather than on the level of the tomb-group, and allowed the close association of the different tombs into even smaller time units, although the rigid tripartite units of the Swedish system could not be followed. The dating by proportional occurrence of the different wares became less important and less applicable as the nature of the wares and their relationships were better understood. The relationships between different regions remained a major problem, and Stewart saw variations as regional rather than temporal[31] and attempted to introduce a concept of cultures into the Cypriot situation.

While Stewart was finalising this study of the Early Bronze Age material, Åström was engaged on a study of the Middle Cypriot Period,[32] working more closely within the Swedish tradition. Although the shape (*type*) is fairly important, the classification is still based on the technological *wares*, which are redefined and developed.[33]

The stratified material used by Gjerstad remains important and the seriation of the tomb groups is still the basis of Åström's dating, although now the first appearance of a new ware is used to mark the beginning of a new period, rather than the less fixed divisions previously employed.[34] Åström also added the important classification of *style* (cutting across the *ware* system, and based primarily on decoration) and the formal similarity of individual pots to one another to give more specific cross–datings. It should however be remembered that these individual correlations do not afford a very close dating for the remainder of the tomb-content, especially with multiple burial tombs. The *style* groups have been developed further by Åström in other studies,[35] and the redefined wares and styles again analysed in terms of the Kalopsidha stratigraphic sequence in order to give more backing to the evolutionary sequence of styles now suggested.[36] In these works the proportional occurrences of the wares continue to be used but the tabular presentation is intented rather as a summary of a chronological model than as a method of arriving at a chronological arrangement of the material (fig. 1e; cf. fig. 1f).[37]

Other problems connecting with the use of Åström's classification will be discussed below (p.6).

Having traced briefly the bases of the Cypriot classifications and chronology, it may be worthwhile to consider the nature of this arrangement of the material, and to assess its meaning and limitations.

The basic divisions which derive from the 3x3 system are in general treated as *periods* (or units of time or contemporaneity) whereas in fact they should be seen rather as *stages* or units of cultural similarity.[38] When material comes from one particular locality, stages are often equivalent to periods, but where correlations between different areas are undertaken, this does not necessarily apply. A further danger in dealing with stages is the common assumption of a universal overall pattern of cultural evolution, where the same sequence is represented in all areas. In the Cypriot situation this particular problem is important in assessing the results of the surface surveys, where the absence of pottery characteristic of a particular *stage* in one part of the island has been taken to demonstrate depopulation during the *period* rather than a regional difference.[39]

The relationships which have been determined between the different groups of material in Cyprus should continue to be critically examined to ensure that they are in fact synchronous, and not just homotaxial.[40] General solutions to the basic problems of relative dating may be found in the use of trade items, in the general similarity of the groups, and in the correlation of other material to a master sequence established by stratigraphy.[41]

The main basis for the cultural periodisation of the Cypriot material is the stratigraphy of a few sites. Although the Late Cypriot Period is now better served with evidence from Myrtou Pighades,[42] Enkomi,[43] and elsewhere[44] to supplement the sequences from Nikolidhes and Nitovikla, the Early and Middle Cypriot Periods still rely on the Alambra and Kalopsidha excavations.[45] The more recent excavations at Kalopsidha do not significantly alter, although they add some detail to, the basic stratigraphic sequence determined by Gjerstad at that site.[46]

It is unfortunate that while most of the stratigraphic evidence for the earlier periods comes from the eastern areas of the island, about half of the tomb material is from the North Coast, and about a third from the western and central areas. The correlation of this master sequence with the tomb seriations must therefore be somewhat suspect, and a general consideration of the problems associated with an independent seriation of the tomb-groups may be of value, although not of direct relevance to the main theme of this study.

Seriation is basically a method of assessing chronological relationships between groups of material on the basis of their similarity (similarity seriation), or on the basis of their development (evolutionary seriation).[47] Most of the Cypriot dating has been carried out by fairly simple calculation of relative frequencies of different wares, the wares themselves originally being seen as developing within an evolutionary seriation sequence. Recently more sophisticated statistical methods have been developed in other areas which give a more accurate assessment of the similarities between groups of data.[48]

The underlying assumption in the seriations is that the more similar an object or group of objects is to another object or group, the closer they are in time. It assumes synchrony on the basis of a homotaxial relationship. Dethlefsen and Deetz have shown in a controlled study[49] the possible spatial distortions which can affect the interpretation of seriations, and other questions of the validity of the method have been discussed by several scholars, most recently by

Dunnell[50] who has laid down some general conditions which should be observed in applying the technique.[51]

1. All groups must be of equal duration.
   It is clear from any analysis of the Cypriot material that with the development of the practice of multiple burial in the tombs the time span of a tomb-group is never a constant or easily determined factor.[52] It is only in those rare cases where smaller burial-groups can be isolated that any precision is possible, and where finer discrimination between groups could be possible; but even here there are too few examples to be of value, and so the Cypriot material does not meet this condition.
2. Groups should be of the same cultural tradition.
   This is a relative condition. Within the Cypriot Bronze Age there is a certain general cultural tradition, but it has been recognised for a long time that major regional differences exist. Comparison between these cultural areas must therefore be suspect, and this condition affects the seriations as well as the stratigraphic correlations within the island.
3. All groups should be from the same local area.
   Again this is a relative term, and is related to the second condition, as most of the culture-areas conform to geographical distribution. Even within a small area such as Cyprus the geographical factor may apply, and questions of time-lag and cultural retardation will affect the results of the seriations.

The major problem is that of controlling the spatial distribution of the material, a factor which is relevant to the second and third conditions.[53] This may be overcome by the use of cross-dating based on imported objects. This is a technique which has been used to a greater extent in the more recent Cypriot studies, where chronological relationships between particular groups are established by locating in them vessels which are so similar in many characteristics as to be certainly the work of a particular craftsman or workshop. The finer dating of the Middle Cypriot Period is often based on this method,[54] which of course has its own limits of accuracy, mainly in the assumption of the contemporaneity of most objects in a group, and an equivalent life-span of pre-burial use of both the objects.[55] This method of cross dating is of course the basic method of correlating the Cypriot sequences with those of other countries. Despite the limitations of the methods, the broad chronological arrangement of the Cypriot Bronze Age can be regarded as reasonably secure.

The relative dating by any of the similarity (seriation) techniques is dependent on the original selection of the attributes or types used in the analysis.[56] Dunnell touches on this in his discussion of possible controls on spatial variation,[57] and it is recognised to a certain extent in other studies of chronological methods.[58] The consideration of this point raises the important question of the basic nature of variation. Although often approached from the point of view of the meaning of similarity,[59] L.R. Binford has provided a useful scheme for considering the nature of variations,[60] and the factors involved in the differences between objects - "culture is multivariate and its operation is to be understood in terms of many causally relevant variables which may function independently or in varying combinations. It is our task to isolate these causative factors and to seek regular, stable, and predictable relationships between them".[61]

Formal variation in pottery may be due to morphological or decorative variation, each of which has two dimensions – technical and design – which affect the way in which the shape is executed. Cross-cutting categories of primary and secondary function are used to place this model into a socio-political situation, affected by the basic use for which the vessel is designed, and the particular effect of the social context of the object.[62] Although the particular object will have different meaning, use or function in different social situations and to different people in the same situation,[63] these variations are of less immediate importance to this study than the understanding of the causes of the formal variation. Even so the meaning and significance of the pottery as trade items, or in the context of the funeral where they function as a symbol of social articulation, is of interest.

The major divisions outlined by Binford may be equated with the stylistic-morphological variables recognised elsewhere,[64] and which have been seen to have different interpretive potential. With the Cypriot situation, the trend toward the isolation of particular *styles* is, generally speaking, a movement toward the style-variable defined by Binford, although they are not so deliberately chosen to give such specific results.

Variation between objects may therefore be seen to

be due to a number of factors, which should if possible be separated, in order to determine how the different processes are operating in each situation. Another way to define the causes of variation is to see them in simpler terms as due to temporal, spatial, or social factors acting on the technological, functional, and decorative aspects of the objects.

The technological variation of Cypriot pottery has a fairly strong correlation to the temporal factor, although because of the problems associated with the dating the precise significance of the spatial dimension cannot be assessed. The decoration has in the past been associated with spatial rather than temporal factors, although again this is not clearly distinct as there is some link between the technological changes and the designs. The diagram below gives an indication of the relationships between the types of variation and their present interpretation in regard to Cypriot White Painted Pottery.

CONTINGENCY TABLE OF CULTURAL VARIATION[65]

Relationships to Cypriot White Painted Pottery
Classifications.

	Primary functional variation	Secondary functional variation
Techno–morphological	No correlation	temporal interpretation of changes to new *wares*
Morphological design	most variation explained by this	minor variation as temporal or spatial
Decorative technique	no correlation	slight changes linked to change in *wares*
Decorative designs	vague correlation	mainly spatial - some temporal interpretations

If it is possible to isolate only one of the types of variation then it may be easier to assess which factors are operating to cause the variations, than is the case where the classification involves the consideration of many types of variation. Similarly, if it is possible to control to some extent the factors causing variation, then the particular significance of the one type of variation may be made much more clear.

The time-variable is the hardest to control. Although precise dating is not normally possible, it is fairly easy to use a broader time-span, and to consider only material from within that period. As most periods are defined by the presence of a particular type or set of types, it is a somewhat circular argument to assess the meaning of the types in terms of such periods. Nevertheless, as each type, broadly classified, does have only a certain time-span, the consideration of that one type is a consideration of that particular period. Divisions within this period are possible, but not essential.

Spatial variation is easier to control. By using only material with known provenance the spatial distribution is fixed, and interpretations may be made in terms of different distributions with some confidence.

The use of pottery of only the one ware or technological type controls the variations due to technology, and most of the primary functional variation can be controlled by considering only those attributes which have little or no relation to the primary function of the vessel. The style-variable (designs) is fairly independent of primary function and within the White Painted wares the techniques of decoration are fairly constant. By considering only the one set of attributes of the general type with its limited time span, and using material from known provenance the results can be regarded as reflecting secondary functional variation and can be more easily interpreted in terms of social relationships.

The classification of decorative styles gives a reflection of a social network and intercommunication within areas, and a measure of the relationship between populations.[66] The full interpretation of these distributions in terms of organised culture groups must eventually use several different artifact-types and sets of attributes[67] and the variations can be analysed in terms of general models derived from geographical trend analyses.[68]

Style-zones can be established, and when considered in relation to each other may give some possibility of assessing not only the traditions involved, but also to some extent the nature of the interaction between areas.[69] Although *traditions* are more commonly used than *interaction spheres* as defined by Binford (these being rather more an assessment of the socio-political and economic significance of interchange), it is possible to see the approach of scholars such as Merrillees as one which seeks to define the political spheres within Cyprus,[70] or the recognition of economic relationships as in the work of Catling,[71] in these terms.

This study is an attempt to distinguish between areas on the basis of stylistic variables, and by assessing the relationship between these areas to reach some conclusions regarding the social articulation between them.[72] Similarity is taken to be a reflection of social rather than temporal or simple geographical relationships, the material being amenable to the application of the idea of interaction spheres, albeit of a social rather than economic nature.[73]

Some form of classification lies behind all archaeological work. Those variables which are considered important will, as has been discussed, determine the meaning of any correlations observed.[74]

Generally typological studies take as their basis the individual object. The manner in which objects are described and classified can vary, making use of different attributes in different ways. Many systems attempt to define types or classes of material on the basis of a great many variables and so present an overall classification. Although this has the advantage of showing the relationships between different aspects of the objects, it confuses interpretation by mixing up the types of variables. There has been a recent movement toward the establishment of statistically defined groups where a large number of variables are considered, and the clustering of certain attributes is taken to reflect a clustering of taxonomic value.[75]

Alongside this development there has been the interest in the assessment of the meaning of the clusters and of the variables,[76] and toward the creation of logical codes to describe the material.[77] The basis of the logical code is that it allows each attribute to be considered independently of the other attributes, and makes correlation between different classes of attributes (or different types of variation) possible.

In the present classification of the Middle Cypriot pottery[78] the typology is far from the logical code. Not only do the same particular attributes have different numbers when in different wares but the fact that each attribute in such an hierarchical system is dependent on other attributes and makes assessment of their independent variation impossible. The types of variation are mixed in the classification, and the material is differentiated on the basis of any or all of the variables without consideration of their different significances.

Ware which is the technological variable is of prime importance, and is generally associated with temporal change. Within the broad ware classes the subdivisions are on the basis of shape, which give the *type*. Some features of shape are considered of greater taxonomic importance than others, and are given greater weight, so that handles are given more importance than shape of neck or mouth, and so on. The variation in the different parts of the vessels may have different meaning in different cases, so that some mouth and rim variation may be due to primary functional variation, and other differences due to secondary functional variation – affected by either time or spatial separation. No attempt is made to allow for this possibility, and the whole classification system is designed primarily for the identification of like vessels and for general historical interpretation rather than for a particular assessment of one aspect. In other words it is a *taxonomic* classification, while that of the present study is *analytic*.[79] – two systems which serve different ends.

The more recent development of the *styles* already begun in *MCBA* does provide the possibility for a better interpretation of the material, especially in terms of the distribution of the various styles.[80] Most of these styles have a purely decorative definition, although they are defined in the overall *ware* system. Some of the styles may be related to particular shapes of vessels, but in general they form an independent classification. Perhaps the least satisfactory of these styles is the "string-hole style" which uses an attribute, at least originally functional, as a decorative element, although this may be seen as an attempt to define one *mode*.[81] The continued refinement of the style as a base for more precise relations between groups is a valuable development, although it is still tied to the concept of classification and identification of individual vessels. Together with a more logical re-coding of the shape attributes, it will provide valuable information regarding secondary functional variation of all types, although, given the lack of standardisation of the pottery, the adequate classification of shape will continue to prove extremely difficult.

Merrillees[82] has recently discussed these problems in a general critique of the Swedish technologically-based classification, and has expressed dissatisfaction with the *ware* groups as they can neither be adequately differentiated nor effectively interpreted. Merrillees recognises the greater value of the design-based style classification, and attempts to develop a regionally-defined style system, mainly in regard to the Karpass material, and including decoration on both White Painted and Red-on-Black and allied wares.

A major difference between the present study and most previous work on the Cypriot material, and also most other archaeology, is that the *type* is not used as the basic classificatory unit. Generally classifications are based on the individual objects which are divided into a set of types. The similarity between groups of material is then determined on the basis of the relative frequency of these types.[83] In this study this intermediate step is left out. Instead the tomb-group is the basis of the classification - not the individual object. The concept and definition of types is complex and difficult,[84] and by bypassing the need to interpose this preliminary classification between the recognition of the attributes and the description of the assemblage, a clearer picture of the nature of the assemblage may be obtained. This is especially relevant in the Cypriot context, where types are very difficult to define in the extremely varied material. In other words, the assemblage is described, and different assemblages are compared, directly in terms of the attributes rather than in terms of the relative frequency of clusters of attributes on individual objects in the assemblages.[85]

Although the calculation of the relative popularity of combinations of attributes (designs) on individual pots within each assemblage (tomb-group) would have been of interest, this was not possible in the present study. This would have given another measure of the differences between vessels or areas, in terms closer to the normal stylistic classifications, but the results from the direct assessment of the relative popularity of designs in tombs gives a precise and more readily interpreted result.

The general method used was to consider only complete vessels from reasonably sized groups of known provenance,[86] and to assess the proportional occurrence of the designs in terms of the number of vessels in each group. The relationship between the different groups is then calculated on the basis of this data.

For the reasons outlined above, only a limited amount of the available material from the period has been used. Only pots of the White Painted Ware series have been used, and the differences between different wares within the series have been ignored. Although some general correlations between certain wares and designs is possible the difficulties in classifying the wares and the meaning of these differences would be too great to make that study worthwhile. Shape too has been left out of the major analyses, although again there are some general correlations possible between designs and shapes (see below Chapter 2.4 and Appendix 2) which have been considered in a general way. Primary functional considerations are therefore only treated in so far as they affect the decoration. The limitation of the material considered to the White Painted Wares, and the fact that the material is all from tombs, makes interpretations of functional variation between areas in economic terms very difficult.

This study is therefore a very specific analysis of selected attributes of one class of pottery, in an attempt to remove most sources of variation and to allow confident assessment of the results.

The designs themselves are fairly easily differentiated and recognition of the designs is fairly easy (see below Chapter 2.2 and fig. 4). The choice of the decoration variable rather than any other was made not only for the general considerations outlined above, but also because this aspect of the pottery was more readily observed from illustrations and the published descriptions, and also because this variable is more likely to be a sensitive indicator of any cultural differences than functional or technological variations.[87] The known Cypriot situation seemed to indicate a correlation between design and regional distribution and the comparative situations indicated this as a normal state.

Considering the large number of design elements and the even larger number of possible combinations, it is clear that the variation between different manufacturing areas should be definite, and have great interpetative potential, especially given the controls on function and technique. This type of close study of particular attributes has been attempted on material within sites, or small regions,[88] and similar results could be expected and have been suggested in the Cypriot context. Besides archaeological studies, relationships between design structure and social interaction have been documented in ethnographic situations, indicating a strong correlation between decorative style and social groupings.[89]

The analysis of similarity between objects or groups is now generally undertaken by one or other of the standard statistical methods using computerised techniques. Various forms of similarity coefficient and correlation coefficient have been applied in different studies, and there has been considerable discussion of the statistical significance of different methods, especially in the ordering or clustering of data.[90] Most early studies made use of a simple linear ordering of the data, reflecting one dimension of change, generally considered to be along the time scale. Various attempts to define other types of variation have been made, and interest in the different methods of linking groups has developed.[91] The simpler analyses have been often replaced with more sophisticated techniques, but given the controls on the data used, much valuable interpretation can be made using any of the methods.

The main analyses in this study make use of factor analysis in order to simplify the complex pattern or relationships between the variables, and a simple clustering technique which gives a measure of the relationships between areas again where there is a complex distribution pattern of variables in the cultural assemblages.[92]

In the present study, as in all archaeological work, some conscious or unconscious use is made of analogies to past and present situations. Analogy can be a dangerous tool, but if used with caution it is a valuable one. The general problems associated with the use of analogies have received much attention during the last few years,[93] and need not be discussed in detail here, although a digression on analogy in the Cypriot context may raise some interesting points.

Cyprus is fairly well served with information regarding the modern and recent rural situation with the valuable study of the land-use pattern by Christodoulou,[94] which also contains much incidental information on Cypriot "life-ways". There is also a wealth of material on Medieval and earlier historical periods, both for demography, economics, and ethnography, all of which are now being studied more systematically by the Society for Cypriot Studies and the Cyprus Research Centre in Nicosia. Studies of present day Cypriot folk pottery are well advanced with the major work of Hampe and Winter,[95] together with other studies.[96] The use of recent potters' practices as an aid to interpreting the ancient material has been a feature of Cypriot archaeology for a long time, but generally this has been in somewhat unsystematic form.[97]

Most of the analogies used in interpreting prehistoric Cypriot life are rather loose. Although based on the intimate knowledge of recent Cypriots, the unsystematic application of social, religious, psychological, and economic behaviour patterns to the ancient societies cannot be accepted.[98] Cyprus has undergone several major changes in population as well as fluctuations in political and social organisation together with many changes in the economic and technological bases. It is therefore unreasonable to use the modern Cypriot as a perfect analogy for the Bronze Age society, although some features may indicate a degree of continuity. Certainly the recent material does give general ideas of the behaviour of some people in the Cypriot situation (although the ecology has changed too) and is therefore of use.

Use may also be made of comparative situations in regard to specific features of social, technological, or economic behaviour patterns. General considerations of the factors involved, for example, in the stability and innovation in pottery manufacture are relevant to the interpretation of the Cypriot material. Summaries of the ethnographic data suggest the wide variety of factors which may be involved in the distribution and manufacture of pottery and the arrangements in trading networks.[99]

In a wider context the ethnographic data related to conservatism and patterns of manufacture within a narrow culturally accepted norm is an aid to reconstructing possible Cypriot situations,[100] and the tendency for complex features such as decoration to diverge in neighbouring manufacturing centres,[101] may be seen in our material. Data on the relationship of individuals and groups to particular styles of pottery is also of use.[102]

Another minor problem which affects the Cypriot material is the relationship between the tomb material and settlement pottery. The cemetery evidence need not be equivalent to the proportional occurence of types in the settlements[103] although this cannot be shown at Kalopsidha.[104] It has been suggested that the pottery in tombs was made specifically for funerary use,[105] although this is in general unlikely. Some of the very small pots and unusual shapes may have been made purely for burial use,[106] but this need not have been the case with the larger vessels. Merrillees has argued that the handles of large jugs could not have taken the weight of the vessels when they were full,[107] however the jugs need not have been carried by the handles[108] which would be used rather to tip the vessel when it was set on the ground.

From most excavations and the work of the Cyprus Survey there seems to be little difference between the cemetery and settlement evidence, although the relative proportions of different shapes cannot be assumed, making economic interpretation suspect. In this particular study, the manufacture of the pottery specifically for burial would not alter its relationship to the locality, or the relationships between localities, as the same factors affecting domestic pottery manufacture would apply.

In short, this study takes as its basis an attitude toward the material which derives from the concept of the *conjunctive approach*.[109] Interest is in an interpretation of factors operating within the cultural system, developing a trend in Cypriot archaeology toward a better understanding of the island's internal structure seen in the studies of settlement pattern and economic relationships by Catling,[110] and the political models of Merrillees,[111] although these are not based on a deliberate organisation of the material. Islands form useful closed systems which give a good opportunity for the investigation of internal articulation,[112] and in this work one set of relationships is investigated.

Ideally all the material should be considered in all different ways, but it seems reasonable to select a particular class of material or attribute mode to be analysed in order to understand its particular significance.[113] Once the specific studies of the different attributes and types of variables within each artifact class are completed these various dimensions can be correlated into a composite model of the prehistoric situation.

1.2. Geographical and Archaeological Considerations

The geography of Cyprus is well known, and the specific problems of the prehistoric situation have been discussed by Catling.[114] The general work by Christodoulou[115] contains basic material for a broad analysis of the pre-industrial cultural geography of the island.

Communications and suitability of land for settlement are of importance in this study, and so a brief note on these features is not out of place.

The Kyrenia Range, which divides the North Coast from the Central Plain, can be crossed in several places, either to the West via Vasilia and Myrtou; through the pass above Kyrenia, or to the north of Lefkoniko. Further east access to the Karpass is possible by way of Phlamoudhi or toward Komi Kebir.

Within the Central Plain access between the sites may have been by way of the river valleys, as suggested by Catling,[116] or across the hard kafkalla (calcrete) plateaus, if these were not too densely overgrown. Although Catling lays stress on the importance of the valleys for communications, the siting of settlements along the rivers has the simpler and more immediate explanation in the presence of water and better alluvial soils.[117] The relationship of settlement to river and trade routes is not a simple one, and the river valleys themselves are difficult to move along.[118] Although more amenable to traffic along their length, rivers in Cyprus were rather a barrier to movement and condusive to isolation of villages.[119]

The location of the main copper sources on the slopes of the Troodos Mountains[120] is a major factor affecting the direction and nature of contacts across the island, as well as the location of some centres of settlement.

The nature of the vegetation in the Middle Cypriot Period is an important but difficult problem. Stewart[121] has suggested heavy forest on the North and South Coasts, and a scrubby vegetation in the Central

Plain, perhaps with marshes to the East and West. The Pasture Research Survey[122] included a map of hypothetical climax vegetation zones, which may give some impression of the situation before human settlement on the island. There is little likelihood that the lowlands were ever covered with dense forest[123] and several cycles of clearing and regeneration of the original forest have been noted.[124]

Any consideration of the extent to which vegetation proved a bar to communication and settlement should take into account the important effects of fire (either deliberate or accidental) in clearing bushland, especially in a dry climate.[125] The effects of locusts and goats in keeping vegetation below the climax should also not be ignored.

Another important ecological factor is the condition of the wetter marshy coastal areas around Morphou and Salamis. The saline soils and high water table[126] would have made these areas less attractive for farming, and one should also consider the presence of malaria in the low lying swampy areas. The increasingly dry conditions and the lowering of the sea level during the second millenium B.C. would have had an effect on the frequency of malaria, and would have allowed greater settlement in the Eastern Mesaoria.[127] This factor may account to some extent for the spread of sites toward the East Coast during the Middle and Late Cypriot Periods.

The general nature of the material of the Middle Cypriot Bronze Age is described at length by Åström in *MCBA* and is summarised in various general works.[128] The beginning of this cultural stage is defined by the appearance of White Painted II Ware, or associated pottery; and its end by the new range of White-Slip and Base-Ring Wares. There is no sharp break between the periods so defined, or between the subdivisions within the period. The series of White Painted Wares develops from the technique of the Red Polished tradition, and the relatively rare White Painted I Ware. The differences between the White Painted Wares are not absolute, and are described by Åström; the Red Polished pottery is dealt with by Stewart.[129]

The length of the period is difficult to establish, but is generally taken to be no more than 200 or 250 years, and possibly less.[130] Its approximate date relative to other areas is fixed by imports and exports both to the Levant and to Crete.[131] There has been a general tendency by both Stewart and Åström to lower the absolute dates of the end of the Early Cypriot and of subsequent periods.[132] Renfrew, in his recent analysis of the Aegean and Cretan material, suggests earlier dates for those areas, and this, together with other evidence may indicate that the Middle Cypriot Period should begin considerably earlier than 1800 B.C.[133] If the period is taken to be short, and with a swift end, this earlier date would disrupt the dating of the end of the period, which is generally considered to be in the sixteenth century B.C.[134]

The present study is not concerned with this complex problem, although the conclusions regarding the short time-span of the popularity of White Painted Pottery will have some bearing on it. Considering the recent discussion of the mainland material, it may be suggested that the higher dating is to be preferred, and that the end of the Middle Cypriot Period is not to be easily defined by the simultaneous appearance of any particular set of new wares, but is rather a slow and gradual change.[135]

The overall settlement pattern is largely dependent on chance finds together with the thorough and detailed survey work by the Archaeological Survey of Cyprus in selected areas.[136] The general results of this work and its implications for this period have been dealt with by Catling.[137] Despite the problems associated with the use of uneven sampling and with survey material in general a reasonable picture of the situation is apparent. Catling suggests a movement, during the Middle Cypriot Period, away from the North Coast, and some of the areas important earlier in the centre of the island also lose their significance. There is a corresponding growth of the settlements toward the East and in the Karpass, as well as in other areas. This Eastward movement may be facilitated by the ecological changes indicated above, as well as the changing economic orientation of the regions.[138] Although not all of the areas of major settlement are represented in the sample of material studied here, the general coverage of those areas of the island where White Painted Pottery was used, is reasonable (cf. Chapter 2.1, Fig. 2).

The Middle Cypriot Period is often seen as transitional between the Early Cypriot Cultures and the more unified Late Cypriot Period, with its new economic structure.[139] The settlement pattern orientation and the nature of the material have been taken to indicate a gradual breakdown of an earlier strong regionalism, a trend which is developed to a greater extent in the Late Cypriot Period.[140]

Åström and Catling[141] interpret the development of fortified sites in the Middle Cypriot Period as related to internal unrest, influenced by a growth in population and possibly aggravated by drought. Some of these walled sites (for example Ayios Sozomenos, *Barsak*) seem too large to be primarily connected with defence, and may be interpreted rather as large animal enclosures.[142] The site mentioned, conveniently placed on the edge of the Kafkalla scarp overlooking the rich Yialias and Alikos Potamos River Valleys, may reflect the pastoral aspect of an economy based on the exploitation of these two distinct ecological zones.

In general, however, the interpretation of the social conditions from the presence of these fortified sites is a reasonable one; but there is no need to postulate any constant or large scale warfare, although there may have been some degree of tension.[143] These sites could have been related mainly to the protection of the agricultural land, with several different villages, or units exploiting different resource zones, combining for this purpose. The function of these fortified sites must have had some influence on developing the relationships within the protected area at the expense of the connections with outside groups.

In spite of the differences, there is a fairly high degree of similarity in the overall material culture and behaviour patterns between most parts of the island (with the Karpass perhaps excepted). Much the same type of pottery was in use, and similar burial practices as well as cult objects[144] indicate common religious symbolism and activities, if not beliefs. There is some movement of individual objects between different areas, which, with the trade in copper,[145] indicates other communication across the pattern of agricultural regionalism.[146]

There is no good evidence of the context of manufacture of the pottery. It is generally assumed, although not discussed in detail, that the pottery was produced in fairly organised workshops.[147] There is no good reason, however, to assume that it was not generally manufactured by women, operating, perhaps, in close conjunction with one another, but within a basic household tradition. To view the craft in terms of artistic development and inspiration of the potters[148] is to ignore its more important relationship to the social context of manufacture. The pottery is best seen in terms of a traditional craft, with the potters repeating standard motifs not because of a particular Cypriot conservatism,[149] but in a normal behaviour pattern seen in most similar situations of local pottery manufacture.[150]

The aesthetic analysis of the White Painted Pottery either reveals a ferment of artistic ideas in a climate of political unrest.[151] or a regretable deterioration due to the lack of outside stimulation.[152] The measurement of the relative quality of art is difficult, if not impossible,[153] and the matter will not be persued here.

A relatively secure basis on which to work has been provided by earlier studies, and it is now possible to attempt finer and more specialised studies of particular problems. Within the broad picture of regionalism and commercial contact in the Middle Cypriot Period there has been little precise analysis of the relationships between sites, or contacts between areas. This study is an attempt to fill in this area, by the particular study of the decoration on the White Painted pottery.

NOTES

CHAPTER 1

1. di Cesnola 1877, 1885–1903; *HCC;* xiii-xx.
2. Sandwith 1880.
3. Sandwith 1880; 128.
4. It was not used by Murray in the introduction to di Cesnola 1885–1903; or by Dümmler (1886); or in the first reports of the Cyprus Exploration Fund (Gardner *et al.* 1888).
5. Gardner *et al.* 1888, 1890, 1891.
6. *Kypros.*
7. Myres 1897; *CCM*: 1–12.
8. Daniel 1968: 90–109; Rowe 1962a: 129–30.
9. *CCM.*
10. Myres 1897.
11. Ohnefalsch–Richter 1899; SPC:262 n.3.
12. *HCC*
13. *SPC*: 262.
14. Petrie 1899, 1901: 4–8.
15. These techniques were in use while Gjerstad worked at Asine in 1922 (Frödin and Persson 1938: 201–2). Compare also the use of comparative stratigraphy by Schmidt in America and later in Anatolia (Schmidt 1928; von der Osten and Schmidt 1930).
16. Evans, A.J. 1905, 1921.
17. Wace and Blegen 1916–18: 176; Renfrew 1972: 53–4.
18. Gjerstad 1924, *SPC.*
19. *SPC*: 263. The data presented by Gjerstad (*SPC*: 273) is shown in fig. 1b, and is drawn out as a histogram in fig. 1c. In this diagram the length of each bar indicates the relative proportion of each stratum which is of each ware. The changing proportions of each ware form "double lenticular ontogeny curves" showing their introduction, growth in importance, and decline in popularity.
20. Myres 1926: 289.
21. *MCBA*: 172; Stewart 1962: 210. It has also been suggested that the periods should be renamed (Catling 1966: 36; cf. Thomas 1967: 79, chart II: 6a).
22. Myres 1926: 210.
23. *SCE* Vols I–III.
24. Daniel 1971: 148.
25. Sjöqvist 1940: 99. There was now also the stratification from Nitovikla for the later period.
26. Sjöqvist 1940.
27. Gjerstad 1931.
28. Dikaios 1938; Stewart and Stewart 1950.
29. Dikaios 1962.
30. Stewart 1962.
31. In regard to the Philia Culture – Early Cypriot relationships he is opposed by Dikaios (*GCM*: 14-15); Merrillees (in Åström 1966: 33-35); and Catling (1966: 24). Cf. also Åström 1968: 87 n. 3.
32. *MCBA.*
33. See comments by Merrillees (1967: 334).
34. *MCBA*: 274; Stewart 1962: 272–3.
35. Åström 1960, 1966.
36. Åström 1966.
37. In figure 1f the relative proportion of pottery in each period which is of each ware is drawn out in the same manner as fig. 1c. Similar patterns of double lenticular ontogeny curves show the changing popularity of the wares through time.
38. Rowe 1962b: 40; Patterson 1963: 389; cf. Childe 1942.
39. *Patterns*: 139.
40. Patterson 1963: 389.
41. Patterson 1963: 390–1; Thomas and Ehrich 1969: 149f.
42. du Plat Taylor 1957.
43. Dikaios 1969–71.
44. Sjöqvist 1940: 98–99; Åström 1972c: 675f.
45. *SPC*: 23, 32; *MCBA*: 163–172.
46. Åström 1966.
47. Rowe 1961: 326.
48. Brainerd 1951; Robinson 1951; Ascher and Ascher 1963; further examples in Clarke 1968.
49. Dethlefsen and Deetz 1966; Deetz and Dethlefsen 1965; Clarke 1968: 199f.
50. Dunnell 1970. See further criticism by McNutt (1973).

51. Dunnell 1970: 311.
52. Rowe 1962a: 134–5; Merrillees 1965: 140.
53. Dunnell 1970: 315.
54. *MCBA*: 187 n. 1.
55. Rowe 1962a: 134–5; cf. Merrillees 1965: 148.
56. Rowe 1961: 326.
57. Dunnell 1970: 315.
58. E.g. Leach 1969: 17–18; cf. Shepard 1968: 343, 348.
59. Leach 1969.
60. Binford, L.R. 1965.
61. Binford, L.R. 1965: 205. Cf. Binford, L.R. 1968a: 22, 27; Binford 1962; Flannery 1967: 119; Renfrew 1972: 16.
62. Binford L.R. 1965: 206-7.
63. Linton 1936; Tippett 1969; Binford 1962; Solheim 1965.
64. E.g. Furumark 1940.
65. Adapted from Binford 1965.
66. Clarke 1968: 252–3; cf. Ford 1954; Weiss 1952: 64–8.
67. Clarke 1968: 289–301.
68. Clarke 1968: 473–90.
69. Binford 1965: 208; cf. Whallon 1968.
70. Merrillees 1971; cf. Åström 1972a, 1972c: 763f.
71. Catling 1964, 1966, 1969.
72. Deetz 1968: 42; Whallon 1968.
73. Struever 1971: 16.
74. Gifford 1960: 346–7.
75. Clarke 1962, 1968; Hodson, Sneath, Doran 1966; Hodson 1970; see chapter 3.5.
76. Binford and Binford 1966; Binford S.R. 1968; note criticisms of their interpretations – Bordes and Sonneville-Bordes 1970, Bordes 1973.
77. Gardin 1958, 1967; Megaw 1967; cf. Delougaz 1952: 1–26.
78. *MCBA*: 11–134.
79. Cf. Rouse 1960, 1970; Sabloff and Smith 1969.
80. *MCBA*: 10; Åström 1966: 138–9.
81. Rouse 1960: 320; Rands 1961: 331.
82. Merrillees 1972.
83. Tugby 1965: 14.
84. Ford 1954; Rouse 1960; McKern 1939; Clarke 1968, 1970; Thomas 1972; Shepard 1968: 306f.
85. Cf. Spaulding 1960; Rouse 1965.
86. See Chapter 2.1.
87. Rands 1961; Patterson 1963: 391; Friedrich 1970.
88. Longacre 1970; Deetz 1965, 1968; Whallon 1968.
89. Friedrich 1970.
90. Hodson 1969a, 1969b, 1970.
91. Hodson 1970; cf. Johnson 1971.
92. Clarke 1968: 246–9; Hodson 1969a; Rowlett and Pollnac 1971. The particular techniques in this study are discussed further in Chapter 3.
93. E.g. Ascher 1961; Binford 1968b; Freeman 1968; Ucko 1969.
94. Christodoulou 1959.
95. Hampe and Winter 1962.
96. Pieridou 1960, 1963–4.
97. E.g. *Kypros*; Casson 1937: 4–7, 1938; Buxton 1920; cf. Ohnefalsch–Richter 1913.
98. As, for example, by Stewart 1962: 292; Merrillees 1965.
99. Foster 1965; Nicklin 1971; Bradley 1971.
100. Nicklin 1971: 24–33; Rands 1961: 331–3.
101. Bunzel 1929.
102. Friedrich 1970; Bunzel 1929.
103. Rowe 1962a; cf. Merrillees 1965: 146; Sjöqvist 1940.
104. As may be deduced from Åström 1966.
105. Weinberg 1956: 112; 1965: 193; Merrillees 1965: 142–3.
106. E.g. the miniature ring–vase A.M. 1933.1687; or the small vessels such as N.M. 58.140 (Ayia Paraskevi, Gladstone Street No. 2).
107. Merrillees 1965: 142–3.
108. The large jugs are most conveniently carried cradled in the arms – as seen with the small White Painted Ware figure holding a "large" jug – C.M. 1941/I–18/1 (described in my forthcoming article "A Middle Cypriote Vessel with modelled figures from Politico *Lambertis*", *RDAC* 1974).
109. Taylor 1948.
110. Catling 1964, 1966, *Patterns*.
111. Merrillees 1971; cf. Åström 1972a, 1972c: 763–8.
112. Evans, J.D. 1973. Cf. Gjerstad, *SCE* Vol. I: xv.
113. Rouse 1960, 1965; Brew 1946: 65.
114. Catling 1966: 4–6, 1964: 14–35, *Patterns*.
115. Christodoulou 1959.
116. Catling 1969: 83–4, *Patterns*: 135, 141.
117. Christodoulou 1959: 205.
118. Cf. Stjernqvist 1966: 40.
119. Christodoulou 1959: 96–7; cf. Merrillees 1965: 140.
120. Catling 1964: 18, 1969; Stewart 1962: 299.
121. Stewart 1962: 286.
122. Jones, Merton, *et al.* 1958; cf. Christodoulou 1959: 226–30 and fig. 117.
123. Christodoulou 1959: 47, 109.
124. Jones, Merton, *et al.* 1958: 57; see also Åström, 1966: 133–4, 141.
125. Stewart, O.C. 1956; Jones 1969.
126. Jones, Merton, *et al.* 1958: 57.
127. For a general discussion of the relationship between these factors, see Angel, 1972, 1971: 77–84.
128. E.g. Åström 1968, 1969; HNM; 140–8; Catling 1966: 34–45, *Patterns*: 139–41.
129. *MCBA*; Stewart 1962.
130. *MCBA*: 273; Catling 1966: 35.
131. Cf. Catling 1966: 35.
132. Åström 1961–2: 148, 1964: 276 post–script, 1967, 1969: 73–4, 1972c: 755f, 851–2, *MCBA*: 257-273; Stewart 1962: 282–5; Cf. Thomas 1967: 79.
133. Renfrew 1972: 211–21; Thomas 1967: 79. At a seminar in Sydney in 1973 (to be published as *Studies in Middle Eastern Archaeology I*, Australian Foundation for Near Eastern and Cypriot Archaeology) Hennessy argued for a very early date for the beginning of the Early Cypriot Period, while Merrillees suggested an early date for the end of the Middle Cypriot Period and the beginning of Late Cypriot.

134. Merrillees 1971; Catling 1968: 35; Hennessy 1964: 50–1; Dikaios 1969–71 Vol. I: chart p. 438; Åström 1972c: 762; cf. Oren 1969: 137, 140.
135. Oren 1969; Thomas 1967: 79; cf. Merrillees 1971. For further discussion on the transition to Late Cypriot forms, and of the development of Late Cypriot fabrics, see Åström, L. 1972: 616; Popham 1972: 431–2, 700; Åström 1972c: 755f; Courtois 1970.
136. *Patterns*; records in the Offices of the Archaeological Survey of Cyprus, and the Survey Collections in Nicosia.
137. Catling 1964: 14–34, 1966: 36–9, *Patterns*.
138. Catling 1966: 65, *Patterns*: 141, 1969.
139. Catling 1966: 36; *MCBA*: 275.
140. For general comments on regionalism, see Stewart 1962: 297; *MCBA*: 275–78; Catling 1966: 36, 45, *Patterns*: 141; Merrillees 1965: 140; Hennessy 1964: 50; Kenna 1971: 7–8.
141. Catling 1966: 38, *Patterns*: 140; Åström 1969: 75, 1972b: 30–44, 1972c: 763–5; Overbeck and Swiny 1972: 25–28; Karageorghis 1969a: 133.
142. Cf. Bradley 1971b.
143. For some observations on the function of hill–forts in other archaeological and ethnographic situations, see Larsen 1972; Bellwood 1971.
144. Karageorghis 1970.
145. Catling 1969, 1964; Stewart 1962: 209f.
146. Åström 1969: 76; Stewart 1962: 292; cf. Hennessy 1964: 50. Cf. Christodoulou 1959: 96–105.
147. Stewart 1962: 291–2; cf. however, Åström 1966: 189.
148. Merrillees 1965; Karageorghis 1969b.
149. Merrillees 1965: 146.
150. E.g. Foster 1965; Bunzel 1927: 60f; Nicklin 1971: 31–33.
151. Karageorghis 1969a: 134.
152. Catling 1966: 42.
153. Wolfe 1969, and discussion.

CHAPTER 2

THE MATERIAL AND ITS CONTEXT

2.1. The Pottery and the Groups

For the reasons given in Chapter 1 only the White Painted Wares are being considered here, and no distinctions are being made between the different wares in the series. 1386 vessels from the basis of the study, and a full list of these is to be found in Appendix I. This is not intented as a complete corpus of Middle Cypriot White Painted pottery, for although it is a somewhat larger sample than that used by Åström in *MCBA* it does not include some 500 vessels listed there: about three–quarters of these because they have no known provenance, and the remainder either because there are no published illustrations, or because the paint is too worn for the decoration to be recognisable. Other pottery not listed by Åström has also been left out of these lists if there is no known provenance.

I have been able to examine the majority of the vessels in Cyprus, England and Australia, and the Appendix contains information to this effect. The other pottery is described from the publications cited.

The use of any archaeological data involves a degree of error resulting from the method of sampling. An attempt has been made to include all the available material in order to reduce such error to the minimum. No attempt has been made to make a random sample of the material, for this would not increase the validity of the results.[1]

As these analyses do not attempt a classification of the pots themselves, but move rather directly from the decorative attributes of the vessels to a classification of the groups of pots, the material has been kept within defined groups. The list below gives the names of the groups (as used in general discussion) and brief information on their size and nature. Further details regarding the identification, composition, location and reliability of the groups is given in Appendix I. The position and relative size of the groups is shown in figure 2.

List of the Groups

Group No	*Group*	*No. of vessels*	*Type of group*
1	Lapithos T. 2	26	suspect composite
2	Lapithos T. 18	66	single tomb
3	Lapithos T. 21	78	composite
4	Lapithos T. 29	29	single tomb
5	Lapithos T. 47	19	single tomb
6	Lapithos T. 49	37	single tomb
7	Lapithos T. 50	82	single tomb
8	Lapithos T. 315 A	25	tomb chamber
9	Lapithos T. 315 B-C	13	tomb chamber
10	Lapithos T. 316[1]	46	burial period
11	Lapithos T. 316[2]	20	burial period
12	Lapithos T. 320	30	single tomb
13	Lapithos T. 4	10	single tomb
14	Lapithos T. 8	9	single tomb
15	Lapithos T. 14	16	single tomb
16	Lapithos T. 51	14	single tomb
17	Lapithos T. 203	17	single tomb
18	Lapithos T. 311	11	single tomb
19	Lapithos T. 313	10	single tomb
20	Lapithos T. 702	13	single tomb
21	Lapithos	82	composite

22	Alambra	7	composite
23	Ayios Iakovos	33	composite
24	Ayia Paraskevi	48	composite
25	Dhali	16	composite
26	Dhenia T. 6	34	single tomb
27	Dhenia	51	composite (3 sites)
28	Dhikomo	10	composite (3 sites)
29	Enkomi	15	composite
30	Galinoporni	39	composite (2 sites)
31	Kalopsidha	37	composite
32	Katydata	8	composite (2 sites)
33	Klavdhia	14	composite
34	Kotchati	19	composite (suspect)
35	Kythrea	15	composite (2 sites)
36	Larnaca	19	composite (5 sites)
37	Leondari Vouno	12	composite
38	Livadhia	8	composite
39	Milia	10	composite
40	Nicosia	119	single tomb
41	Palaealona	9	composite
42	Politico T. 4	41	single tomb
43	Politico	58	composite
44	Myrtou	8	composite (2 sites)
45	Vounous	23	composite
46	Yeri	27	composite
47	?Alambra	53	museum

Some of the groups (Groups 2, 4-20, 26, 40, 42) are composed of material from a single tomb, although not, of course from a single burial. In some cases individual chambers of a tomb have been kept separate (Groups 8 and 9 – Lapithos T. 315) or different burial periods within a tomb have been isolated (Groups 10 and 11 – Lapithos T. 316). Most of the other groups are composed of material from several tombs in the same cemetery or at the same site, where the individual tomb–groups are too small to be useful on their own. Although there are some exceptions (especially where these composite groups draw on material from a great many tombs (as Group 21)) these composite groups can be taken to have almost the same value as the single–tomb groups.

A few other groups include material from several cemeteries within the same region, where otherwise the area would be poorly represented, or not represented at all. The results based on these regional groups are less valid than those using the better defined cemetery–groups but they do give some indication of the situation in the area. The Group 47 (?Alambra) is the least satisfactory group and should be treated with extreme caution.

Of the groups thus defined, 17 have more than 30 pots, and with a further 6 having at least 20 pots, about half of the groups contain at least 1.5 per cent of the total sample. Those with less than 19 pots are progressively less reliable, and the size of the groups should be considered as well as the reliability of their composition in the interpretation of their relationships to one another. Figure 2 illustrates the relative size of the groups, and indicates that there is a reasonable coverage of the island (except, of course, for the Troodos and the South–Western areas) with well constituted groups of reasonable size, and the results regarding geographical distributions may therefore be considered as fairly reliable (compare also fig. 6b).

Because all the groups are composed of material from more than one burial, they cannot be dated with great precision, although some groups cover a larger time span than others. The presence of White Painted Ware necessitates their being placed after the end of the Early Cypriot Period according to Åström's definition of the stages,[2] and some of the material may pass into the early part of the Late Cypriot Period. Within the Middle Cypriot Period (stage) the dating of the groups follows that put forward by Åström on the basis of similarity of frequency of wares and the cross–dating by similarity of individual pieces, together with the limited amount of stratigraphic evidence available and suggested evolution of certain designs.[3]

Despite the problems associated with these methods of dating (see Chapter 1) the general arrangement of the material is useful and does give an indication of the general chronological relationship of the groups. This information is contained in Appendix I, and is summarised in figure 3.[4]

2.2. Decoration and the Design Motifs

The designs on the Cypriot Bronze Age White Painted Wares were painted on the vessels before firing, generally using a thin slip of a darker colour than the pot itself. The colour of the vessels varies from a very light yellow to a slightly greenish colour, with the majority of vessels being various shades of light brown. The painted decoration varies from red to black, depending mainly on the quantity of iron or manganese in the clay used, and the variation in oxidation or reduction during firing.[5]

The lustrous surface and paint of the "earlier" wares (especially W.P. II) is not found later in the period, when most pottery has a matt surface. This change is due largely to the higher firing temperature of the later wares, which tends to destroy burnishing or polishing,[6] leading to a change in surface treatment.

The designs were painted with some form of brush, which varied in thickness from about 0.1 cm to at least 1.0 cm. Different sized brushes were sometimes used on the same vessel to produce different aspects of the decoration and multiple brushes were also used.[7] The pots were generally painted while being rotated in a clockwise direction, and most commonly from the neck downwards; although there are exceptions to this, and in many cases the order and direction of painting cannot be determined.

The painters attempted to produce regular and symmetrical patterns, and there is a high degree of uniformity in the size and shape of the design elements on a vessel, although there are numerous examples of mistakes and miscalculations. Although a few pots exhibit particular characteristics of design and execution which allow them to be grouped together as the products of one individual, the range of designs and method of application is too simple and common to make this possible with the great majority of vessels.

The geometric design motifs which commonly cover the entire vessel, repeatedly used in a regular fashion, are easily differentiated. These motifs are themselves built up by the repeated use of standard design elements.

It is possible to group the elements themselves on the basis of general shape (lozenge, triangle, etc.) or of filling (plain, hatched, cross–hatched, etc.) but these differences have all been treated as of equal importance, and each motif is differentiated on the basis of both shape and filling. The motifs are differentiated by the various manners of use, or orientation, of the elements; so that to be considered as the same motif, two designs must be similar in all three respects. While some subdivision is possible within the series of motifs defined here, and schematically drawn in figure 4, most of these motifs are clearly distinct from the others, and each forms an independent unit of design on the vessels.[8]

Although 81 motifs are described in this chapter and in figure 4, only the first 70 of these have been considered in the later analyses, partly because of the nature of the material originally used, and partly because most of these other designs are extremely rare and therefore of little use in assessing the relationships between several sites. A few of the designs included in the analyses are also rare, and this should be borne in mind when assessing results where they feature as important. There are other motifs which were used on White Painted Pottery, but if none of the pots in the sample are decorated in that way, then these other motifs have not been described here. Designs on the handles of vessels have also been ignored.

A classification of the *style* of decoration of the pottery would need to take into consideration the positioning of the different motifs, and the common use of two or more motifs on the same vessel, as well as the repeated use of one motif. As this form of classification of the individual pot would not necessarily lead to any greater understanding of the problems considered here, and would involve far more complex analyses, such a style classification is not used; nor are factors such as the positioning of the decoration taken into consideration.

In some later analyses, each motif is counted only once for each pot on which it appears (see Table 3 a and b). In other analyses a measure of the relative popularity of the motifs is used. This is assessed as the ratio of the number of occurrences of each motif in a group to the number of vessels in the group.

There is some correlation of different designs with different groups and shapes, and this information is summarised in section 6 of this chapter, where each design is discussed in turn.

2.3. Group Size and Motif Occurrence

Figure 5 demonstrates the relationship between the number of vessels in a group and the number of different motifs found in that group.

It is clear that as the groups get larger so does the number of motifs, and that the rate of increase in this number is greater untill there are about 20 pots in the group. After this the rate of increase in the number of designs lessens, although larger groups still have more designs than smaller ones

This correlation will affect the analyses regarding the relationships between designs and groups, and, in general, the larger the group, the more reliable the results.

As well as this it would appear that composite groups tend to have more different designs than single–tomb groups, and this factor will also be affecting the similarity studies to some degree, although the proportional occurrence used still gives a useful indication of the preferred designs in the cemetery or area.

Another interesting point may be observed from figure 5. The two groups from Politico (Groups 42 and 43) have relatively more designs in them than any of the other groups, indicating a somewhat more differentiated style of decoration, and the frequent use of many different motifs on the one vessel. In contrast to this the Eastern and Karpass sites have relatively fewer designs than the other groups, reflecting the generally recognised East–West (linear–tectonic) stylistic differences.

The difference is due mainly to the tendency in the Eastern areas to use such design systems as the "Wavy Line" and "Cross–Line" styles, which cover the entire vessel with only one or two motifs. This feature will affect some of the analyses by reducing the possible degree of similarity between sites within the Eastern bloc, where the similarity coefficient is dependent on the number of common occurrences, and not percentage occurrence.

The imbalance between sites with different numbers of pots is reduced to a certain extent by considering the proportional occurrence of the motifs in relation to the size of the groups, to give some measure of the relative frequency (or popularity) of the motifs. This percentage figure itself causes some problems, as rare designs in small groups receive undue weighting.

2.4. The Shapes

Åström has classified most of the shapes of White Painted Pottery[9] and some of the problems with this classification have been discussed in Chapter 1.

The shapes used in this study are simply defined into the major classes, roughly corresponding to basic functional types. The more important aspect of the shape classification here is the different surface each shape presents to the painter. The only real exception to this is the jug–juglet differentiation, which is not clear–cut. Many of the small jugs could well be classified as juglets in terms of the field of decoration, but the general classification does serve to give an idea of the relative frequency of different shapes in different areas, and the relationship between certain shapes and designs. These correlations should be borne in mind when assessing the relative popularity of shape–linked designs in areas where the shape is rare, absent, or in large quantity.

The exact nature and range of variation within each of the general shape classes may be determined by reference to the publications listed in Appendix I – but they may be simply defined as follows:

Jug A small or large jug, with an open mouth. (*MCBA*, figs. III: 3–9; XI: 7, 8; XVI: 14–16).

Juglet A small jug with a lateral mouth and tubular spout. (*MCBA*, figs. XI: 4–6; XIII: 12).

Cup A small deep bowl with vertical handle; either hemispherical or with a flat bottom and straight sides. (*MCBA*, fig. V: 9–11).

Bowl An open vessel, usually hemispherical body without neck or distinct rim; generally with a horizontal handle. (*MCBA*, figs. III: 1, 2; X: 1–5; XVI: 1–4).

Amphora Usually a fairly large vessel, with a vertical neck, wide flat mouth, and two vertical handles. (*MCBA*, figs. V: 2–4; XV: 1–6).

Jar A smaller vessel, with a wide flat mouth and without handles. Often with two holes pierced below the rim. (*MCBA*, figs. XVI: 7–9; 11, 12).

Tankard A fairly large vessel, with wide vertical neck and flat mouth, with a single tall vertical handle from the neck base or body to the rim. (*MCBA*, fig. XVIII: 5–8).

Flask A tall, fairly narrow vessel, often oval in section, with a narrow neck. Generally a fairly large handle from rim to shoulder. (*MCBA*, figs. XI: 10, 11;XIV: 1–3, 5–9).

Bottle A smaller vessel with a narrow neck, and either globular or cylindrical body. A string–hole lug or small handle at the neck base. Some examples have two small handles (amphoriskos). (*MCBA*, figs. IX: 8; XI: 9; XIV: 4).

Other Includes the more unusual shapes such as

ring–vases, animal and bird vases, and composite vessels. (*MCBA*, figs. VIII: 7–10; IX: 11; XV: 8; XVIII: 1–3).

In Appendix II a list of the shapes on which each motif is found is given, and Table 1 lists the number of vessels of each shape in the groups. Table 2 gives this number as a percentage of the pots in the group. This information is summarised in figure 6a which gives the relative frequency of the different shapes in the eight major regions defined below.

The most common shape is the jug (both large and small) followed by the bowl. Less frequent are the bottles, amphorae, flasks, cups, juglets and jars. Jugs and bowls are found at nearly all the sites, and are only absent from very small groups. Cups, bottles, amphorae, and flasks occur in over half the groups, the other shapes are less common.

The meaning of the different distribution of the shapes is not easy to assess, considering that one is dealing with tomb material and only with the one class of pottery. There are several possible explanations of the observed distribution, which are really more valuable in assessing the significance of the occurrence of shape–linked designs.

It may be possible to indicate a few trends in the shapes preferred for White Painted ware in some regions. There are no cups from the Karpass, the Eastern, or the Larnaca areas, and juglets are rare in those parts. There are also no amphorae in the Larnaca groups, but this may again be due to the small body of material available. The indication of fewer shapes in White Painted Ware in the Eastern part of Cyprus may be significant, but may be due to the size of the samples. The Nicosia group (40) has a large quantity of juglets and many small jugs, but the meaning of this is impossible to assess.

2.5. The Regions

In his study of settlement patterns Catling[10] has defined 11 major areas within Cyprus, developing the system devised by Gjerstad.[11] These may be compared to the 12 major morphological regions discussed by Christodoulou[12] or those of Osmond.[13]

For purposes of general discussion I have used 8 main areas, which conform more or less to the regions defined by Catling and Christodoulou, and which allow the sites used in this study to be easily grouped into larger geographical units. The classification is therefore fairly specific to the present work, and is not to be taken as a cultural division, or implying necessary cultural unity within these areas, even though there are some clear and obvious cultural differences between the areas. It is primarily a geographical division.

The relative numbers of vessels in each of these areas is shown in figure 6b.

Unlike the other studies, and for convenience, I have not used a numbered system to refer to the regions, but use instead the following terms:

The North Coast. The northern slopes of the Kyrenia Range, and the Kyrenia Lowlands, extending from Kormakiti to Ephtagonia. (Catling 1, Christodoulou 8). This includes here the sites of Lapithos, Vounous and Palaealona.

The Southern Foothills. The southern slopes of the Kyrenia Range, and the Kyrenia Belt. (Catling 2, Christodoulou 6). This area is represented by the groups from Kythrea and the Dhikomo area.

Western Region. The western half of the central plain – the alluvial fan region, including Myrtou to the north and the sites in the Karyotis river valleys. (Catling 4 and 5, Christodoulou 5). This includes Dhenia, Myrtou, and Katydata groups.

The Central River Valleys. The areas of the Pedieos Drainage Basin around Nicosia. (Part of Catling 7, and Christodoulou 7b.). This is taken to include Yeri and Leondari Vouno as well as the Nicosia groups.

The Southern River Valleys. The more southern parts of the Pedieos and Yialias Basin, and including the area of the pillow–lavas along the north–east side of the Troodos Range. (Catling 7, Christodoulou 7b and 1c.) The Politico, Kotchati, Alambra, and Dhali groups fall within this region.

The Eastern Area. The eastern half of the central plain, from Nicosia to Salamis Bay, the Mesarka, the Bottomlands, and the Peristeronopiyi Trachonas areas. (Catling 6, Christodoulou 4, 4a and 7a.) Includes the sites of Milia, Enkomi, and Kalopsidha.

The Karpass. The Karpass peninsula. (Catling 3, Christodoulou 9.) Includes the Ayios Iakovos and Galinoporni groups.

The Larnaca Region. Larnaca and the Lowlands. (Catling 8, Christodoulou 3, 3a.) Includes Klavdhia, Livadhia and the Larnaca sites.

2.6. The Motifs and their Distribution

In this section each of the 81 motifs is briefly discussed. It is mainly a commentary on Appendix II, where the exact data is presented. It is intended as a general guide to the information in the two appendices. See also Table 3 which summarises the number of vessels in each group with each design.

As the discussion is limited to the material listed in the Appendices, and does not consider the large amount of material of unknown provenance, comments as the shapes decorated with certain motifs must be treated with some caution, although occasionally other material is referred to.

The comments are not intended to be precise, and no special significance should be attached to the use of "common", "frequent", "normal" and the like, beyond their ordinary usage.

A schematic representation of the designs is to be found in figures 4a and b. Some idea of the range of variation within each motif–type may be gained by reference to the illustrations noted in each case.

Motif 1

The design consists of one or more broad horizontal lines, generally over 0,5 cm wide. (*MCBA*, figs. II: 8; IX: 10–12.)

This is a common motif, and is found on 18 per cent of all vessels studied: on 42 per cent of the jugs, 12 per cent of bottles, and 10 per cent of amphorae, as well as on all other shapes, except jars. Over 80 per cent of vessels with this design are jugs.

It is most commonly used on White Painted II and III pottery, although it does occur on the other wares.

It is a little more common at Lapithos than in the centre of the island, and is also common at the Eastern sites. It is found on the necks of jugs with Cross–Line Style decoration (motif 48) and is therefore common at Kalopsidha, while a similar use with 'Pendent Line Style' jugs accounts for its frequency elsewhere in the Eastern areas. On the Lapithos examples it is more common on the bases of the vessels (often in conjunction with motif 8) than on the necks. The use of this design on bowls is not common, and is fairly distinctive of the Ayios Iakovos material, and of the wide dishes from Kalopsidha and Enkomi.

Motif 2

A broad horizontal band flanked by parallel straight lines. (*MCBA*, figs. XVI; 11, 15, 17; XVIII: 10).

This design occurs on jugs and amphorae and to a lesser extent on jars and bowls.

Åström has noted this design as characteristic of White Painted V ware, especially in Eastern Cyprus. It is, however, also found in the Larnaca Region, and in the Southern River Valley Region. It is present (together with design 4) in large quantity at the settlement site of Enkomi.[14] Together with motif 4 it forms Åström's White Painted V Framed Band Style.[15]

Motif 3

A set of vertical parallel straight lines. (*MCBA*, figs. I: 1, 2; V: 7, 8; IX: 3–8).

In *MCBA* Åström has used this element as one of the distinguishing features of Pendent Line Style[16] (see also notes to motif 9). In this analysis any independent set of lines is classified as this motif, and it is therefore commonly noted on bowls as well as jugs and bottles. On bowls it is used both as external and internal decoration, and also occurs on the bases of jugs, tankards, amphorae, and jars (*MCBA*, fig. XVI: 11, 12), as well as on the body of jugs.

It is a very common design, occuring on nearly 30 per cent of vessels studied (20 per cent of jugs, 50 per cent of bowls, 40 per cent of bottles, and 85 per cent of jars) and is found on all shapes.

It is found all over the island, and is only absent from the small groups of Palaealona (Group 41) and L313 (Group 19).

The common feature of vertical lines dividing a vessel into two or four segments along or across the handle axis has been ignored in this analysis.

Motif 4

A broad vertical band flanked by parallel straight lines (cf. motif 2; *MCBA*, figs. XVI: 17; XVIII: 10).

The design is similar to motif 2 and occurs in approximately the same quantities at the same range of sites – mainly in the Eastern and Southern River Regions – although never in large quantity. As with motif 2 it is commonest on jugs and amphorae, and, with it forms Åström's Framed Band Style.[15]

Motif 5

A short detached wavy line, occurring singly or in groups; either horizontal or vertical. (*MCBA*, fig. XII: 5, 3.)

It is a reasonably common design, occurring on about 3 per cent of all vessels. It is most common on bowls (60 per cent of vessels) and jugs (20%) and occurs in small quantities on most other shapes as well. On bowls it is used both internally and externally as a filling ornament, and on other vessels is most common as a filling ornament on the base.

The design as classified here differs in the various parts of the island. In the Karpass it is rather a part of the Wavy Line Style, and its use at Lapithos differs from elsewhere (cf. *MCBA*, fig. XVI: 13). The two bottles from Anglisidhes (Larnaca Group 36) are here described as having this design, although they have been classified as "Pendent Line Style" by Åström.[17]

Although not found at all sites the motif occurs in all areas. At Lapithos its use is restricted rather more to bowls than in the other areas, where it is used with greater frequency on the bases of other shapes.

Motif 6

A single horizontal wavy line. (*MCBA*, figs. III: 5; IV: 2; V: 8; XII: 1–4.)

This design is a common one, occurring on about 28 per cent of all vessels. It is most common on bowls, generally used on the interior, either simply around the rim, or as a set of widely spaced concentric rings. It occurs in some form on nearly half of the bowls, and is equally frequent on jars. About a third of most other shapes are decorated with this motif, but it is rare on bottles.

The design is widely distributed in similar proportions over all of the island, and is only absent from Ayios Iakovos. The numerical proportions of bowls to jugs with this design at Kalopsidha may be significantly different from that in other areas.

Motif 7

Two or more horizontal parallel wavy lines drawn close together and forming a unit. (*MCBA*, figs. III: 8; VII: 11; VIII: 3; IX: 10.)

The motif is used mainly on jugs and bowls, and also on tankards (more commonly in the West) and amphorae (North and Karpass).

While in other areas this motif may be seen as a variant of motif 6, in the Karpass it is different, and together with motif 10 forms the Wavy Line Style, which, in relation to other regional fabrics, may be considered a part of a regional "Karpass Style".[18]

Motif 8

Broad wavy lines around lower body and base. (*MCBA*, figs. VI: 2, 5–7, 13, 15; XIV: 7; XVII: 11.)

Because of the classification of this design partly by position it cannot normally be found on bowls or jars, and is rare on vessels other than jugs – 18 per cent of which have this design, which is often used in conjunction with motif 1, in alternating bands around the base.

It is not normally found at the Eastern sites, but does occur in most other areas. It is twice as common at Lapithos than elsewhere, and at that site is more often used on shapes other than jugs than is the case in other parts of the island.

Motif 9

A single vertical wavy line. (*MCBA*, figs. III: 5–8; V: 6–8.)

This is a common design, occurring on 20 per cent of the vessels studied, and appears in all groups (except the small Group 13 – Lapithos T.4).

Over half of the vessels with this design are jugs, 20 per cent are bowls and 10 per cent bottles, and it is used less frequently on all other shapes.

At Lapithos about 70 per cent of the vessels other than bowls with this design also have motif 28, while only about 10 per cent have design 3 in conjunction with motif 9, this reflecting different combinations on jugs and bottles. A similar proportion is found at Dhenia, Vounous, Palaealona, and Kotchati. Elsewhere in the island the combination of 3 and 9 is the more common one on jugs as well as bottles, this forming what Åström classifies as the "Pendent Line Style",[19] which is most frequently used in the Eastern and Southern Areas. This style is considered to be earlier than, and ancestral to, the Cross Line Style in those regions.[20]

Motif 10

Two or more parallel vertical wavy lines. (*MCBA*, figs. VI: 15; X: 1, 2, 6.)

This motif is most common on bowls and jugs; on amphorae it is used more often on the bases than the sides, while on flasks it is used within the "Pendent Line Style".

The motif is most common in the Karpass, where it has a different form from the rest of the island, and where, together with motif 7 it constitutes a part of the distinctive "Wavy Line Style" which may be seen in the context of a regional Karpass Style including the other fabrics.[21] Elsewhere motif 10 is less common and is more like a variant of motif 9.

Motif 11

A set of closely spaced wavy and straight lines, similar to what Åström terms the "Framed Caduceus" design.[22] (*MCBA*, figs. IX: 1; XVI: 14.)

It is found on most shapes, although in small quantity, and with no particular popularity.

Åström notes its occurrence at Kalopsidha (*MCBA*, fig. IA) and at Galinoporni (on trichrome ware – fig. IX. 2), and suggests it is an early motif which develops into the "Pendent Line Style".[23] The early occurrence of the motif in the East and Karpass may perhaps be seen as a development from some of the designs on White Painted I wares,[24] while in the other areas it is a late design, and is found on White Painted V ware and is a precursor of some aspects of Proto White Slip Wares.[25]

Motif 12

A set of parallel vertical straight lines flanked by wavy lines.

This is a variant of design 11, and is also connected to the development of the Pendent Line Style. It is perhaps to be associated with the later wares (White Painted IV and V) but there are too few examples to give a clear indication.[26]

It is found in different parts of the island in spite of being a rare design. The jugs from Galinoporni (1953/II–3/1) and Politico (T.4–132) are in many ways quite similar.

Motif 13

A single horizontal zig–zag line. (*MCBA*, figs. VIII: 6, 10; XVI: 5, 6; XVII: 3.)

This is not a common design, and occurs on only about 3 per cent of the sample. It is most common on amphorae, and cups, where it is usually used on or near the base, and on jugs, where it is used on the neck. It occurs in smaller quantities on most other shapes.

Although not common it does occur in most parts of the island and there is no clear trend of areas where it is a preferred design.

Motif 14

A pair of horizontal parallel zig–zag lines. (*MCBA*, figs. VIII: 11; XI: 4; XII: 13.)

This is a reasonably common design, occurring on about 8 per cent of the sample. It is used on all shapes, and is most common on juglets (40 per cent of juglets – related to popularity in the Nicosia Group 40) flasks, amphorae, and jugs (nearly half the vessels with this design are jugs).

On jugs it is generally used on the neck, while on flasks and juglets etc. it is rather used on the body, or near the base, and occasionally it is used on the outside of bowls.

The design has no particular distribution, and is found in most areas of the island, perhaps a little more commonly in the central and southern river valley areas, than elsewhere.

Motif 15

A band of multiple parallel zig–zag lines, or of chevrons. (*MCBA*, figs. XVI: 7; V: 1.)

The multiple chevron band is found on White Painted V vessels rather than other wares (Kythrea, L702 examples).

Multiple zig–zags, either framed or open are commonest on jugs and amphorae, usually on the neck or body.

The use of this design on amphorae may be a feature of the North Coast, and total distribution is confined to that area, the Southern foothills, and the Karpass, as well as the central sites.

Motif 16

Horizontal or vertical band of concentric zig–zags – a more complex form of design 15 (cf. also design 56). (*MCBA*, fig. V: 4.)

This is a rare motif, occurring only on 3 amphorae, 2 from Palaealona and 1 from L. T 313.

Motif 17

A band of three parallel zig–zag lines, usually overlapping or intersecting at the junctions. (*MCBA*, figs. XII: 1, 3–7; XVI: 18.)

It is most commonly used as a border on the external rim of bowls (70 per cent of examples – 34 per cent of bowls) and more rarely on all other shapes except bottles.

It is found at most sites, but is a little more common at Lapithos than elsewhere in the island, and is least common in the Karpass and the Southern Foothills. It may be more popular in the Western sites (Myrtou, Katydhata) than the Central ones.

Motif 18

A pair of horizontal parallel zig–zag lines with the space between filled with vertical or horizontal hatching. (Cf. design 20.) (*MCBA*, figs. XVIII: 5; XVII: 1.)

This design is not associated with any particular shape, but may be generally associated with White Painted V or other of the later wares. The two vessels from Lapithos with this motif (L 316^2.64 and L2.36) are similar and probably by the same craftsman. The jug and juglet from Politico and Yeri are less similar; and the Politico bowl has a very different version of this design, and is closer to White Painted VI or Proto White Slip Wares.

The design also occurs on the White Painted I vessel, L4A.674.

Motif 19

Three horizontal parallel zig–zag lines, with the space between the upper two filled with vertical hatching. (*MCBA*, fig. XI: 3.)

This motif only occurs on one jug from Ayia Paraskevi – compare however vessels with designs 18 and 20, especially those from Politico T.4 (Group 42).

Motif 20

A horizontal cross–hatched zig–zag band (compare motifs 19 and 18). (*MCBA*, figs. XV: 7; XVII: 7.)

This motif is used on jugs, juglets, amphorae, tankards and flasks, and occurs on one deep spouted bowl. Many of the White Painted IV and V vessels with this motif have other features in common, and it is often used with motifs 34 and 59; these vessels forming a fairly good although widespread group, generally more common on the North Coast, in the West and the Central and Southern River Valleys than elsewhere. The combination of 20 with motifs 34, 51, 59 is characteristic of the decoration of the large Nicosia group (40) – many of these small jugs and juglets are probably products of the same workshop. A similar style of decoration is apparent at Politico (cf. Politico T.4.49, 50, 59).

Motif 21

A single vertical zig–zag line.

This is not a common design, and is generally either a variant of the wavy line motif 9 or a simple version of motif 22.

It is most common on jugs, flasks, and bottles, and generally only occurs on the North Coast and in the Southern Foothills, as well as the Central and Southern River Valley areas.

Motif 22

A pair of parallel vertical zig–zag lines. (*MCBA*, figs. XIII: 7; XIV: 4.)

This motif appears most frequently on the sides of jugs and bottles, but also occurs on most other shapes. On bowls it is a variant of motif 24.

It is found in most groups, but is rare in the Karpass and the Eastern sites. It is most common in the Nicosia Group, and is more frequent south of Kyrenia Range than to the North.

Motif 23

A vertical unframed set of parallel zig–zags. (*MCBA*, figs. VIII: 5; VII: 3.)

This is a rare design, similar to motif 24, but more complex and generally unframed. It is used most often on the sides of jugs.

It occurs too infrequently to show any clear trend in distribution, but is more common on the North Coast and Centre than in other areas of the island.

Motif 24

A framed set (usually of 3) vertical parallel zig–zag lines, usually with the intersections crossed or interlocked. (*MCBA*, figs. XII: 1; XIII: 8.)

This is not a very common design, and is most frequently used underneath bowls, but also occurs on most other shapes, fairly often on bottles.

It is fairly widely distributed over the island, but rare or absent from the Karpass and Eastern sites.

Motif 25

A vertical cross–hatched zig–zag (cf. design 20).

This is a rare motif, and is mainly restricted to three of the Southern River Valley sites, with one occurrence at Lapithos.

It is used on jugs, flasks and bottles.

Motif 26

A horizontal row of crossed zig–zags; or crosses formed by double zig–zag lines. (*MCBA*, fig. XIV: 3.)

This motif is very rare. It is used on a flask from Lapithos, and on a composite White Painted II vessel of three bowls from Ayia Paraskevi. It also appears on a zoomorphic vessel (A.M. inv 1933–1686) and on a bowl from Lapithos T.50.

This motif is not clear on the photograph of the Ayia Paraskevi example in *SPC* from which Åström was working, and he therefore regarded it as a new motif in White Painted IV. Its use on the composite vessel is a variant of motif 14 (as on CM invA904) or a single zig–zag as at Alambra (*MCBA*, fig. VIII: 10).

This motif could also be seen as a variant of the plain lozenge row (motif 57).

Motif 27

A horizontal lattice band. (*MBCA*, figs. IV: 1, 2; V: 1, 3–5; VIII: 7, 8, 10.)

This element occurs predominantly on amphorae, mainly on the bodies and necks, as well as on jugs (more commonly on the necks) and to a lesser extent on all other shapes.

It is reasonably common in the centre of the island, and in the Southern River Valley System, as well as at Lapithos, where it is common in Tomb 313. It is very much a particular feature of Palaealona, Vounous, and Lapithos T.313.

Motif 28

A vertical lattice (cross–hatched) panel. (*MCBA*, figs. III: 3, 5–8; VI: 1, 2, 4–8, 10, 11, 13–15.)

This design is very common, and is used on 20 per cent of the vessels. It appears on 42 per cent of the jugs (that is, nearly 80 per cent of all occurrences of the motif) and is used on all other shapes except jars and tankards (see, however, Herscher 1972: 30).

Åström divides off a separate type of this motif with an empty triangle at the top of the lattice. This form is related to White Painted IV ware, while the standard type is used on the earlier wares. Another variant has vertical lines crossed by diagonals. It is found both on "earlier" material (e.g. Lapithos T.2.37; Nicosia.50; Dhiorios *Aloupotrypes* A.M. 1953.1126) and on "later" wares – being particularly common on White Painted V vessels. In these analyses the variants have not been separated.

The motif is more common on the North Coast than elsewhere on the island, but is only absent from the small groups from Leondari Vouno (Group 37) and Milia (Group 39).

At Lapithos it is usually (on about two–thirds of the jugs) used together with a vertical wavy line (motif 9), the two motifs alternating on the body of the vessel. This combination is used in most other areas, but in smaller proportions, and is entirely absent in the Karpass and Eastern Areas.

Motif 29

An unframed lattice (cross–hatch) pattern, covering a large area of the vessel. (*MCBA*, figs. XI: 5; XVIII: 8.)

This is not a common design, but does occur on most shapes except jars and tankards. It is found on bottles at Lapithos and is used on animal–shaped vessels elsewhere, although never in great quantity.

It is generally confined to the North Coast, and the Central and Southern River Valley sites, but it does appear on one bowl from Ayios Iakovos.

Motif 30

A chequer pattern of latticed diamonds (cf. design 32). (Grace, 1940, fig. IA.73; *GCM*, pl.VI.7.)

A rare design, being one of the determinants of Åström's Lattice Diamond Style:[27]

The Lapithos example is not the same as the Politico ones, having a more complex arrangement within the lattice pattern (cf. designs 60 and 79) although the small jug CM A715 from *Chomazoudhia* does also have that form (design 60) as a vertical band.

The Politico examples are clearly closely related, especially the two from Tomb 4, but their connection to the Lapithos and Yeri vessels is less certain.

Motif 31

A panel of rectilinear cross–hatching. (*MCBA*, fig. XIII: 4.)

This design is generally similar to design 28, and is a particular variety of that motif, although not always used in the same way (for example, the flask from Nicosia Group 40 has this design on the flat base).

It is commonest on jugs, amphorae, and flasks, but is also used on animal shaped vessels, bottles and bowls.

The small jugs from Galinoporni are similar to the one from Lapithos ($T.316^1.78$).

The distribution has no particular or easily discernible trend.

Motif 32

A rectilinear chequer with alternate squares cross–hatched. (*MCBA*, figs, X: 9, 10; XIII: 15; XIV: 1, 5.)

This is more common than the variant motif 30,

and is also a determinant of the Lattice Diamond style.[27]

It is most common on flasks, jugs and amphorae, but does also appear on other shapes.

It is not common at Lapithos, and several of the examples from there (L.316[1].176, L.315A.86) have a good deal in common with the amphora from Politico (Tomb 4.49). The design is found in small quantity in most parts of the island, and has no immediately significant overall distribution.

Motif 33

A single horizontal stripe of alternate open and filled in squares. (*MCBA*, fig. V: 4.)

This design occurs only on six vessels, all of different shape.

It is found at six different sites, on the North Coast, Central and Larnaca Districts.

Motif 34

A horizontal chequer band, two rows deep. (*MCBA*, figs. IV: 1, 5; XI: 1, 3; XIII: 9; XIV: 5.)

This a fairly common design, and is used more frequently than the simpler design 33 or the more complex designs 35 and 36.

It is used mainly on amphorae, flasks and jugs, but is only absent from cups and jars.

It is found in most areas of the island, except in the Larnaca and Eastern sites, and is rare in the Karpass. At Nicosia it is used with motifs 20, 51, 59 in a fairly individual style of decoration, which is also in evidence at Politico and other sites in those regions.

Motif 35

A horizontal chequer design, three rows deep. (*MCBA*, figs. IV: 1–3:, 5; XV: 3.)

This design is less common than the simpler design 34, but more common than designs 36 and 33.

As with the other designs it is commonest on amphorae, jugs, and flasks, and does occur also on bowls.

Design 35 is mainly found on the North Coast, most commonly at Palaealona and Lapithos T.313, but is also known from the Central and Southern River Valley Sites, and appears on one (probably imported) jug from Ayios Iakovos (T. 6.1).

Motif 36

A horizontal chequer band, four or more rows deep. (*MCBA*, figs. IV: 3; V: 1.)

This design is rare, much less common than the related designs 34 and 35, but like them it occurs on jugs and amphorae.

Its occurrence is restricted to Lapithos and Vounous, with one example from Dhikomo.

Motif 37

A horizontal chequered zig–zag. (*MCBA*, fig. XI: 14.)

This design is found only on the one amphora from Lapithos (T.311.14).

Motif 38

A vertical single chequered stripe. (*MCBA*, fig. VIII: 1.)

This design only occurs on one jug from Lapithos (T.320.111) and on the base of a bowl from Nicosia (T.8.208).

Motif 39

A vertical chequer band, two or more rows wide. (*MCBA*, figs. IV: 2, 7; V: 3; XI: 1.)

This more complex form of motif 38 is much more common. It is used mainly on jugs, but also appears on other shapes (except juglets, jars, and tankards).

It is found mainly on the North Coast, and in the Central and Southern River Valley Areas.

Motif 40

A vertical chequered zig–zag band. (*MCBA*, fig. III: 9.)

This design, as with motif 37, is very rare. It occurs only on three vessels (two jugs and a bottle) from Lapithos.

Motif 41

A set of thick parallel vertical lines (*MCBA*, figs. XVI: 9; XVII: 6, 7.)

This design is most common on jars, nearly half of which are decorated with this motif. It is also used on other shapes, especially the more squat, wider, or larger vessels. It does not appear on juglets, cups or bowls.

Its distribution is confined to the North Coast (Lapithos), where it is most common on amphorae, and the Central and Southern River Valley Sites, with one jar from Kalopsidha, and one from Dhenia outside of this area.

Motif 42

A complex chequer pattern, with long vertical panels intersected by horizontal bands of narrower chequered squares. (*MCBA*, figs. V: 9; VIII: 4; XIV: 7; XV: 2.)

The design is used on most shapes, except bowls and jars (where design 41 is preferred), and is most common on tankards and flasks.

As with other chequer motifs it is commonest at Lapithos, where it occurs on a wide variety of shapes. It is also found on the southern slopes of the Kyrenia range (at Krini), and in the Southern River Valley Area on a more restricted range of shapes.

Motif 43

A complex chequer pattern, with long horizontal panels intersected by vertical bands of narrower chequer squares. (*MCBA*, figs. XI: 12; XVII: 11.)

This design, the reverse of design 42, is less common, and its use is more restricted. It appears on tankards, flasks and bottles in 6 groups from Lapithos, most of which also contain vessels with motif 42.

Motif 44

A rectilinear chequer pattern, covering a large part of the vessel. (*MCBA*, fig. VI: 9; XI: 2; XVII: 5.)

This decoration is found on all shapes, and is commonest on tankards, flasks and juglets.

Its distribution, as with other chequer patterns is mainly confined to Lapithos, with appearences in the Central and Southern River Valley Sites, and is also found toward the West.

Motif 45

An angled chequer pattern, covering large parts of the vessel – a variant of design 44, but with diamonds rather than squares.

This is a rare design, appearing on only one vessel in each of 5 Lapithos tombs, generally those also with design 44.

Motif 46

Crosses formed by sets of broad parallel bands meeting in a chequer pattern. (*MCBA*, figs. VI: 14; XVII: 7.)

This design appears on all the normal shapes except jars. It is most common on amphorae. It is used either on the base or the sides of vessels.

The design is restricted to the Lapithos groups, but is found at Politico, and is fairly frequent on the bases of small jugs and juglets from the Nicosia Group 40. A cup from Aghirda (Kyrenia District) has a variety of this design on the base.

Motif 47

A cross formed by two broad bands. (*MCBA*, figs. III: 7; XVI: 11.)

The design is found on all of the standard shapes, most often on jugs and bowls, but never in large quantity. It is generally found on the bases of the vessels, but occasionally appears on the sides.

It occurs in half of the groups, and in all areas of the island.

Motif 48

Sets of parallel straight lines crossing each other diagonally. (*MCBA*, figs. VIII: 3; IX: 10–14.)

This motif is the characteristic of Åström's "Cross Line Style", which he suggests is derived from the Pendent Line Style.[28] It is possible to subdivide this motif into different forms[29] but this has not been done in this study.

The design appears on 6 per cent of the jugs and bottles (generally small globular amphoriskoid bottles) as well as one tankard. The taller narrower bottles tend to have "Pendent Line Style" decoration rather than the "Cross–Line Style" as it is more suited to their shape.

About one third of the examples used here come from Kalopsidha, where over 40 per cent of jugs are decorated in this manner. This style of decoration is common at Milia, Kythrea and Enkomi, and reasonably common in the Larnaca district. It is found elsewhere on the island, but in smaller quantity, and is clearly an Eastern trait.[30]

This type of decoration had considerable influence on some of the styles of "Palestinian" Bichrome Ware.[31]

Motif 49

A row of hatched triangles. (*MCBA*, figs. VI: 3; VIII: 11; XII: 7, 10, 11; XIII: 2.)

This motif is found on all shapes, but is more common on jugs and bowls. Nearly a third of all cups have this motif, and it is reasonably common on juglets and amphorae.

It is fairly common at Lapithos, where it is more frequently used on bowls and amphorae than the other shapes. Elsewhere it is more common on jugs. The design is not used in the Karpass or at any of the Eastern sites.

Motif 50

A row of hatched triangles, with a framing line along one side. (*MCBA*, figs. V: 6; XIII: 1; XVIII: 5.)

This design, while still fairly popular (7 per cent of vessels) is less common than design 49.

Its use is restricted to fewer shapes, and although found on cups, juglets and jugs, it is much more common on bowls, which account for two–thirds of all occurrences. Twice as many bowls have this design than have the similar motif 49.

Motif 50 has much the same distribution as motif 49, and although one bowl from Kalopsidha is decorated in this way it is generally absent from the Karpass and Eastern sites.

Motif 51

A row of cross–hatched triangles. (*MCBA*, figs. V: 10; VI: 3, 16; X: 6; XI: 4, 14, 15; XII: 12; XV: 4.)

This is a reasonably common design, a little more frequent than motif 49. It appears on all shapes except jars, and is most common on juglets, cups, amphorae and jugs.

It is found in most groups and in all parts of the island, being most common in the Nicosia group (40) where it is popular on the small jugs and juglets, and used there with motifs 20, 34 and 59, with related material at Politico and other sites.

One may compare the preference at Galinoporni and other sites for this more complex filling of triangles with a similar preference for the cross–hatched filling of lozenges (see motif 59).

Motif 52

A row of filled–in triangles. (*MCBA*, figs. XI: 15; XVIII: 5; XVII: 6.)

The design is rare, occurring only on two tankards, a jug, a flask and a bottle, all from Lapithos.

At least three of these vessels, L.316[2].64, L.2.36, L.316[1].4 may be by the same craftsman. (See note on design 18.)

Motif 53

A row of inverted triangles. (*MCBA*, figs. III:4; XVI: 7.)

This is not a common design, appearing on several different shapes, and with no clear pattern of distribution.

Motif 54

A vertical row of cross–hatched triangles. (*SPC*, p. 152, flask 1; *BSA*, 41, pl. 28.1, row 3.7.)

A rare design used on only one vessel in each of six groups, at Lapithos, and the Central and Southern River Valley Areas.

Motif 55

Two opposing and interlocking rows of cross–hatched triangles, either horizontal or vertical. (*MCBA*, figs. VII: 10; XVIII: 4.)

Only one vessel used in the analysis has this design (Lapithos T.315 B–C) but it also occurs at Dhiorios *Aloupotrypes* (A.M.1953.1121).

Motif 56

A set of plaited hatched triangles, either vertical or horizontal. (*MCBA*, figs. III: 2; 7; IV: 3, 7; XII: 9, 13.)

This is not a common design, and is usually found on bowls either around the exterior rim or underneath the base; on jugs as a vertical or horizontal panel, and to a lesser extent on juglets, cups and flasks.

It is not normally used in the Karpass (one bowl from Ayios Iakovos), the Southern Slopes, or the Eastern sites, but appears in all the other areas of the island.

Motif 57

A horizontal row of plain lozenges. (*MCBA*, figs. VI: 1; XIII: 13; XVII: 1.)

This is not a common design, but is used on all shapes except jars. It is commonest at Lapithos, Nicosia and Politico, but also is found in the East in small quantity.

Motif 58

A horizontal row of hatched lozenges. (*MCBA*, figs. VIII: 6; XIV: 2; XV: 5.)

This is a reasonably common motif, and is used on all shapes (except cups). It is most popular for amphorae, tankards, jugs and flasks.

This design is fairly evenly distributed over all areas of the island except the Karpass and the Eastern sites.

Motif 59

A horizontal row of cross hatched lozenges. (*MCBA*, figs. XI: 3, 13, 14; XIV: 5, 8; XV: 3, 7.)

This motif is much more common than the simpler designs 57 and 58. As with 58 it is commonest on amphorae, flasks, and tankards, but it is also common on juglets (mainly in the Nicosia group 40), and occurs on all other shapes.

This design is more widely distributed than the two related designs, and it occurs in all parts of the island. It is most popular at Dhali and Galinoporni, where the simpler designs were not used at all, and is an important motif in the Nicosia style of decoration (cf. motif 51).

Motif 60

A diamond divided into four, with two complementary quarters cross–hatched. (*GCM*, pl. VI. 7.)

This is a rare design, and is related both to design 30 and to the 'butterfly' design 79. In the analysis it appears on 2 jugs from Politico (but see also Lapithos T.6A.73).[32]

Motif 61

A horizontal row of solid lozenges. (*MCBA*, figs. XV: 5; XVII: 6, 7.)

This is a rare design, but appears on most shapes.

It is fairly well confined to Lapithos pottery, except for one jug in the ? Alambra group (47).

It may be related to the use of the solid triangle, motif 52.

Motif 62

A vertical set of plain lozenges. (*MCBA*, fig. XIV: 1.)

This is not a common design, but is used on most shapes (except cups and jars). It is commonest on flasks and jugs, occurring generally as a minor design in an axial stripe dividing the main panels.

It is used occasionally in all areas except the Eastern and Larnaca districts.

Motif 63

A vertical set of hatched lozenges. (*MCBA*, figs. IV: 6; V: 2.)

This is not a common design. It is used most frequently on bottles, and occasionally on jugs, bowls, amphorae and flasks.

It is confined to the North Coast, the Western Mesaoria, and the Southern slopes and the Central and Southern River Valley areas.

Motif 64

A vertical set of cross–hatched lozenges. (*MCBA*, figs. IV: 5; V: 3; XVII: 2, 3.)

This design is more common than the simpler designs 62 and 63, and is found at more sites. It appears commonest on bottles, flasks and amphorae, but is also used on all the other shapes except jars and juglets.

It occurs in all parts of the island, but is less common toward the East, in the Larnaca district and the Karpass.

Motif 65

A large area of the vessel covered with paint. (*MCBA*. figs. III: 5, 6, 9; IV: 1–6; V: 1–5, 10.)

This decoration is generally used on the base, as a large blob or covering the lower third of the body of jugs, cups and amphorae, but it does appear on other shapes as well. It is not used on jars and tankards, and the one bowl decorated in this way is a deep shape.

It is most common on the North Coast, but also appears in all other areas except the East and Karpass.

This covering of a large portion of the vessel with paint develops from the standard Red Polished techniques.

Motif 66

A dot or set of dots.[33] (*MCBA*, figs. III: 1; IV: 6; XVI: 7, 11.)

This dot is not a standardised motif, and appears normally as a filling ornament. Although not very common it is not restricted to any particular shapes; but seems more common on the later wares.

It is found in all areas except the Karpass.

Motif 67

A small circle, with or without a central dot.[34] (*MCBA*, figs. VI: 16; VII: 1; VIII: 11; XII: 2, 4, 7; XV: 1, 9; XVI: 14, 15.)

This is a reasonably common motif. Nearly half of the occurrences are on bowls (23 per cent of bowls have this design) and it is also used frequently on juglets, amphorae and jugs (especially those of White Painted V Type V B 1 b and similar shape) as well as occurring on all other shapes.

On bowls it serves as a central motif on the interior

or as a filling ornament on the base, and appears commonly an the bases of other shapes as well.

It is found at most sites and in all areas.

Motif 68

A pair of small concentric circles. (*MCBA*, figs. V: 5; VI: 15; XVI: 16.)

This design is quite rare, and is used in different ways in different parts of the island. It is generally a variant of the design 67 circle with a central dot.

At Lapithos it appears on the sides of the vessels, at Dhenia, Nicosia and Politico on the bases, and at Enkomi, Milia and Trikomo on the shoulders of the small jugs (White Painted V, type V Bl b).

Motif 69

A wavy line with a circle in the centre – either with or without a central dot. (*MCBA*, fig. IV: 4.)

This is not a common design; it is used on the sides of 9 jugs, on the bases of 2 bowls, and on 2 cups (the one from Yeri has a line only below the circle, and the Lapithos example has the circle at the base of the handle which is decorated with a wavy line).

Åström has noted the occurrence of this design in discussing the Dhenia examples and includes the White Painted V animal from Livadhia (CM 1942/IV–17/2 = MLA 164) which is not included in the analyses.[35] The design on that vessel is different from the other examples, and has straight, not wavy, lines joining a series of dotted circles. One vessel from Lapithos (T.702.150) is not classified as having this motif as it is used on the side of the handle, with the circle painted around a large string–hole.

The distribution of design 69 is confined to Dhenia, Stephania and Lapithos.

Motif 70

A chequer or similar pattern with alternate squares hatched in different directions.

This is a rare design and occurs on only four vessels from Lapithos, Ayia Paraskevi, Larnaca, and Politico.

Motif 71

A band of angled, cross–hatched rectangles.

A rare design occurring only twice, once at Lapithos and once at Galinoporni.

Motif 72

A vertical arrow. (*MCBA*, fig. X: 8.)

This design occurs on only one vessel – Yeri B.M. C263.

Motif 73

An animal. (*MCBA*, fig. VII: 11.)

There is only one example of a painted animal among the pots studied – Ayios Iakovos T.6.1. This jug does not fit into the normal Ayios Iakovos range, and is most likely an import from the North Coast (perhaps Vounous – note the use of motifs 27 and 35 – while the animal design may be related to decoration on White Painted I vessels[36]).

There may be some connection to the possible development of the regional Karpass Style Wavy Line Motifs from the White Painted I designs.

Motif 74

A herring–bone pattern. (*MCBA*, fig. XVII: 5.)

This design appears on only two vessels, a juglet and a tankard from Lapithos.

Motif 75

A wide hatched band or panel. (Villa, 1969, pl. IV. 59; Dikaios, 1938, pl. LVI. 1, 4.)

The design is not common, but is used on most shapes.

It is found mainly on the North Coast and in the Central and Southern River Valley Areas, used in different ways at different sites (for example, at Vounous it is related to motif 27 as a horizontal hatched band).

It is generally to be regarded as in use in the later stages of White Painted Pottery manufacture.

Motif 76

A stitch pattern (Åström and Wright, 1963, fig. IV.8.)

This design is similar to motif 18, but only has the narrow hatched panels in one direction, not two, to make the zig–zag.

Only one amphora with this design is included here (Dhenia T.6.22). Compare the White Painted I jug – L.4A.674.[37]

Motif 77

A horizontal row of lozenges with vertical hatching.

This variant of motif 58 occurs on only one amphora, L.18.183.

Motif 78

A cross formed by a broad band and a cross–hatched

panel. (*MCBA*, fig. XIV: 6.)

This only occurs on one flask – L.320.76.

Motif 79

"Butterfly" motif – complementary triangles of a quartered rectangle filled with cross–hatching. (*MCBA*, fig. XVI: 11.)

A rare design, found toward the East (compare however Politico T.4.133) and generally associated with the later White Painted Wares.

Motif 80

Small crosses or asterisks.

These are not common, and are generally used as filling motifs.

It has no particularly significant distribution.

The simpler cross is associated with earlier wares (and is found on White Painted I vessels[38]); the asterisk is used toward the end of the period on White Painted V and later pottery.

Motif 81

Hatched or cross–hatched chevrons, large triangles with each half hatched in the opposite direction. Sometimes associated with a complex arrow or tree motif.

This is a rare type of motif on most of the White Painted Wares, and is associated with the latest White Painted pottery.

2.7. **Summary**

The material comes from 47 defined Groups which represent individually or in groups a total of 33 sites. Pairs of groups from some sites, and the 21 groups from Lapithos provide some possibility of distinguishing smaller variations, while the reasonable representation in at least 6 of the 8 main geographical areas used in this survey allow for general consideration of regional variation.

Although there is some correlation of design to shape this is not strong enough to upset the potential distribution of the motifs.

It is clear from the general discussion of each of the motifs that many of them have strong associations with particular regions. A simple histogram illustrating the relative popularity of certain of the motifs or sets of motifs in the eight geographical regions is presented in fig. 7.

Although this study does not involve the isolation of particular styles of decoration on the individual pots, the general structural differences in motif arrangement are clear from thc visual analysis of the data assisted by the notes on the individual motifs and Appendix II, especially when considered in the light of indications from the computer studies in the next chapter. These trends may be seen in fig. 7.

Åström has defined two main styles – Western "tectonic" and Eastern "linear".[39] The Wavy Line Style (motifs 7 and 10) characterises the Karpass.[40] Kalopsidha and neighbouring sites are linked by the use of the Cross Line Style (motif 48) as well as others such as the Framed Broad Band Style[41] (motifs 2 and 4). These styles can be said to exhibit a more linear, or generally a less complex structure from the rest of the island, and differentiate the Eastern areas. There are some links, however, as may be seen in the use of such motifs as horizontal triangles and lozenges (motifs 49–51, 57–59) in the Karpass as well as the centre of the island.

These particular motifs are commonest in the central and Southern Regions, together with other lozenge motifs (motifs 62–4). The Nicosia Group, with its large proportion of small jugs and juglets, displays the very characteristic structural style of the pottery from the sites in these regions, with much use of motifs 20 and 34 together with 51 and 59 on the one vessel in a series of horizontal bands.

Nearby Politico has a high proportion of these motifs, and the complex horizontal structure is in evidence there. It is also distinguished by the presence of different motifs which reflect in part Åström's Lattice Diamond Style, which was noted as typical of Yeri.[42] Some of the vessels may definitely be grouped as the products of an individual craftsman –for example, CM A715 from *Chomazoudhia*[43] and CM 1958/I–17/4 from Ayia Paraskevi[44] which display a common use of cross–hatched chequers (motifs 30 and 32) as well as other motifs, and have a characteristic smooth surface and somewhat thick black paint, with careful decoration where the motifs are outlined in wider lines than the finer hatching. Politico T.4.49 and 59 are among other vessels closely related to these pots, in the use of the motifs and the string–hole lugs on the handle and neck, and are clearly within a Central Cypriot tradition.

The horizontality of this tradition reflects that of Vounous and Palaealona, where the motifs are larger and simpler. In general the North Coast (here dominated by the size of the Lapithos sample) is characterised by the use of large formally structured decoration, with emphasis on vertical panels, seen in fig. 7 in the popularity of motif 28. This motif and the use of the broad wavy line (motif 8) link Lapithos to the West (Dhenia), but the greater popularity of the chequer patterns (motifs 40–45) separate them. Other motifs indicate the links between the Western and Central regions.

This simple analysis indicates the divisions within the island in terms of motif popularity and design structure, and points toward the possibility of finer divisions of the material. From figure 7 it is clear that each general area has some differences and similarities to each of its neighbours, giving an impression of the cultural linkages between them. The histogram only treats 9 motifs or classes of motif in the major geographical (not necessarily cultural) areas. In the following chapter an attempt is made to isolate motifs from the total range which are most important in differentiating between each of the groups, and to assess the nature of the relationships more accurately.

NOTES

CHAPTER 2

1. Tugby 1965: 12, 1969: 645–6.
2. *MCBA*: 172.
3. Åström 1966: 83–6, 1960a: 81.
4. *MCBA*: 172–199; Stewart 1962: Index III.
5. Cf. Shepard 1968: 36–42.
6. Courtois 1970: 82; Eslick 1972: Vol 2, 63–4.
7. Boardman 1960: 85–6; Åström 1964: 210.
8. Cf. Shepard 1968: 266f. Compare the more recent classiications of Late Cypriot designs by Åström (e.g. 1972b: 65–9).
9. *MCBA*: 12–78.
10. *Patterns*: 134.
11. Gjerstad 1924, *SPC*.
12. Christodoulou 1959: fig 2.
13. Christodoulou 1959: 225.
14. Dikaios 1969–71: 223, 224, pls 53, 54, 198.7.
15. Åström 1966: 90.
16. *MCBA*: 30–1
17. Popham 1963a: 89.
18. Merrillees 1972; *MCBA*: 30–32.
19. *MCBA*: 29–30.
20. Åström 1960a: 81, 1966: 82–3.
21. Merrillees 1972; *MCBA*: 30–32.
22. *MCBA*: 17–8, Åström 1960a: 81.
23. Åström, *loc cit*.
24. E.g. Stewart 1962: fig. CLVI; Dikaios 1938: pls. LV.3,7,9,10,LVIII.1–3.
25. For a general discussion of this ware see Popham 1963b, 1972.
26. Stewart 1965: 161.
27. *MCBA*: 34.
28. *MCBA*: 18, 66, 274, Åström 1960a: 81, 1966: 83.
29. Åström 1966: 83–6.
30. Åström 1966: 88, *MCBA*: 277.
31. Epstein 1965, 1966: 83f. See also Artzy, Asaro, Perlman 1973.
32. Compare Milia T. 10.91 (Westholm 1939: pl IV.2).
33. Cf. Åström's White Painted V Eyelet Style (1966: 86)
34. See previous note.
35. Åström and Wright 1963: 244.
36. E.g. Vounous T.2.32, T. 41.15 (Dikaios 1938: pl LVIII). For a discussion of this type of motif and other figured decoration, see Åström 1971.
37. Stewart 1965: 158.
38. E.g. C.M. A671 (*Archaeologia Viva* 3: pl. 135)
39. *MCBA*: 275; Åström 1960a: 81.
40. Cf. Merrillees 1972.
41. Åström 1966: 83f, 90.
42. *MCBA*: 32.
43. CMN C2326.
44. CMN C.11.360. Professor Åström has shown me a photograph of Bonn 781 which must also be by this potter.

CHAPTER 3

COMPUTER ANALYSES

3.1. Factor Analysis

The various procedures included in the general term "factor analysis" aim to reduce a set of variables referring to subjects to a smaller set of new, uncorrelated, variables, defined solely in terms of the original dimensions, and which retain the most "important" information contained in the original data.[1] This simplification may consist of the production of a set of classificatory categories, or the creation of a smaller number of hypothetical variables. It is most valuable where a great array of phenomena are multiply determined and where the conceptual independent variables are not easily located and agreed upon.[2] Its role is more important in classifying manifestations or variables rather than producing a taxonomy.[3]

Factor analyses allow one to approach problems as a whole, instead of putting together pieces of evidence from single differences. Although as with all hypothesis testing there is a certain amount of trial and error, factor analysis can remove much of this and apply immediate information of the nature and significance of the underlying factors at work.[4]

It is therefore suited to the problem in this study – that of reducing the independent variables in the different groups to some more easily understood set of major factors.

Factor analysis has been used in other archaeological situations[5] and the general applications have been discussed in several general reviews.[6] Tugby[7] has discussed the covariation between the different dimensions of criteria, situations, and archaeological units,[8] in an attempt to define different analytical possibilities in the data. Although the units and situations in his discussion differ from those considered here, the general pattern is the same. In this study the two major types of analysis were used:

R–mode: This gives a correlation between the members of a set of criteria scored on a series of cultural units. In this case the criteria are the design motifs, and the cultural units the tomb or cemetery–groups.

Q–mode: This correlates cultural units on the series of criteria – the transpose of the R–mode analysis. In this study the Groups are correlated on the basis of the motifs in them.

The other techniques, although of potential value, have not been applied at the present time.

As this study is only dealing with the one type of variable (design) and scoring on the basis of proportional occurrence of the variable in the groups, objections to the use of factor analysis techniques such as those put forward by Sackett[9] can be set aside, as none of the variables are necessarily either mutually interdependent or mutually exclusive. The choice and limitation of the type of variation also overcomes the problems which Sackett sees in the lack of ability of the R–mode technique to accommodate the qualitative variables supplied by a typological attribute system, or to isolate and measure the interactions that influence their multivariate patterning.[10]

The factor analysis program used here is that written by P.F. Sampson and R.I. Jennrich (Health Science Computing Facility, University of California, Los Angeles), BMDX72, and operating on the IBM 7040 computer at the University of New South

Wales. I would like to acknowledge the assistance I received from Dr. D. Jeffrey (Department of Geography, University of New South Wales), in the running of this program, and discussion concerning its meaning.

The data, as with other main programs, was in the form of percentage occurrence of the motifs in the groups.

3.2. The R–Mode Principal Components Analysis

A preliminary run of the R–mode analysis demonstrated that a great many factors would be required to account for the total variation in the data. 22 factors with eigenvalues above 1.0 accounted for only 86% of the variance.

A second program, using only the first 10 factors (eigenvalues above 2.5, accounting for 58% of total variance) was then run. This program also performed a varimax rotation of the factors to maximize the column–variation criteria. This program also produced estimated factor scores for the subjects (tomb–groups).

The 10 factors considered are all orthogonal (they have extremely low correlation with one another). The table below lists the eigenvalues and the proportion of total variance accounted for by these ten factors.

factor	1	2	3	4	5	6	7	8	9	10
eigenvalue	7.6	5.6	4.7	4.0	3.6	3.4	3.2	2.9	2.8	2.7
percentage of variance	10.9	8.0	7.3	5.7	5.1	4.8	4.5	4.2	4.0	3.8

The rotated factor matrix, and the factor scores of the subjects (groups) are presented in tables 5 and 6.

In interpreting these results, it is possible to consider only those variables which exhibit strong positive or negative correlations with each factor, indicating that their respective presence and absence is important in isolating that particular variation. The other variables although they have some weight are considered as less important, and can be generally ignored.

The factor scores of the subjects (tomb–groups) indicate the correlation between each of these and the particular factor, and by comparing the important variables (motifs) with the important subjects (groups) it is possible to interpret the meaning of each of the factors.

A high negative correlation of a variable with a factor indicates it is at one extreme, where the positive correlations are at the other. Such a ("negative") variable will generally be absent from groups with high positive scores, and present in groups with high negative scores. Conversely "positive" variables will tend to be present in groups with high positive scores, and absent from groups with high negative scores. In effect the symbols – and + are interchangeable.

From the table of eigenvalues above some idea of the relative importance of each factor can be assessed. The lists below isolate the more important variables and their associated groups, and a brief interpretation of the meaning or significance of each of these factors is attempted, bearing in mind other archaeological data and theories. Figure 8 gives a visual presentation of the factors and their related distribution – a simple summary of this economical way of explaining the total variation in the data.

FACTOR 1 (fig. 8a)

motif	*corr*	*group*	*score*
35	0.93	41 Palaealona	5.7
16	0.91	19 L.313	2.9
64	0.77	45 Vounous	0.7
39	0.72		
27	0.62		
33	0.62		
15	0.59		
65	0.56		
no high –ve correlations		11 L.316^2	-1.0
		26 Dhenia 6	-1.0
		28 Dhikomo	-1.0
		8 L.315A	-0.7
		40 Nicosia	-0.7

This factor has the highest correlation with the horizontal motifs 35 and 16. There are no motifs which are normally absent when these motifs are present, or which especially characterise the sites with high negative scores. Although there are other links between those sites they are here rather grouped by the absence of those motifs which may be found in large proportion at the three sites with high positive scores. In interpreting the relationship between these three sites and their relative importance it must be remembered that both L.313 and Palaealona are small groups.

Most of the motifs which correlate strongly with this factor are found at the three sites with high scores, and the significance of this factor may be understood. Vounous is an important cemetery in E.C. and continues into the earlier part of M.C.; the same may be true for Palaealona; and L.313 is also considered early in the conventional system. This factor may have isolated a certain degree of temporal variation within the North Coast Region.

In regard to the use of motifs such as 27, 35 and 36, one should note the White Painted II jug (C.M. inv 1970/VI–26/4.14)[11] and other vessels of unknown provenance on the antiquities market. These could well come from a North Coast cemetery to be associated with a regional or temporal group including Palaealona and Vounous.

FACTOR 2 (fig. 8b)

motif	*corr*	*group*	*score*
3	0.45	36 Larnaca	2.4
5	0.41	24 Ay. P.	1.6
70	0.41	14 L.8	1.2
		37 Leondari	1.0
		31 Kalopsidha	0.9
		33 Klavdhia	0.9
		16 L.51	0.9
		20 L.702	0.8
14	-0.69	28 Dhikomo	-4.0
51	-0.63	40 Nicosia	-1.9
59	-0.56	25 Dhali	-1.2
21	-0.55	45 Vounous	-1.0
34	-0.55	8 L.315A	-0.8
47	-0.52		

Fig. 8b appears to indicate two main areas associated with the positive incidence of this factor, but it must be remembered that the Lapithos groups in question are all small and so percentage occurrence of motifs will be abnormally high. The factor may be seen rather as related to the Larnaca District, with extensions toward the north (to Kalopsidha and Ayia Paraskevi).

The sites associated with the other aspect of this factor, differentiated from the positive–correlated variables, is largely constituted by groups important also in factor 1 – Dhikomo, Nicosia, L.315A, here joined with Dhali to the south and Vounous to the north. Most of the important motifs are horizontal – accounting for the link to Vounous.

This factor represents some distinction between areas in the central plain – a south–easterly and a more northerly unit, the latter to be closely associated with the complex horizontally structured design style which is characteristic of the Nicosia material.

FACTOR 3 (fig. 8c)

motif	*corr*	*group*	*score*
62	0.57	28 Dhikomo	2.4
29	0.45	37 Leondari	2.3
57	0.45	39 Milia	1.6
		43 Politico	1.4
		36 Larnaca	1.2
		40 Nicosia	1.2
		24 Ay. P.	1.1
		29 Enkomi	1.0
1	-0.75	18 L.311	-2.2
28	-0.64	9 L.315 B–C	-3.0
9	-0.73	17 L.203	-1.4
8	-0.45	15 L.14	-1.3
55	-0.40	10 L.316^1	-1.1
55	-0.40	22 Alambra	-1.0
		11 L.316^2	-0.8

The negative aspect of this factor may be seen as the more important one – it is associated with all but 4 of the Lapithos groups, and the strongest scores are all of Lapithos groups; the only exception is the small Alambra group. In this regard the factor places most weight on the motifs 1, 8, 9, 28, which often combine to form the standard Lapithos style of decoration (broad bands around the base, a vertical wavy line alternating with a cross–hatched panel on the body of most jugs).

The relative absence of these designs, together with the presence of the two forms of open lozenge and the unbounded cross–hatching separates off the other aspect of the factor. This has its own geographical extent – central and eastern Cyprus.

As with factor 2, this can therefore be seen as a geographical factor, indicating different design–styles in these two areas.

FACTOR 4 (fig. 8d)

motif	*corr*	*group*	*score*
4	0.76	22 Alambra	4.8
31	0.75	29 Enkomi	1.4

32	0.68	46 Yeri	1.4
2	0.45	38 Livadhia	0.9
44	0.45	31 Kalopsidha	0.9
		32 Katydata	0.8
		34 Kotchati	0.6
49	-0.51	16 L.51	-1.8
67	-0.55	15 L.14	-1.4
		26 Dhenia 6	-1.3
		37 Leondari	-1.1
		20 L.702	-0.9
		21 Lapithos	-0.8

This factor appears to be another geographical one – linking sites in the Eastern and Larnaca Districts with others along the northern foothills of the Troodos Range – and separating them from most of the Lapithos groups, which have some connection to Dhenia in regard to the motifs considered. The small Leondari Vouno group should probably be ignored.

The use of motifs 2 and 4 are normally regarded as an Eastern trait, although they do have a wider distribution: the other three motifs here associated with them are all forms of chequer or cross–hatch, different from these forms on the North Coast.

There is no immediate significance in the relationship of the other motifs to the factor, and it is probably the absence of the other motifs rather than the presence of these which here group the Lapithos and Dhenia tombs.

FACTOR 5 (fig. 8e)

motif	*corr*	*group*	*score*
69	0.68	19 L.313	3.7
6	0.66	44 Myrtou	3.3
36	0.49	1 L.2	1.0
63	0.48	11 L.316[2]	1.0
17	0.40	8 L.315A	0.9
		26 Dhenia 6	0.9
		35 Kythrea	-1.9
15	-0.40	41 Palaealona	-1.4
48	-0.35	31 Kalopsidha	-1.2
		39 Milia	-1.2
		38 Livadhia	-1.1
		37 Leondari	-1.0
		17 L.203	-0.9
		23 Ay. Iak.	-0.9
		30 Galinoporni	-0.7

This must be seen as another geographical factor, where the variables weighted in this way indicate a separation between the North Coast, together with the West; and the Eastern sites.

Although the negative aspect does not have many heavily weighted motifs the Cross–Line Style may be seen as of some importance in this factor. The variables with strong positive correlations with this factor are more readily seen as closely related to Lapithos, Dhenia and Myrtou – note the occurrence of the distinctive motif 69 (wavy line with a circle in the centre) which is found in most of the groups noted here, and indicates some contact around the Kyrenia Range via Vasilia.

FACTOR 6 (fig. 8f)

motif	*corr*	*group*	*score*
54	0.71	11 L.316[2]	1.9
40	0.68	13 L.4	4.2
58	0.64	19 L.313	1.6
8	0.44		
29	0.42		
44	0.42		
no high –ve		18 L.311	-1.5
correlations		44 Myrtou	-1.4
		16 L.51	-1.0
		32 Katydata	-1.0

This factor seems only to be significant in regard to Lapithos and Western groups, and it is tempting to interpret it as a temporal factor, especially as the Myrtou and Katydata groups must be late in the period. However L.311 is conventionally placed early in the period, as is L.313, and there is no recognised correlation between the other groups.

Although the motifs with high positive correlations to this factor may in fact define some particular relationship within the Lapithos material (a family matter if not a temporal one), the negative scoring sites are only characterised by the absence of those motifs. The positive aspect of the factor makes use of rare designs such as 29 and 40, and the motifs 8 and 54 are very unlikely to be found at Katydata as there are no jugs or bottles in that group.

It is distinctions seen within the Lapithos cemetery that may be of interest, but again the groups with high negative scores are both small ones.

FACTOR 7		((fig. 8g)	
motif	*corr*	*group*	*score*
25	0.83	42 Politico 4	4.2
30	0.82	46 Yeri	2.9
60	0.72	43 Politico	2.5
18	0.55	11 L.316^2	1.2
57	0.32	1 L.2	0.7
no high –ve		32 Katydata	-1.3
correlations		44 Myrtou	-1.2
		20 L.702	-1.1
		45 Vounous	-1.1

One aspect of a central Cypriot style has been separated out as part of Factor 1. This factor isolates another focus centered around Politico and Yeri. The motifs such as 30 and 60 constitute what Åström has referred to as "Lattice Diamond Style" which is one noticeable feature of pottery important in relation to this factor, some of which can be regarded as the product of a single craftsman or workshop.

The three sites with the highest negative scores are generally considered to be late in the period. Vounous is early, and the sites closely related to it (Palaealona and L.313) also have fairly high negative scores.

This factor may therefore, in separating out the designs characteristic of the Southern River Valley area, also give an indication of its probable dating in the middle of the period, and have some reference to relationships within Lapithos.

FACTOR 8		(fig. 8h)	
motif	*corr*	*group*	*score*
7	0.55	30 Galinoporni	1.8
48	0.52	39 Milia	1.8
		29 Enkomi	1.7
		35 Kythrea	1.5
		44 Myrtou	1.5
		31 Kalopsidha	1.2
		23 Ay. Iak.	1.2
		43 Politico 4	1.0
26	-0.55	12 L.320	-3.0
42	-0.50	24 Ay. P.	-1.8
38	-0.48	37 Leondari	-1.1
		6 L.49	-1.0
		2 L.18	-0.9

This factor places most weight on the mutually exclusive distribution of motifs 7 and 48 from motifs 26, 38, 42.

The first of these are the distinguishing features of the well known "Cross Line" and "Wavy Line" styles, and the scores of the groups against this factor confirm their importance in the East and Karpass. Politico T.4 has a fairly high proportion of both motif 7 and the related motif 10 (also with a reasonably high correlation with this factor). However the use of this motif at this site is very different from that of the Karpass, and the apparent clustering on this basis should not be considered significant. The Myrtou group scores highly as its size allows the single occurrence of motifs to show as a high proportion.

The other aspect of this factor isolates designs which link Ayia Paraskevi to some of the Lapithos groups, and which separate them from the East and Karpass.

This factor is therefore to be seen as a simple geographical situation.

FACTOR 9		(fig. 8i)	
motif	*corr*	*group*	*score*
52	0.88	20 L.702	5.1
61	0.81	11 L.316^2	2.1
43	0.69	10 L.316^1	1.3
17	0.63	1 L.2	1.1
41	0.56	35 Kythrea	0.8
no high –ve		38 Livadhia	-1.1
correlations		24 Ay. P.	-1.0
		26 Dhenia T.6	-1.0
		30 Galinoporni	-0.8

The series of heavy – filled–in – designs has a high correlation with this factor, and the sites with high scores form a small unit within Lapithos, with Kythrea less significant. The use of motifs 41 and 43 as with most other chequer patterns is a feature of Lapithos, and motifs 52 and 61 may characterise the works of a particular workshop (cf. L.2. 36; L.316^2. 64; .316^1. 4; with perhaps some relationship to the ?later vessels L.702.144 and150).

Although basically a major geographical interpretation is clear in the overall use of the motifs (most other motifs are negatively correlated with this factor), this factor perhaps selects out the designs favoured by a particular workshop or family group.

FACTOR 10		(fig. 8j)	
motif	*corr*	*group*	*score*
66	0.68	19 L.313	3.9
36	0.48	32 Katadyta	1.3
65	0.47	38 Livadhia	1.3
68	0.47	39 Milia	1.3
12	-0.59	44 Myrtou	-3.0
53	-0.36	30 Galinoporni	-1.7
59	-0.35	41 Palaealona	-1.3
		13 L.4	-1.1

There is no immediately apparent interpretation of this factor possible. There does not appear to be any temporal or spatial characteristics related to it. The factor's relative importance may be due to the fact that most of the design motifs with high correlation to the factor are rare, and that most of the groups with high scores are small.

Other Factors

Twelve other factors in the preliminary run of this program each account for less than 1.5% of the total variance, and have no immediately apparent cultural significance, and therefore need not be discussed further, although it is worth noting the large number of factors needed to account for the total variance, indicating that there is no simple structure underlying the distribution of many of variables in this mode.

3.3 **The Q–mode Analysis**

This technique is the transpose of the R–mode analysis, based on the correlation coefficients between each pair of variables (tomb–groups) scored on the subjects (motifs). It attempts to reduce the variation between these variables (tomb–groups) in the same way as the R–mode analysis and to construct a simpler set of variables to account for the distribution of the motifs.

As with the R–mode analysis, only factors with eigenvalues above 2.0 were considered, and here the computer drew out 3 factors. The table below gives their eigenvalues and the proportion of variance accounted for by each factor.

factor	Q1	Q2	Q3
eigenvalue	28.1	3.6	2.1
percentage of variance	59.8	7.6	4.4

Unlike the R–mode factors, these 3 factors are not orthogonal, and the table below gives the correlations between them.

factor	Q1	Q2	Q3
Q1	1.0	0.37	0.57
Q2	0.37	1.0	0.34
Q3	0.57	0.34	1.0

The full factor correlation matrix and the list of factor scores is presented in the tables 7 and 8.

As with the R–mode factors, a summary of these factors is given here, with a visual presentation of the selected data in figure 9.

FACTOR Q1		(fig. 9a)	
group	*corr*	*motif*	*score*
31 Kalopsidha	0.91	1	2.1
36 Larnaca	0.88	3	5.8
14 L.8	0.86	6	3.1
20 L.702	0.86	9	2.4
35 Kythrea	0.85	17	1.7
39 Milia	0.82	28	1.0
37 Leondari	0.81	48	1.1
29 Enkomi	0.76		
47 ?Alambra	0.73		
all other groups have a positive correlation except:			
45 Vounous	-0.13	65	-0.68
41 Palaealona	-0.12	27	-0.67
28 Dhikomo	-0.12	34	-0.63
40 Nicosia	-0.07	36	-0.57
19 L.313	-0.06	35	-0.54
13 L.4	-0.03	54	-0.52

This factor accounts for 60% of the total variance, and has most variables (tomb–groups) correlated positively with it – those few groups with negative correlations all have low correlations. The importance of this factor indicates there is a basic structure underlying the total body of data scored in terms of the proportional occurrence of the motifs.

This factor has a definite geographical/temporal significance.

The negatively correlated groups may be the same as those connected with the first two factors of the R–mode analysis, and again the Palaealona–Vounous–L.313 group (and L.4) show up as different from the other groups, and associated with the horizontal motifs. The use of some of these motifs on the small jugs and juglets in the Nicosia Group, and at Dhikomo, align them with this factor; reflecting the Nicosia variant of a Central Cypriot Style.

The strongest correlations with the positive aspect of this factor are with the later Lapithos groups (e.g. L.702) and with the Eastern and Larnaca District sites, associated with the "tectonic" and "linear" motifs respectively.

This factor does, to a certain extent, differentiate between the major areas, and also isolates the "early" North Coast groups from the "later" ones.

FACTOR Q2		(fig. 9b)	
group	*corr*	*motif*	*score*
9 L.315 B–C	0.75	28	4.6
17 L.203	0.75	9	4.0
18 L.311	0.74	1	2.5
19 L.313	0.72	6	2.3
5 L.47	0.69	8	1.5
21 Lapithos	0.63	65	1.5
10 L.316[1]	0.62	27	1.0
41 Palaealona	0.61		
45 Vounous	0.60		
all other groups have a positive correlation except:			
37 Leondari	-0.27	48	-1.1
39 Milia	-0.26	3	-0.89
30 Galinoporni	-0.19	7	-0.87
23 Ay. Iak.	0.18	10	-0.86
28 Dhikomo	-0.12	2	-0.85
31 Kalopsidha	-0.05	32	-0.59
36 Larnaca	-0.05	5	-0.53
29 Enkomi	-0.03	18	-0.53
20 L.702	-0.02	4	-0.50

This factor differentiates between the North Coast and the Karpass and Eastern Regions. It is a clear geographical separation.

The motif scores indicate the Eastern "linear" style and the Northern "tectonic" style discussed by Åström. The North Coast sites are to be associated with the motifs 1, 8, 9, 28, 65 (which often occur on the same vessel – cf. Factor 3). The other area is connected with the presence of the Cross–Line style (motif 48), the Framed Broad Band (motifs 2 and 4), and Pendent Line Style (motifs 3 and 11), as well as the Wavy Line Style (motifs 5, 7, 10). The stray Lapithos group (T.702) is probably late in the period.

FACTOR Q3		(fig. 9c)	
group	*corr*	*motif*	*score*
40 Nicosia	0.93	6	4.2
28 Dhikomo	0.92	3	2.8
26 Dhenia T.6	0.64	51	2.4
42 Pol. 4	0.57	59	2.4
25 Dhali	0.56	10	1.7
13 L.4	0.51	9	1.6
43 Politico	0.50	14	1.6
		22	1.6
most other groups have positive correlations except:		67	1.6
		49	1.3
35 Kythrea	-0.19	48	-1.2
14 L.8	-0.10	35	-0.85
31 Kalopsidha	-0.10	16	-0.76
41 Palaealona	-0.10	61	-0.71
17 L.203	-0.06	37	-0.69
29 Enkomi	-0.05	33	-0.68
36 Larnaca	-0.05	55	-0.68
19 L.313	-0.02	69	-0.68
39 Milia	-0.02	19	-0.64
20 L.702	-0.01	52	-0.64
34 Kotchati	-0.01	70	-0.63
		26	-0.60
		43	-0.60

This factor differentiates the sites in the Centre and West of the island from those to the North and East.

The Central sites are to be associated with the use of the hatched triangle and lozenge etc. which have high scores. The motif 48 of course is important in the East, and many of the other designs with the negative scores are associated with the North Coast, although not necessarily associated with the particular sites with high negative correlations.

As with the previous factor, this is to be seen as a spatial differentiation, based on the main types of style already discussed.

3.4 Factor Analysis – Summary

The two techniques used here reveal certain structures underlying the covariation in the data, and allow for their simple explanation.

Although the correlations between the variables (motifs) in the R–mode analysis are not great, and therefore need a large number of factors to explain the variance, the ten factors considered here do appear to have understandable significance. On the one hand they confirm the ideas of a basic distinction between the tectonic and linear styles of decoration, but they also indicate that this simple binary distinction is inadequate, and that there is a more subtle relationship between the motifs, with more motif–areas (rather than style areas). The relationship between the different areas or groups on the basis of the factors distinguished in this analysis reveals a complex pattern of similarities and differences, with sites having different relationships with one another in regard to different factors.

Some of the factors may be taken to isolate motifs which characterise the work of a certain manufacturing unit, others may indicate temporal differences, but in the main these factors can best be explained by the geographical aspects of the distribution of the criteria.

The Q–mode analysis separates out first of all a partly temporal, partly geographical distinction between the "early" North Coast sites together with the Central ones; and the North Coast and the Eastern bloc. The second factor distinguishes between the North Coast and the rest of the island, while the third shows the Centre of the island as different from the East. Three main style– (motif–) distribution areas are therefore presented, together with a certain temporal (?) distinction. The scores of the subjects (motifs) against these factors reiterates the now clear concepts of the nature of the design structure in these zones. Formal, thick, and simple decoration characterises the North Coast; linear and open design is seen in the East; and an eclectic, complex and highly structured set of motifs are popular in the Central Plain.

The two factor analysis techniques present much the same picture, which is one easily fitted into the conventional concept of the styles of the pottery, but demonstrate as well the complexity of the relationships, giving a more formal and secure basis for discussion, with some idea of the relative significance of the different aspects of the material.

3.5 Cluster Analysis

Although factor techniques can be used to classify variables in groups according to their resemblance, this is a secondary usage,[12] and for such clustering other techniques are available. Most of these classificatory techniques are based on the methods of Numerical Taxonomy.[13] The use and problems of different clustering techniques in archaeological situations have been discussed in many recent works.[14]

Generally the clustering techniques have been applied to the classification of objects into types, and the clarification of differences and similarities in the data. Some application to the problem of relationships between sites and data has been attempted.[15] Archaeological units may be arranged according to their relative similarity on the basis of the variables in them (Q–mode) or the relationships between the variables assessed on the basis of their distribution in the units (R–mode).

The Q–mode cluster analysis is useful, therefore, in arranging the sites into groups or clusters on the basis of the motifs in them, and such an analysis can give an idea of the relative similarity between individual sites or groups of sites, and therefore be of value in defining areas of greater or lesser contacts, in time or in space.

3.6 Q–mode Clusters using a presence-absence Similarity Coefficient

This was a preliminary analysis, and used only the presence or absence of the motifs to calculate a similarity coefficient on which to base the cluster analysis.

There are of course many problems associated with such a coefficient, especially as the number of motifs is so closely tied to the number of pots (cf chapter 2.3, fig. 5) and this limits the possible similarity in relation to larger groups. Also the Eastern and Karpass sites which have fewer designs will therefore have low similarities to one another as well as to the rest of the island. In order to overcome a few of these problems, a formula was used which takes no account of cases where neither group has a particular variable, but used cases where they have a variable in common, or one site has a motif absent in the other. This formula may be referred to as the Jaccard Coefficient of similarity,[16] and is calculated by the formula:

$$\text{Similarity Coefficient} = \frac{\text{no. of positive matches}}{\text{no. of positive matches} + \text{no. of mismatches}}$$

Although not a perfect formula, it does allow the consideration of the relationship between the groups simply on the basis of the appearance of the motifs, and where all motifs have the same value.

This coefficient was calculated using a program written by Mrs. J. Bubb of the Computing Department, Commonwealth Scientific and Industrial Research Organization, and run on the C.S.I.R.O. computer.

The full similarity matrix is presented in table 4 (a & b).

Because the nature of the Jaccard coefficient is such that small groups have comparatively low similarities to any other groups, these have been left out of the following analysis of the table of similarity coefficients. In order to see basic patterns within the matrix use was made of a form of the simple ordering technique described by Renfrew and Sterud.[17] This involves the simple plotting of the two units most similar to each of the units, which are thus grouped into clusters or linear patterns, presumably related to temporal, geographical, or other causes.

The results of this analysis are presented in figure 10; the arrows indicate the direction of the linkages between groups.

Although there is a bias toward large groups (such as L.50 and Ayia Paraskevi) which tend to "attract" other groups, some basic geographical clustering is evident. The Lapithos groups tend to form distinct interrelated clusters, with two main foci, one with groups such as L.18, 29, 47, 320; the other with groups L.316^1, 316^2, 315A. The latter is connected to the group Dhenia T.6. The other Dhenia group links L.50 to Nicosia, which in turn is linked to the Ayia Paraskevi group.

Strong links join the Politico groups (but note their tendency to have many different motifs) and link them with Nicosia, with Yeri tagged on. Dhali and Kotchati form a small cluster attached to Ayia Paraskevi, which also has links from the Larnaca district and the Eastern sites, which form their own cluster. With so few motifs Ayios Iakovos has low similarity to any site, and its position is really meaningless.

The main geographical areas are apparent in this simple clustering. A similar analysis based on a proportional occurrence correlation matrix is discussed in section 3.10 (fig. 16).

A somewhat more complex analysis also based on the presence–absence (Jaccard) similarity coefficient was undertaken using a technique of average–linkage clustering.[18] This involves the initial grouping of the two most similar units on the basis of the matrix of coefficients. These are thereafter considered as a unit. The next highest similarity is then sought for, to link two other units, or, if the *average* similarity of a third unit to the first pair is higher than any other, to link it to them. This process continues, repeatedly linking the individuals with the highest or the groups with the highest average similarity, until all are within the one cluster.

The technique involves some important problems, which lead to a certain distortion of the results. An odd high similarity can link two subjects at an early stage and trap them together, when their main similarities to other units differ. Also a fairly high similarity of one unit to another may be obscured by the slightly higher similarity of a third unit, which, when joined to the second unit, prevents the first from approaching it.

By comparing the average–linkage analysis with the Close–Proximity Analysis some of these distortions may be apparent.

The results of this cluster analysis are presented as a dendrogram in figure 11 a.

The chaining effect and lack of a clear cut–off point of main clusters at a particular level of similarity is due largely to the lower level of similarities among the Eastern sites, where fewer motifs are used.

Six main clusters are, however, apparent in fig. 11. For convenience the linkages have been drawn out as a series of isopleths on the map in figure 11b.

The Lapithos groups display the tendency seen in the Close–Proximity Analysis to cluster together, and the distinction between the two sets (L.18, 29, 47, 49, 50, 320; L.316^1, 316^2, 2, 315A) is again apparent, as well as the linkage between Dhenia and the latter group. The Politico and Nicosia groups again link with Dhenia and are close to the Lapithos groups. Yeri now groups with Dhali and Kotchati, while the Eastern and Larnaca sites form their own interrelated clusters.

This technique shows a slightly different structure from that of the close proximity analysis, although they both display the same patterns of geographical separation, inherent in the similarity coefficient on which they are based.

It can be seen from fig. 11b that there are definite differences between the various areas on the basis of which designs were used, but the nature of the similarity coefficient is such that it would be unwise to attempt to assess the relative degree of intercommunication between the regions on that basis, although the main style–zones are fairly clear.

3.7 Q–mode clusters using proportional occurrence

Although programs similar to those used above are possible using a correlation matrix based on the proportional occurrence of the variables (such as are the basis of the factor programs), the technique used here is that devised by Ward.[20] This is a procedure for forming hierarchical groups of mutually exclusive subjects, each of which has members that are maximally similar with respect to the specified characteristics. Given N sets, the procedure permits their reduction to N–1 mutually exclusive sets by uniting the 2 sets which will, when united, produce the least impairment of the optimal value of the objective function. This is taken to contain the greatest amount of information when the original set of N members is ungrouped. The N–1 groups are then examined to determine whether a third member should be associated with the first pair, or another different pairing made to secure the optimal value of the objective function for N–2 groups. This is continued until all N members of the original array are in the one group, the groups formed by this process being "hierarchical clusters".[21]

This procedure is in many ways similar to the Average–Linkage Cluster Analysis, and has many of the problems associated with that technique, although its bases are somewhat different. The distortions which can affect the Average–Linkage Analysis are also apparent in these clusters, and these must again be considered in interpreting the results.

The computer program to perform this hierarchical cluster analysis was based on the HGROUP program set out by Veldman,[22] slightly adapted for, and run on, the IBM 7040 computer in the Basser Department of Computing Science, Sydney University.[23]

This program allows for an option to standardise the raw data matrix by the variables, in order to avoid the distortion caused where variables with smaller variabilities contribute less to the index of group distance than variables which are scaled with larger variances.[24]

The exercise of this option is not an obviously necessary step with the problem considered here. It may be advisable, or at least interesting, to consider both situations, where the variables (motifs) which are most common affect the analysis to a greater or lesser extent.

Accordingly two series of programs were run, one with standardised variables, the other without. In order to remove distortions caused by the effects of small group–size, two of each of these analyses were run, the one with all the groups, the other with selected (generally larger) groups.

The results of these 4 programs are presented in figures 12 to 15. The numbers at the sides of the dendrograms indicate the relative error generated in the optimal value of the objective function by linking the groups at each level. As with the average–linkage analysis, isopleth maps indicate the geographical aspect of the clusters. Although not all the clusters are indicated the main geographical relationships are clear.

3.8 Hierarchical Cluster Analysis – Variables not Standardised

(fig. 12 main analysis, all sites; fig. 13 minor analysis, selected sites.)

Although the lower level linkages (where the error is comparatively great) are not of great significance, it is clear that the Vounous–Palaealona–L.313 cluster is very distinct (compare Factors 1 and Q1); and again may be explained in temporal/spatial terms as an early North Coast group. The Karpass and Eastern sites also join together before linking to the other sites. It is, however, most useful to consider the clusters separated when the error level in these particular analyses is below about 0.4.

At this stage 8 main clusters are differentiated in the analysis using all of the material, and 6 in the other, where only selcted sites are used. The two clusters missing from the latter contained mostly small groups, which were removed for this reason.

The first of these small clusters is composed of the Klavdhia, Leondari, Mytou, and L.702 groups. Three of these are considered to be late, and their clustering would seem to confirm this arrangement. The Leondari group is small, and may not really belong here, although it often is linked with the same factors as L.702 (cf Factors 2 and 4). The other small cluster is formed by L.315 B–C, L.311, and L.203. These three groups are found together with very high scores in relation to Factor 3, and the cluster may indicate some temporal or other distinction within the Lapithos cemetery.

The close relationship between most other Lapithos groups is clear in both versions of this analysis. L.316[1] and L.316[2] are closer to one another than to any other of the Lapithos groups, suggesting a stronger continuity of pottery design within one family through time than between family groups at a particular time. Most of the other Lapithos groups are joined in a main cluster which includes Dhenia, which has much Lapithos–style pottery, and Kotchati, where 4 of the 19 pots would not be out of place on the North Coast (note the reasonably high score for Kotchati in Factor 3).

L.315A and L.320 which are separated from the other Lapithos groups, join with L.4 in the complete analysis, and with Dhenia T.6 in both analyses; and this cluster is closely related to a cluster grouping sites in the centre of the island. This cluster, with the two Politico groups, Nicosia, and Dhali, is neatly geographical, with outlying links to Dhikomo and Katydata (cf Factor Q3).

Yeri has close relations with Ayia Paraskevi, and the pair link with the small group L.51, and with both Alambra groups, one of which demonstrates a connection to Livadhia in the south–east. In the minor analysis, Klavdhia, displaced by the removal of other members of its original cluster, joins this cluster in the place of Livadhia, reiterating the southeastern orientation (cf Factor 2).

Galinoporni and Ayios Iakovos cluster together, demonstrating the unity within the Karpass and its relative isolation; although the pair later join to the Eastern cluster. In that cluster Kalopsidha, Milia, and Enkomi form a unit, with Kythrea and Larnaca, half–way between the Centre and the East, joining them (cf Factors 8 and 5).

3.9 Hierarchical Cluster Analysis – Variables Standardised

(figure 14: main analysis, all groups; figure 15: minor analysis, selected groups.)

A slightly different picture is presented by the analysis where all the variables carry the same weight, although the results are still close to the other analysis (and a little closer to the results of the average–linkage analysis).

All but four of the Lapithos groups now join into one cluster in the main analysis, involving Dhenia and Kotchati as before, but now also including the ?Alambra group. Although they do not form a cluster of their own, the three of these stray Lapithos groups, L.315A, L.320, L.4, were differentiated from the other Lapithos groups in the earlier analysis, where they joined with Dhenia T.6. The link between L.315A and Dhenia T.6 remains.

In the analysis eliminating small groups, the L.315A and L.320 groups join into the main Lapithos cluster. This selected analysis also reestablishes the distinctions within the Lapithos material, which were not apparent in the main program. L.316[1] and L.316[2] are again seen as a unit; L.29, L.47, L.49 link together; and so do L.18 and L.50.

This difference between the two analyses demonstrates the distortion caused by small groups, which force close groups apart by biased correlations due to the small number of motifs represented. This imbalance is more in evidence in this standardised analysis than in the earlier analyses where rare designs carried less weight. In this regard the present analysis is more similar to that based on the presence–absence (Jaccard) similarity coefficient.

Dhenia T.6, linked with L.315A in the main analysis (cf Factor 5) joins with a central cluster in the minor one. This cluster is based around a Nicosia-Dhali link, and at a lower level also takes in Vounous in both analyses (forced away from Palaealona and L313) by the method's distortion. The Politico groups in this analysis join with Yeri, and this cluster links with the Nicosia one, representing the two foci of a central style area. In the main analysis other small groups such as Dhikomo reiterate their relationship to these clusters.

Ayia Paraskevi, still with some links to Lapithos in the main analysis, demonstrates again the south–eastward links, especially in the minor study.

The pattern of relationships within the Eastern cluster is a little different from those in the earlier analyses, and again the links to Kythrea and the Larnaca district are in evidence, as well as the lower level linkage to the familiar Karpass cluster.

3.10 Close Proximity Analysis based on proportional occurrence

A close–proximity analysis, similar to that discussed in section 3.6, was performed using the correlation matrix on which the Q–mode factor analysis was based, in order to compare the results with that earlier analysis.

The diagram indicating the two highest correlations of the main groups is presented in figure 16.

The now familiar pattern of clusters is again apparent, and the general impression is the same as in the other analyses, although clearly better than that in the clustering based on the Jaccard similarity coefficient, and more similar to the results of the hierarchical clusters.

All the main geographical groups are obvious, as well as some of the finer clustering at Lapithos. The variable relationships of groups like Kotchati and Ayia Paraskevi, with some connections to the West and North, and others to the South–East are shown; and generally the results of this analysis indicate that, given a good similarity coefficient as a base, this method of rapid ordering of the data is very valuable.

3.11 R–mode clusters

As a complement to the R–mode factor analysis, an R–mode hierarchical cluster program was run, in order to group the motifs on the basis of their distribution. As most of the motifs have little correlation to one another in this regard, few of the clusters have any significance, and they do not add at all to the results of the factor analysis.

As a general guide to the relationships of occurrence of the motifs, the highest linkages between them in the correlation matrix on which the R–mode factor analysis was based, are shown in figure 17.

The main groups in this extremely simple representation can easily be related to the results of the factor analysis, and demonstrate the main geographical or individual style groupings. It may be worth pointing out that the highest correlations of some of the triangle and lozenge forms are with motifs having the same filling, rather than the same shape (e.g. 52 and 61; 30 and 60; 51 and 59; 49 and 58) and that in other stylistic studies this could be a useful distinction.

This simple diagram, although interesting, is no substitute for the factor analysis of such a complex situation.

3.12 Cluster Analysis – Discussion and Summary

It is of interest to compare the results of the analyses using all the groups and those using only the main ones. In the latter cases, not only are the results easier to see, but also the tendency of small groups to distort the results by reducing the overall or average similarity to clusters of which they are members, and by their unexpected low–level linkages, is clear. This distortion is more important when the presence/absence of motifs is the basis of the correlation matrix or analysis, and is also greater when all variables carry equal weight in the standardised hierarchical cluster programs.

It is unfortunate and probably inevitable that groups from the earlier or latest phases of the life–span of the wares studied are smaller than those which were formed when the wares were most popular. The same is true for peripheral areas. Because of this the relationships between these groups and the others cannot be assessed as well as the relationships between major groups, although it is of equal or perhaps greater, interest to study the fringe areas as well as the main ones. Nevertheless some indication of the temporal divisions can be seen in these analyses, as well as the position of poorly represented areas; especially in the cluster program using unstandardised variables.

It is possible that the somewhat different picture presented in that analysis from those using standardised variable weighting, or based on a presence/absence similarity coefficient, may demonstrate the not unlikely situation where the occurrence of a motif is a stronger determinant of geographical relationship than the relative proportions of the motifs. This proportional popularity will change within an area through time, while most motifs will reflect only the basic distribution pattern. The proportional occurrence analyses will tend, therefore, to give temporal as well as spatial groupings while the presence/absence studies show mainly spatial patternings.

If this method of interpreting the cluster analyses is valid, then the simpler patterns of the latter analyses are to be understood as showing basic style– (or motif–) areas, and their relative contacts with one another. Although the clusters are fairly well defined, from the tendency of sites like Dhenia and Nicosia to provide two groups with differing orientations suggests that the different areas do not have tightly controlled relations with other areas. The general picture is of closer relationships with the neighbouring sites, and lesser contacts with areas further away, with the main zones discussed in the factor analysis where there is greater sharing of motifs.

The analysis where the more common motifs carry greater weight isolates a few temporal groups. L.702, Myrtou, Klavdhia, are at the latest part of the period of use of White Painted Wares; Vounous, Palaealona and L.313 are at the beginning. L.315 B–C, L.311, L.203 may also be considered as fairly early, in relation to the other Lapithos groups, where clusters may be familial rather than temporal. $L.316^1$ and $L.316^2$ indicate strong unity in a presumably family group, and the same may be interpreted for the relationships between L.47 and L.49, and the different degree of similarity between this pair and other groups such as L.29, L.18 and L.50.

Most of the clusters can be related to similar factors in the other analyses, giving mutual corroboration and confirmation of the basic patterns underlying the distribution of the motifs in the groups. These techniques, in considering the totality of the data and suggesting the most satisfactory arrangement of it, give a more solid basis for the interpretation of the prehistoric situation, and also provide general insights into the material to show profitable avenues for future research.

NOTES

CHAPTER 3

1. Veldman 1967: 206.
2. Cattell 1965: 190.
3. Cattell 1965: 191.
4. Cattell 1965: 424–6.
5. E.g. Binford and Binford 1966; Glover 1969; Binford 1972; Rowlett and Pollnac 1971.
6. Tugby 1965: 7–8, 1969; Cowgill 1968: 370f; Sackett 1969; Hodson 1969a.: 93f; Clarke 1968: 562–4.
7. Tugby 1965: 7, 1969: 639.
8. Cf. Cattell 1965: 414–416.
9. Sackett 1969: 1126. For other discussions of problems of interdependent criteria, see Johnson 1971 and Christenson 1972.
10. Sackett 1969: 1129.
11. Nicolaou 1970: pl. 63.8.
12. Cattell 1965: 431–2.
13. Sokal and Sneath 1963; Sneath 1966.
14. Hodson, Sneath, Doran 1966; Hodson 1969a, 1969b, 1970; Cowgill 1968; Thomas 1971, 1972; Clarke 1968: 512f. For a simple introduction to these techniques, see my forthcoming article "The pot–marks of Vounous: Simple Clustering Techniques, their problems and potential" *Opuscula Atheniensia*, 1974.
15. E.g. Thomas 1971; Rowlett and Pollnac 1971.
16. Sokal and Sneath 1963: 128f. It has been used in other archaeological situations (e.g. Irwin 1972: 88).
17. Renfrew and Sterud 1969; Renfrew 1972: 142–7.
18. Hodson, Sneath, Doran, 1966: 322; Hodson 1970: 306–8; Cowgill 1968: 369–70.
19. Cf. Hodson 1970: 307–8.
20. Ward 1963; Rowlett and Pollnac 1971: 56.
21. Ward 1963: 312. These analyses are, for convenience, referred to here as "hierarchical cluster analyses" and the other cluster analysis as "average–linkage analysis". This is not intended to imply that the average–linkage method is not an hierarchical one.
22. Veldman 1967: 308–17.
23. I have applied this particular program to other archaeological problems – e.g. on a body of data on pre– and proto–historic sites in the South Island of New Zealand, supplied by Mr. W. Orchiston of the Department of Anthropology, Sydney University. This series of well dated sites was classified according to the proportional occurrence of formally defined adze and fish–hook types; the results, as in this analysis, showed some predictable clusters of temporal and spatial significance.
24. Veldman 1967: 311.

CHAPTER 4

DISCUSSION AND CONCLUSIONS

The analyses discussed in the previous chapter indicate the main trends in the relationships between the groups and the characteristics of the different areas of Cyprus.

Instead of the two main cultural areas described by Åström[1] it is possible to divide the island into a series of overlapping regions, each of which can be characterised by the greater popularity of specific design motifs and structure, although similar vessels may be found in the other areas.

The Karpass is the most distinct region, with a very high frequency of the Wavy Line Style.[2] Other motifs and designs are used there as well, especially those of the Eastern sites. These sites tend to have linear decoration, either the earlier Pendent Line and Cross Line Styles or later types such as the Framed Broad Band Style.[3] In the Larnaca District, there is no specific local style of decoration recognisable in the small sample of material available, and the pottery tends to have some of the characteristics of the Eastern sites and some of the more central ones. The same is true for Kythrea.

The Centre of the island is characterised by a complex style using small motifs in horizontal bands, commonly with double chequer rows alternating with cross–hatched zig–zags, lozenges or triangles. This style of decoration is most common in the large Nicosia Group, but is frequent at Dhikomo and other central sites. A related but somewhat different style may have its centre at Politico, where there is more use of angled cross–hatched chequers and diamonds.

Dhenia, toward the west, has no recognisable individual characteristics, but the Central Styles are fairly popular, as are those common on the North Coast. The main North Coast style is that of Lapithos, which is a more formal style, using larger and heavier decoration than elsewhere. The use of vertical cross–hatched panels is popular, especially associated with vertical wavy lines, and with broad bands around the bases. A variety of chequer patterns are also characteristic of Lapithos, but many of the aspects of the Central Style are also frequent.

An earlier form of North Coast decoration is that most common at Vounous and Palaealona, as well as occurring on many Lapithos vessels, especially in L.313. Here the simple large–scale decoration is horizontal rather than vertical as in the later Lapithos material.

This picture of regional styles is based to a large extent on the analysis of the relative frequency of occurrence of the motifs in the groups, and not on the individual vessels. No particular account in the earlier analyses is taken of the transport of individual pots from their place of manufacture, although this contributes to the total measure of relationships.

The concept of a trade in pottery is a common interpretation, and is used to explain the distribution of many individual vessels. The pots may, however, be transported for a variety of reasons, and may function as trade–goods, gifts, souveniers, loot, booty, or other symbols of social intercourse. The spread of some distinctive wares may well indicate a trade or other reciprocal interchange, as is suggested for the Red–on–Black wares.[4]

Other vessels may reflect situations not directly concerned with a pottery trade. These more casual movements of objects are more difficult to interpret. Within the framework of general similarity and style areas already established, some further attempt to assess the nature of these exchanges and influences is possible.

A useful starting point in the examination of the relationships of the different styles is the Group 34 from Kotchati, comprising three groups in the Cyprus Museum (1950/V–18/1; 1950/VI–16/1; 1970/X–7/10–22).[5] The first two of these groups contain some later White Painted Vessels, the other would appear to be earlier, and is made up of vessels of much the same fabric and colour, probably being local products. One cup (CM 1970/X–7/17, figure 19a) is decorated with horizontal chequer and cross–hatched bands (motif 27 and 35) and should be compared with material from Ayia Paraskevi[6] as well as the groups which have been especially characterised by these motifs – Palaealona and Vounous[7] and some Lapithos pottery, as in L.313. These, and related motifs, have , as has been seen, a general distribution on the North Coast and in the centre of the island.

The horizontal emphasis in decoration may be seen in the incised decoration of earlier Red Polished vessels at Vounous especially in E.C. II,[8] and is repeated in a somewhat different form in these later wares. It is most likely that the earlier White Wares and White Painted I wares of E.C. III develop from the techniques of the Red Polished Wares, using the general visual concepts of the painted Chalcolithic pottery, if not the specific motifs; and that the White Painted II ware derives from the earlier painted wares on the North Coast.[9] The White Painted I ware may be most strongly associated with Vounous than other sites, although pottery of this type has been found at Ayia Paraskevi, Kalopsidha, and elsewhere.[10]

Stewart has suggested an E.C. – M.C.I. movement of copper from the Troodos sources to Vounous via Ayia Paraskevi and Dhikomo,[11] and considering the similarity of the Kotchati and Ayia Paraskevi vessels with the Vounous–Palaealona style of decoration, the use of this route must be considered a strong possibility. Other similarities between these sites may be seen in the possible relationships between the shrine model from Vounous and those from Kotchati, which can be compared to the carvings on the Palaealona tomb dromoi.[12]

The E.C. – M.C.I contacts between Vounous, Palaealona, and Kotchati may be inferred from the vessel from that site showing the characteristics of the primary North Coast style.[13] This earlier style influences the earliest White Painted II pottery of Lapithos as well, and in the cluster analyses, the Kotchati group is placed with the main Lapithos cluster, but for other reasons. Vessels from Kotchati such as 1970/X–7/11, 13, 15 and 1950/V–8/1a (fig. 19b) are all decorated in the standard panelled Lapithos style, and these contacts must again be connected with the copper trade. The route is not necessarily that used in the (earlier) contacts to Vounous, for with the close relationship between Dhenia and Lapithos, the Western route through the Vasilia passes may be seen to have been in use for most of the time.[14]

This is not to say that the various Kotchati pots were brought from Lapithos or Dhenia. The general contact and fairly constant communication in regard to the copper trade could lead to an exchange of ideas as much as of material, or to the migration of people, either permanently or for short periods. As a possible alternative hypothesis to explain the pottery similarities in the context of the main resource–based contact, one may postulate a situation where pottery–making women were exchanged between the North Coast and the Centre of the island, either in one direction in exchange for copper, or more reasonably, in a reciprocal exchange, whereby the kinship ties thus established could be used as a basis for trading systems. In such a system, the women would bring to their new homes the concepts in pottery manufacture and decoration common in their native villages. Some of the other contacts between sites or similarities between tomb–groups, as well as the spread of new pottery styles or techniques may also be explained by similar models of virilocal marriage systems.

Kotchati and the surrounding areas may also be seen to have affinities with the Eastern sites, again mainly to be associated with the copper sources. If the salt–lakes had formed to some extent at this early date, then one may postulate a reciprocal trade in salt. CM 1950/VI–16/a is a fairly standard Cross–Line Style vessel. CM 1970/X–7/12, although Cross–Line Style, is different from the usual type (figure 19c).[15] This vessel has a row of large blobs around the neck, with thin horizontal lines above and below, and has broad bands around the base, indicating, perhaps, a local product, influenced a little by North Coast design. Some of the White Painted VI vessels in the Kotchati groups also indicate the eastern trends.

Besides these other orientations, Kotchati also has pottery similar to its near neighbours. CM 1970/X–7/10 is clearly within the Central tradition (figure 19d),[16] as is CM 1950/VI–16/1b which may be related to the Politico–Yeri version of this style.

This small group, in a fairly important economic position not far from the copper sources, indicates some of the complex interactions to be seen in the material, and it also affords some clues to the development of the regional styles in the White Painted Ware, with a primary spread of the Vounous–Palaealona style of pottery decoration and manufacture to the Central Plain. Even if the model of trade contact and exchange is not accepted, it is possible to demonstrate some evolutionary developments in the other material.

The general horizontal emphasis and use of chequer bands seen in the Vounous White Painted pottery may also be found on vessels such as CM 1938/XI–15/5 from Mavro Nero[17] or Vounous T.8.47[18] which show some of the motifs common later at Nicosia and Dhikimo. The horizontal bands, using techniques of incision from the Red Polished tradition on these unusual wares, have parallels in the standard Central Cypriot White Painted styles. The horizontal hatched zig–zag is repeated on the unusual vessel from Lapithos T.4A.6/4[19] and the general style must again be related to the Central sites, demonstrating once more an influence from the North Coast in technique and style, operating on a central Red Polished tradition.

Another evolutionary sequence, again beginning from the assumed North Coast origins of the White Painted Wares may be drawn up for the Karpass Style. The unconnected and broken nature of some Red Polished and the normal White Painted I decoration may be seen as the source for the character of the Wavy Line Styles, and some of the open lattice motifs found at Vounous provide the motifs for the range of triangles and lozenges on the Karpass pottery.[20] The jug from Ayios Iakovos (T.6.1) must be an import from the North Coast, possibly Vounous, Palaealona, or similar site, indicating one specific contact between these areas.[21] The animal motif on this vessel must be seen again in relation to the animals on White Painted I pottery.[22]

The Karpass has, however, greater affinities with the Eastern sites especially in the use of the Pendent Line and Cross Line Styles; and one may suggest that an early contact with the areas toward Vounous on the North Coast was replaced with a southern orientation.

The Pendent Line Style, fairly characteristic of the Eastern sites, can also be derived from White Painted I decoration, perhaps by way of the Framed Caduceus Style.[23]

Åström has also suggested the evolution of the Cross Line Style from the Pendent Line Style.[24] This evolution is suggested on the basis of the jug CM A798[25] and other material.[26] Such a simple genetic relationship is not necessary, and the decoration on CM A798 can be seen together with that on other vessels[27] to be a combination of the two styles, rather than as an intermediate transitional form. There are several other developments of regional or late forms of the Cross Line Style, and the later redevelopment of the Framed Caduceus and breakdown of the Cross Line Style is possible.[28]

The general evolutionary picture presented above is not really adequate to explain the process of pottery style spread and development, which must be placed in a more human situation of social contact and exchange. The simple model suggested above for the development of the relationships between Central and North Coast pottery styles is one possible solution, and some relationship of the contacts seen in the pottery to other exchange systems must be inferred. The copper trade is the most obvious of these other aspects, and can explain most of the long distance contacts between different regions, through the centres at places like Nicosia, Ayios Sozomenos, or Politico as well as the settlements closer to the mines, like Kotchati.

With the development of the White Painted tradition, and its local variants the several regions can be placed in a general system of greater and lesser similarity to one another. The distribution of the different motifs indicates a basic and reasonable model of greatest contact beween near neighbours and less contact with further groups. The figures 18 a–l which plot the general similarity (correlation) of selected sites (from the Q–mode analysis) against the approximate straight line distance between them show a steady fall off in similarity with greater distance. The range of similarity is too large to allow any attempt to define the size of a local area distinct from an outside area in this way, and there is no sudden obvious fall off in similarity after a certain distance, to reflect such internal or external cultural contacts.

The factor analyses, demonstrating the structure underlying the variation, and cluster analyses which show the general relationships between the groups indicate this general pattern of greater and lesser contacts between groups and its relationship to geographical factors.

The Kotchati material, as has been shown, includes a complex of designs from all parts of the island, perhaps locally made, but reflecting the various contacts to the North and the East. The Politico groups form a close unit, and have connections with many other parts of the island. Some of the pottery there is characterised by a neatness of decoration developed from the Central Cypriot tradition, and uses a wider range of motifs than is common elsewhere. The main relationships of these groups are to Yeri and Dhali, as well as the Nicosia and other central groups. The Nicosia Group (in which the pottery is extremely homogeneous) is a standard of Central Cypriot design, exhibiting patterns used in the North and West as well as in the upper reaches of the Yialias and Pedeios Rivers. Strong connections with Dhikomo demonstrate the relevance of the trade route north through the Kyrenia Pass.

The contacts to Dhenia, and of Dhenia to Lapithos, indicate the use of the Vasilia Pass, as well as communication across the Kafkalla Plateau west of Nicosia (on the south side of the Ovgos Valley).

The Ayia Paraskevi composite group reflects a different orientation, with its closest contacts toward the south and east, as well as some northerly communication. The Alambra and Kotchati groups also show the relationships of the central sites to the Larnaca District, as does some of the Politico pottery.

The Larnaca sites also have strong connections with the Eastern sites, and are, as with Kythrea, between the Central and Eastern clusters.

Because of the accident of excavation, Kalopsidha is seen as the focus of the Eastern zone. Besides general contacts with the peripheral sites, there are very strong links to the other two Eastern sites of Milia and Enkomi. The Karpass has links to these sites, and also to the central ones – Nicosia and Politico, but mainly forms a distinctly different region, with some outside contact also seen in the distribution of the Red–on–Black Wares.

The Lapithos groups have their links with Dhenia and the Central and Southern River Valley sites, as well as with the earlier material from Vounous and Palaealona, which is perhaps ancestral to many of the other White Painted pottery styles.

It is possible to interpret some of the clusters of tomb–groups at Lapithos as demonstrating either temporal or family groupings within this one social unit. The two burial periods of L.316 are closely related, showing a unity in the family tomb gifts. Some of these vessels may be regarded as by the same individual[29] and may be associated with pots from L.2 and L.702, the latter probably being later examples of this individual style. L.2 generally is grouped with L.29, L.47, L.49, representing another social unit at Lapithos, as do L.315A and L.320.

The nature of the material and the analysis makes it difficult to place much reliance on the links between some of the other sites and individual Lapithos tomb groups, although it may be suggested that L.47 and L.49 have the stronger links with Kotchati and Dhenia, while L.315A and L.320 demonstrate greater affinity with Nicosia – showing, perhaps, different kinship links within the main trading networks.

Other specific contacts between sites may be seen in the products of individual potters, as with the flasks from Livadhia (CM1942/IV–17/2 = MLA 166) and Ayia Paraskevi (CM 1958/I–17/4) which must have been made at Politico.[30] Most similarities between Nicosia, Politico, and Lapithos cannot be taken to be the result of the transportation of products of individual craftsmen as the overall stylistic similarities are too great to isolate individual styles. Where there is less basic stylistic similarity, however, the movement of the similar individual pots can be suggested.[31]

Some of the clusters isolated in the analyses may be taken to be associated with temporal as well as other factors, as is seen not only with the Vounous–Palaealona – L.313 cluster, but with another reasonably early group of tombs at Lapithos – L.315 B–C, L.311, L.203. The Klavdhia, Myrtou, L.702 cluster may be interpreted as reflecting their late date.

The explanation of most of the variation in the White Painted tradition in terms of geographical and cultural factors rather than temporal ones is an indication that the probable length of the period is certainly no more than the 200 years normally allowed; with an initial development on the North Coast followed by the spread to the rest of the island where the local characteristics developed. The later stages of the breakdown of these regional styles are hard to document at the moment; and this problem is connected with the development of the new "Late Cypriot" Wares.[32] There are two main tendencies to be seen; the one toward the refinement and closer attention to neat and exact design as seen in the vessels from Politico which form the source for the Proto–White Slip vessels such as AM 1968.1155 (from Magounda).[33] This primarily Western development of the White Painted VI and White Slip Wares as seen in the types common at Stephania, Akhera, and Toumba tou Skourou, is in contrast with the general trend toward a breakdown in the design structure in most of the pottery decoration. The developments from the Cross–Line and Framed Broad Band ("Tangent") Styles generally appear to represent simplification and a less careful approach, with larger and less controlled decoration on late White Painted V vessels, as well as the movements toward the finer lines of White Slip Wares.

The fall–off in popularity of the main White Painted tradition must be seen as a fairly slow process, with contemporary developments of the other wares, together with the introduction of the "foreign" Tell–el–Yehudiyeh and Bichrome Wares.[34] This period of change should be seen as almost as long as the main period of popularity of the White Painted Wares, and not as a brief precursor to the main Late Cypriot Period.[35]

Within the period of greatest popularity of the White Painted Wares, an overall pattern of regionalism is clear, with an important unifying factor in the copper trade. That sites in the centre of the island and toward the Troodos Mountains have relatively more different motifs than other sites[36] must be seen as related to their contacts with all the other regions. The further sites are from this economic centrepoint the greater their isolation, which can be measured in terms of the relative number of different motifs used.

Although comparative work on the other aspects of the material culture of the period can expand and develop the ideas in this study, the main outline of the regional structure of the island is clear. Local units, mainly inward looking as regards design style and structure can be distinguished. The combination of several villages or residence units into larger units in regard to the defensive–offensive clusters implied by the fortified sites, would allow the exploitation of different resource zones by each of these complexes; and the probable kinship and marriage structures within this framework would keep a general style within each such unit. The relationships between neighbouring units are fairly strong, implying that there was no little communication between villages in different defensive–economic clusters. These relationships should also be seen in terms of reciprocal exchange of different produce and probable intermarriage. While other goods must have been exchanged, the main known economic factor unifying the whole of Cyprus was the copper production, and much of the social interaction between the fairly isolated regions can be related to it.

NOTES

CHAPTER 4

1. *MCBA*: 275; Åström 1969: 76.
2. *MCBA*: 30–32; Merrillees 1972.
3. Cf. Åström 1967: 82–90.
4. Åström 1964: 79; cf. Herscher 1972: 29–31.
5. The reader is reminded that there may be some doubt concerning the provenience of the Kotchati material.
6. E.g. *Kypros*: pl. CLXX Tombs 9 and 10.
7. Compare Vounous T. 64.107.
8. Stewart 1962: 271.
9. Stewart 1962: 231, 269. See C.M. 1967/X–27/4 (Karageorghis 1968: 267–9, fig. 14a–b) and compare the shape with Stewart 1962: pl.CXIX. 2, 3.
10. Åström 1960a: 79–80; MLA 23 (Karageorghis 1962: 237, pl. VII.2).
11. Stewart 1962: 299.
12. Karageorghis 1970; Frankel and Tamvaki n.d.
13. Compare also Margi T. 1.3 (Karageorghis 1958: pl. xi.6).
14. Cf. Stewart 1962: 299.
15. For a discussion of this style, see Åström 1966: 84.
16. The closest parallels for this pot may be at Lapithos – e.g. L.47.45.
17. Stewart 1962: pl. CLIV. 19, 20. *HNM*: 134–6, fig. 36; *RDAC* 1937–39: 200, pl XLI; CMN F392; Buchholz and Karageorghis: no. 1563.
18. Dikaios 1938: pl. XXIX.
19. Stewart 1965: 157–9; *GCM*: pl VI.1; CMN C2283.
20. Compare the pottery from Galinoporni T.2; Cf. *MCBA* fig. VIII.8.
21. *MCBA*: 177.
22. Åström 1971.
23. Åström 1960a: 81, fig 12, *MCBA*: 276. Cf. Stewart 1962: pl.CLVI.2,5.
24. Åström loc cit.
25. *MCBA* : fig IX.10; SPC: 169 jug 1; Åström notes this jug as from Kythrea T.1, after a photograph by Gjerstad. It is catalogued in the Cyprus Museum as from Kalopsidha T.25. See below n.28.
26. Åström 1960: 82–3.
27. E.g. Politico T.4. 51, 132.
28. Local variants include CM A782 (Kythrea T.1 – similar shape to A798); Dhenia *Potamos tou Merikas* (CM 1937/III– 31/3) – compare CM 1963/XI–4/14. The Framed Caduceus motif may be seen on Politico T.4. 132. Cf. Stewart 1965.
29. L.316^1.4, 106, L.316^2.64, L.2.36, L.702.144, 150. For a discussion of other potters' works in these tombs see Herscher 1972.
30. Cf. Politico T.4.152, CM A715 and A714 (Politico *Chomazoudhia*), Bonn 781.
31. E.g. AM C55 – a Central or Politico vessel found at Enkomi.
32. Popham 1963b, 1972.
33. Compare, for example CMN C7096, and Akhera T.1.70 (Popham 1972: 436, pl. LXXIX.9).
34. Analysis of clays has recently shown that Bichrome Ware is almost certainly of local (Cypriot) manufacture (Artzy, Asaro, Perlman 1973). The indication of different clay sources for different sites in Eastern Cyprus may be taken to confirm the model of local manufacture of pottery evident from the analyses of decorative motifs, upon which these conclusions are based. Cf. also, Åström 1972c: 767–8.
35. Cf. Popham 1963b: 286–91; Karageorghis 1965: 61.
36. Cf. Chapter 2.3, figure 5.

APPENDIX I

This Appendix lists the data used in the analyses. It is not intended as a complete Corpus of the material, but rather to indicate the composition of the sample used. Although not designed for the purpose it may also serve as a partial concordance of *MCBA* and museum inventory numbers.

The material is presented here within the groups used in the analyses and discussion. Further information regarding location and publication of the sites may be found by reference to Catling's lists in *Patterns*. The serial numbers of sites in his Middle Cypriot list are given with the prefix MC. The nomenclature of sites follows that in *Patterns*; a short list of the groups is placed before the main body of the Appendix for quick reference, indicating their composition and the short names used in the general text (see also Chapter 2.1 and figure 2).

Only basic information on the general shape and the motifs is given for each vessel, together with reference to an illustration or a mention in *MCBA*. Where no publication is cited the vessel is otherwise unpublished and is included in this list by courtesy of the relevant museum authorities.

A reference to a museum in the right hand column indicates that I have examined the vessel in question: other pots are described from publications.

The following abbreviations refer to museum or other collections:

A.M. Ashmolean Museum, Oxford.
B.M. British Museum, London.
C.M. Cyprus Museum, Nicosia.
C.M.F. Famagusta District Museum, Cyprus.
C.M.L. Larnaca District Museum, Cyprus.
N.M. Nicholson Museum, Sydney.
W.F. Material from the late J.R. Stewart's excavation, at present stored at Wentworth Falls, N.S.W.

References to publications are the same as those in the main text, with the following additional abbreviations:

BSA 41 Myres, J.L. "Excavations in Cyprus, 1913", *Annual of the British School at Athens*, 41, 1940–5, 53–98.
JHS 17 Myres, J.L. "Excavations in Cyprus in 1894", *Journal of Hellenic Studies*, 17, 1897, 134–173.
CMN Cyprus Museum Negative.

The reader is reminded of the following equivalents:
BSA 41 pl. 28.1: CMN G609
BSA 41 pl. 28.2: CMN G616
BSA 41 pl. 29.1: CMN G577
BSA 41 pl. 29.2: CMN G614
CMN G576: CMN G608

SHORT LIST OF SITES IN THE GROUPS

The name in upper case letters is that used to identify the group in the analyses and general discussion.

Group	Site
1–19	LAPITHOS, *Vrysis tou Barba.*
20	LAPITHOS, *Kylistra.*
21	LAPITHOS, *Vrysis tou Barba.*
22	ALAMBRA, *Asproge.*
23	AYIOS IAKOVOS, *Melia.*
24	Nicosia, *AYIA PARASKEVI.*
25	DHALI, *Drakontospilios.*
26	DHENIA, *Kafkalla.*
27	DHENIA, Kafkalla; Mali, *Potamos tou Merikas.*
28	DHIKOMO, *Onishia, Bademli Bogaz*; Krini, *Merra.*
29	ENKOMI, *Ayios Iakovos.*
30	GALINOPORNI, Village, *Trachonas*; Korovia, *Nitovikla.*
31	KALOPSIDHA, *Tsaoudhi Chiflik.*
32	KATYDATA; Pendayia, *Mandres.*
33	KLAVDHIA, *Tremithios.*
34	KOTCHATI, *Ayia Varvara, Kalamoudhia.*
35	KYTHREA, *Potamos tis Viklis*; Bey Keuy, *Mandra tou Vasili.*
36	LARNACA, *Laxia tou Riou*; Arpera Chiflik, *Ayios Andronikos*; Arpera *Mosphilos*; Anglisidhes, *Solia*; Alaminos, *Stavroti*;, Hala Sultan Tekke, *Kremnos, Angathia, Vounaropoulos.*
37	Eylenja, *LEONDARI VOUNO.*
38	LIVADHIA, *Kokotes.*
39	MILIA, *Vikla Trachonas.*
40	NICOSIA, *Ayia Paraskevi (Dhasoupolis).*
41	Karmi, *PALAEALONA.*
42	POLITICO, *Lambertis.*
43	POLITICO, *Lambertis, Chomazoudhia.*
44	MYRTOU, *Stephania*; Dhiorios, *Aloupotrypes.*
45	Bellapais, *VOUNOUS.*
46	YERI, *Phoenikes.*
47	? ALAMBRA, *Asproge.*

GROUP 1 LAPITHOS T.2

Lapithos Vrysis tou Barba Tomb 2

MC110

This is a group of pottery in the Cyprus Museum which includes the 26 White Painted vessels used here, and which bears the marking "Lapithos 1913 T2?". There is no published record of this tomb group from Myres' excavations in 1913, and although this material has been kept separate the interpretation of the group must be tentative.

The pottery in this group is probably MC II-III.

Lapithos tomb 2:

36	flask	6 9 18 52 63	C.M.
37	jug	8 9 28	C.M.
38	jug	1 8 9 28	C.M.
40	amphora	22 42	C.M.
41	jug	3 9 63	C.M.
42	jug	1 6 8 28	C.M.
43	jug	1 6 8 28	C.M.
44	jug	6 42 58 57 67	C.M.
45	jar	3 14	C.M.
46	jug	1 3	C.M.
47	jug	3 41	C.M.
48	jug	1 6 14 50	C.M.
49	bottle	9 63	C.M.
50	jug	3 6	C.M.
51	jug	20 34 59	C.M.
52	comp.	6 51	C.M.
53	jug	9 28 32	C.M.
56	cup	10 17 23	C.M.
58	cup	6 49 65	C.M.
61	bowl	3 6 17	C.M.
62	bowl	2 6 50 67	C.M.
63	bowl	3 5 17	C.M.
64	bowl	3 6 10 50 67	C.M.
65	bowl	3 5 6 17	C.M.
66	bowl	5 6 10 17	C.M.
67	bowl	23 28	C.M.

Number of pots in this group: 26

Designs occurring in this group: 1 3 5 6 8 9 10 14 17 18 20 22 23 28
32 34 41 42 49 50 51 52 57 58 59 63 65 67.

GROUP 2 LAPITHOS T.18

Lapithos, Vrysis tou Barba, Tomb 18 A and B

MC110

SPC, pp.61, 79, 274; BSA 41, p.79.

140 pots were found in this tomb, including 81 White Painted vessels (SPC, p.274). Only 66 of these have been identified and used in the analyses.

This group has been assigned to MCII to late MC III (MCBA, p.184).

Lapithos tomb 18:

101	bowl	6 24 49	C M.
102	bowl	3 9 56	C.M.
103	bowl	56	C.M.
104	bowl	3 9 17 67	C.M.
106	bowl	3 6 9 17	C.M.
107	bowl	3 17 24	C.M.
108	bowl	3 6 17	C.M.
109	bowl	3 5 6 17	C.M.
111	bowl	3 6 9 50	C.M.
112	bowl	3 5 6 50 66	C.M.
114	bowl	3 6 17 66	C.M.
116	bowl	3 6 9 17 67	C.M.
128	cup	8 50	C.M. MCBA, p.50; BSA 41, pl.29.1 hanging 29.2 row 2.3.
120	bowl	3 6 17	C.M.
121	bowl	3 9 17	C.M.
122	bowl	3 6 17	C.M.
124	bowl	3 5 17	C.M.
125	bowl	9 17 67	C.M.
127	bowl	3 6 17	C.M.
133	jug	1 8 9 28	C.M.
135	jug	1 6 10 28	C.M.
136	jug	1 6 9 28	C.M. MCBA,p.22; BSA 41, pl.29.2 row 4.8.
138	jug	1 48	C.M. MCBA,p.64; BSA 41, pl.29.1 row 2.8. 29.2 row 4.9.
139	jug	1 9 28	C.M.
141	jug	1 3 9 28	C.M.
142	jug	1 14 58	C.M. MCBA, p.53; BSA 41, pl.29.2 row 3.7. SPC, p.157, jug 5.
143	jug	1 28	C.M.
145	juglet	14 51 66	C.M. A754, MCBA, p.55; BSA 41, pl.29.2 row 3.8.
147	juglet	3 14 49 58	C.M. MCBA, p.55; BSA 41, pl.29.2 row 2.6.
148	juglet	14 58	C.M.
149	jug	6 8	C.M. MCBA, p.54; BSA 41, pl.29.2 row 2.4.

Group 2 (contd.)

150	jug	1 28	C.M. MCBA, p.13; BSA 41, pl.29.2 row 3.4.
151	jug	1 8 51	C.M. MCBA, p.52; BSA 41, pl.29.2 row 3.13.
152	jug	1 8 28	C.M. MCBA,p.20; BSA 41, pl.29.2 row 2.13.
153	juglet	11 49 58 67	C.M. MCBA,p.23; BSA 41, pl.29.2 row 3.1.
154	juglet	49 51 66 74	C.M. MCBA,p.23; BSA 41, pl.19.2 row 3.2.
155	juglet	6 49	C.M. MCBA,p.56; BSA 41, pl.29.2 row 1.1.
156	jug	1 8 9 28	C.M.
158	jug	49 57 66	C.M. MCBA,p.52; BSA 41, pl.29.2 row 2.14.
160	jug	14 49	C.M.
163	flask	14 51 59 62	C.M. A852 MCBA, p.74; BSA 41, pl.29.2 row 4.5.
165	bottle	1 3 8 9	C.M. A872 MCBA, p.28; BSA 41, pl.29.2 row 3.9.
166	flask	49	C.M. MCBA,p.44; BSA 41, pl.29.2 row 2.7.
167	flask	8 9 42	C.M. MCBA,p.74; BSA 41, pl.29.2 row 3.5.
174	amphora	8 24 34 51 59	C.M. MCBA,p.45; BSA 41, pl.29.2 row 4.3.
177	amphora	59	C.M.
178	amphora	1 6 8 17 49 51 28	C.M. A836 MCBA, p.61; BSA 41, pl.29.2 row 4.4; SPC, p.159, amphora 2.
178	amphora	3 6 41	C.M. MCBA,p.61; BSA 41, pl.29.1 row 2.4; A840 pl.29.2 row 2.8.
179	amphora	6 41	C.M. MCBA, pp.75-76; BSA 41, pl.29.2 row 2.11.
182	tankard	3 14 44 45 61	C.M. MCBA, p.33; BSA 41, pl.29.2 row 4.1.

Group 2 (contd.)

183	amphora	58 62 77	C.M. MCBA,p.57; BSA 41, pl.29.2 row 4.2.
184	jug	51 62	C.M. MCBA,p.56; BSA 41, pl.29.2 row 3.3.
185	tankard	14 49 58	C.M. MCBA,p.57; BSA 41, pl.29.2 row 2.9.
186	jar	3 6 41 65	C.M. MCBAp.68; BSA 41, pl.29.2 row 2.12.
-	bottle	3 9	MCBA, p.29; BSA 41, pl.29.2 row 1.4.
-	bottle	29	MCBA, p.58; BSA 41, pl.29.2 row 1.5.
-	jug	14	MCBA, p.52; BSA 41, pl.29.2 row 1.7.
-	bowl	3 74	MCBA, p.13; CMN G 615 row 1.8.
-	jug	28	MCBA, p.38; BSA 41, pl.29.2 row 2.5.
-	jar	3 6 41 67	MCBA, p.68; BSA 41, pl.29.2 row 2.10.
-	amphora	3 6 41	MCBA, p.76 and p.61; BSA 41, pl.29.2 row 2.8.
-	flask	32	MCBA, p.33; BSA 41, pl.29.2 row 3.6.
-	jug	9	MCBA, p.20; BSA 41, pl.29.2 row 3.11.
-	jug	28	MCBA, p.43; BSA 41, pl.29.2 row 3.12.
-	jug	1 8 28 47	MCBA, p.54; BSA 41, pl.29.2 row 4.7.
-	jug	1 9 56	MCBA, p.13; BSA 41, pl.29.1 row 3.6; 29.2 row 4.6.

Number of pots in group 2: 66

Designs occurring in group 2: 1 3 5 6 8 9 10 11 14 17 24 28 29 32 34 41 42 44 45 47 48 49 50 51 56 58 59 61 62 65 66 67 68 74 77.

GROUP 3 LAPITHOS T.21

Lapithos, Vrysis tou Barba, Tomb 21

MC 110

SPC, pp.62, 79, 274; CMN G590

Gjerstad records 36 White Painted vessels as coming from this tomb. Besides the 24 listed in MCBA the other vessels used here are those marked "Lapithos 21 (913)" and stored with the other Lapithos material in the Cyprus Museum. As there is no certainty of the provenance of the extra 42 pots, this group should be regarded as a composite collection rather than a single tomb group, and therefore treated with caution.

The basic Tomb 21 material has been assigned to MC II (MCBA. p.184).

Group 3 Lapithos tomb 21:

23	bowl	3 9 56 67	C.M.
24	bowl	3 6 9 17	C.M.
25	bowl	3 6 9 17 67	C.M.
26	bowl	6 9 10 17 67	C.M.
27	bowl	6 44 58	C.M.
28	bowl	3 7 50 67	C.M.
29	bowl	17 22 56	C.M.
30	bowl	3 9 17 67	C.M.
31	bowl	3 6 17 66	C.M.
32	bowl	3 9 17	C.M.
33	bowl	3 17	C.M.
34	bowl	3 6 50 67	C.M.

Group 3 (contd.)

36	cup	3 6 17 66	C.M.
37	cup	13 17 65	C.M.
38	cup	6 13 51 22	C.M. MCBA,p.50; CMN G590 row 1.1.
39	cup	6 49 66	C.M.
40	cup	3 51	C.M.
42	cup	3 50	C.M.
43	cup	3 49	C.M.
44	cup	3 49 66	C.M.
45	cup	3 17	C.M.
46	jug	1 6 9 28	C.M. MCBA, p.22; CMN G590 row 4.5.
47	jug	1 6 9 28 56	C.M.
48	jug	1 6 8 9 28 65	C.M.
49	jug	1 9 28	C.M.
50	jug	1 8 9 28	C.M.
53	jug	1 9 28	C.M.
54	jug	1 8 9 24 28	C.M.
55	jug	1 28	C.M. MCBA, p. 54; CMN G590 row 2.10
56	jug	6 9 41 67	C.M.
57	jug	61 65	C.M.
58	jug	1 6 28 46	C.M. MCBA, p.21; CMN G590 row 3.8.
59	jug	1 9 28 67	C.M.
60	jug	3 9	C.M.
61	jug	3 8 9	C.M.
62	jug	9 28	C.M.

Group 3 (contd.)

63	juglet	6 9	C.M.
64	jug	1 9 28	C.M.
66	jug	9 28	C.M.
67	jug	1 8 28	C.M.
69	jug	1 6 8 9 28	C.M.
70	juglet	54 59	C.M.
71	Jug	9 13 17	C.M.
72	jug	1 8 28	C.M. MCBA, p.55; CMN G590 row 3.9.
73	juglet	6 10 42	C.M. MCBA, p. 39; CMN G548 row 1.3; G590 row 2.11.
74	jug	51	C.M.
75	flask	58	C.M. A858 MCBA,p.42; CMN G590 row 4.10.
76	flask	20 41 57 59	C.M. MCBA, p.60, CMN G590 row 4.6.
77	flask	6 14 20 34 59 62	C.M. MCBA, p.42; CMN G590 row 4.8.
78	flask	14 23 64	C.M.
79	flask	6 58	C.M.
80	flask	8 9 28	C.M.
81	bottle	1 8 9 28	C.M. MCBA, p.58; CMN G590 row 4.12.
82	bottle	22 64	C.M.
83	bottle	9 29	C.M.
84	bottle	22 63	C.M.
84B	bottle	1 21 40 45	C.M.
85	bottle	9 28	C.M.
86	jug	21 24 28	C.M.

Group 3 (contd.)

88	bottle	3 9	C.M.
89	bottle	1 3 28	C.M.
90	flask	28 39 47 46	C.M. MCBA, p.59; CMN G590 row 1.4.
91	amphora	8 35 58 64	C.M. MCBA, p.61; CMN G590 row 4.4.
92	amphora	6 7 15 17 22	C.M. MCBA, p.61; CMN G590 row 4.2.
93	amphora	14 22 51	C.M. MCBA, p.61; CMN G590 row 4.3.
94	amphora	7 49	C.M.
97	jar	3 6 10 41	C.M. MCBA, p.68; CMN G590 row 3.3.
98	amphora	14 34 59	C.M.
99	bowl	9 20 34 49 59 64	C.M. A654a MCBA, p.34; SPC, p.157 bowl 15.
100	tankard	3 58	C.M. MCBA, p.72; CMN G590 row 3.4.
102	tankard	3 7 58	C.M.
103	tankard	6 17 67	C.M. CMN G590 row 3.6.
104	tankard	52 59	C.M. MCBA, p.57; CMN G590 row 2.12
105	bowl	3 58 67	CM A654 MCBA, p.51; SPC, p.157 bowl 14; CMN G590 row 3.7.
107	composite	9 44	C.M. MCBA, p.47; BSA 41, p.83; SPC, p.160 comp 1.
-	cup	3 51	MCBA, p.50; CMN G590 row 1.5.
-	bottle	3 9	MCBA, p.29; SPC, p.176.1.
-	cup	3 51	MCBA, p.50; CMN G590 row 1.3.

Number of pots in group 3: 78

Designs occurring in group 3: 1 3 6 7 8 9 10 13 14 15 17 20 21 22 23 24 28 29 34 35 39 40 41 42 44 45 46 47 49 50 51 52 54 56 58 59 61 62 63 64 65 66 67.

GROUP 4 LAPITHOS T.29

Lapithos, Vrysis tou Barba, Tomb 29

MC 110

SPC, pp.79f, 274; BSA 41, p.79; CMN G599, G601.

50 White Painted vessels came from this tomb (SPC, p.274). Only 29 of these have been identified and used in the analyses.

This group has been assigned to MC II-III (MCBA, p.184).

Lapithos tomb 29:

55	jug	3	C.M.
60	bowl	3 9 17	C.M.
61	bowl	24 56	C.M.
62	bowl	3 5 7 9 10 17	C.M.
65	bowl	3 6 9 67	C.M.
66	bowl	3 46 50 67	C.M.
67	bowl	3 6 9 17 66 67	C.M.
68	bowl	6 24 50 67	C.M.
72	bowl	3 6 9 17 67	C.M.
73	bowl	3 5 6 17	C.M.
75	cup	9 75	C.M. MCBA, p.35; CMN G599 row 1.12.
76	cup	1 50	C.M. MCBA, p.50; CMN G601 row 1.7.
77	bowl	3 6 17	C.M. MCBA, p.49; CMN G601 row 1.3.
79	bowl	3 6 17	C.M. MCBA, p.49; CMN G601 row 1.8.
80	jug	1 3 9	C.M. MCBA, p.54; SPC, p.158 jug 14.
82	jug	1 8 9 28 46	C.M. MCBA, p.23; CMN G601 row 4.7.
83	jug	1 8 9 28 42	C.M. MCBA, p.24; CMN G599 row 3.3; SPC, p.157 jug 3.

Group 4 (contd.)

84	jug	1 8 22 57	C.M. MCBA, p.53; CMN G601 row 3.3.
85	jug	1 9 28	C.M. MCBA, p.22; CMN G601 row 3.5.
86	jug	1 6 8 22 28	C.M. MCBA, p.23; CMN G599 row 1.8.
87	jug	1 8 9 28	C.M.
92	jug	50 66	C.M.
93	jug	1 6 28 69	C.M.
94	bottle	3 6 9	C.M. MCBA, p.29; CMN G601 row 2.8.
95	bottle	1 3 8 29	C.M. MCBA, p.58; CMN G601 row 2.9.
98	amphora	42 46 64	C.M. MCBA, p.45; CMN G599 row 2.6.
99	jar	41	C.M.
100	jar	3 6 41	C.M. MCBA, p.68; CMN G601 row 2.4.
101	tankard	3 9 27 49 51	C.M. MCBA, p.73; SPC, p.158 jug 23.

Number of pots in group 4: 29

Designs occurring in group 4: 1 3 5 6 7 8 9 10 17 22 24 27 28 29 41 42 46 49 50 56 57 64 66 67 69 75

GROUP 5 LAPITHOS T.47

Lapithos, Vrysis tou Barba, tomb 47

MC 110

SPC, p.274; CMN G598

Gjerstad notes 20 White Painted pots from this tomb (SPC, p.274). 19 of these have been used in the analyses.

This group has been assigned to MC II (MCBA, p.185).

Lapithos tomb 47:

25	bowl	14 28 56	C.M.
26	bowl	10 50 67	C.M. MCBA, p.18; CMN G598
27	bowl	50	C.M.
28	cup	3 6 49 67	C.M. MCBA, p.50; CMN G598 row 1.2.
29	cup	3 6 9 17 67	C.M. MCBA, p.49; CMN G598 row 1.5.
31	cup	13 51 66	C.M. MCBA, p.50; CMN G598 row 1.4.
32	jug	1 28 39	C.M. MCBA, p.14; CMN G598 row 3.2.
33	jug	1 8 10 28 69	C.M. MCBA, p.23; CMN G598 row 3.1.
34	jug	1 6 9 28	C.M.
35	flask	6 9 42	C.M. MCBA, p.42; SPC, p.159 flask 1; GCM[3], pl. VI.3.
36	jug	27 28 34 35 57 65	C.M. A 677 MCBA, p.14; SPC, p.152 jug 2.
37	bottle	1 8 9 42	C.M. MCBA, p.73; CMN G598 row 2.2.
38	bottle	1 9 28	C.M.
39	bottle	24	C.M.
40	bottle	22 64	C.M.
42	amphora	8 59	C.M.
43	amphora	6 8 41	C.M. MCBA, p.45; CMN G598 row 2.8.
44	amphora	6 9 50 47	C.M. MCBA, p.57; SPC, p.158 jug 21.
45	amphora	22 28 34 59 46	C.M.

Number of pots in group 5: 19

Designs occurring in group 5: 1 3 6 8 9 10 13 14 17 22 24 27 28 34 35 39 42 46 47 49 50 51 56 57 59 64 65 66 67 69.

GROUP 6 LAPITHOS T.49

Lapithos, Vrysis tou Barba, tomb 49

MC 110

SPC, pp.80, 274; CMN G575, 576

Gjerstad notes 41 White Painted vessels in this tomb (SPC, p.274). 37 of these have been used in the analyses.

This group has been assigned to MC III, and may be one of the latest MC groups at Lapithos (MCBA, p.175 n.10, pp.192-3.)

Lapithos tomb 49:

52	bowl	6 9 10 50 67	C.M. CMN G575 row 1.3.
53	bowl	6 24 50 66	C.M. CMN G576
54	bowl	6 24 50 66	C.M. CMN G576
55	bowl	6 24 50 66	C.M. CMN G576
56	bowl	6 24 50 67	C.M. CMN G576
57	bowl	3 6 9 24 50 67	C.M.
61	bowl	3 5 6 17	C.M. CMN G576
63	bowl	3 9 50 64 67	C.M. CMN G576
65	bowl	3 17 80	C.M. CMN G576 row 1.3.
66	bowl	3 5 17 67	C.M. CMN G576 row 1.6.
68	bowl	3 5 14	C.M.
70	jug	17 51 65	C.M.
71	jug	1 6 9 28	C.M. CMN G576 row 4.5.
72	jug	1 6 9 28	C M. MCBA, p.13; CMN G575 row 3.4.
74	jug	1 8 9 28 46	C.M. A712 MCBA, p.23; CMN G575 row 3.5.
75	jug	1 9 28	C.M.

Group 6 (contd.)

76	jug	1 9 28	C.M. MCBA, p.53; GMN G576 row 3.2.
77	jug	1 8 9 28	C.M. MCBA, p.54; CMN G576 row 3.1.
78	jug	1 8 9 28 66	C.M. MCBA, p.22; CMN G576 row 2.15.
81	jug	3 6 14 44	C.M. A717 MCBA, p.54; CMN G576 row 2.4; G575 row 1.2.
82	bottle	1 9 28 45	C.M. MCBA, p.58; CMN G576 row 2.5.
83	Bottle	1 8 9 29	C.M. MCBA, p.59; CMN G576 row 3.6.
84	jug	59	C.M.
85	flask	6 24 28 41 42 43 56 59	C.M. A856 MCBA, p.42; SPC, p.159 flask 3.
86	bottle	51 54 59	C.M. MCBA, p.73; CMN G576 row 2.8.
87	bottle	1 8 9 28	C.M. A879 MCBA, p.73; CMN G575 row 1.1; G576 row 2.7.
88	bottle	6 41 46	C.M. MCBA, p.73; CMN G576 row 2.9.
90	bottle	3 9	C.M. MCBA, p.41; CMN G576 row 2.11.
92	bottle	3 9	C.M. MCBA, p.29; CMN G576 row 3.12.
93	bottle	9 24	C.M.
94	amphora	6 51	C.M. A844 MCBA, p.61; CMN G576 row 3.7; SPC, p.159 amphora 3
95	tankard	3 8 59	C.M. MCBA, p.57; CMN G576 row 3.8.
96	tankard	22 34 58 59	C.M. MCBA, p.57; CMN G576 row 3.9.
97	jar	6 41 47	C.M. MCBA, p.68; CMN G576 row 2.14.
98	amphora	6 50	C.M. MCBA, p.61; CMN G576 row 2.13.
-	jug	14 44	MCBA, p.36; CMN G575 row 1.4; G576 row 2.3.
-	bottle	42	MCBA, p.73; CMN G576 row 2.10.

Number of pots in group 6: 37

Designs occurring in group 6: 1 3 5 6 8 9 10 14 17 22 24 28 29 34 41 42 43 44 45 46 47 50 51 54 56 58 59 64 65 66 67 80.

GROUP 7 LAPITHOS T.50

Lapithos, Vrysis tou Barba, tomb 50

MC 110

SPC, pp.62, 80 274; CMN G569, 570, 590, 593, 627 (others in MCBA G568, 584 533).

Gjerstad notes 105 White Painted vessels in this tomb (SPC, p.274). 83 of these are used here.

This group has been assigned to MC II-III (MCBA, p.185).

Lapithos tomb 50:

1	jug	6 17 66	C.M. Inv 1958/VII-31/1 MCBA, p.53; CMN G569 row 1.4.
59	bowl	3 6 50 22	C.M. A636 MCBA, p.19; CMN G593 row 4 right
151	bowl	24 50	C.M.
158	bowl	3 6 9 24 50	C.M.
163	bowl	3 6 17 67	C.M. CMN G593 row 5.5.
164	bowl	3 6 17	C.M. CMN G593 row 5.4.
166	bowl	3 17	C.M. A1920 MCBA,pp.19 or 48; CMN G590 row 4.5.
169	bowl	3 5 6 17	C M. CMN G593 row 5.1.
174	bowl	3 6 17	C.M. CMN G593 row 3.2.
177	bowl	3 6 17 67	C.M.
180	bowl	3 5 17	C.M.
192	cup	22 42	C.M.
193	bowl	6 17 67	C.M.
195	cup	56 57	C.M.
196	cup	6 51	C.M. MCBA, p.51; CMN G593 row 1.5.
201	cup	14 51 65	C.M.
203	cup	3 6 49 67	C.M. A659 MCBA, p.19; CMN G593 row 1.4.

Group 7 (contd.)

207	jug	1 6 9 28	C.M. MCBA, p.22; CMN G570 row 3.4.
208	jug	1 9 28 65	C.M. A682 MCBA, p.13; CMN G570 row 3.1.
209	jug	1 6 9 28	C.M.
210	jug	1 9 13 28	C.M. MCBA, p.22; CMN G570 row 2.3.
211	jug	1 9 28	C.M.
212	jug	1 6 9 28	C.M. A742
213	jug	1 6 8 9 28	C.M.
215	jug	1 8 9 28	C.M.
220	jug	3 50	C.M.
222	jug	1 8 9 28 69	C.M.
223	jug	1 8 9 28	C.M.
224	jug	51 57 65	C.M.
226	jug	9 28	C.M.
227	jug	3 49 67	C.M. MCBA, p.21; CMN G593 row 1.1.
228	jug	1 6 17	C.M.
229	jug	1 10 28	C.M. MCBA, p.53; CMN G593 row 1 right
231	juglet	14 51	C.M. MCBA, p.40; CMN G593 bottom row, 5.
235	jug	1 8 9 28	C.M. CMN G593 row 6.9.
236	jug	1 9 28	C.M. MCBA, p.55; CMN G593 bottom row, 8.
237	juglet	3 58	C.M.
238	flask	1 8 24 31	C.M. A857 MCBA, p.74; CMN G627 row 3.3.
239	flask	10 20 34 58	C.M.
241	flask	42	C.M. CMN G627 row 4.2.
242	flask	6 8 9 17 65 75	C.M.

Group 7 (contd.)

244	flask	44	C.M. MCBA, pp.42-3; CMN G627 row 3.1.
245	bottle	9 44	C.M. MCBA, p.73; CMN G627 row 1.4.
246	bottle	44 45	C.M.
247	bottle	6 9 63	C.M. MCBA, p.58; CMN G627 row 1.2.
248	bottle	22 63	C.M.
249	bottle	1 8 9 43	C.M. MCBA, p.73; CMN G627 row 1.3.
250	bottle	9 61	C.M.
251	bottle	22	C.M.
252	bottle	9	C.M.
254	bottle	6	C.M.
255	jug	1 28 62	C.M.
256	amphora	14 34 22 59	C.M. A835 MCBA, p.61; CMN G570 row 2.4.
257	amphora	3 6 20 32 51 58 67 70	C.M. MCBA, p.61; CMN G570 row 2.2.
258	amphora	13 27 65	C.M. MCBA, p.25; CMN G569 row 2.4.
259	amphora	3 10 14 58	C.M. A838 MCBA, p.61; CMN G570 row 2.5.
260	amphora	10 14 59 67	C.M. A837 MCBA, p.61; CMN G570 row 2.1.
261	amphora	1 9 32 51 67	C.M.
262	amphora	6 41	C.M. A841 MCBA, p.75; CMN G570 row 1.2.
266	tankard	9 51 59	C.M. MCBA, p.57 fig 8; CMN G569 row 3.4.
267	tankard	9 10 14 17 22 41 49	C.M.
268	tankard	3 6 9 58	C.M. A770
269	tankard	6 44	C.M. A776; CMN G570 row 1.5.
270	amphora	1 6 32 43 59	C.M.

Group 7 (contd.)

272	ring-vase	6 9 32	C.M. MCBA, p.46; SPC, p.160 ring-vase 1.
-	cup	13 49	MCBA, p.19; SPC, p.157 bowl 9
-	tankard	6 44	MCBA, p.57; SPC, p.158 jug 20.
-	jar	3 6 41	MCBA, p.68; CMN G570 row 1.1.
-	amphora	6 41	MCBA, p.76; CMN G570 row 1.3.
-	jar	3 6 41	MCBA, p.68; CMN G570 row 1.4.
-	jug	1 9 28	MCBA, p.13; CMN G570 row 3.2.
-	jug	1 10 28 49	MCBA, p.13; CMN G570 row 3.3.
-	cup	3 49	MCBA, p.51; CMN G593 row 1.1.
-	cup	13 51	MCBA, p.50; CMN G593 row 1.2.
-	jug	3 49	MCBA, p.70; CMN G593 row 3.1.
-	jug	1 5 8 28	MCBA, p.70; CMN G593 row 3.2.
-	jug	1 3 28	MCBA, p.70; CMN G593 bottom row 3
-	jug	14 51 62	MCBA, p.55; CMN G593 bottom row 4
-	jug	9 22 28	MCBA, p.37; CMN G593 bottom row 6
-	jug	1 8 9 28	MCBA, p.55; CMN G593 bottom row 7
-	bottle	3 9	MCBA, p.29; CMN G627 row 1.1.
-	flask	58	MCBA, p.60; CMN G627 row 3.7.

Number of pots in group 7: 82

Designs occurring in group 7: 1 3 5 6 8 9 10 13 14 17 20 22 24 27 28 31 32 34 41 42 43 44 45 47 49 50 51 56 57 58 59 61 62 63 65 67 69.

GROUP 8 LAPITHOS T.315A

Lapithos, Vrysis tou Barba, tomb 315 Chamber A

MC 110

SCE I, pp.105 ff.

25 of the 33 White Painted vessels in this group have been used.

This group has been assigned to MC II-III (MCBA, pp.181, 192).

Lapithos tomb 315 Chamber A;

2	bowl	8 49	MCBA, p.51 fig XII.10; SCE I pl.XXIX.1 row 3.5; CVI.8.
4	bowl	6 9 24 49	MCBA, p.49; SCE I pl.XXIX.1 row 3.19.
6	jug	1 8 9 28	MCBA, p.22 fig VII.6; SCE I pl.XXIX.1 row 2.1.
10	cup	51 65	MCBA, p.19 fig V.10; SCE I pl.XXIX.1 row 3.4.
14	flask	59	MCBA, p.60 fig XIV.8; SCE I pl.XXIX.1 row 2.11.
18	bottle	22 63	MCBA, p.58 fig XIV.4; SCE I pl.XXIX.1 row 3.14.
20	bowl	6 49	MCBA, p.13; SCE I pl.XXIX.1 row 4.1.
22	flask	6 34	MCBA, p.44 fig XI.1; SCE I pl.XXIX.1 row 3.10.
24	bottle	47 63	MCBA, p.58; SCE I pl.XXIX.1 row 3.16.
26	jug	1 6 7 9 28 47	MCBA, p.14 fig III.8; SCE I pl.XXIX.1 row 2.4.
29	jug	1 6 9 28	MCBA, p.13 fig III.3; SCE I pl.XXIX.1 row 3.12.
30	flask	8 42	MCBA, p.60 fig XIV.7; SCE I pl.XXIX.1 row 2.9.
37	tankard	6 59 64	MCBA, p.33 fig X.11.
43	jug	1 9 28	MCBA, p.22 fig VII.4; SCE I pl.XXIX.1 row 2.2.
46	jug	3 6 51	MCBA, p.52 fig XIII.5; SCE I pl.XXIX.1 row 2.16
58	amphora	7 49 58	MCBA, p.61; SCE I pl.XXIX.1 row 3.11; pl.CVIII.3.

Group 8 (contd.)

67	bowl	3 17 67	MCBA, p.49; SCE I pl.XXIX.1 row 3.22.
70	cup	8 49 67	MCBA, p.50 fig XII.11; SCE I pl.XXIX.1 row 3.18.
74	bowl	6 9 17 67	MCBA, p.49; SCE I pl.XXIX.1 row 3.20.
77	jug	1 6 9 28 47	MCBA, p.13; SCE I pl.XXIX.1 row 2.5.
86	flask	6 34 59	MCBA, p.60 fig XIV.5; SCE I pl.XXIX.1 row 2.12.
92	bottle	47 63	MCBA, p.58; SCE I pl.XXIX.1 row 3.15.
94	bowl	3 17 24 67	MCBA, p.49 fig XII.1; SCE I pl.XXIX.1 row 3.2.
95	bowl	17 47 67	MCBA, p.48; SCE I pl.XXIX.1 row 3.21.
97	amphora	6 13 51	MCBA, p.61 fig XV.4; SCE I pl.XXIX.1 row 2.15.

Number of pots in group 8: 25

Designs occurring in group 8: 1 3 6 7 8 9 13 17 22 24 28 34 42 47 49 51 58 59 63 65 66 67.

GROUP 9 LAPITHOS T.315 B-C

Lapithos, Vrysis tou Barba, tomb 315 Chambers B-C

MC 110

SCE I, pp.105 ff.

13 vessels from this part of the tomb, and from the dromos cupboard have been used.

The group has been assigned to MC I-II (MCBA, pp.181,182).

Lapithos tomb 315 Chambers B and C:

5	amphora	3 9 44 67	MCBA, p.61 fig XV.1; SCE I pl.XXX.1 row 1.12.
6	jug	6 8 9 28 65	MCBA, p.13 fig III.5; SCE I pl.XXX.1 row 1.10; CV.9
18	jug	1 8 9 28 55	MCBA, p.22 fig VII.10; SCE I pl.XXX.1 row 1.9; CV.10.
25	bowl	22 24	MCBA, p.49 fig XII.6; SCE I pl.XXX.1 row 2.12.
26	animal	56	MCBA, p.26 fig VIII.9; SCE I pl.XXX.1 row 2.9; CVIII.5; CXLVIII.10.
27	amphora	1 8 9 14 49 67	MCBA, p.25 fig VIII.11; SCE I pl.XXX.1 row 1.11.
31	cup	14 56	MCBA, p.50 fig XII.13; SCE I pl.XXX.1 row 1.14.
34	jug	1 8 9 28 67	MCBA, p.22 fig VII.1; SCE I pl.XXX.1 row 1.1.
35	bowl	6 9 49 67	MCBA, p.49 fig XII.2; SCE I pl.XXX.1 row 2.13; CVI.10.
39	jug	6 9 28	MCBA, p.13; SCE I pl.XXX.1 row 1.2.
49	bowl	9 17	MCBA, p.49 fig XII.3; SCE I pl.XXX.1 row 2.14; CVI.9.

Lapithos tomb 315 cupboard

1	jug	1 6 9 28	MCBA, p.20 fig VI.1; SCE I pl.XXX.1 row 2.3.
2	bowl	17	MCBA, p.50; SCE I pl.XXX.1 row 2.1.

Number of pots in group 9: 13

Designs occurring in group 9: 1 3 6 8 9 14 17 22 24 28 44 49 55 56 65 67.

GROUP 10 LAPITHOS T.316[1]

Lapithos, Vrysis tou Barba, tomb 316 burial 1

MC 110

SCE I, pp.115-121. See also Herscher 1972: 32.

Of the 50 White Painted pots associated with this burial group 46 are used here. One vessel from the group (L316.38) has accidently been placed with the other group in the tomb (Group 11).

The group has been assigned to the end of MC II and into MC III (MCBA, pp.181-2).

Lapithos tomb 316 burial 1:

2	bowl	6 17	MCBA, p.18; SCE I pl.XXXI.1 row 5.27.
3	bowl	3 6 17	MCBA, p.48; SCE I pl.XXXI.1 row 4.24.
4	amphora	1 6 8 13 51 52	MCBA, p.45 fig XI.15; SCE I pl.XXXI.1 row 3.10.
6	amphora	3 14 58 61 67	MCBA, p.61 fig XV.5; SCE I pl.XXXI.1 row 3.1.
12	jug	1 8 9 28	MCBA, p.35 fig XI.7; SCE I pl.XXXI.1 row 4.5.
18	juglet	6 9 14 51 59	MCBA, p.38 fig XI.4; SCE I pl.XXXI.1 row 5.11.
21	jug	8 28 48	MCBA, p.22 fig VII.2; SCE I pl.XXXI.1 row 4.15.
34	jug	1 8 9 28	MCBA, p.22 fig VII.9; SCE I pl.XXXI.1 row 2.6.
35	jug	1 7 8 28 48 14	MCBA, p.23 fig VIII.3; SCE I pl.XXXI.1 row 2.8; CVII.7.
36	bowl	6 17	MCBA, p.49; SCE I pl.XXXI.1 row 6.1.
37	jug	1 8 9 28	MCBA, p.52; SCE I pl.XXXI.1 row 5.20.
39	bowl	3 6 9 49	MCBA, p.66; SCE I pl.XXXI.1 row 6.12.
41	bowl	6 9 49	MCBA, p.48; SCE I pl.XXXI.1 row 6.4.
46	bottle	9 46	MCBA, p.58; SCE I pl.XXXI.1 row 3.19.

Group 10 (contd.)

68	bowl	6 14 17	MCBA, p.49; SCE I pl.XXXI.1 row 5.26
70	bowl	6 9 49	MCBA, p.18; SCE I pl.XXXI.1 row 6.11.
78	jug	7 9 31	MCBA, p.52 fig XIII.4; SCE I pl.XXXI.1 row 5.12.
79	flask	3 6 14 58	MCBA, p.43 fig XI.11; SCE I pl.XXXI.1 row 2.14.
81	amphora	42 46	MCBA, p.61 fig XV.2; SCE I pl.XXXI.1 row 3.14; CVIII.4.
85	tankard	3 6 22 42	MCBA, p.24 fig VIII.4; SCE I pl.XXXI.1 row 3.9; CVIII.1.
93	tankard	6 9 42 43	MCBA, p.41 fig XI.12; SCE I pl.XXXI.1 row 3.15.
106	jug	28 51 52	MCBA, p.54 fig XIII.10; SCE I pl.XXXI.1 row 4.14.
107	jug	1 8 9 28	MCBA, p.21 fig VI.4; SCE I pl.XXXI.1 row 2.11; CVII.9.
114	bowl	6 9 17 67	MCBA, p.49; SCE I pl.XXXI.1 row 5.3.
117	amphora	1 6 8 59	MCBA, p.45 fig XI.13; SCE I pl.II; XXXI.1 row 3.13.
118	jug	1 8 28	MCBA, p.21 fig VI.6; SCE I pl.XXXI.1 row 4.6.
119	tankard	6 14 47	MCBA, p.72 fig XVII.4; SCE I pl.XXXI.1 row 5.13.
120	jug	1 8 9 28	MCBA, p.23 fig VIII.2; SCE I pl.XXXI.1 row 4.11.
122	jug	1 8 9 28	MCBA, p.22 fig VII.5; SCE I pl.XXXI.1 row 4.8.
126	jug	1 6 8 9 28	MCBA, p.21 fig VI.7; SCE I pl.XXXI.1 row 4.2; CV.8.
127	amphora	41	MCBA, p.75; SCE I pl.XXXI.1 row 3.6.
130	jug	1 6 8 28 47	MCBA, p.23; SCE I pl.XXXI.1 row 3.21.
132	bowl	6 9 49	MCBA, p.50 fig XIII.2; SCE I pl.XXXI.1 row 5.28.
133	bowl	6 17	MCBA, p.49 fig XII.4; SCE I pl.XXXI row 6.14; CVII.2.
134	bottle	3 9	MCBA, p.29 fig IX.8; SCE I pl.XXXI.1 row 5.15; CVII.4.

Group 10 (contd.)

144	jug	1 6 8 9 28	MCBA, p.22 fig VII.7; SCE I pl.XXXI.1 row 4.13.
150	jug	1 8 9 28	MCBA, p.23 fig VI.13; SCE I pl.XXXI.1 row 4.10.
152	jug	1 9 28	MCBA, p.22; SCE I pl.XXXI.1 row 2.5.
154	bowl	6 9 51	MCBA, p.48; SCE I pl.XXXI.1 row 4.1.
161	bowl	3 6	MCBA, p.48; SCE I pl.XXXI.1 row 6.2.
162	bowl	3 9 49	MCBA, p.19 fig V.7; SCE I pl.XXXI.1 row 5.4; CVI.6; CVII.1.
176	flask	32 57 58 62	MCBA, p.59 fig XIV.1; SCE I pl.XXXI.1 row 2.7; CVII.11.
178	jug	1 8 13 14 32 57 59	MCBA, p.56 fig XIII.13; SCE I pl.XXXI.1 row 2.9.
181	bowl	6 9 49	MCBA, p.49; SCE I pl.XXXI.1 row 5.5.
182	amphora	8 44 47	MCBA, p.61; SCE I pl.XXXI.1 row 3.7.
183	bowl	6 17	MCBA, p.18; SCE I pl.XXXI.1 row 5.2.

Number of pots in group 10: 46

Designs occurring in group 10: 1 3 6 8 9 13 14 17 22 28 31 32 41 42 43 44 46 47 48 49 51 52 57 58 59 62 67.

GROUP 11 LAPITHOS T.316[2]

Lapithos, Vrysis tou Barba, tomb 316 burial 2

MC 110

SCE I, pp.115-121. See also Herscher 1972.

There are 20 pots in this group, including the material from the cupboards, and the vessel (L316.38) which should be in the other burial group in this tomb.

The group has been assigned to MC II-III (MCBA, pp.181-2).

Lapithos tomb 316 burial 2:

13	bowl	3 6 17	MCBA, p.48; SCE I pl.XXXI.1 row 6.3.
14	bottle	9 63	MCBA, p.58: SCE I pl.XXXI.1 row 3.2.
15	jug	1 8 9 28	MCBA, p.20 fig VI.5; SCE I pl.XXXI.1 row 4.17.
23	bowl	6 17 47	MCBA, p.19; SCE I pl.XXXI.1 row 5.25.
25	tankard	10 14 58 67	MCBA, p.57 fig XV.9; SCE I pl.XXXI.1 row 5.14.
33	bowl	3 9 49 6	MCBA, p.66; SCE I pl.XXXI.1 row 6.5.
38	bowl	6 17 47	MCBA, p.19; SCE I pl.XXXI.1 row 6.13.
53	bowl	6	MCBA, p.48; SCE I pl.XXXI.1 row 5.24.
54	jug	1 6 8 10 28 68	MCBA, p.23 fig VI.15; SCE I pl.XXXI.1 row 2.10.
55	jug	1 8 28 44	MCBA, p.38 fig XI.2; SCE I pl.XXXI.1 row 2.12; CVII.10.
60	juglet	1 8 28	MCBA, p.37 fig XI.6; SCE I pl.XXXI.1 row 4.16; CVII.6.
64	bottle	1 8 9 18 51 52	MCBA, p.73 fig XVIII.5; SCE I pl.XXXI.1 row 4.9; CVII.3.
75	bottle	3 9	MCBA, p.29; SCE I pl.XXXI.1 row 5.21.
95	tankard	1 6 44 74	MCBA, p.72 fig XVII.5; SCE I pl.XXXI.1 row 3.8; CVIII.2.
97	bowl	9 6 14 17	MCBA, p.48; SCE I pl.XXXI.1 row 5.24.
102	flask	6 14 32 58	MCBA, p.59 fig XIV.2; SCE I pl.XXXI.1 row 2.13.
104	amphora	3 10 13 22 58 67	MCBA, p.25 fig VIII.6; SCE I pl.XXXI.1 row 3.12.

Lapithos 316 cupboard 1

2	bowl	6 17 47	MCBA, p.19; SCE I pl.XXXI.1 row 6.18.

Lapithos 316 cupboard 2

1	bowl	5 6 17	MCBA, p.49; SCE I pl.XXXI.1 row 6.17.
2	bottle	1 8 9 43	MCBA, p.73 fig XVII.11; SCE I pl.XXXI.1 row 6.15.

48	jug	1 28 46 47	MCBA, p.23 fig VI.14; SCE I pl.XXXIV.1 row 3.13.
63	bowl	3 6 17	MCBA, p.48; SCE I pl.XXXIV.1 row 5.9.
64	bottle	51 57	MCBA, p.41 fig XI.9; SCE I pl.XXXIV.1 row 3.2.
65	bowl	6 49 67	MCBA, p.49 fig XII.7; SCE I pl.XXXIV.1 row 5.13.
66	juglet	22 29	MCBA, p.38 fig XI.5; SCE I pl.XXXIV.1 row 3.10.
67	jug	1 8 9 28	MCBA, p.20 fig VI.2; SCE I pl.XXXIV.1 row 2.5.
68	bottle	42	MCBA, p.73; SCE I pl.XXXIV.1 row 3.15.
76	flask	6 28 39 78	MCBA, p.60 fig XIV.6; SCE I pl.XXXIV.1 row 2.3.
79	flask	41 44	MCBA, p.43 fig XI.10; SCE I pl.XXXIV.1 row 3.6.
81	bowl	6 49	MCBA, p.49; SCE I, p.136.
85	bowl	17 21 28	MCBA, p.48; SCE I pl.XXXIV.1 row 5.12.
86	cup	51 57	MCBA, p.51 fig XII.12; SCE I pl.XXXIV.1 row 4.7.
87	amphora	3 8 51	MCBA, p.61; SCE I pl.XXXIV.1 row 3.8.
88	jug	14 49 51	MCBA, p.21 fig VI.3; SCE I pl.XXXIV.1 row 2.6.
89	bowl	17	MCBA, p.49; SCE I pl.XXXIV.1 row 5.8.
111	jug	1 8 28 38	MCBA, p.23 fig VIII.1; SCE I pl.XXXIV.1 row 2.9.
135	jug	22 56	MCBA, p.53 fig XIII.7; SCE I pl.XXXIV.1 row 2.10.

Lapithos tomb 320, cupboard 3

1	bowl	6 9 17	MCBA, p.48; SCE I pl.XXXIB.1 row 5.2.

Number of pots in group 12: 30

Designs occurring in group 12: 1 3 5 6 8 9 14 17 21 22 23 26 27 28 29 34 38 39 41 42 44 46 47 49 50 51 56 57 59 67 78.

Group 11 (contd.)

Number of pots in group 11 20

Designs occurring in group 11: 1 3 5 6 8 9 10 13 14 17 18 22 28 32 43 44 47 49 51 52 58 63 67 68 74.

GROUP 12 LAPITHOS T.320

Lapithos, Vrysis tou Barba, tomb 320

MC 110

SCE I, pp.132-139.

Of the 35 White Painted vessels in this tomb 30 have been used in this analysis.

The group has been assigned to MC II-III (MCBA, p.182).

Lapithos tomb 320

23	bottle	1 8 42 41	MCBA, p.73 fig XVII.10; SCE I pl.XXXIV.1 row 2.14.
24	jug	34 59	MCBA, p.53 fig XIII.9; SCE I pl.XXXIV.1 row 2.7.
25	jug	1 23 28	MCBA, p.22 fig VII.3; SCE I pl.XXXIV.1 row 2.12.
26	bowl	6 17	MCBA, p.49; SCE I pl.XXXIV.1 row 5.6.
27	flask	1 27	MCBA, p.59 fig XIV.9; SCE I pl.XXXIV.1 row 1.11.
28	amphora	14 59	MCBA, p.61 fig XV.6; SCE I pl.XXXIV.1 row 3.7.
29	bowl	9 50	MCBA, p.18; SCE I pl.XXXIV.1 row 5.11.
34	cup	14 42	MCBA, p.19 fig V.9; SCE I pl.XXXIV.1 row 5.15.
36	bowl	5 6 17	MCBA, p.49; SCE I pl.XXXIV.1 row 5.10.
38	bowl	6 9 49 67	MCBA, p.18; SCE I pl.XXXIV.1 row 5.7.
39	cup	3 17	MCBA, p.19 fig V.11; SCE I pl.XXXIV.1.
47	flask	6 22 26 49	MCBA, p.59 fig XIV.3; SCE I pl.XXXIV.1 row 2.15.

GROUP 13 LAPITHOS T.4

Lapithos, Vrysis tou Barba, tomb 4

MC 110

SPC, p.274; BSA 41, pls. 28.1 and 2, p. 79.

Of the 19 White Painted pots listed from this tomb only 10 are used in the analysis.

This group has been assigned to MC II + MC III (MCBA, p.183).

Lapithos tomb 4

CM A675	jug	1 8 10 28	C.M. MCBA, p.14; SPC , p.152 jug 1.
CM A675a	jug	6 8 15 27 28 34 40 65	C.M. BSA 41, pl.28.2 row 3.2.
-	cup	3 49	MCBA, p.49; BSA 41, pl.28.1 row 1.5.
-	jug	51 59	MCBA, p.54; BSA 41, pl.28.1 row 3.5; SPC, p.157 jug 1.
-	flask	58 59	MCBA, p.60; BSA 41, pl.28.1 row 3.6.
-	flask	22 28 54 71	C.M. MCBA, p.42; BSA 41, pl.28.1 row 3.7.
-	tankard	3 58	C.M. MCBA, p.57; BSA 41, pl.28.1 row 2.5; pl.28.2 row 1.3.
-	bowl	6 49	MCBA, p.50; BSA 41, pl.28.1 row 1.3; pl 28.2 2nd hanging bowl.
-	tankard	44	MCBA, p.57; BSA 41, pl.28.2 row 1.4.
-	bowl	51	MCBA, p.51; BSA 41, pl.28.2 row 1.2.

Number of pots in group 13; 10

Designs occurring in group 13: 1 3 6 7 10 15 22 27 28 34 40 44 49 51 54 58 59 65 71.

GROUP 14 LAPITHOS T.8

Lapithos, Vrysis tou Barba, tomb 8

MC 110

SPC, pp.79, 274; CMN G602

Gjerstad notes 15 White Painted pots in the tomb (SPC, p.274). Only 9 of these have been used.

The group has been assigned to MC III (MCBA, p.192).

Lapithos tomb 8:

15	bowl	3 6 17	C.M. MCBA, p.48; CMN G602 row 2.2.
19	cup	1 8 17 69	C.M. CMN G602 row 2.11.
21	jug	3 44	C.M. MCBA, p.54; CMN G602 row 3.10.
22	bottle	1 8 28	C.M. MCBA, p.58; CMN G602 row 3.11.
24	jug	3 50	C.M. MCBA, p.23; CMN G602 row 2.7.
27	jug	9 28	C.M. MCBA, p.53; CMN G602 row 2.10.
-	bowl	3 9 17	MCBA, p.48; CMN G602 row 2.3.
-	amphora	6 41 49	MCBA, p.61; CMN G602 row 3.5.
-	bottle	3 9	MCBA, p.29; CMN G602.

Number of pots in Group 14: 9

Designs occurring in group 14: 1 3 6 8 9 17 28 41 44 49 50 69.

GROUP 15 LAPITHOS T.14

Lapithos, Vrysis tou Barba, tomb 14

MC 110

SPC, pp.61, 76, 274; CMN G591, 606.

Group 15 (contd.)

The material from the three groups, Lapithos tombs 14, 14D and 14E has all been placed together to give a larger group, which still only comprised 16 pots.

This material can be assigned to MC II-III (MCBA, pp.178, 184, 192).

Lapithos tomb 14:

9	amphora	6 46 49 58 67	C.M.
10	amphora	3 9 17 49 58 67	C.M.
11	amphora	22 34 59	C.M.
12	jug	1 8 28 46 69	C.M. MCBA, p.23; CMN G606 row 3.5.
13	juglet	14 51	C.M.
14	cup	3 6 13 51 67	C.M.
15	bottle	1 8 9 28	C.M.
16	jug	3	C.M.
17	jug	3 28 46	C.M.
18	bowl	3 5 7 67	C.M.
25	jug	1 8 9 28	C.M. A711 MCBA, p.23; CMN G606 row 3.6.
CM A673	jug	5 48 65 66 67	C.M.

Lapithos tomb 14 E:

24	jug	1 9 28	C.M.
-	bowl	44	MCBA, p.18; CMN G606 row 1.7.
-	jug	28	MCBA, p.28; CMN G606 row 2.1.
27	jug	1 8 9 28	C.M. MCBA, p.20; CMN G606 row 2.9.

Number of pots in group 15: 16

Designs occurring in group 15: 1 3 5 6 7 8 9 13 14 17 22 28 34 44 46 48 49 51 58 59 65 66 67 69.

GROUP 16 LAPITHOS T.51

Lapithos, Vrysis tou Barba, tomb 51

MC 110

SPC, pp.58, 84, 274; CMN G600

14 of the 15 White Painted pots in this group have been used.

The group has been assigned to MC II-III (MCBA, p.185).

Lapithos tomb 51:

15	jug	3 50	C.M. MCBA, p.34; CMN G600 row 2.6.
16	bowl	3 6 9 10 50 67	C.M.
17	bowl	3 9 17	C.M.
18	bowl	3 9 49 56	C.M.
19	bowl	6 9 50 67	C.M.
20	bowl	6 9 10 50	C.M.
21	bowl	9 49 67	C.M.
24	composite	49	C.M.
27	jug	1 9 28 67	C.M. MCBA, p.22; CMN G600 row 3.6. CM A1970
28	jug	1 8 28 46	C.M. MCBA, p.20; CMN G600 row 1.10.
32	flask	49 51 58	C.M.
36	bottle	9 22 24	C.M.
-	flask	28 43 53 67	MCBA, p.44; CMN G600 row 3.5; SPC, p.159 flask 4.
-	bowl	3 6 49 67	MCBA, p.49; CMN G600.

Number of pots in group 16: 14

Designs occurring in group 16: 1 3 6 8 9 10 17 22 24 28 43 46 49 50 51 53 56 58 67.

GROUP 17 LAPITHOS T.203

Lapithos, Vrysis tou Barba, tomb 203

MC 110

SPC, pp. 62, 80 274; CMN G583, 604, 822

The group is made up of material from L203 A and C which share a common dromos, together with that from L203B, a neighbouring tomb. This gives a total of 21 White Painted vessels; however only 17 of these are used here.

The groups have been assigned to MC I-III (MCBA, pp.175, 185) but predominantly MC I-II.

Lapithos tomb 203 A, B, C

5	jug	1 9 28	C.M. MCBA, p.22; CMN G604 row 1.4.
9	cup	13 49 66	C.M. MCBA, p.19; CMN G604 row 2.1.
10	jug	1 3	C.M. MCBA, p.53; CMN G604. CM A781.
11	jug	1 9 28	C.M. MCBA, p.14.
12	amphora	9 14 51 59	C.M. MCBA, p.61; CMN G604 row 2.5.
14	bowl	9 56 67	C.M.
16	cup	3 51 66	C.M. MCBA , p.50; CMN G583 row 1.8.
18	jug	1 6 17 28 39 65	C.M. A680 MCBA,p.22; CMN G583 row 2.3.
19	jug	1 9 28	C.M. MCBA, p.13; CMN G583 row 2.4.
20	jug	1 9 13 28	C.M. MCBA, p.22; CMN G583 row 2.2.
21	jug	1 9 28	C.M. MCBA, p.22; CMN G583 row 2.1.
22	jug	1 9 13 28	C.M. MCBA , p.13; CMN G583 row 2.5.
23	jug	9 28 65	C.M. MCBA, p.13; CMN G583 row 2.6.
24	jug	9 20 46 51 67	C.M. MCBA, p.56; CMN G583 row 1.6.

Group 17 (contd.)

25	jug	28 51	C.M. A713a MCBA, p.56; CMN G583 row 1.7.
26	cup	51 66	C.M. A660 MCBA, p.19; CMN G583 row 2.7.
-	jug	1 8 9 28	MCBA, p.13; CMN G604 row 3.2; SPC, p.152 jug 4.

Number of pots in group 17: 17

Designs occurring in group 17: 1 3 6 8 9 13 14 17 20 28 39 46 49 51 56 59 65 67.

GROUP 18 LAPITHOS T.311A

Lapithos Vrysis tou Barba, tomb 311A

MC 110

SCE I, pp.76 ff.

All 11 vessels in this group are used.

The group has been assigned to MC I-II (MCBA, p.173).

Lapithos tomb 311A:

4	jug	1 6 9 28	C.M. MCBA, p.22 fig VII.8; SCE I pl.XXII.1 row 3.8; CVII.8.
9	bowl	1 6 9 28 47	C.M. MCBA, p.13; SCE I pl.XXII.1 row 2.9.
12	jug	1 9 28 65	MCBA, p.13; SCE I pl.XXII.1 row 2.5.
13	jug	1 9 14 28 65	C.M. MCBA, p.13 fig III.6; SCE I pl.XXII.1 row 2.4.
22	jug	21 22 49	C.M. MCBA, p.21; SCE I pl.XXII.1 row 3.6.
26	bowl	3 5 6 9 47 67	MCBA, p.19; SCE I pl.XXII.1 row 4.2; CVI.1.
27	jug	1 9 28	C.M. MCBA, p.13; SCE I pl.XXII.1 row 2.10.
30	bowl	56	C.M. MCBA,p.13 fig III.2; SCE I pl.XXII.1 row 4.3; CV. row 4.5.

Group 18 (contd.)

31	amphora	6 17 37 51 59	C.M. MCBA, p.45 fig XI.14; SCE I pl.XXII.1 row 3.7.
35	jug	9 28	C.M. MCBA,p.21; SCE I pl.XXII.1 row 3.10.
36	bowl	6 10 24 50 67	C.M. MCBA, p.19; SCE I pl.XXII.1 row 4.1.

Number of pots in group 18: 11

Designs occurring in group 18: 1 3 5 6 9 10 14 17 21 22 24 28 37 47 49 50 51 56 59 65 67.

GROUP 19 LAPITHOS T.313

Lapithos, Vrysis tou Barba, tomb 313

MC 110

SCE I, pp.85-99.

All 10 White Painted vessels in this group have been used.

The groups in the tomb have been assigned to MC I-II (MCBA, pp.173-4, 179-180).

Lapithos tomb 313 A, B:

21	jug	27 34 35 36 56 57 65	MCBA, p.14 fig IV.3.
22	jug	6 28 63 65 66	MCBA, p.15 fig IV.6; SCE I pl.XXV.1 row 2.10.
23	bowl	6 17 49 66	MCBA, p.13 fig III.1; SCE I pl.XXVI.1 row 3.7.
47	jug	6 27 28 35 39 65	MCBA, p.14 fig IV.2; SCE I pl.XXV.1 row 2,5; CV.7.
71	jug	27 34 35 36 65	MCBA, p.14 fig IV.1; SCE I pl.XXV.1 row 2.9.
79	jug	1 6 9 28	MCBA, p.13; SCE I pl.XXVI.1 row 2.4.

Group 19 (contd.)

82	jug	1 28 69	MCBA, p.15 fig IV.4; SCE I pl.XXXVI.1 row 2.3.
113	askos	6 27 33 58 65 68	MCBA, p.16 fig V.5; SCE I pl.XXV.1 row 2.11.
101	jug	6 28 40 65	MCBA, p.13 fig III.9; SCE I pl.XXVI.1 row 2.5.
114	amphora	9 16 27 28 33 65	MCBA, p.16 fig V.4; SCE I pl.XXV.1 row 2.6.

Number of pots in group 19: 10

Designs occurring in group 19: 1 6 9 16 17 27 28 33 34 35 36 39 40 49 56 57 58 63 65 66 68 69.

GROUP 20 LAPITHOS T.702

Lapithos, Kylistra, tomb 702

MC 114a

SCE I, pp.164 ff.

13 of the 16 White Painted vessels in this tomb are used here.

This group has been assigned to MC II-III (MCBA, pp.192, 198).

Lapithos tomb 702

14	bowl	3 6 17	MCBA, p.67; SCE I pl.XL row 7.5.
55	jug	3 17	MCBA, p.70 fig XVI.18; SCE I pl.XL row 5.19.
69	jug	3 5 6 17 50	MCBA, p.69 fig XVI.13; SCE I pl.XL row 3.8.
70	jug	1 8 9 24 28	MCBA, p.53 fig XIII.8; SCE I pl.XL row 4.11.
81	bowl	3 17	MCBA, p.67 fig XVI.2; SCE I pl.XL row 7.4.
98	jar	3 15 53 66	MCBA, p.68 fig XVI.7; SCE I pl.XL row 7.13.
99	bowl	3 6 17	MCBA, p.67 fig XVI.3; SCE I pl.XL row 7.6.

Group 20 (contd.)

117	jug	9 28 47	MCBA, p.71; SCE I pl.XL row 5.18.
136	bottle	43 61	MCBA, p.73; SCE I pl.XL row 5.14 CVII.5.
144	tankard	3 9 41 52 64	MCBA, p.73 fig XVII.6; SCE I pl.XL row 3.9.
150	tankard	6 20 41 46 61	MCBA, p.72 fig XVII.7; SCE I pl.XL row 2.5.
153	bowl	3 6 17	MCBA, p.66 fig XVI.1; SCE I pl.XL row 5.26.
178	jug	6 11 67	MCBA, p.69 fig XVI.14.

Number of pots in group 10: 13

Designs occurring in group 10: 1 3 5 6 8 9 11 15 17 20 24 28 41 43 46 47 50 52 53 61 64 66 67.

GROUP 21 LAPITHOS

Lapithos, Vrysis tou Barba. Other material

MC 110

This is a composite group made up of the smaller tomb groups and the other Lapithos material in the Cyprus Museum. This makes up a total of 82 pots, but the group must be used with caution.

The pottery in the group can be assigned to all MC periods.

Tomb 6A:

2 vessels from the Pennsylvania Museum Excavations (Grace, 1940). MC II (MCBA, p.189). See also A.J.A. 77: 195 (1973).

Tomb 9

2 White Painted vessels. MC II (MCBA, pp.183 and 189).

Tomb 10B

2 White Painted vessels, MC II (MCBA, pp.184 and 189).

Group 21 (contd.)

Tomb 13

Myres' T13, and Markides T13B; 7 vessels. MC II-III (MCBA, p.185).

Tomb 15

SPC, p.79; CMN G581; 1 vessel. MC III (MCBA, p.192).

Tomb 16A

A large White Painted II bowl in the Cyprus Museum ("L16a (1917)"). Cf. the similar bowl CM A624 (no provenance).

Tomb 28

SPC, pp.62, 79 274; BSA 41, pl.27.1. 2 vessels. MC II (MCBA, p.184).

Tomb 35

CMN G602. 1 vessel. MC III (MCBA, p.192).

Tomb 42

CMN G607. 1 vessel. MC II (MCBA, pp.185-189).

Tomb 43

6 White Painted vessels in the Cyprus Museum.

Tomb 45

SPC, pp.60, 76, 265; CMN G592. 2 White Painted vessels. MC II or earlier (MCBA, pp.175, 179).

Tomb 46 A and B

2 vessels. MC I-II (MCBA, pp.175, 179, 185).

Tomb 52

CMN G613. 1 vessel in the Cyprus Museum.

Tomb 201B

CMN G611; SPC, pp.61, 77, 265. MC II (MCBA, p.186).

Group 21 (contd.)

Lapithos tomb 6A

3	bowl	3 6 9 67	MCBA, p.49; Grace, 1940, p.30 fig 22.
73	jug	1 6 8 28 30	MCBA, p.24; Grace, 1940, pl.IA:73, p.30.

Lapithos tomb 9

CM A678	jug	1 6 9 15 28 65	C.M.
-	jug	9 14 28 65	MCBA, p.15; SPC, p.152 jug 3.

Lapithos tomb 10B

5	jug	1 49 57	C.M. CMN G581 row 2.9.
6	amphora	8 24 49	C.M. MCBA, p.45; CMN G581 row 2.10

Lapithos tomb 11

A 1	jug	1 9 28	C.M.
2	jug	1 28 69	C.M.
A 2	jug	1 9 28	C.M.

Lapithos tomb 13

CM A679	jug	1 23 27 28 65	C.M.
2	jug	9 28 65	C.M.
3	amphora	14 17 49	C.M. MCBA, p.25.
5	cup	6 9 23 51 69	C.M. MCBA, p.50.
6	jug	51 57	C.M.
7	cup	6 51 66	C.M. MCBA, p.50.
8	cup	22 51	C.M. MCBA, p.50; SPC, p.157 bowl 5.

Group 21 (contd.)

Tomb 204

CMN G603; SPC, p.62. 3 vessels. MC II-III (MCBA, p.186).

Tomb 303B

SCE I, pp.24-38. MC II.

Tomb 306

SCE I, pp.57-62. 4 White Painted vessels. MC II (MCBA, p.181).

Tomb 307

SCE I, pp 1 vessel. MC I (MCBA, pp.173-179).

Tomb 319B

SCE I, pp 1 vessel. MC I-II (MCBA, p.179).

Tomb 322D

SCE I, pp 4 vessels. MC I-II (MCBA, p.174).

Tomb 323

SCE I, pp 1 vessel. MC II + III (MCBA, pp.182 ff).

Tomb 410

This is a large jug labelled "Lapithos T410 No.5" in the Cyprus Museum, but it is not the White Painted vessel from the SCE excavations at Lapithos Kastros.

Other pottery

Other material from Myres' and Markides' excavations in the Cyprus Museum, a total of 32 vessels.

Group 21 (contd.)

Lapithos tomb 15

CM A686	jug	1 7 8 9 28	C.M.

Lapithos tomb 16a

CM A625	bowl	27 28 36	C.M.

Lapithos tomb 28

20	amphora	34 46 59 62	C.M.
-	bottle	3 9	MCBA, p.29; BSA 41, pl.27.1.

Lapithos tomb 35

6	amphora	20 22 34 58	C.M. MCBA, p.61; CMN G613 row 1.2.

Lapithos tomb 42

3	bowl	10 50 67	C.M. CMN G607 row 3.3.

Lapithos tomb 43

3	bottle	28	C.M.
7	jug	10 25 28	C.M.
11	amphora	17 22 59	C.M. A839
12	amphora	13 59 65	C.M.
cupb.1	amphora	51	C.M.

Lapithos tomb 45

-	cup	27	MCBA, p.19; CMN G592 row 1.2.
16	cup	6 27 33	C.M.

Group 21 (contd.)

Lapithos tomb 46

A 11	amphora	13 27 28 39	C.M. A829 MCBA, p.16; SPC. p.152 amphora 1.
B 11	amphora	7 10 58 67	C.M. MCBA, p.61; CMN G613 row 1.5.

Lapithos tomb 52

6	bowl	3 5 6 49	C.M. MCBA, p.50; CMN G591 row 2.10.

Lapithos tomb 201B

6	tankard	1 8 24 27 42	C.M. MCBA, p.57; CMN G611 vase 4.

Lapithos tomb 204

27	bowl	3 9 17	C.M. CMN G603 row 1.8.
29	bowl	3 9 50 67	C.M.
31	tankard	9 42	C.M. MCBA, p.57; GMN G603 row 2.5.

Lapithos tomb 303B

4	jug	6 21 28 63 65	MCBA, p.15; SCE I pl.XIV.3 4.
9	jug	6 23 28 31 65	MCBA, p.23 fig VIII.5; SCE I pl.XIV.3 ?. pl.CV.6.

Lapithos tomb 306

-	jug	6 28 39 56 65	MCBA , p.15 fig IV.7.
6	amphora	27 28 39 64 65	MCBA, p,16 fig V.3; SCE I pl.XVIII.2 row 2.8; CVI.4.
7	amphora	6 9 28 63 65	MCBA, p.16 fig V.2; SCE I pl.XVIII.1 row 2.3.
14	jug	6 7 9 28 34 35 64 65	MCBA, p.15 fig IV.5; SCE I pl.XVIII.1 row 1.2; pl.CVI.2.

Group 21 (contd.)

65	bowl	3 17	C.M.
66	bowl	3 46 50 67 69	C.M.
67	bowl	3 5 6 17	C.M.
68	bowl	6 9 10 50 67	C.M.
69	bowl	6 28 51 59 61	C.M.
70	bowl	10 56 67	C.M.
71	bowl	14 56	C.M.
72	bowl	3 50 69	C.M.
73	bowl	3 6 9 17 67	C.M.
74	bowl	3 9 17	C.M.
75	bowl	3 6 17	C.M.
79	jug	1 9 28 69	C.M.
80	jug	1 6 9 28	C.M. SPC, p.158 jug 10.
81	jug	9 28 45	C.M.
82	jug	1 8 9 28	C.M.
84	jug	28	C.M.
85	jug	1 8 28	C.M.
86	jug	8 28	C.M.
88	jug	8 17 41 65	C.M.
89	jug	51 67	C.M.
90	bottle	9 63	C.M.
91	bottle	22 64	C.M.
92	flask	1 8 9 27 28 42	C.M.
93	flask	6 9 41 42	C.M.

Group 21 (contd.).

Lapithos tomb 307

14	jug	1 9 47 56	MCBA, p.13 fig.III.7; SCE I pl.XIX.1 row 2.1.

Lapithos tomb 319B

41	bowl	6 47 49	MCBA, p.19; SCE I pl.XXXIII row 4.12.

Lapithos tomb 322 D

33	bowl	3 5 6 17	C.M. MCBA, p.49 fig XII.5; SCE I pl.XXXVII.1 row 5.1.
36	bowl	3 9 46 50 66 67	C.M. MCBA, p.18 fig V.6; SCE I pl.XXXVII.1 row 5.2.
41	jug	1 8 9 28	C.M. MCBA, p.54 fig XIII.11; SCE I pl.XXXVII.1 row 2.10.
86	amphora	15 27 36 57 65	C.M. MCBA, p.15 fig.V.1; SCE I pl.XXXVII.1 row 1.3; pl.CVI.3.

Lapithos tomb 323 D

3	amphora	3 8 13 14 49 58	C.M. MCBA, p.61; SCE I pl.XXXIX.4 no.6.

Lapithos tomb 410

5	jug	9 10 21 62 75	C.M.

Lapithos

59	bowl	3 9 50	C.M.
60	bowl	3 50 63	C.M.
61	bowl	3 6 10 50 67	C.M.
62	bowl	3 6 56 67	C.M.
63	bowl	3 9 56 67	C.M.
64	bowl	3 6 56 67	C.M.

Group 21 (contd.)

94	amphora	9 27 49 58 67	C.M.
96	amphora	1 6 51 59 64	C.M.

Number of pots in group 21: 82

Designs occurring in group 21: 1 3 5 6 7 8 9 10 13 14 15 17 20 21 22 23 24 25 27 28 29 30 31 33 34 35 36 39 41 42 45 47 49 50 51 56 57 58 59 61 62 63 64 65 66 67 68 69 75.

GROUP 22 ALAMBRA

Alambra, Asproge

MC 4

SPC, p.6; CCM, p.2.

A small group of 7 vessels, mainly from Cesnola's excavations at Alambra, and comprising only those vessels which are most certainly from Alambra.

Alambra:

-	amphora	2 4	MCBA, p.76 fig XVIII.10; di Cesnola 1885-1903 II, pl.LXXXVIII.769; SPC, p.173 amphora 4.
-	jug	3 6 44	MCBA, p.21 fig VI.9; di Cesnola 1885-1903 II, pl.LXXXIX.771; HCC, p.26 fig 177.
-	amphora	1 14 17 32	MCBA, p.25; di Cesnola 1885-1903 II, pl.LXXXIX.772; HCC, fig 174.
-	composite	6 31	MCBA, p.47; di Cesnola 1885-1903 II,pl.LXXXVII.768.
-	bowl	1 3 9	MCBA, p.28; di Cesnola 1885-1903 II, pl.CX.875.

Group 22 (contd.)

-	composite	22 27 28	MCBA, p.26; di Cesnola 1885-1903 II, pl.LXXXIX.767.
-	amphora	3 6 9 28 31	C.M. inv 1939/II-27/3 MCBA, p.75; RDAC 1937-39 (1951) pl.XLI.7, p.200.

Number of pots in group 22: 7

Designs occurring in group 22: 1 2 3 4 6 9 14 17 22 27 28 31 32 44.

GROUP 23 AYIOS IAKOVOS

Ayios Iakovos, Melia

MC 19

SPC, p.9; SCE I, pp.302-355.

A composite group using almost all of the SCE material from the cemetery. Generally dating to MC II-III.

Tomb 1

SCE I, pp.302-306. All 4 White Painted vessels used. MC III (MCBA, p.193).

Tomb 2

SCE I, pp.306-308. All 3 White Painted vessels used. MC II (MCBA, p.193).

Tomb 4A

SCE I, pp.309-313. 3 White Painted vessels used. MC I-II (MCBA, p.186).

Tomb 4B

SCE I, pp.309-313. All 7 vessels used. MC III(MCBA, p.193).

Tomb 6

SCE I, pp.314-322. 6 of the 7 White Painted vessels used. MC II (MCBA, pp.177-8, 186).

Group 23 (contd.)

Ayios Iakovos tomb 4A

-	bowl	56	MCBA, p.49 fig XII.9.
3	bowl	10	MCBA, p.30 fig X.3; SCE I pl.LX.3, 10.
4	bowl	10 47	MCBA, p.30; SCE I pl.LX.3 16.

Ayios Iakovos tomb 4B

2	bowl	10	MCBA, p.30; SCE I pl.LX.3, 8.
3	bowl	3 10	MCBA, p,30; SCE I pl.LX.3, 4; CVIII.8.
5	bowl	1 5 10	MCBA, p.30 fig X.4; SCE I pl.LX.3, 2; CVIII.10.
6	amphora	7 10	MCBA, p.31 fig X.7; SCE I pl.LX.3, 1; CIX.2.
7	bowl	5 7	MCBA, p.66; SCE I pl.LX.3, 6.
8	bowl	10	MCBA, p.30; SCE I pl.LX.3, 5.
9	bowl	10 47	MCBA, p.30; SCE I pl.LX.3, 7.

Ayios Iakovos tomb 6

1	jug	1 7 27 28 35 73	MCBA, p.22 fig VII.11; SCE I pl.LXI row 3.1; CVI.1. Åström 1968: 73.
26	bowl	10	MCBA, p.30; SCE I pl.LXI row 8.8.
84	bowl	31	MCBA, p.49; SCE I pl.LXI row 8.4; CIX.4.
127	bowl	5 10	MCBA, p.30 fig X.1; SCE I pl.XLI row 9.3.
51	bowl	10 47	MCBA, p.31 fig X.5; SCE I pl.LXI row 6.1.
159	bowl	10 47	MCBA, p.66; SCE I pl.LXI row 9.5; CIX.5.

Tomb 7

SCE I, pp.322-325. All 3 White Painted vessels used. MC II-III (MCBA, p.186).

Tomb 9

SCE I, pp.335-337. Both White Painted vessels used. MC III (MCBA, p.193).

Tomb 12

SCE I, pp.341-345. Both White Painted vessels used. MC III (MCBA, p.193).

Tomb 13

SCE I, pp.345-348. 2 of the 4 White Painted vessels used. MC III (MCBA, p.193).

Tomb 14

SCE I, pp.349-354. 2 of the 4 White Painted vessels used. MC III-LC (MCBA, p.163).

Ayios Iakovos tomb 1

4	bowl	1 9	MCBA, p.30; SCE I, pl.LX.1, 10.
7	bowl	9	MCBA, p.30; SCE I, pl.LX.1,8.
8	bowl	10	MCBA, p.30 fig X.2; SCE I pl.LX.1, 12 CVIII.7.
9	bowl	1 10	MCBA, p.30; SCE I pl.LX.1, 11.

Ayios Iakovos tomb 2

3	bowl	3	MCBA, p.30; SCE I pl.LX.2, 8.
4	bowl	3	MCBA, p.30; SCE I pl.LX.2, 7.
9	bowl	10	C.M. MCBA, p.30; SCE I pl.LX.2, 6 CVIII.6.

Group 23 (contd.)

Ayios Iakovos tomb 7

1	bowl	7 9 10	C.M. MCBA, p.31; SCE I pl.LX.4 row 2.1; CVIII.9.
7	bowl	3	MCBA, p.30; SCE I pl.LX.4 row 3.6.
14	bowl	3 7	C.M. MCBA, p.30; SCE I pl.LX.4 row 3.2.

Ayios Iakovos tomb 9

2	bottle	3 9 51	MCBA, p.73 fig XVII.9; SCE I pl.LXII.2.
8	jug	18 32 57	MCBA , p.69 fig XVII.1; SCE I pl.CIX.1.

Ayios Iakovos tomb 12

3	bowl	3 9 29 47 10	C.M. MCBA, p.30; SCE I pl.CXIII.4 row 2.11.
32	bowl	3	MCBA, p.30; SCE I pl.LXII.4 row 2.5.

Ayios Iakovos tomb 13

33	bowl	10	MCBA, p.30; SCE I pl.LXIV.1 row 4.12.
38	tankard	7 8 10 51	MCBA, p.31 fig X.6; SCE I pl.LXIV.1 row 4.9.

Ayios Iakovos tomb 14

48	tankard	20 32	C.M. SCE I pl.LXV.1 row 4.1.

Number of pots in group 23: 33

Designs occurring in group 23: 1 3 5 7 9 10 18 20 27 28 29 31 32 35 47 51 56 57 73

GROUP 24 AYIA PARASKEVI

Nicosia Ayia Paraskevi

MC 134

SPC, p.4; Myres, 1897, pp.136-38; CCM, p. 1; Kypros.

A composite group made up of various small groups and individual pots from the cemetery, giving a total of 48 vessels. The material dates from most MC periods, but the bulk of it is likely to be MC III (MCBA, p.188).

The material comes from Myres' excavations in 1894, together with other material in the Ashmolean, Cyprus, and Istanbul Museums. Other pottery from the excavations carried out by the late Professor J.R. Stewart for the Melbourne Cyprus Expedition, now in the Nicholson Museum or at present stored at Wentworth Falls, N.S.W., and shortly to be published by J.B. Hennessy, is also included.

Note other pottery from this site in Group 40 (Nicosia).

Ayia Paraskevi:

-	jug	59	MCBA, p.20; Kypros pl.CL.7.
CM A685	jug	13 27 34 58	C.M. MCBA, p.15: SPC, p.152 jug 5; Kypros pl.CLXX.10c.
-	jug	17 23 28 65	MCBA, p.23; Kypros pl.CLXX.10d.
-	jug	15 28 65	MCBA, p.14; Kypros pl.CLXX.10e; CCM, p.49 no.415, pl.III.
-	basket	27	MCBA, p.19; Kypros pl.CLXX.10f.
-	jug	3 9	MCBA, p.27; Kypros pl.CLXX.10g.
-	flask	6 54	MCBA, p.74; Kypros pl.CLXXI.14d.
-	composite	51	MCBA, p.47; Kypros pl.CLXXII.15d.
-	bowl	9 10 67	MCBA, p.31; Kypros pl.CLXXIII.22f.
-	animal	39	MCBA, p.25; Kypros pl.CLXXIII.22i.

Group 24 (contd.)

Ayia Paraskevi - Gladstone Street:

2	jug	14 51	N.M. 58.140
3	cup	3 49	N.M. 58.141; MCBA, p.50.
4	bowl	9 50 66 67	W.F. MCBA, p.19.
5	bottle	9 70	N.M. 58.142; MCBA, p.58.
6	bottle	3 24	N.M. 58.148; MCBA, p.58.
7	cup	3 49 67	W.F. MCBA, p.19.
8	jug	1 9 27 56	N.M. 58.144; MCBA, p.20 fig VI.12.
9	jug	1 8 9 28	W.F. MCBA, p.54.
11	jug	3 6 49 58 67	W.F. MCBA, p.37.
12	jug	14 19 34 51 59 62 67	W.F. MCBA, p.36 fig XI.3.

Ayia Paraskevi Theophanides Street, tomb 13:

-	cup	6 50	W.F.
3	bowl	3 10 50	W.F.
5	bowl	6 17 39 67	W.F. MCBA, p.49.
11	bowl	3 6 17	W.F. MCBA, p.50.
12	bowl	3 6 9 17 66	W.F. MCBA, p.49.
14	bowl	3 50	W.F. MCBA, p.51 fig XIII.1.
15b	bowl	3 5 6 17	W.F. MCBA, p.49.

Ayia Paraskevi - Theophanides Street, tomb 14:

1	bowl	3 6 17	W.F.

Number of pots in group 24: 48

Designs occurring in group 24: 1 3 5 6 8 9 10 13 14 15 17 19 22 23 24 26 27 28 29 32 33 34 35 39 49 50 51 54 56 58 59 62 64 65 66 67 70 75 80.

Group 24 (contd.)

AM C15	jug	3 9	A.M.
AM C17	juglet	6 9 75	A.M.
AM C39	jug	3 17 50	A.M.
AM C40	jug	5 9 28	A.M. MCBA, pp.70-1.
AM C41	jug	3 6 75 80	A.M. MCBA, p.71
AM C43	jug	3 5 50	A.M.
AM C45	juglet	3 6 9 24	A.M. MCBA, p.55.
AM C51	juglet	6 9 50 66 67	A.M.
AM C56	bottle	22 64	A.M. MCBA, p.58.
AM C60	jug	6 39 75	A.M. MCBA, p.35.
AM C63	animal	3 6 29	A.M. MCBA, p.47.
CM A728	jug	3 9 28	C.M.
CM A733	jug	3	C.M.
CM A744	jug	5 9 10 49	C.M.
CM A827	amphora	27 33 65	C.M. MCBA, p.16; Kypros pl.CLXX.10a; CCM, p.49 no.412, pl.III.
CM A903	composite	26 27 35	C.M. MCBA, p.16; Kypros pl.CLIII.13; CLXX.9c; CCM no.411, pl.III; SPC, p.152.
CM 1958/1-17/4	flask	6 9 32	CMN, C II.360. Buchholz and Karageorghis No. 1564.
BM C310	ring-vase	27 39	B.M. MCBA, p.25; CVA BM pl.5.11; Kypros, pl.CXLVIII.10e; CLXX.9e; SPC, p.152.
Instanbul 1180	flask	6 28	MCBA, p.75 fig XVIII.7.
-	bottle	3 9	MCBA, p.29 fig IX.7.

GROUP 25 DHALI

Dhali Drakontospilios.

MC 39

CCM, p.3.

A composite group of 16 vessels: 7 from C.M. excavations in 1943 (material in Nicosia) and most of the rest from excavations carried out by Ohnefalsch-Richter for Sir Charles Newton (material in London).

Idalion Drakontospilios tomb 1:

11	jug	9 56	C.M.
12	jug	1 6 28	C.M.
13	jug	6 22 32 59	C.M.
18	flask	20 34 51 59 62	C.M.
19	bottle	14 34 59	C. M.
20	bottle	39 64 67	C.M.
22	cup	3 49 67	C.M.

Dhali:

BM C306	animal	6 3 14 29	B.M. MCBA, p.46; CVA BM pl.5.4.
BM C289	jug	3 6 28 64	B.M. MCBA, p.39;CVA BM pl.5.5.
BM C303	flask	9 28 65	B.M. MCBA, p.75; CVA BM pl.5.15; SPC, p.159 flask 6.
BM C280	jug	1 6 9 14 22 47 51	B.M. MCBA, p.37; CVA BM pl.5.39.
BM C301	flask	6 28	B.M. MCBA, p.44; CVA BM pl.6.11.
BM 84 12.10 44	bottle	22 27 59	B.M. MCBA, p.58; CVA BM pl.6.19.
BM C293	bottle	48	B.M. MCBA, p.65; CVA BM pl.6.23.
BM 84 12.10 192	bottle	3 9	B.M. MCBA, p.29; CVA BM pl.6.28
-	bottle	3 9 24	MCBA, p.59; CVA Louvre 4 pl.3.20.

Group 25 (contd.)

Number of pots in group 25: 16

Designs occurring in group 25: 1 3 6 9 14 20 22 24 27 28 29 32 34 39 47 48 49 51 56 59 62 64 65 67.

GROUP 26 DHENIA T.6

Dhenia, Kafkalla, tomb GW 6

MC 41

Åström and Wright, 1963, pp.225-276.

A group of 34 White Painted pots from this tomb. Other pottery from this tomb in the Cyprus Museum and labelled GW2 has accidently been considered with the other material in the analyses (cf. Åström and Wright, 1963, p.241 n.3).

The group has been assigned to MC II-III (Åström and Wright, 1963, pp.275-6).

Dhenia tomb 6: All references to Åström and Wright, 1963.

1	jug	1 6 8 9 28	p.243 pl.II.1.
2	jug	1 6 9 28	p.243 pl.II.2.
3	jug	1 8 9 28	p.243 pl.II.3.
4	jug	3 5 6 28 64 69	p.244 pl.II.4.
5	jug	1 28 56	p.245 pl.III.1.
6	jug	6 13 49 58	p.245 pl.III.2.
7	jug	13 14 49 67	p.245 pl.III.3.

Group 26 (contd.)

8	jug	49 58	p.245 pl.III.5.
9	jug	59 67	p.245 pl.III,4.
10	jug	6 49 58	p.245 pl.III.6.
12	jug	9 22 49 59 67	p.246 pl.III.7.
13	jug	6 22 49	p.246 pl.III.8.
14	jug	22 51 59 67	p.246 pl.III.9.
15	jug	3 6 49 58 67	p.246 pl.IV.1-2.
15a	jug	13 22 58	p.247 pl.IV.3.
16	tankard	6 9 49 67	p.247 pl.IV.4.
17	tankard	7 49 58	p.247 pl.IV.5.
18	tankard	13 58	p.248 fig 9.
19	tankard	22 49 58	p.248 pl.IV.6.
19a	tankard	28 44	p.248.
20	amphora	6 9 51 59 67	p.248 pl.IV.7.
21	amphora	3 8 58 67	p.248 fig.9.
22	amphora	6 13 20 59 76	p.248 pl.IV.8.
23	flask	22 63	p.249 fig 9.
24	bowl	6 49 63 67	p.249 pl.IV.9.
25	bowl	3 6 10 50 58 68	p.249 pl.V.1.
26	cup	3 9 17	p.250 pl.V.2.
26a	cup	9 51	p.250.
26d	bowl	51	p.250.
26d	bowl	6 9 50	p.250.
27	bowl	56	p.251 pl.V.3.
28	bowl	3 6 50	p.250 pl.V.4.
28a	cup	13 49	p.250 pl.V.5.
29	composite	34 56	p.250 fig 9.

Number of pots in group 26: 34

Designs occurring in group 26: 1 3 5 6 7 8 9 10 13 14 17 20 22 28 34 44 49 50 51 56 58 59 63 64 67 68 69 76.

GROUP 27 DHENIA

Dhenia, Kafkalla, Mali, Potamos tou Merikas

MC 41, 42, 43

SPC , pp.7 ff; HNM, p.142; Åström and Wright, 1963.

Material from several localities in small groups or as individual objects; in the Cyprus, Nicholson and Ashmolean Museums (the latter material largely collected by H.W. Catling). Comments and discussion of most of this material may be found in Åström and Wright, 1963, pp.227-30).

A total of 51 pots, mainly from MC II-III (cf. Åström and Wright, 1963, pp.240-41).

Dhenia Tomb GW 1: All references for this tomb to Åström and Wright, 1963.

6	jug	1 6 8 9 28	p.235 pl.I.16.
7	jug	1 6 8 9 28	p.235 fig 7.
8	jug	1 6 8 9 28	p.335 fig 7.
9	jug	1 9 28	p.236 fig 7.

Group 27 (contd.)

12	jug	1 8 28 66 69	p.238 fig 7.
13	jug	3 6 59 67	p.236 fig 7.
14	amphora	3 7 9 67	p.237 pl.I.12.
16	flask	22 59 62	p.237 pl.I.13-14.
19	bowl	3 17	p.237 fig 7.
20	bowl	3 6 50 67	p.239 fig 7.
22	bowl	3 9 50 67	p.239 fig 7 pl.I.11.
23	bowl	3 17	p.239 fig 7.
25	bowl	3 6 9 58	p.239 fig 7.
26	flask	3 63	p.239 pl.I.15.

Dhenia tomb C

	jug	6	MCBA, p.23; HNM, p.142 fig 28 row 2.1.
	bowl	56	MCBA, p.19; HNM, p.142 fig 28 row 3.1.

Dhenia tomb F

	bowl	3 50	MCBA, p.51; HNM, p.142 fig 28 row 3.2.

Dhenia tomb G

	bottle	3 9	MCBA, p.29; HNM, p.142 fig 28 row 3.4.

Dhenia tomb 1

67	cup	6 9 13 22 51	N.M. 51.387.

Dhenia tomb 2

20	jug	1 8 9 28	C.M.

Group 27 (contd.)

21	bowl	6 9 14 50	C .M.
21a	bowl	3 17	C.M.
22	jug	1 6 8 9 28	C.M.

Dhenia tomb 3

9	bowl	3 6 50	C.M.

Dhenia Mali

AM 1953.820	jug	1 9 28	A.M.
AM 1952.821	jug	28	A.M.
AM 1953.827	jug	6 22 28	A.M.
A.M. 1953.830	jug	6 24	A.M.
AM 1953.833	jug	3 13 28	A.M.
AM 1953.835	bowl	3 17 44 67	A.M.
AM 1953.836	bowl	3 6 17	A.M.
AM 1953.837	bowl	3 14 28	A.M.
AM 1953.854	bowl	3 5 6 17	A.M.
CM 1960/IV-19/4	bowl	6 51 65	C.M.

Dhenia Kafkalla

AM 1953.826	jug	1 8 9 28	A.M.
CM 1933/V-22/1	flask	21 28	CM inv book
CM 1933/V-22/6	cup	28 39 51	CM inv book
CS 1390	jug	7 23 32 44 51 59	C.M. Karageorghis, 1966, pp.302-3 fig 10. Bucholz and Karageorghis 1971: No 1559.

Group 27 (contd.)

Potamos tou Merikas

CM 1937/III-31/3	bowl	1 48 47	C.M.

Dhenia

AM 1953.822	juglet	14 22 28	A.M.
AM 1953.838	bowl	49 50 63	A.M.
AM 1953.841	cup	6 49	A.M.
AM 1953.842	cup	3 17 80	A.M.
AM 1953.1004	bowl	6 9 17 67	A.M.
AM 1953.1009a	bowl	3 6 49	A.M.
AM 1953.1095	bowl	3 6 17	A.M.
NM 51.351	bowl	3 5 9	N.M. (CM1951/III.14/3).
NM 51.353	jar	2 6 41	N.M. (CM1951/III.14/3).
	jug	6	MCBA p.22; HNM, p.142 fig 28 row 1.1.
CM A1949	bowl	56 39	C.M.
CM 1937/III.31/5	amphoriskos	6 31	C.M.

Number of pots in group 27: 51

Designs occurring in group 27: 1 3 5 6 7 8 9 13 14 17 21 22 23 24 28 31 32 39 41 44 47 48 49 50 51 56 58 59 62 63 65 66 67 69 80.

GROUP 28 DHIKOMO

Dhikomo Onishia, Bademli Bogaz; Krini, Merra

MC 44, 101-2

Group 28 (contd.)

5 vessels from Onishia T.4 (CM 1953/VIII-21/1); 4 from Bogaz Bademli (C.M. excavations, 1935); and one vessel from Krini Merra (Ashmolean Museum - collected by H.W. Catling; other material from this site was not included as the sherds were too small to indicate the total range of decoration). 1 amphora from Bogaz near the East Coast was accidently included in this group in the analyses.

Dhikomo Onishia tomb 4:

1	jug	20 22 34 47 51 59	C.M. inv 1953/VIII.21/1.
2	jug	6 14 49 62	C.M. inv 1953/VIII.21/1.
3	jug	14 22 28	C.M. inv 1953/VIII.21/1.
18	bottle	3	C.M. inv 1953/VIII.21/1/
19	cup	3 13 21	C.M. inv 1953/VIII.21/1/

Krini Merra:

AM 1970. 874	bowl	3 6 9 50	A.M.

Bademli Bogaz tomb 3

3	cup	51 57	C.M.
8	jug	14 34 36 47 51 59	C.M.
21	cup	13 51	C.M.

Bogaz area

-	amphora	6 10 32 59	MCBA, p.75 fig XVIII.8.

Number of pots in group 28: 10

Designs occurring in group 28: 3 6 9 10 13 14 20 21 22 28 32 34 36 47 50 51 59 62.

GROUP 29 ENKOMI

Enkomi Ayios Iakovos

MC 54b

SCE I, pp.467 ff; Schaeffer, 1936, pp.67 ff; Schaeffer, 1952; Dikaios, 1969-71.

A composite group of material mainly from the SCE excavations together with some from the British excavations (T.10), and other pottery in the Cyprus Museum, together with one (late) vessel from Salamis.

This material is all at least MC III in date (MCBA, pp.194, 195 ff.).

Enkomi tombs

2.22	jug	4	MCBA, p.71; SCE I pl.LXXVI.1 row 3.7.
5.291	jug	48	MCBA, p.64; Schaeffer, 1952, pl.XXXVIII.
10.	bottle	48	B.M. C292 MCBA, p.65; CVA BM, pl.6.24.
11.	jug	48	MCBA, p.64; Schaeffer 1936 fig 30.3 pl.XXXI.a.
12.	bowl	3 6	MCBA, p.66; Schaeffer 1952, p.25 fig r1.2.
12.	bowl	3 17	MCBA, p.66; Schaeffer 1952, p.25 fig r2.1.
19.60	jug	1 48	MCBA, p.66; SCE I pl.XCI row 10.6; CIX.3.
20.2	tankard	14 20 59	MCBA, p.57 fig XV.7; SCE I pl.LXXXVII.3.
20.3	jar	3 6 9 28 47 66 79	MCBA, p.68 fig XVI.11; SCE I pl.LXXXVIII.3 no.1; CIX.9.
21.1	jug	1.48	MCBA, p.65 fig IX.13.

Group 29 (contd.)

Enkomi

CM 1939/VII.18/1	jug	17	C.M.
CM 1939/VII.18.1	jug	28 67 68	C.M.
CM 1939/VII.18/1	jug	1 3	C.M.
AM C55	flask	14 20 32 57 59 64	A.M. MCBA, p.42.

Salamis

CM A805	jug	1 3 6 7 28	C.M.

Number of pots in group 29: 15

Designs in group 29: 1 3 4 6 7 14 17 20 28 32 47 48 57 59 64 66 67 68 79.

GROUP 30 GALINOPORNI

Galinoporni Village, Trachonas, Korovia Nitovikla

MC 59, 62, 98.

Material from these different localities in the Cyprus Museum (CM 1953/II-23/1; CM 1956/III-7/6) and the Ashmolean Museum (AM 1953.); together with pottery from the SCE excavations at Nitovkla (SCE I, pp.407-415).

These latter vessels date to MC III (MCBA, p.194).

Group 30 (contd.)

37	jug	6 7 10 31 67	C.M.
39	jug	10 51	C.M.
40	jug	3 28 59	C.M.
47	amphora	5 6 7 10 51 59	C.M.
48	amphora	7 10 31 67	C.M.
49	bowl	3 10	C.M.
50	bowl	5 9 13 51	C.M.
51	bowl	3 51	C.M.

Galinoporni Trachonas

AM 1953.225	jug	7 10 32 67 71	A.M. MCBA, p.31
AM 1953.832	jug	3 9	A.M.
AM 1953.860	jug	6 10 59	A.M.

Nitovikla tombs

1.9.	bowl	1 3 9 67	C.M. MCBA, p.27; SCE I pl.LXIX.1 row 1.7.
1.42	jug	3 53 59	C.M. MCBA, p.54; SCE I pl.LXIX.1 row 2.10.
2.40	bowl	1 3 9	MCBA, p.28 fig IX.4; SCE I pl.LXIX.3 row 1.8.
2.47	bowl	7 10 59 67	MCBA, p.30; SCE I pl.LXIX.3 row 1.1; CVIII.11.
3.1.	jug	7 10 51	C.M. MCBA, p.31
3.2.	bowl	3 9	C.M. MCBA,p.27; SCE I, p.415.

Number of pots in group 30: 39

Designs occurring in group 30: 1 3 4 5 6 7 9 10 12 13 14 15 17 24 28 31 32 34 48 51 53 59 64 67 71.

Group 30 (contd.)

Galinoporni tomb 2 CM inv 1956/III-7/6

1	jug	3 10 51	C.M.
8	jug	6 21 51	C.M.
17	amphora	6 7 10 59 67	C.M.
16	amphora	17 59	C.M.
28	amphora	3 9 13	C.M.
30	bowl	7 10 59	C.M.F. MA.357
31	bowl	3 7 51 59	C.M.F. MA.363
49	jug	1 48	C.M.
50	jug	1 3 4	C.M.
62	jug	1 3 9	C.M.
63	jug	1 24 48	C.M. F. MA.360
67	jug	1 3 9	C.M.
72	jug	3	C.M.
103	jug	7 10	C.M.
131	jug	7 10	C.M.
150	flask	14 32 34 59 62	C.M.F. MA.372
240	bowl	3 10 64	C.M.
241	bowl	7 10 64	C.M.

Galinoporni CM inv 1953/II-23/1

33	jug	1 48	C.M.
34	jug	1 12	C.M.
35	jug	10 15	C.M.
36	jug	7 10 31 67	C.M.

GROUP 31 KALOPSIDHA

Kalopsidha, Tsaoudhi Chiflik

MC 67-69

Myres 1897, pp.138, 147; SPC, pp.12, 27-37; Åström, 1966.

A composite group made up of material from various tombs, principally those excavated by Myres in 1894, together with other material in the Cyprus Museum (Nicosia and Famagusta) and elsewhere.

The tombs generally are dated to MC III (MCBA, p.196).

Kalopsidha tomb 11:

CM A801	juglet	1 48	C.M. MCBA, p.64; JHS 17 fig 4.2.
-	bottle	48	MCBA, p.65; JHS 17 fig 4.4.
AM C59	jug	14 51 47	A.M. MCBA, p.38; JHS 17 fig 4.14.
-	bowl	3 6	MCBA, p.67; JHS 17 fig 4.17.
-	bowl	11	MCBA, p.66; JHS 17 fig.4.18.
CM A665	bowl	3 6	C.M. MCBA, p.66; JHS 17 fig 4.18.
-	jug	2 3 6 66 67	MCBA, p.69; JHS 17 fig 4.22.
-	tankard	48	MCBA, p.65; JHS 17 fig 5.1.
-	jug	48	MCBA, p.64; JHS 17 fig 5.2.
-	bowl	3 9	MCBA, p.27; JHS 17 fig 5.3.
-	jar	41	MCBA, p.68; JHS 17 fig 5.4; CCM, no.331 pl.III
-	bowl	3 9	MCBA, p.27; JHS 17 fig 5.5.
CM A901	bottle	3	C.M. MCBA, p.29; JHS 17 fig 5.10.
CM A791	jug	48	C.M. MCBA, p.64; JHS 17 fig 5.13.
CM A787	jug	1 48	C.M. MCBA, p.64; JHS 17 fig 5.14.

Group 31 (contd.)

-	jug	48	MCBA, p.64; JHS 17 fig 5.15; SPC p.169 jug 2.
-	jug	48	MCBA, p.64; JHS 17 fig 5.16.
-	jug	1 48	MCBA, p.64; JHS 17 fig 5.17.
-	bowl	6	MCBA, p.67; JHS 17 fig 5.26; SPC p.172 bowl 1.
-	bowl	3 6	MCBA, p.67; JHS 17 fig 5.27.
AM C38	jug	1 48	A.M.
AM C46	bottle	1 48	A.M.
AM C49	bowl	3 6 9	A.M.
AM C50	bowl	3 6	A.M.
AM C52	jug	2 3 28 67	A.M.

Kalopsidha tombs

17.	bowl	3 50	C.M. A657 MCBA, p.51; SPC, p.157 bowl 16.
17.	bowl	3 6	C.M. A667 MCBA, p.67.
25	jug	1 7 48	C.M. A789 MCBA, p.65.
25.	jug	1 6 7 48	C.M. A798 MCBA, p.64 fig IX.10; SPC,p.169 jug 1.
27.	jug	1 48	A.M. C37 MCBA, p.64; JHS 17 p.142.

Kalopsidha

-	bowl	3 13	MCBA, p.67 fig XVI.5.
Stat.Hist. M.18082	jug	1.48	MCBA, p.65 fig IX.11.
Stat.Hist. M.18082	jug	2 4	MCBA, p.71 fig XVI.17.
Stat.Hist. M.18082	bowl	3 6	MCBA, p.51 fig XIII.3.
CMF 1967.5	bowl	1 6 9	C.M.F.

Group 31 (contd.)

CMF 967.1	bowl	1 6 9	C.M.F. Karageorghis 1968 fig 66.
CM 1954/XII-2/2	amphora	3 6 9 29	C.M.

Number of pots in group 31: 37

Designs occurring in group 31: 1 2 3 4 6 7 9 10 11 13 14 28 41 47 48 50 51 66 67.

GROUP 32 KATYDATA

This is a small composite group, with only 8 vessels.

Katydata

MC 88

CCM 4; ARDA 1915, p.15; 1916, pp.4 ff; SPC, p.8.

Most of the Katydata material dates from MC II, but some of the tomb 88 material may be MC III (MCBA, p.188).

Pendayia, Mandres

Karageorghis, 1965, pp.2-70.

3 White Painted vessels from this site have been used.

Katydata tombs

42.6	juglet	6 28 66	C.M.
48.	juglet	14 22 51 66	C.M.
55.10	bowl	9 24 56	C.M.
85.24	juglet	34 59	C. M. MCBA, p.55.
88	bowl	3 10 56	C.M.

Group 32 (contd._

Pendayia Mandres

CM 1966/VIII-8/1	bowl	3 17	C.M.
CM 1966/VIII-8/2	bowl	17	C.M.
CM 1965/VII-27/1	bowl	6 32	C.M.

Number of pots in group 32: 8

Designs occurring in group 32: 3 6 9 10 14 17 22 24 28 32 34 51 56 59 66.

GROUP 33 KLAVDHIA

Klavdhia Tremithios

MC 89

Material from the British Museum excavations in 1899 in Nicosia and London. A relatively small group of only 14 pots.

Klavdhia tombs

A12 (10)	flask	32 51	B.M. C298 MCBA, p.43.
15.	jug	6 59 47	B.M. C275 MCBA, p.55; CVA BM pl.6.25.
A15.	bottle	22 32 66	B.M. C290 MCBA,p.33; CVA BM pl.5.7.
A31.	jug	3 6 50 67	B.M. 99 12.29 116; MCBA, p.71; CVA BM pl.5.37.
-	jug	1 8 22 28 33	B.M. C329 MCBA, p.52; CVA BM pl.5.31.
CM A718a	jug	3 5 50 80	C.M.
CM A722	jug	3 6 17 50 67	C.M.
CM A751	juglet	3 6 17 50 67	C.M.
CM A755	juglet	3 10 65	C.M.
CM A758	juglet	6 23 59	C.M.
CM A806	jug	6 27 28 67 79	C.M.

Group 33 (contd.)

CM A876	bottle	3 9 65	C.M. MCBA, p.29; SPC, p.159 bottle 2a.
CM A877	bottle	3	C.M.
CM A898	bottle	1 3 6 9	C.M.

Number of pots in group 33: 14

Designs occurring in group 33: 1 3 5 6 8 9 10 17 22 23 27 28 32 33 47 50 51 59 65 66 67 79 80.

GROUP 34 KOTCHATI

Kotchati, Ayia Varvara, Kalamoudhia

MC 100

ARDA, 1950, p.14. Åström 1972b,c.

Material from three groups in the Cyprus Museum (all purchased).

Kotchati Ayia Varvara CM inv 1950/V-8/1

a	jug	1 8 9 28	C.M.
b	jug	3 6	C.M.

Kotchati Kalamoudhia CM inv 1950/VI-16.1

a	jug	1 48	C.M.
b	jug	6 14 22 51	C.M.
e	juglet	3 14	C.M.
g	jar	3 13 20	C.M.
k	bowl	1 3 6	C.M.

Group 34 (contd.)

Kotchati		CM inv 1970/X-7/	
10	amphora	28 34 54 58	C.M.
11	jug	1 8 9 28	C.M.
12	jug	1 47 48 66	C.M.
13	jug	1 8 9 28	C.M.
14	jug	3 49 51	C.M.
15	jug	1 28	C.M.
17	jug	27 35 65	C.M.
18	bowl	6 24 56	C.M.
19	bowl	3 17	C.M.
20	bowl	3 6 17	C.M.
21	bowl	3 6 17	C.M.
22	cup	3 17	C.M.

Number of pots in group 34: 19

Designs occurring in group 34: 1 3 6 8 9 13 14 17 20 22 24 27 28 34 35 47 49 51 54 56 58 65 66.

GROUP 35 KYTHREA

A composite group from the two sites:

Kythrea Potamos tis Viklis (MC 106). SPC ,pp.7, 276. Material in the Cyprus Museum.

Bey Keuy Mandra tou Vasili (MC 37). 4 White Painted vessels in the Ashmolean Museum.

Probably early MC III (MCBA, p.197).

Group 35 (contd.)

Kythrea tomb 1			
CM A710	jug	6 23 13 28 64 66	C.M. MCBA, p.70 fig XVII.3; SPC, p.158 jug 15.
CM A729	jug	3 15 66 81	C.M.
CM A739	jug	3 11 28	C.M. MCBA, p,70.
CM A740	jug	3 11 28	C.M. MCB A , p.70.
CM A741	jug	3 9 49	C.M.
CM A775	bowl	1 3 9	C.M. MCBA, p.28
CM A777	bowl	1 3 9 8	C.M. MCBA, p.28.
CM A782	jug	1 48	C.M. MCBA, p.64.
CM A796	jug	48	C.M.
CM A782	jug	1 48	C.M. MCBA, p.64; SPC, p.169 jug 1.
CM A911	animal	22 28 64	C.M. MCBA, p. 77; CMN C.II.352; Buchholz and Karageorghis No. 1571.

Bey Keuy			
AM 1953.844	cup	17 49 65	A.M.
AM 1953.1025b	jug	9 24 58 67	A.M.
AM 1953.1025e	jug	1 3 9 10	A.M.
AM 1953.1028d	jug	48	A.M.

Number of pots in group 35: 15

Designs occurring in group 35: 1 3 6 8 9 10 11 13 15 17 22 23 28 48 49 58 64,65 66 67 81.

GROUP 36 LARNACA

A composite group of 19 vessels from 5 sites near Larnaca.

Arpera Chiflik Ayios Andronikos (MC 7a). ARCA 1914, p.41; 1915, pp.4 ff; SPC, p.14; MCBA, p.16.

The three vessels from tombs 203, 204, 103 are MC III (MCBA, pp.188, 197).

Arpera Mosphilos Tomb IA. BSA 58, p.90. This vessel is MC III (MCBA, p.197, n.6).

Anglisidhes Solia (MC 6). Material in the Cyprus Museum (BSA 58, p.89).

Alaminos Stavroti (MC 5a). Material in the Cyprus Museum.

Hala Sultan Tekke, Kremnos, Angathia, Vounarapoulos (MC 64). SPC, p.13; CMC, p.188. Material from Walters excavations in 1897 - 98 in the Cyprus Museum.

Larnaca Laxia tou Riou. CMC, p.58; Myres, 1897, pp.147-152; SPC, p.13. (Excavated by Myres, 1894.)

These groups generally are to be dated about MC II-III (MCBA, pp.188, 196).

Arpera tombs			
203.	jug	48	MCBA, p.64.
205A.24	animal	5 17 29	C.M. A912.
103.	jug	1 8 24 28 33	MCBA, p.52.
AM 1953.945	bowl	9 68	A.M.
1A.13	jug	3 9 22	C.M. Popham,1963a, p.90.

Group 36 (contd.)

Anglisidhes C.M. inv 1939/III-4/3			
a	bottle	3 5	C.M. Popham, 1963a, p.89
b	bottle	3 5	C.M. Popham, 1963a, p.89
-	bowl	28 35 51	C.M.
-	bowl	3 6 49 67	C.M.

Alaminos C.M. inv 1933/XII-18/			
6	jug	1 48	C.M.
7	jug	1 3 9	C.M. Popham, 1963a, p.89.

Hala Sultan Tekke			
CM A726	jug	3 5	C.M.
CM A795	jug	3 4	C.M.
CM A859	flask	6 70	C.M.

Laxia tou Riou			
CM A842	jar	3 5 14 17 53	C.M. (tomb 2)
-	jug	51	MCBA, p.39; CCM no.360 pl.III (tomb 1)
-	jug	64	MCBA, p.37; CCM no.345, p.48; CMN 6480.
CM 757	juglet	22 49	C.M. MCBA, p.55
AM C76	tankard	3 58 75	A.M. MCBA, p.72

Number of pots in group 36: 19

Designs occurring in group 36: 1 3 4 5 6 8 9 14 17 22 24 28 29 33 35 48 49 51 53 58 64 67 68 70 75.

GROUP 37 LEONDARI VOUNO

Eylenja, Leondari Vouno

MC 57

JHS, IX 1888, pp.6 ff; SPC, p.4; CMC, 8.

Excavated by James for Cyprus Exploration Fund in 1885. Material in Fitzwilliam Museum, Cambridge, and the Ashmolean Museum, Oxford.

Leondari Vouno

-	jug	9 50 56	MCBA, p.37; CVA Cambridge pl.VIII.2.
-	jug	3 50 62 67	MCBA, p.70; CVA Cambridge pl.VIII.3.
-	jug	10 39	MCBA, p.55; CVA Cambridge pl.VIII.4.
-	jug	8 9 41	MCBA, p.55; CVA Cambridge pl.VIII.6.
-	bottle	3 62 47	MCBA, p.58; CVA Cambridge pl.VIII.15.
-	bowl	3 6 17 67	MCBA, p.19; CVA Cambridge pl.VIII.38.
-	bowl	3 6 15	MCBA, p.19; CVA Cambridge pl.VIII.39.
AM 1888.1246	jug	3 75	A.M. MCBA, p.36
AM 1888.1247	jug	6 41	A.M. MCBA, p.70.
AM 1888.1247A	jug	3 17	A.M. MCBA, p.70.
AM 1888.1248	juglet	3 5 7 29	A.M. MCBA, p.37.
AM 1888.1249	flask	21 57 75	A.M.

Number of pots in group 37: 12

Designs occurring in group 37: 3 5 6 7 8 9 10 15 17 21 29 39 41 47 50 56 57 62 67 75.

GROUP 38 LIVADHIA

Livadhia Kokotes

MC 122

Tomb 1, CM inv 1942/IV-17/2, material in the Larnaca Museum.

A small group of only 12 vessels.

Livadhia tomb 1 C.M. inv 1942/IV-17/2

5	juglet	3 6 50 66	C.M.L. MLA 149
6	jug	1 2 28 67	C.M.L. MLA 150
7	bottle	3 9	C.M.L. MLA 151 (BSA 58, p.90).
8	bowl	3 6 22 58	C.M.L. MLA 152
9	bowl	2 51	C.M.L. MLA 153
10	bowl	6 10 50 56	C.M.L. MLA 154
-	flask	22 32	C.M.L. MLA 166
-	jug	1 48	C.M.L. MLA 168

Number of pots in group 38: 8

Designs occurring in group 38: 1 2 3 6 9 10 22 28 32 48 50 51 56 58 66 67.

GROUP 39 MILIA

Milea, Vikla Trachonas

MC 128

Westholm, 1939.

A small group of 10 vessels, comprising those published by Westholm (SCE excavations) together with three other vessels in the Cyprus Museum (inv 1934/II-12/6) which probably come from this site (Patterns, p.159).

Group 39 (contd.)

Milia tombs

			References to Westholm, 1939
10.58	bowl	13 21	MCBA, p.67; pl.1.
10.72 (38)	bottle	48	MCBA, p.65; pl.I, V.7.
10.73 (8)	jug	48	MCBA, p.64; pl.I, V.5.
10.86 (5)	bottle	3 51 58	MCBA, p.59; pl.I
11.4 (39)	bowl	6	MCBA, p.66; pl.VI.
11.9 (22)	jug	48	MCBA, p.64; pl.VI.
13.4 (17)	bowl	2	MCBA, p.67; pl. VI.

C.M. inv 1934/II-12/

6	bowl	3 5 6 17	C.M.
7	jug	1 3 9	C.M.; Popham, 1963a.
8	jug	2 7 62 66 67 68	C.M.

Number of pots in group 39: 10

Designs occurring in group 39: 1 2 3 5 6 7 9 13 17 21 48 51 58 62 66 67 68.

GROUP 40 NICOSIA

Nicosia, Ayia Paraskevi

MC 134

ARDA 1949, p.14.

A very large tomb group, which includes the 119 White Painted vessels used here. This group was excavated by the Cyprus Museum in 1949

Group 40 (contd.)

and is labelled as Nicosia Dhasoupolis Tomb 8 CM 1949/IX-14/2.

Nicosia Dhasoupolis tomb 8

3	askos	1 3 6 32 57 59	C.M.
5	jug	8 59	C.M.
7	jug	3 6 49 68	C.M.
8	jug	3 49 58 68	C.M.
9	jug	17 49 62	C.M.
11	jug	3 14 50 58	C.M.
12	flask	14 51 59	C.M.
13	cup	3 49 67	C.M.
14	jug	20 22 34 46 51 59	C.M.
15	jug	6 28 66	C.M.
16	jug	6 7 9 50 58 67	C.M.
19	bowl	6 10 49 22	C.M.
20	juglet	14 20 22 46 51 59 67	C.M.
21	jug	10 15 22 51 59	C.M.
22	cup	3 49	C.M.
23	bowl	3 9 50	C.M.
26	bottle	22 64	C.M.
28	ring vase	28 59 62	C.M.
30	juglet	51 67	C.M.
32	juglet	14 22 49 58	C.M.
37	juglet	3 14 22 51 59 67	C.M.
39	bowl	9 24 49	C.M.
40	flask	6 34 59 67	C.M.

Group 40 (contd.

41	amphora	22 32 35	C.M.
46	juglet	3 14 58	C.M.
47	jug	22 34 51 62	C.M.
48	bottle	6 22 63	C.M.
49	jug	8 49 65	C.M.
50	jug	1 6 8 9 28	C.M.
51	jug	6 44	C.M.
58	bowl	3 6 24 50	C.M.
65	jug	6 9 14 63 67	C.M.
70	jug	14 20 46 59 62	C.M.
75	jug	3 22 51 59	C.M.
81	jug	20 22 51 57 47	C.M.
82	jug	3 51	C.M.
83	animal	56	C.M.
87	juglet	14 59	C.M.
91	juglet	14 20 22 51 59 46	C.M.
94	bowl	56 57	C.M.
96	animal	56	C.M.
97	jug	8 49 65	C.M.
101	bottle	22 28	C.M.
102	jug	22 54 65	C.M.
107	bowl	56 62	C.M.
113	juglet	14 51	C.M.
120	bottle	22 63	C.M.
130	jug	1 3 6 8 28	C.M.
131	composite	34 64 67	C.M.

Group 40 (contd.)

137	cup	22 28	C.M.
140	cup	8 49	C.M.
141	bottle	22 64	C.M.
142	cup	9 39 51	C.M.
143	jug	13 44	C.M.
144	bowl	9 56 62	C.M.
146	bowl	56 68	C.M.
149	bottle	22 64	C.M.
207	bowl	3 6 17 67	C.M.
208	bowl	6 9 24 38 50	C.M.
209	bowl	6 10 50 67	C.M.
211	bowl	6 24 50	C.M.
213	bowl	9 24 49	C.M.
214	bowl	6 10 49 63 67	C.M.
215	bowl	6 9 50 67	C.M.
216	bowl	6 10 50 67	C.M.
217	bowl	6 10 50 67	C.M.
218	cup	6 9 14 51 64 67	C.M.
221	cup	3 51 67	C.M.
225	flask	9 20 22 31 44 59	C.M.
226	flask	10 20 59	C.M.
227	flask	6 27 57 59	C.M.
230	flask	6 9 34 59	C.M.
232	bottle	3 64	C.M.
234	bottle	3 9 64	C.M.
235	bottle	3 64	C.M.

Group 40 (contd.)

236	bottle	9 41	C.M.
237	bottle	22 64	C.M.
239	bottle	9 63	C.M.
240	bottle	3 28	C.M.
241	bottle	41 44	C.M.
256	cup	13 14	C.M.
257	jug	6 22 49 58 62	C.M.
258	jug	6 49 67	C.M.
259	jug	6 14 22 58	C.M.
260	juglet	8 20 22 46 51 59	C.M.
261	juglet	9 14 20 59	C.M.
262	juglet	9 14 34 51 59 46	C.M.
263	jug	6 27 59	C.M.
264	juglet	22 34 46 59 51	C.M.
265	juglet	3 6 14 58 67	C.M.
266	amphora	20 34 46 51 59 64	C.M.
267	juglet	3 49 58	C.M.
268	jug	10 14 51	C.M.
269	juglet	3 6 9 44 67	C.M.
270	juglet	6 10 20 51 59	C.M.
283	juglet	9 34 49 58 67	C.M.
284	juglet	6 13 20 21 22 51	C.M.
285	juglet	57	C.M.
286	juglet	14 51	C.M.

287	juglet	51 57	C.M.
288	juglet	14 17 46 51	C.M.
289	jug	9 13 14 22 58 67	C.M.
290	jug	1 56	C.M.
291	jug	1 6 8 9 28	C.M.
292	jug	14 49 58 62	C.M.
293	jug	3 14 49 50 67	C.M.
294	jug	7 9 14 58	C.M.
295	jug	20 22 51 59	C.M.
296	jug	10 41 67	C.M.
297	jug	1 6 9 28	C.M.
298	jug	6 10 58 67	C.M.
299	jug	6 14 51	C.M.
300	animal	29	C.M.
301	animal	31	C.M.
302	animal	17	C.M.

Nicosia Dhasoupolis tomb 8B

1	jug	14 46 51	C.M.
3	bowl	3 17	C.M.
5	jug	13 20 22 27 51 57 59	C.M.

Nicosia Dhasoupolis tomb 8C

2	bottle	3 6 22 67	C.M.

Number of pots in group 40: 119

Designs occurring in group 40: 1 3 6 7 8 9 10 13 14 15 17 20 21 22 24 27 28 29 31 32 34 35 38 39 41 44 46 47 49 50 51 54 56 57 58 59 62 63 64 65 66 67 68.

GROUP 41 PALAEALONA

Karmi Palaealona

MC 82a

Stewart, 1963, pp.197 ff.

A small group of 9 vessels from 4 of the tombs excavated by Stewart in 1961. The material is to be published shortly by J.B. Hennessy, and is at present stored at Wentworth Falls, N.S.W.

Palaealona Tombs

2.	jug	9 28 51	W.F.
2.60	amphora	51 64	W.F.
3a.140	jug	21 23 28 64 39	W.F.
3a.142	jar	15 16 33 65	W.F.
3a.143	amphora	1 13 27 35	W.F.
3a.144	amphora	28 35	W.F.
14.16	amphora	27 34 35 64	W.F.
11.4	jug	6 9 27 28 35 65	Stewart, pl.V fig. 6
11.5	amphora	16 35	Stewart, 1963 fig.7.

Number of pots in group 41: 9

Designs occurring in group 41: 1 6 9 13 15 16 21 23 27 28 33 34 35 39 51 64 65.

GROUP 42 POLITICO T.4

Politico Lambertis, tomb 4

MC 141

Group 42 (contd.)

A fairly large tomb group including the 41 White Painted vessels used here. Excavated by the Cyprus Museum in 1963. (CM inv 1963/XII-20/2).

The material is probably MC II-III, with some later material.

Politico tomb 4

49	amphora	1 6 20 30 32 51 59	C.M.
50	jug	9 20 25 34 59 67	C.M.
51	jug	1 10 48	C.M.
52	tankard	14 22 28 51 59	C.M.
53	jug	3 7 57 59 65	C.M.
56	jug	6 9 50	C.M.
57	tankard	3 7	C.M.
59	jug	6 14 18 22 30 34 57 66	C.M.
60	flask	22 64	C.M.
61	bottle	22 64	C.M.
109	cup	56 62	C.M.
110	jug	6 7 9 58 67	C.M.
111	cup	3 6 49 67	C.M.
112	bowl	6 10 17 67	C.M.
113	cup	8 49 65	C.M.
114	bowl	3 50	C.M.
116	jug	1 13 49	C.M.
117	jug	49 51 65	C.M.
118	jug	1 13 58 47	C.M.
119	jug	1 10 49	C.M.
120	jug	1 6 8 9 28	C.M.

Group 42 (contd.)

130	jug	6 7 9 49 58 67	C.M.
131	jug	3 10 28	C.M.
132	jug	1 3 4 12	C.M.
133	jug	3 25 41 60 81	C.M.
134	jug	7 12 22 59	C.M.
138	juglet	3 41 75	C.M.
139	flask	6 14 59 64	C.M.
142	jug	3 11	C.M.
143	jug	3 11 28	C M.
144	jug	1 6 8 28	C.M.
146	bowl	1 6 7 10 8 39 49 63 67	C.M.
147	bowl	3 6 18	C M.
148	tankard	1 9 10 42 75	C.M.
149	jug	9 14 58 67	C.M.
150	jug	28 62	C.M.
151	jug	44	C.M.
152	jug	6 9 34 51 67 68	C.M.
164	bowl	6 10 17 67	C.M.
165	bowl	9 10 17 67	C.M.
166	bowl	5 6 9 10 50	C .M.

Number of pots in group 41: 41

Designs occurring in group 41: 1 3 4 5 6 7 8 9 10 11 12 13 14 17 18 20 22 25 28 30 32 34 39 41 42 44 47 48 49 50 51 56 57 58 59 60 62 63 64 65 66 67 68 75 81.

GROUP 43 POLITICO

Politico Lambertis, Chomazoudhia

MC 141, 143

A composite group of individual pots and smaller groups from the area of Politico.

Most of the material is from the locality Lambertis - excavated by Ohnefalsch-Richter. CCM 12; SPC 9; Kypros, fig.37, 38. The other groups are from more recent Cyprus Museum excavations (CM invs 1940/XII-23/1, 1941/I-18/1).

Two vessels come from the locality Chomazoudhia.

Lambertis tomb ME 6

-	jug	3 28	MCBA,p.54; CVA Cambridge pl.VIII.9.

Lambertis tomb 8

CM A 849	flask	1 6 54	C.M. MCBA, p.42; SPC, p.152 flask 1.

Lambertis tomb 9

CM A 704	jug	1 3 6 49 63	C.M. MCBA, p.35.
CM A788	jug	1 3 9	C.M.
-	juglet	58	MCBA, p.35; Kypros pl.CCXVI.22.
-	bottle	14 57	MCBA,p.58; CVA Cambridge pl.VIII.17.
-	cup	51	MCBA, p.50; CVA Cambridge pl.VIII.34.

Lambertis tomb 12

-	jug	3 5 6 7 28	MCBA, p.69; CVA Cambridge pl.VIII.23.

Group 43 (contd.)

Lambertis tomb 14

-	jug	29	MCBA, p.35; Ohnefalsch-Richter, 1899, VIII.9.

Lambertis tomb 18

-	jug	1 7 8 9 46	MCBA, p.35; CVA Cambridge pl.VIII.22
-	jar	34 59	MCBA, p.62; SPC, p.160 jar 1.

Lambertis tomb 28

CM A703	jug	3 49 58 67	C.M. MCBA, p.35
-	bowl	2 6 50 67	MCBA, p.49; CVA Cambridge pl.VIII.37.

Lambertis tomb 31

CM A634	bowl	3 6 50 67	C.M.
CM A637	bowl	3 6 17 22	C.M. MCBA, p.34; CCM, p.48 no.312.
CM A702	jug	1 2 8 9 28	C.M. MCBA, p.36; SPC, p.158 jug 13.
CM A762	juglet	51 57 62	C.M. MCBA, p. 39; CMN 6480.
CM A799	jug	1 48 67	C.M. MCBA, p.65.

Lambertis tomb 38

CM A690	jug	51 57	C.M.
CM A723	jug	3 6 14 49	C.M.
CM A763	juglet	10 14 51 67	C.M. MCBA, p.40.
CM A765	jug	51	C.M. MCBA, p.37; Ohnefalsch-Richter, 1899, fig.III.8.
CM A861	flask	29	C.M.
CM A875	flask	34 35 51	C.M.
-	jug	3 6 14 49	C.M.

Group 43 (contd.)

-	flask	1	MCBA, p.42;CVA Cambridge pl.VIII.10.
-	flask	42	MCBA, p.43; CVA Cambridge pl.VIII.11.
-	animal	22 29	MCBA, p.47; CVA Cambridge pl.VIII.12.
-	composite	6 14 41	MCBA, p.47; CVA Cambridge pl.VIII.13.
-	composite	44	MCBA, p.47; CVA Cambridge pl.VIII.14.
-	flask	51	MCBA, p.44; CVA Cambridge pl.VIII.18.
-	jug	6 66	MCBA, p.35; CVA Cambridge pl.VIII.21.
-	jar	2	MCBA, p.68; CVA Cambridge pl.VIII.24.
-	bowl	3 6 9 50	MCBA, p.50; CVA Cambridge pl.VIII.35.
-	bowl	3 6 11	MCBA, p.67 fig XVI.5; CVA Cambridge pl.VIII.36.
-	jug	25 51	MCBA, p.36; Kypros, pl.XXXVI.21.

Chomazoudhia

3.IV	jug	3 14 22 29 44 57	C.M. A714 MCBA, p.36; SPC, p.157 jug 4.
CM A715	jug	9 14 30 47 60 62	C.M. MCBA, p.37; GCM VI.7; CCM no.334 pl.III; Archaeologia Viva pl.139.

Number of pots in group 43: 58

Designs occurring in group 43: 1 2 3 4 5 6 7 8 9 10 11 12 13 14 17 20 21 22 25 27 28 29 30 32 34 35 39 41 42 44 46 47 48 49 50 51 54 57 58 59 60 62 63 64 66 67 70.

Group 43 (contd.)

Lambertis tomb 43

CM A772	tankard	3 6 58	C.M.

C.M. inv 1940/XII-23/1

-	bottle	9 62	C.M.
-	bottle	22	C.M.
-	jug	6 14 22 32	C.M.
-	jug	1 9 28	C.M.
-	composite	14 39 44	C.M.

C.M. inv 1941/I-18/1

-	bottle	21 64	CM inv book
-	bottle	9	CM inv book
-	bottle	3 10	CM inv book
-	jug	51	CM inv book
-	jug	6	CM inv book
-	bowl	3 17	CM inv book
-	bowl	3 6 50	C.M.
-	bowl	17	CM inv book
-	jug	51	CM inv book
-	tankard	3	CM inv book
-	bottle	6 9 13 70	C.M.
-	tankard	4 6 11 57	C.M.

Lambertis

-	jug	3 20 27	MCBA, p.70;CVA Cambridge pl.VIII.1
-	jug	3 13 14 44	MCBA,p.36 fig XI.8;CVA Cambridge,pl.VIII.8

GROUP 44 MYRTOU

A small composite group of 8 pots, from the two sites:

Myrtou Stephania (MC 131). 5 vessels from tombs 10 and 13 excavated by Hennessy in 1951. Hennessy, 1964. MC III (MCBA, p.198, Hennessy, 1964, p.51).

Dhiorios Aloupotrypes (MC 51). Three of the vessels collected by H.W. Catling and in the Ashmolean and Nicholson Museums.

Stephania tombs

10.4	tankard	3 7 59	N.M. MCBA, p.57 fig XV.10.
10.5	tankard	3 6 17 20	N.M., MCBA, p.72 fig XVII.8.
10.7	amphora	3 6 12 59	N.M. MCBA, p.75 fig XVIII.9.
13.1	jug	6 9 28 69	MCBA, p.55
13.7	bowl	3 6 17	MCBA, p.49; Hennessy, 1964, pl.LIV.7

Dhiorios

AM 1953.1121	jug	6 9 49 53 67	A.M.
AM 1953.1122a	jug	3 9 28	A.M.
NM 54.36	bowl	3 6 17	N.M.

Number of pots in group 44: 8

Designs occurring in group 44: 3 6 7 9 12 17 20 28 49 53 59 67 69

GROUP 45 VOUNOUS

Bellapais Vounous

MC 35a

Dikaios, 1938; Schaeffer, 1936; Stewart and Stewart, 1950.

Group 45 (contd.)

A composite group of 23 of the White Painted vessels from the several excavations at the sites.

Most of the material can be assigned to MC I-II (MCBA, pp.186-7, 176).

Vounous tombs

37.77	jug	28	MCBA, p.13; Dikaios, 1938, pp.78,135e.
37.96	amphora	13 27 36	MCBA, p.25; Dikaios, 1938, pl.LVI.2.
37.98	bowl	3 10	MCBA, p.30; Dikaios, 1938, pl.LVI.3a.
38.19	amphora	9 27 28	MCBA, p.16; Dikaios, 1938, p.80; CMN G908 row 1.2.
40.2	amphora	27 56 75	MCBA, p.15; Dikaios, 1938, pl.LVI.1.
40.4	amphora	27	MCBA, p.27; Dikaios, 1938, p.84
40.7	bowl	14 56 75	MCBA, p.19; Dikaios, 1938, pl.LVI.4.
50 SSC 1	jug	20 22 34 59	MCBA, p.23; Schaeffer, 1936, pl.XXIV.1.
50 SSC 2	jug	14 20 34 51	MCBA, p.24; Schaeffer, 1936, pl.XXIV.2.
56.93	jug	1 6 32 67	MCBA, p.14 fig 7.
57A	animal	27	MCBA, p.25; Schaeffer, 1936, pl.XXII.
64.32	amphora	13 27 65	C.M.
64.107	jug	13 27 36 65	C.M.
64.108	jug	6 9 28 65	C.M.
64.112	jug	9 28	C.M.
64	jug	6 9 17 23 28	C.M.
64	jug	27 36 58	C.M.
64.138	askos	14 27 28 36 65	C.M. MCBA, p.16; Schaeffer, 1936, pl.XXII; GGM^{3}, pl.VI. Bucholz and Karageorghis, 1971: No. 1562.

Group 45 (contd.)

68.6	amphora	27 56 75	Sketch in microfilm Vounous 3 in Fisher Library, Sydney University
68.29	askos	28 63	N.M.
68.31	amphora	3 9 28 65	N.M.
99.4	amphora	59	MCBA, p.45; Stewart and Stewart, 1950 pl.XIe.4.
37.117	cup	53 59	MCBA p.13; fig III.4; Dikaios 1938 pl.LV.12.

Number of pots in group 45: 23

Designs occurring in group 45: 1 3 6 9 10 13 14 17 20 22 23 27 28 34 36 51 53 56 58 59 63 65 67 75.

GROUP 46 YERI

Yeri Phoenikies

MC 169

SPC, p.5; Kypros, p.33; CMC, p.10.

27 vessels from the excavations by Ohnefalsch-Richter carried out in 1883. Most of the material is now in London. Some of the tombs may be dated to MC III (MCBA, p.197).

Yeri

BM C286	juglet	13 27 56	B.M. MCBA, p.56; CVA BM pl.5.1.
BM C265	bowl	3 14 22 32	B.M. MCBA, p.32 fig X.10; CVA BM pl.5.12.
BM C263	cup	6 9 30 47 67 72	B.M. MCBA, p.33 fig X.8; CVA BM pl.5.13; SPC, p.157 bowl 13.
BM C274	jug	1 3 9	B.M. MCBA, p.28; CVA BM pl.5.15.
BM C328	flask	25 39 64	B.M. MCBA, p.43; CVA BM pl.5.17.

Group 46 (contd.)

BM C299	flask	6 9 44	B.M. MCBA, p.44; CVA BM pl.5.20.
BM C260	bowl	3 6 17	B.M. MCBA, p.67; CVA BM pl.5.22.
BM C264	cup	6 51	B.M. MCBA, p.52; CVA BM pl.5.28.
BM C296	bottle	3 9 21	B.M. MCBA, p.29; CVA BM pl.5.30.
BM C283	jug	3 6 75	B.M. MCBA, p.71; CVA BM pl.5.32.
BM 84 12.10.195	jug	9 24 75	B.M. MCBA, p.36; CVA BM pl.5.34.
BM C281	juglet	14 51	B.M. MCBA, p.39; CVA BM pl.5.38.
BM C287	juglet	6 9 18 50 67	B.M. MCBA, p.38; CVA BM pl.5.42.
BM C294	flask	6 9 42	B.M. MCBA, p.59; CVA BM pl.6.6.
BM C326	jug	1 3 9	B.M. MCBA, p.28; CVA BM pl.6.7; Kypros, pl.CLII.8.
BM 84 12.10.8	jug	1 3 9	B.M. MCBA, p.27; CVA BM pl.6.9.
BM C276	juglet	22 75	B.M. MCBA , p.70; CVA BM pl.6.18.
BM C284	jug	3 28 80	B.M. MCBA, p.70; CVA BM pl.6.22.
BM 84 12.10.6	amphora	2 4 10 31	B.M. MCBA, p.76; CVA BM pl.6.28; SPC, p.173 amphora 3.
BM C259	bowl	3 9 50 67	B.M. MCBA, p.48; CVA BM pl.8.13.
BM C266	bowl	3 6 50	B.M. MCBA, p.19; CVA BM pl.6.20.
BM C262	bowl	3 6 17	B.M. MCBA, p.49; CVA BM pl.8.24.
BM	bowl	3	B.M. MCBA , p.48; CVA BM pl.8.26.
BM C297	bottle	13 64 65 67	B.M. MCBA , p.58; CVA BM pl.6.27.
BM C300	flask	6 28 30 32	B.M. MCBA , p.33; CVA BM pl.6.30.
-	flask	44	MCBA, p.43; Kypros pl.CL.18.
-	juglet	6 9 14 34 58	MCBA, p.38; Kypros pl.CXLVI.3 B, k; CLXXIII.20, 21, k.

Number of pots in group 46: 27

Designs occurring in group 46: 1 2 3 4 6 9 10 13 14 17 18 21 22 24 25 27 28 30 31 32 34 39 44 47 50 51 56 58 64 65 67 75 76 80.

GROUP 47 ?ALAMBRA

Alambra Asproge

MC 4

Villa, 1969.

This is a dubious group, and uses 53 White Painted vessels in the Stanford Museum, recently published by P. Villa. As there was some slight chance that they do in fact constitute a proper group from Cesnola's excavations at Alambra the material was included as an independent group. If the patterning of designs is compatible with its location then there is some value in its use. If not then the group should be ignored.

Alambra? Cesnola Collection in Stanford

			All references to Villa, 1969
36	jug	9 28 63 67	pl.II, XII
37	jug	1 3 9	pl.II
38	jug	1 3 9	pl.II
39	juglet	44	pl.II
40	juglet	9 44	pl.II
41	jug	29	pl.II
42	juglet	17 51	pl.III
43	jug	3 22 28	pl.III
44	jug	3 9 28	pl.III
45	jug	9 28	pl.III
46	jug	9 31	pl.III
47	jug	22 51 59 67	pl.III
48	jug	22 61 66	pl.III

Group 47 (contd.)

49	jug	1 3 8 50	pl.IV
50	jug	3 14 17 50	pl.IV
51	jug	1 6	pl.IV
52	jug	9 28	pl.IV
53	jug	22 76	pl.IV
54	jug	28	pl.IV
55	jug	3 6 9 49 67	pl.IV
56	jug	3 50	pl.IV
57	jug	3 22 49	pl.IV
58	jug	9	pl.IV
59	jug	9 75	pl.IV
60	jug	9 24 28	pl.IV
61	jug	3 17 50	pl.IV
62	jug	3 6 9 17 50	pl.V
63	jug	3 24 50	pl.V
64	jug	3 17 50	pl.V
65	jug	1 3 6	pl.V
74	flask	3 9	pl.V
75	flask	22 64	pl.V
76	flask	22 64	pl.V
77	flask	3 63	pl.VI
78	flask	9 22	pl.VI
79	flask	3 75	pl.VI

Group 47 (contd.)

Alambra (Villa)

80	flask	14 64	pl.VI
81	flask	24	pl.VI
82	flask	3 14 25 64	pl.VI
83	flask	11 25 64	pl.VI
84	flask	20 33 34 59	pl.VI
85	flask	9 28	pl.VI
86	flask	3 6 7 28	pl.VI
87	flask	3 9 28	pl.VI
88	bottle	1 48	pl.VI
89	bottle	1 48	pp.23-4
90	cup	6 9 44 67	pl.VII
91	cup	3 9 42 67	pl.VII
92	bowl	3 49	pl.VII
93	amphora	6 13 22	pl.VII
94	amphora	1 2 6 7	pl.VII
95	jar	3 5 6 17	pl.VII
97	animal	3 5 9 28	pl.VII

Number of pots in group 47: 53

Designs occurring in group 47: 1 2 3 5 6 7 8 9 11 13 14 17 20 22 24 25 28 29 31 33 34 42 44 48 49 50 51 59 61 63 64 66 67 75.

APPENDIX II

This appendix lists the occurrence by group and shape of each of the motifs, giving also the totals and percentages.

Besides the pots listed in Appendix I, which are used in the analyses, other vessels are occasionally included where they show the motif at a different site or on a different shape from the main sample.

For convenience in drawing up the tables the names of the sites and of the shapes have been abbreviated; there should be no problems in recognising these abbreviations. Similar abbreviations are also used in some of the tables and figures.

MOTIF 1

	Group	jug	jlt	cup	bwl	amp	jar	tnk	flk	btl	oth	total	% of group
1	L2	5										5	19
2	L18	14				1			1			16	24
3	L21	14								2		16	23
4	L29	8		1						1		10	34
5	L47	3								2		5	26
6	L49	7								2		9	27
7	L50	20				2			2			24	32
8	L315 A	5										5	20
9	L315 B-C	2				1						3	31
10	L316[1]	14				1						15	35
11	L316[2]	3	1					1		1		6	35
12	L320	4										4	20
13	L4	1										1	10
14	L8			1					1			2	22
15	L14	4								1		5	31
16	L51	2										2	14
17	L203	7										7	47
18	L311	5										5	45
19	L313	2										2	20
20	L702	1										1	8
21	Lapithos	14				1		1				16	21
22	Alambra	1				1						2	29
23	Ay Iak	1			3							4	12
24	Ay P.	3										3	4
25	Dhali	2										2	13
26	Dhenia 6	4										4	12
27	Dhenia	9										9	20
29	Enkomi	3										3	27
30	Gal.	9										9	23
31	Kalops.	8			2					1		11	30
33	Klavdhia	1								1		2	14
34	Kotchati	6			1							7	37
35	Kythrea	5										5	33
36	Larnaca	3										3	16
38	Livadhia	2										2	25
39	Milia	1										1	10
40	Nicosia	5	1								1	7	5
41	Palaeal.					1						1	11
42	Pol. 4	7				1		1				9	24
43	Politico	5							2			7	14
45	Vounous	1										1	4
46	Yeri	3										3	11
47	?Alambra	5				1				2		8	15
TOTAL		219	2	2	6	10		3	6	13	1	262	18
Percentage of shape		42	3	2	1	10		6	13	12	3		

MOTIF 2

	Group	jug	jlt	cup	bwl	amp	jar	tnk	flk	btl	oth	total	% of group
22	Alambra					1						1	14
29	Enkomi						1					1	6
31	Kalops.	3										3	8
38	Livadhia				1							1	25
39	Milia	1			1							2	20
43	Politico					1	1					2	3
46	Yeri					1						1	4
47	?Alambra					1						1	2
TOTAL		4			2	4	2					12	1
Percentage of shape		1			1	1	5						

A White Painted V type V B 1 b α Jug from near Trikomo also has this design (MCBA fig.XIV.15).

MOTIF 3

	Group	jug	jlt	cup	bwl	amp	jar	tnk	flk	btl	oth	total	% of group
1	L2	4			5		1					10	38
2	L18		1		14	2	2		1	1		21	38
3	L21	3		6	8		1	1	1		2	21	33
4	L29	3			9		1			2		15	52
5	L47			2								2	11
6	L49	1			5			1		2		9	27
7	L50	4		2	9	1		1				17	27
8	L315A	1			2							3	12
9	L315 B-C					1						1	8
10	L316[1]				5	1		1	1			8	17
11	L316[2]				2	1				1		4	20
12	L320			1	1	1						3	10
13	L4				1			1				2	20
14	L8	2			2					1		5	56
15	L14	2		1	1	1						5	31
16	L51				4							4	36
17	L203	2		1								3	12
18	L311				1							1	9
20	L702	1			4		1	1				7	62
21	Lapithos				19	1				1		21	26
22	Alambra	2				1						3	43
23	Ay. Iak.				7					1		8	24
24	Ay. P.	7	1	2	6					3		19	42
25	Dhali			1				1		2	1	5	31
26	Dhenia 6	2		1	2	1						6	18
27	Dhenia	1		1	15	2	1		1	1		21	43
28	Dhikomo			1	1					1		3	30
29	Enkomi	1			2		1					4	33
30	Gal.	9			2		1					12	41
31	Kalops.	4			9	1				1		15	41
32	Katyd.				2							2	25
33	Klavdhia	3	2							2		7	57
34	Kotchati	3	1	4		1						9	47
35	Kythrea	7										7	47
36	Larnaca	4			1		1	1		2		9	47
37	Leondari	3	1		2					1		7	58
38	Livadhia		1		1					1		3	30
39	Milia	1			1					1		3	38
40	Nicosia	7	6	2	4					5	1	25	21
42	Pol. 4	8			2			1				11	27
43	Politico	10			6			2		1		19	34
44	Myrtou	1			1	1		2				5	75
45	Vounous				1	1						2	9
46	Yeri	4			6					1		11	44
47	?Alambra	14		1	1		1		3	3	1	24	45
TOTAL		114	12	23	168	17	11	13	6	36	3	403	29
Percentage of shape		22	19	30	51	17	55	24	7	32	8		

MOTIF 4

	Group	jug	jlt	cup	bwl	amp	jar	tnk	flk	btl	oth	total	% of group
22	Alambra					1						1	14
29	Enkomi	1										1	7
30	Gal.	1										1	3
31	Kalops.	1										1	3
36	Larnaca	1										1	5
42	Pol. 4	1										1	2
43	Politico							1				1	2
46	Yeri					1						1	4
TOTAL		5				2		1				8	1
Percentage of shape		1				2		2					

MOTIF 5

	Group	jug	jlt	cup	bwl	amp	jar	tnk	flk	btl	oth	total	% of group
1	L2				4							4	12
2	L18				3							3	5
4	L29				2							2	7
6	L49				3							3	8
7	L50	1			2							3	4
11	L316[2]				1							1	5
12	L320				1							1	3
15	L14	1			1							2	13
18	L311				1							1	9
20	L702	1										1	8
21	Lapithos				3							3	4
23	Ay. Iak.				3							3	9
24	Ay. P.	3			1							4	8
26	Dhenia 6	1										1	3
27	Dhenia				1							1	4
30	Gal.				1	1						2	5
33	Klavdhia	1										1	7
36	Larnaca	1					1			2	1	5	26
37	Leondari		1									1	8
39	Milia				1							1	10
42	Pol. 4				1							1	2
43	Politico	1										1	2
47	?Alambra						1				1	2	4
TOTAL		10	1		29	1	2			2	2	47	3
Percentage of shape		2	2		8	1	10			2	6		

This design is also found on a small jug from Syriankhori T1.2 (C.M. 1963/VI-3/1) (Karageorghis, 1963, p.313)

See also Enkomi T.5. 16 (Dikaios 1969-71, pl.198.7)

MOTIF 6

	Group	jug	jlt	cup	bwl	amp	jar	tnk	flk	btl	oth	total	% of group
1	L2	3		1	5				1		1	11	42
2	L18	4			10	4	2					20	32
3	L21	5	2	2	7	1	1		2			20	27
4	L29	2			7		1			1		11	38
5	L47	1		1	1	2			1			6	32
6	L49	3			7	2	1		1			14	41
7	L50	7		2	6	4	2	3	1	1	1	27	37
8	L315 A	4			3	1		1	2			11	44
9	L315 B-C	3			1							4	31
10	L316¹	3	1		14	2		3	1			24	52
11	L316²				8			1	1			10	55
12	L320				7				2			9	30
13	L4	1			1							2	20
14	L8			1		1						2	22
15	L14					1				1		2	13
16	L51				4							4	29
17	L203	1										1	6
18	L311	1			3	1						5	45
19	L313	4			1						1	6	60
20	L702	2			3			1				6	46
21	Lapithos	7		2	3	2			1			15	30
22	Alambra	1				1					1	3	43
24	Ay.P.	2	3	1	4				3			13	33
25	Dhali	4							1		1	6	38
26	Dhenia 6	6	1		4	1		2				14	41
27	Dhenia	8			6	1	1					16	45
28	Dhikomo				1	1						2	30
29	Enkomi	1			1		1					3	20
30	Gal.	3				2						5	13
31	Kalops.	1			10	1						12	32
32	Katyd.		1		1							2	25
33	Klavdhia	4	2							1		7	50
34	Kotchati	2			4							6	32
35	Kythrea	1										1	13
36	Larnaca				1				1			2	11
37	Leondari				2							2	25
38	Livadhia		1		2							3	38
39	Milia				1							1	20
40	Nicosia	13	6		10				2	2	1	34	30
41	Palaeal.	1										1	11
42	Pol. 4	5		1	5	1			1			13	34
43	Politico	3			5	1		2	1			12	31
44	Myrtou	2			2	1		1	.			6	75
45	Vounous	3										3	13
46	Yeri	2	1	1	4				3			11	41
47	?Alambra	4				1	1					6	17
TOTAL		117	18	12	154	32	10	14	25	6	6	394	28
Percentage of shape		22	29	15	46	32	50	31	30	5	17		

MOTIF 8

	Group	jug	jlt	cup	bwl	amp	jar	tnk	flk	btl	oth	total	% of group
1	L2	4										4	15
2	L18	7				2			2			11	17
3	L21	2				1			1	1		5	13
4	L29	4								1		5	21
5	L47	1				2						3	21
6	L49	3						1		2		6	16
7	L50	6							3			9	12
8	L315 A	2							1			3	16
9	L315 B-C	3				1						4	31
10	L316¹	15				2						17	37
11	L316²	3	1							1		5	30
12	L320	2				1			1			4	13
13	L4	2										2	20
14	L8			1					1			2	22
15	L14	4										4	25
16	L51	2								1		3	7
17	L203	1										1	6
20	L702	1										1	8
21	Lapithos	4				1		1				6	13
23	Ay. Iak.	1										1	3
24	Ay. P.	1										1	2
26	Dhenia 6	2				1						3	9
27	Dhenia	5										5	12
33	Klavdhia	1										1	7
34	Kotchati	3										3	16
35	Kythrea	1										1	7
36	Larnaca	1										1	5
37	Leondari	1										1	8
40	Nicosia	6		1								7	7
42	Pol.4	2		1	1							4	10
43	Politico	2										2	3
47	?Alambra	1										1	2
TOTAL		94	1	3	1	11		2	9	6		126	9
Percentage of shape		18	2	3	1	11		4	9	5			

MOTIF 7

	Group	jug	jlt	cup	bwl	amp	jar	tnk	flk	btl	oth	total	% of group
3	L21	1			1	2						4	5
4	L29				1							1	3
8	L315 A	1				1						2	8
10	L316¹	2										2	4
15	L14				1							1	6
21	Lapithos	1				1						2	4
23	Ay. Iak.	1			3	2						6	18
26	Dhenia 6	1						1				2	3
27	Dhenia	1				1						2	4
29	Enkomi	1										1	13
30	Gal.	5			5	2						12	33
31.	Kalops	1										1	5
37	Leondari		1									1	8
39	Milia	1										1	10
40	Nicosia	2										2	2
42	Pol. 4	3			1			2				6	12
43	Politico	1										1	3
44	Myrtou							1				1	13
47	?Alambra					1			1			2	4
TOTAL		21	1		12	10		4	1			48	4
Percentage of shape		4	2		3	10		9	1				

A sherd in the Cyprus Survey collection from Dhikomo <u>Onishia</u> (MC 44) has this design

MOTIF 9

	Group	jug	jlt	cup	bwl	amp	jar	tnk	flk	btl	oth	total	% of group
1	L2	4							1			5	23
2	L18	8			6				2	1		17	26
3	L21	17			7				1	1		26	40
4	6		1	4						1		12	45
5	L47	1		1		1			1	2		6	32
6	L49	7			3					6		16	43
7	L50	17			1	1		2	2	5	1	29	34
8	L315 A	5			2							7	28
9	L315 B-C	5			2	2						9	69
10	L316¹	10		1	6					2		19	50
11	L316²	1			2					4		7	35
12	L320	1			3							4	13
14	L8	1			1					1		3	33
15	L14	4				1				1		6	[illegible]
16	L51	1			6					1		8	57
17	L203	9			1	1						11	65
18	L311	6			1							7	64
19	L313	1				1						2	20
20	L702	2						1				3	23
21	Lapithos	13		1	9	2		1	1	1		28	37
22	Alambra	1										1	29
23	Ay. Iak.				5							5	15
24	Ay. P.	8	3		3				1	2		17	33
25	Dhali	2							1	2		5	31
26	Dhenia 6	4		2	1	1		1				9	26
27	Dhenia	9		1	5	1				1		17	33
28	Dhikomo				1							1	10
29	Enkomi						1					1	6
30	Gal.	6			1	1						8	21
31.	Kalops.	1			2	1						4	16
32	Katyd.				1							1	13
33	Klavdhia									2		2	14
34	Kotchati	3										3	16
35	Kythrea	5										5	27
36	Larnaca	2			1							3	16
37	Leondari	2										2	17
38	Livadhia									1		1	13
39	Milia	1										1	10
40	Nicosia	7	4	2	6				2	1		22	20
41	Palaeal.	2										2	22
42	Pol. 4	7			2			1				10	27
43	Politico	5			1				3			9	16
44	Myrtou	3										3	38
45	Vounous	2				1						3	22
46	Yeri	4	2	1		1			2	1		11	41
47	?Alambra	12	1	2					1	3	1	20	38
TOTAL		205	10	12	81	16	1	6	18	39	2	390	28
Percentage of shape		39	17	15	24	16	5	13	21	36	6		

MOTIF 10

Group	jug	jlt	cup	bwl	amp	jar	tnk	flk	btl	oth	total	% of group
1 L2			1	2							3	12
2 L18	1										1	2
3 L21		1		1		1					3	4
4 L29				1							1	3
5 L47	1										1	11
6 L49				1							1	3
7 L50	3				1			1			5	7
11 L316[2]	1				2						3	15
13 L4	1										1	10
16 L51				2							2	14
18 L311				1							1	9
21 Lapithos	2			4	1						7	9
23 Ay. Iak				17	2						19	58
24 Ay. P.	1			2							3	6
26 Dhenia 6				1							1	3
28 Dhikomo					1						1	10
30 Gal.	9			5	3						17	46
32 Katyd.				1							1	13
33 Klavdhia		1									1	7
35 Kythrea	1										1	7
37 Leondari	1										1	8
38 Livadhia				1							1	13
40 Nicosia	4	1		6				1			12	9
42 Pol. 4	1			3			1				5	22
43 Politico								1			1	3
45 Vounous				1							1	4
46 Yeri					1						1	4
TOTAL	26	3	1	49	11	1	1	3			95	7
Percentage of shape	4	5	1	14	11	5	2	3				

MOTIF 11

Group	jug	jlt	cup	bwl	amp	jar	tnk	flk	btl	oth	total	% of group
2 L18		1									1	2
20 L702	1										1	8
31 Kalops.				1							1	3
35 Kythrea	2										2	13
42 Pol. 4	2										2	5
43 Politico				1			1				2	3
47 ?Alambra								1			1	2
TOTAL	5	1		2			1	1			10	1
Percentage of shape	1	2		1			2	1				

MOTIF 12

Group	jug	jlt	cup	bwl	amp	jar	tnk	flk	btl	oth	total	% of group
30 Gal	1										1	3
42 Pol. 4	2										2	2
44 Myrtou							1				1	13
TOTAL	3						1				4	1
Percentage of shape	1						2					

MOTIF 13

Group	jug	jlt	cup	bwl	amp	jar	tnk	flk	btl	oth	total	% of group
3 L21	1		2								3	4
5 L47			1		1						2	5
7 L50	1			2	1						4	5
8 L315 A					1						1	4
10 L316[1]	1				1						2	4
11 L316[2]					1						1	5
15 L14			1								1	6
17 L203	2		1								3	18
21 Lapithos					3						3	4
24 Ay. P.	1										1	2
26 Dhenia 6	2		1		1		1				5	18
27 Dhenia	1		1								2	6
28 Dhikomo			2								2	20
30 Gal.			1		1						2	8
31 Kalops.			1								1	3
34 Kotchati	1										1	5
35 Kythrea	1										1	7
39 Milia				1							1	10
40 Nicosia	2	2									4	4
41 Palaeal.					1						1	11
42 Pol. 4	2										2	5
43 Politico	1								1		2	3
45 Vounous					3						3	13
46 Yeri	2										2	7
47 ?Alambra					1						1	2
TOTAL	18	2	11	3	15		1		1		51	3
Percentage of shape	3	3	12	1	15		2		1			

This motif is also found on a jug from the Larnaca District (C.M. 1940/VIII-26/1)

MOTIF 14

Group	jug	jlt	cup	bwl	amp	jar	tnk	flk	btl	oth	total	% of group
1 L2	1					1					2	12
2 L18	1	3					2	1			7	14
3 L21	1				2			2			5	5
5 L47	2			1							3	5
6 L49	2										2	8
7 L50	1	1	1		3						6	9
9 L315 B-C			1		1						2	15
10 L316[1]	2	1		1	2		1				7	15
11 L316[2]				1			1	1			3	15
12 L320	1		1		1						3	10
15 L14		1									1	6
17 L203					1						1	6
18 L311	1										1	9
21 Lapithos	1			2	1						4	5
22 Alambra					1						1	14
24 Ay. P.	2										2	4
25 Dhali	1								1	1	3	19
26 Dhenia 6	1										1	3
27 Dhenia		1		2							3	4
28Dhikomo	3										3	30
29 Enkomi							1	1			2	13
30 Gal.								1			1	3
31 Kalops		1									1	3
32 Katyd.		1									1	13
34 Kotchati		1				1					2	11
36 Larnaca						1					1	5
40 Nicosia	12	12	1					1			26	23
42 Pol. 4	3							1			4	10
43 Politico	6	1						1	2		10	17
45 Vounous	1										1	13
46 Yeri		2		1							3	11
47 ?Alambra								2	1		3	6
TOTAL	42	25	4	8	12	3	5	11	4	1	115	8
Percentage of shape	7	40	5	2	12	15	11	13	4	3		

MOTIF 15

Group	jug	jlt	cup	bwl	amp	jar	tnk	flk	btl	oth	total	% of group
3 L21					1						1	1
13 L4	1										1	10
20 L702						1					1	8
21 Lapithos	1				1						2	2
24 Ay. P.	1										1	2
30 Gal.	1										1	3
35 Kythrea	1										1	7
37 Leondari				1							1	8
40 Nicosia	1										1	1
41 Palaeal.					1						1	11
TOTAL	6			1	3	1					11	1
Percentage of shape	1			1	2	5						

Also on an amphora from Marki Vounaros (Karageorghis, 1958, pl.XI.b)

MOTIF 16

Group	jug	jlt	cup	bwl	amp	jar	tnk	flk	btl	oth	total	% of group
19 L313					1						1	10
41 Palaeal.					2						2	22
TOTAL					3						3	1
Percentage of shape					3							

MOTIF 17

Group	jug	jlt	cup	bwl	amp	jar	tnk	flk	btl	oth	total	% of group
1 L2			1	4							5	23
2 L18				13	1						14	21
3 L21	1		2	9	1	1					14	18
4 L29				6							6	24
5 L47			1								1	5
6 L49			1	3							4	14
7 L50	3			8				1			12	15
8 L315 A				3							3	16
9 L315 B-C				2							2	15
10 L316[1]				6							6	15
11 L316[2]				6							6	30
12 L320			1	6							7	23
14 L8			1	2							3	33
15 L14					1						1	8
16 L51				1							1	7
17 L203	1										1	6
18 L311					1						1	9
19 L313				1							1	10
20 L702	2			4							6	46
21 Lapithos	1			7	2						10	12
22 Alambra					1						1	14
24 Ay. P.	2			5							7	15
26 Dhenia 6			1								1	3
27 Dhenia			1	8							9	18
29 Enkomi	1			1							2	13
30 Gal.					1						1	3
32 Katyd.				2							2	25
33 Klavdhia	1	1									2	14
34 Kotchati			1	3							4	21
35 Kythrea			1								1	7
36 Larnaca						1				1	2	11
37 Leondari	1			1							2	17
39 Milia				1							1	10
40 Nicosia	1	1		2						1	5	4
42 Pol. 4	1			3							4	7
43 Politico				3							3	5
44 Myrtou				2			1				3	25
45 Vounous	1										1	4
46 Yeri				2							2	7
47 ?Alambra	3	1				1					5	11
TOTAL	19	3	10	113	8	3	1	1		2	160	12
Percentage of shape	3	5	13	34	8	15	2	1		6	12	

MOTIF 18

Group	jug	jlt	cup	bwl	amp	jar	tnk	flk	btl	oth	total	% of group
1 L2								1			1	4
11 L316[2]									1		1	10
23 Ay. Iak.	1										1	3
42 Pol. 4	1			1							2	5
46 Yeri		1									1	4
TOTAL	2	1		1				1	1		6	1
Percentage of shape	1	1		1				1	1		1	

MOTIF 19

Group	jug	jlt	cup	bwl	amp	jar	tnk	flk	btl	oth	total	% of group
24 Ay. P	1										1	2
TOTAL	1										1	1
Percentage of shape	1										1	

MOTIF 20

Group	jug	jlt	cup	bwl	amp	jar	tnk	flk	btl	oth	total	% of group
1 L2	1										1	4
3 L21				1				2			3	4
7 L50					1			1			2	2
17 L203	1										1	6
20 L702							1				1	8
21 Lapithos					1						1	1
23 Ay. Iak.							1				1	3
25 Dhali								1			1	6
26 Dhenia 6					1						1	3
28 Dhikomo	1										1	10
29 Enkomi							1	1			2	13
34 Kotchati	1										1	5
40 Nicosia	5	6			1			2			14	12
42 Pol. 4	1				1						2	5
43 Politico	1										1	2
44 Myrtou							1				1	13
45 Vounous	2										2	9
47 ?Alambra								1			1	2
TOTAL	13	6		1	5		4	8			37	3
Percentage of shape	2	9		1	5		9	9			3	

MOTIF 21

Group	jug	jlt	cup	bwl	amp	jar	tnk	flk	btl	oth	total	% of group
1 L21									2		2	3
12 L320				1							1	3
18 L311	1										1	9
21 Lapithos	2										2	2
27 Dhenia								1			1	2
28 Dhikomo			1								1	10
37 Leondari								1			1	8
39 Milia				1							1	10
40 Nicosia	1										1	1
41 Palaeal.	1										1	11
43 Politico									1		1	2
46 Yeri									1		1	4
TOTAL	5		1	2				2	4		14	1
Percentage of shape	1		1	1				2	4		1	

MOTIF 22

	Group	jug	jlt	cup	bwl	amp	jar	tnk	flk	btl	oth	total	% of group
1	L3					1						1	4
3	L21			1	1	1				2		5	8
4	L29	2										2	7
5	L47					1				1		2	11
6	L49							1				1	3
7	L50	2		1	1	1				2		7	9
8	L315 A				1					1		2	4
9	L315 B-C				1							1	8
10	L316[1]							1				1	2
11	L316[2]					1						1	5
12	L320		1			1			1			3	10
13	L4								1			1	10
15	L14					1						1	6
16	L51									1		1	7
18	L311	1										1	9
21	Lapithos				1	2				1		4	5
22	Alambra										1	1	14
24	Ay. P.									1		1	2
25	Dhali	2										2	19
26	Dhenia 6	3	1						1			5	18
27	Dhenia	2		1					1			4	8
28	Dhikomo	2										2	20
32	Katydhata		1									1	13
33	Klavdhia	1								1		2	7
34	Kotchati		1									1	5
35	Kythrea										1	1	7
36	Larnaca	1	1									2	11
40	Nicosia	11	6	1	1	1			2	7		29	24
42	Pol. 4	3							1	1		5	12
43	Politico	2			1					1	1	6	9
45	Vounous	1										1	4
46	Yeri	1			1							2	7
47	?Alambra	5				1				2		8	17
TOTAL		39	11	4	8	11		2	7	21	3	107	8
Percentage of shape		8	17	5	2	11		4	8	19	9	8	

MOTIF 23

	Group	jug	jlt	cup	bwl	amp	jar	tnk	flk	btl	oth	total	% of group
1	L2			1	1							2	8
3	L21	1										1	1
12	L320	1										1	3
21	Lapithos	2		1					1			4	4
24	Ay. P.	1										1	2
27	Dhenia	1										1	2
33	Klavdhia		1									1	14
35	Kythrea	1										1	7
41	Palaeal.					1						1	11
45	Vounous	1										1	4
TOTAL		8	1	2	1	1			1			14	1
Percentage of shape		1	1	2	1	1			1			1	

MOTIF 24

	Group	jug	jlt	cup	bwl	amp	jar	tnk	flk	btl	oth	total	% of group
2	L18				2	1						3	5
3	L21	1								1		2	3
4	L29				2							2	7
5	L47									1		1	5
6	L49				5				1	1		7	19
7	L50				2				1			3	4
8	L315 A				2							2	8
9	L315 B-C				1							1	8
16	L51									1		1	7
18	L311				1							1	9
20	L702	1										1	8
21	Lapithos					1		1				2	2
24	Ay. P		1							1		2	4
25	Dhali									1		1	6
27	Dhenia	1										1	2
30	Gal.	1										1	3
32	Katyd.				1							1	13
34	Kotchati				1							1	5
35	Kythrea				1							1	7
36	Larnaca	1										1	5
40	Nicosia				5							5	4
46	Yeri	1										1	4
47	?Alambra	2								1		3	6
TOTAL		8	1		23	2		1	2	7		44	2
Percentage of shape		1	1		6	2		2	2	6		2	

MOTIF 25

	Group	jug	jlt	cup	bwl	amp	jar	tnk	flk	btl	oth	total	% of group
21	Lapithos	1										1	1
42	Pol. 4	2										2	5
43	Politico	1										1	2
46	Yeri								1			1	4
47	?Alambra								2			2	4
TOTAL		4							3			7	1
Percentage of shape		1							3			1	

The design is also known on bottles: e.g., a bottle without known provenance in the Ashmolean Museum (inv 1885-1954).

MOTIF 26

	Group	jug	jlt	cup	bwl	amp	jar	tnk	flk	btl	oth	total	% of group
12	L320								1			1	3
24	Ay. P.										1	1	2
TOTAL									1		1	2	1
Percentage of shape									1		3	1	

Also on a zoomorphic vessel. (A.M. inv 1933.1686), and a bowl from Lapithos T.50 (CMN G593 row 5-6).

MOTIF 27

	Group	jug	jlt	cup	bwl	amp	jar	tnk	flk	btl	oth	total	% of group
4	L29	1										1	3
5	L47	1										1	5
7	L50					1						1	1
12	L320								1			1	3
13	L4	1										1	10
19	L313	3				1					1	5	50
21	Lapithos	1		2	1	4		1	1			10	12
22	Alambra										1	1	14
24	Ay. P.	2					1				1	4	10
25	Dhali								1			1	6
33	Klavdhia	1										1	7
34	Kotchati	1										1	5
40	Nicosia	2							1			3	3
41	Palaeal.	1				2						3	33
45	Vounous	2				7				2		11	48
46	Yeri		1									1	4
TOTAL		17	1	2	1	15	1	1	4	2	3	47	4
Percentage of shape		3	1	2	1	15	1	2	5	2	9	4	

MOTIF 28

	Group	jug	jlt	cup	bwl	amp	jar	tnk	flk	btl	oth	total	% of group
1	L2	5			1							6	23
2	L18	8				1						9	20
3	L21	16							2	4		22	28
4	L29	6										6	21
5	L47	5			1					1		7	37
6	L49	7							1	2		10	27
7	L50	21										21	26
8	L315 A	5										5	20
9	L315 B-C	5										5	38
10	L316[1]	14										14	33
11	L316[2]	3	1									4	20
12	L320	4			1				1			6	20
13	L4	2							1			3	20
14	L8	1							1			2	22
15	L14	5								1		6	44
16	L51	2							1			3	21
17	L203	9										9	59
18	L311	6										6	55
19	L313	5				1						6	60
20	L702	2										2	15
21	Lapithos	22			2	3			1	1		29	35
22	Alambra					1					1	2	29
23	Ay. Iak.	1										1	3
24	Ay. P.	6							1			7	15
25	Dhali	2							2			4	25
26	Dhenia 6	5										5	18
27	Dhenia	11	1	1		1			1			15	31
28	Dhikomo	1										1	10
29	Enkomi	2					1					3	20
30	Gal.	1										1	3
31	Kalops.	1				1						2	5
32	Katyd.		1									1	13
33	Klavdhia	2										2	14
34	Kotchati	3				1						4	26
35	Kythrea	3									1	4	27
36	Larnaca	1			1							2	11
38	Livadhia	1										1	13
40	Nicosia	3	2	1						2	1	9	8
41	Palaeal.	3				1						4	44
42	Pol. 4	5										5	15
43	Politico	4										4	7
44	Myrtou	2										2	25
45	Vounous	4				2					2	8	35
46	Yeri	1							1			2	7
47	?Alambra	7							2	1	1	11	21
TOTAL		222	5	2	6	12	1		15	12	5	280	20
Percentage of shape		42	8	2	2	12	5		17	11	15	20	

MOTIF 29

	Group	jug	jlt	cup	bwl	amp	jar	tnk	flk	btl	oth	total	% of group
2	L18									1		1	2
3	L21									1		1	1
4	L29									1		1	3
5	L49									1		1	3
12	L320		1									1	3
21	Lapithos					1						1	1
23	Ay. Iak.				1							1	3
24	Ay. P.										1	1	2
25	Dhali										1	1	6
36	Larnaca										1	1	5
37	Leondari		1									1	8
40	Nicosia										1	1	1
43	Politico	2							1		1	4	7
47	?Alambra	1										1	2
TOTAL		3	2		1	1			1	4	5	17	1
Percentage of shape		1	2		1	1			1	4	15	1	

MOTIF 30

	Group	jug	jlt	cup	bwl	amp	jar	tnk	flk	btl	oth	total	% of group
21	Lapithos	1										1	1
42	Pol. 4	1				1						2	5
43	Politico	1										1	2
46	Yeri			1					1			2	7
TOTAL		3		1		1			1			6	1
Percentage of shape		1		1		1			1			1	

MOTIF 31

	Group	jug	jlt	cup	bwl	amp	jar	tnk	flk	btl	oth	total	% of group
7	L50								1			1	1
10	L316[1]	1										1	2
21	Lapithos	1										1	1
22	Alambra					1					1	2	29
23	Ay. Iak.				1							1	3
27	Dhenia									1		1	2
30	Gal.	2				1						3	8
40	Nicosia								1		1	2	2
46	Yeri					1						1	4
47	?Alambra	1										1	2
TOTAL		5			1	3			2	1	2	14	1
Percentage of shape		1			1	3			2	1	6	1	

MOTIF 32

	Group	jug	jlt	cup	bwl	amp	jar	tnk	flk	btl	oth	total	% of group
1	L2									1		1	4
2	L18								1			1	2
7	L50					3					1	4	5
10	L316[1]	1							1			2	4
11	L316[2]								1			1	5
22	Alambra					1						1	14
23	Ay. Iak.	2										2	6
24	Ay. P.								1			1	2
25	Dhali	1										1	6
27	Dhenia	1										1	2
28	Dhikomo					1						1	10
29	Enkomi								1			1	7
30	Gal.	1										1	5
32	Katyd.				1							1	13
33	Klavdhia								1	1		2	7
38	Livadhia								1			1	13
40	Nicosia	1									1	2	2
42	Pol. 4					1						1	2
43	Politico	1										1	2
45	Vounous	1										1	4
46	Yeri					1			1			2	7
TOTAL		9			1	7			8	2	2	29	2
Percentage of shape		2			1	7			9	2	6	2	

MOTIF 33

	Group	jug	jlt	cup	bwl	amp	jar	tnk	flk	btl	oth	total	% of group
19	L313										1	1	20
21	Lapithos			1								1	1
24	Ay. P.					1						1	2
33	Klavdhia	1										1	1
41	Palaeal.						1					1	11
47	?Alambra								1			1	2
TOTAL		1		1		1	1		1		1	6	1
Percentage of shape		1		1		1	5		1		3	1	

MOTIF 34

	Group	jug	jlt	cup	bwl	amp	jar	tnk	flk	btl	oth	total	% of group
1	L2	1										1	4
2	L18					1						1	2
3	L21				1	1			1			3	4
5	L47	1				1						2	11
6	L49							1				1	3
7	L50					2			1			3	4
8	L315 A								2			2	8
12	L320	1										1	3
13	L4	1										1	10
15	L14					1						1	6
19	L313	2										2	20
21	Lapithos	1				2						3	4
24	Ay. P.	2										2	4
25	Dhali								1	1		2	13
26	Dhenia 6										1	1	3
28	Dhikomo	2										2	20
30	Gal.								1			1	3
32	Katyd.	1										1	13
34	Kotchati				1							1	5
40	Nicosia	2	3			1			2		1	9	8
41	Palaeal.					1						1	11
42	Pol. 4	3										3	7
43	Politico					1			1			2	3
45	Vounous	2										2	9
46	Yeri		1									1	4
47	?Alambra								1			1	2
TOTAL		19	4		1	12		1	10	1	2	50	4
Percentage of shape		4	6		1	12		2	12	1	6	4	

MOTIF 35

Group	jug	jlt	cup	bwl	amp	jar	tnk	flk	btl	oth	total	% of group
3 L21					1						1	1
5 L47	1										1	5
19 L313	3										3	30
21 Lapithos	1			1							2	2
23 Ay. Iak.	1										1	3
24 Ay. P.										1	1	2
34 Kotchati	1										1	5
36 Larnaca				1							1	5
40 Nicosia					1						1	1
41 Palaeal.	1				4						5	56
43 Politico								1			1	2
TOTAL	8			2	6			1		1	18	1
Percentage of shape	1			1	6			1		3	1	

MOTIF 36

Group	jug	jlt	cup	bwl	amp	jar	tnk	flk	btl	oth	total	% of group
19 L313	2										2	20
21 Lapithos					1						1	2
28 Dhikomo	1										1	10
45 Vounous	2				1					1	4	17
TOTAL	5				2					1	8	1
Percentage of shape	1				2					3	1	

MOTIF 37

Group	jug	jlt	cup	bwl	amp	jar	tnk	flk	btl	oth	total	% of group
18 L311					1						1	9
TOTAL					1						1	
Percentage of shape					1							

MOTIF 38

Group	jug	jlt	cup	bwl	amp	jar	tnk	flk	btl	oth	total	% of group
12 L320	1										1	3
40 Nicosia				1							1	1
TOTAL	1			1							2	
Percentage of shape	1			1								

MOTIF 39

Group	jug	jlt	cup	bwl	amp	jar	tnk	flk	btl	oth	total	% of group
3 L21								1			1	1
5 L47	1										1	5
12 L320								1			1	3
17 L203	1										1	6
19 L313	1										1	10
21 Lapithos	1				2						3	4
24 Ay. P.	2			1						1	4	8
25 Dhali									1		1	6
27 Dhenia			1	1							2	4
37 Leondari			1								1	1
40 Nicosia			1								1	1
41 Palaeal.	1										1	11
42 Pol. 4				1							1	2
43 Politico								1			1	1
46 Yeri								1			1	1
Total	8		2	3	2			3	1	2	21	2
Percentage of shape	1		2	1	2			3	1	6	2	

MOTIF 40

Group	jug	jlt	cup	bwl	amp	jar	tnk	flk	btl	oth	total	% of group
3 L21									1		1	1
13 L4	1										1	10
19 L313	1										1	10
TOTAL	2								1		3	1
Percentage of shape	1								1		1	

MOTIF 41

Group	jug	jlt	cup	bwl	amp	jar	tnk	flk	btl	oth	total	% of group
1 L2	1										1	4
2 L18					3	2					5	8
3 L21	1					1				1	3	4
4 L29						1					1	7
5 L47					1						1	5
6 L49						1		1	1		3	8
7 L50	1				2	2					5	6
10 L316^1					1						1	2
12 L320								2			2	7
14 L8					1						1	11
20 L702							2				2	15
21 Lapithos	1							1			2	2
27 Dhenia						1					1	2
31 Kalops						1					1	3
37 Leondari	2										2	17
40 Nicosia	1								2		3	3
42 Pol. 4	2										2	5
43 Politico										1	1	2
TOTAL	9				8	9	2	4	3	2	37	3
Percentage of shape	2				8	45	4	5	3	6	3	

MOTIF 42

Group	jug	jlt	cup	bwl	amp	jar	tnk	flk	btl	oth	total	% of group
1 L2	1				1						2	8
2 L18								1			1	2
3 L21		1									1	1
4 L29	1				1						2	7
5 L47								1	1		2	11
6 L49								1	1		2	5
7 L50			1					1			2	2
8 L315 A								1			1	4
10 L316^1					1		2				3	7
12 L320			1					1	1		3	10
21 Lapithos							2	2			4	5
42 Pol. 4							1				1	2
43 Politico							1				1	2
46 Yeri							1				1	4
47 ?Alambra			1								1	2
TOTAL	2	1	3		3		7	8	3		27	2
Percentage of shape	1	1	4		3		15	9	3		2	

MOTIF 43

Group	jug	jlt	cup	bwl	amp	jar	tnk	flk	btl	oth	total	% in group
6 L49								1			1	3
7 L50								1			1	1
10 L316^1							1				1	2
11 L316^2									1		1	5
16 L51								1			1	7
20 L702									1		1	8
TOTAL							1	3	2		6	1
Percentage of shape							2	4	2		1	

MOTIF 44

Group	jug	jlt	cup	bwl	amp	jar	tnk	flk	btl	oth	total	% in group
2 L18							1				1	2
3 L21		1							1		2	3
6 L49	2										2	5
7 L50							2	1	2		5	6
9 L315 B-C					1						1	8
10 L316^1					1						1	2
11 L316^2	1							1			2	10
12 L320	1							1			2	3
13 L4					1						1	10
14 L8	1										1	11
15 L14				1							1	6
22 Alambra	1										1	14
26 Dhenia 6							1				1	3
27 Dhenia	1			1							2	4
40 Nicosia	2	1						1	1		5	3
42 Pol. 4	1										1	2
43 Politico	2									2	4	5
46 Yeri								3			3	11
47 ?Alambra		2	1								3	6
TOTAL	12	4	1	2	3		4	7	4	2	39	3
Percentage of shape	2	6	1	1	3		9	8	4	6	3	

MOTIF 45

Group	jug	jlt	cup	bwl	amp	jar	tnk	flk	btl	oth	total	% of group
2 L18							1				1	2
3 L21									1		1	1
6 L49									1		1	3
7 L50									1		1	1
21 Lapithos	1										1	1
TOTAL	1						1		3		5	1
Percentage of shape	1						2		3		1	

This design also occurs on a zoomorphic vessel (C.M. A915 - unknown provenance).

MOTIF 46

Group	jug	jlt	cup	bwl	amp	jar	tnk	flk	btl	oth	total	% of group
3 L21	1			1				1			3	4
4 L29	1			1	1						3	10
5 L47					1						1	5
6 L49	1								1		2	5
10 L316[1]					1				1		2	4
12 L320	1										1	3
15 L14	2				1						3	19
16 L51	1										1	7
17 L203	1										1	6
20 L702							1				1	8
21 Lapithos				2	1						3	4
40 Nicosia	3	6			1						10	8
43 Politico	1										1	2
TOTAL	12	6		4	6		1	1	2		32	2
Percentage of shape	3	9		1	6		2	1	2		2	

This design is found on a cup from Aghirda (C.M.1966/X-14/5).

MOTIF 47

Group	jug	jlt	cup	bwl	amp	jar	tnk	flk	btl	oth	total	% of group
3 L21								1			1	1
5 L47					1						1	5
6 L49						1					1	3
8 L315 A	2			1					2		5	20
10 L316[1]	1				1		1				3	7
11 L316[2]				3							3	15
12 L320	1										1	3
18 L311	1			1							2	18
20 L702	1										1	8
21 Lapithos	1			1							2	2
23 Ay. Iak.				5							5	18
25 Dhali	1										1	6
27 Dhenia	1										1	2
28 Dhikomo	2										2	20
29 Enkomi						1					1	7
31 Kalops.		1									1	3
33 Klavdhia	1										1	7
34 Kotchati	1										1	5
37 Leondari									1		1	8
40 Nicosia	1										1	1
42 Pol. 4	1										1	2
43 Politico	1										1	2
46 Yeri			1								1	4
TOTAL	16	1	1	11	2	2	1	1	3		38	3
Percentage of shape	3	2	1	3	2	10	2	1	9		3	

MOTIF 48

Group	jug	jlt	cup	bwl	amp	jar	tnk	flk	btl	oth	total	% of group
2 L18	1										1	2
10 L316[1]	2										2	4
15 L14	1										1	6
25 Dhali									1		1	6
27 Dhenia	1										1	2
29 Enkomi	3								1		4	33
30 Gal.	3										3	8
31 Kalops.	11						1		2		14	41
34 Kotchati	2										2	11
35 Kythrea	4										4	27
26 Larnaca	2										2	11
38 Livadhia	1										1	13
39 Milia	2								1		3	30
42 Pol. 4	1										1	2
43 Politico	1										1	2
47 ?Alambra									2		2	4
TOTAL	35						1		7		43	3
Percentage of shape	6						2		6		3	

There are further occurrences of this design at Enkomi - e.g. Dikaios, 1969-71, Vol.I, p.134, pl.59.3 (Level IIA)

MOTIF 49

Group	jug	jlt	cup	bwl	amp	jar	tnk	flk	btl	oth	total	% of group
1 L2			1								1	4
2 L18	2	4		1	1	1		1			10	15
3 L21			3	1	1						5	8
4 L29	1										1	3
5 L47			1								1	5
7 L50	3		3								6	9
8 L315 A	1		1	2	1						5	20
9 L315 B-C				1	1						2	15
10 L316[1]			1	5							6	13
11 L316[2]				1							1	5
12 L320	1			3				1			5	17
13 L4			1	1							2	20
14 L8					1						1	11
15 L14					2						2	13
16 L51				3				1		1	5	36
17 L203			1								1	6
18 L311	1										1	9
19 L313				1							1	10
21 Lapithos	1			2	4						7	9
24 Ay. P.	2		2								4	8
25 Dhali			1								1	6
26 Dhenia 6	6	1	1	1			3				12	35
27 Dhenia			1	2							3	3
28 Dhikomo	1										1	10
35 Kythrea	1		1								2	13
36 Larnaca		1		1							2	11
40 Nicosia	10	2	2	4							18	16
42 Pol. 4	4		1	1					1		7	17
43 Politico	4										4	7
44 Myrtou	1										1	13
47 ?Alambra	2			1							3	6
TOTAL	41	8	21	31	11	1	3	3	1	1	121	9
Percentage of shape	8	13	27	9	11	5	7	3	1	3	9	

This motif also appears on a cup from near Kyrenia (C.M. 1940/I-11/2 - from a drawing in the C.M. inventory book) and a cup from Kaimakli (C.M. 1963/VII-11/4).

MOTIF 50

Group	jug	jlt	cup	bwl	amp	jar	tnk	flk	btl	oth	total	% of group
1 L2	1			2							3	12
2 L18	1			2							3	5
3 L21			1	2							3	4
4 L29	1		1	2							4	14
5 L47				2	1						3	16
6 L49				7	1						8	22
7 L50	1			2							3	5
12 L320				1							1	3
14 L8	1										1	11
15 L51				4							4	29
18 L311	1										1	9
20 L702	1										1	8
21 Lapithos				9							9	11
24 Ay. P.	2	1	1	3							7	15
26 Dhenia 6				3							3	9
27 Dhenia				4							4	12
28 Dhikomo				1							1	10
31 Kalops.				1							1	3
33 Klavdhia	3	1									4	29
37 Leondari	2										2	17
38 Livadhia		1		1							2	25
40 Nicosia	3			8							11	9
42 Pol. 4	1			2							3	7
43 Politico				4							4	7
46 Yeri		1		2							3	11
47 ?Alambra	7										7	13
TOTAL	25	4	3	62	2						96	7
Percentage of shape	5	6	4	19	2						7	

This design appears on a jar (C.M.A649 - no known provenance).

MOTIF 51

	Group	jug	jlt	cup	bwl	amp	jar	tnk	flk	btl	oth	total	% of group
1	L2										1	1	4
2	L18	1	2			2					1	6	11
3	L21		1	4		1						6	8
4	L29	1										1	3
5	L47			1								1	5
6	L49			1		1			1			3	8
7	L50	2	1	1		2		1				7	11
8	L315 A	1		1		1						3	12
10	L316[1]		1		1	1						3	9
11	L316[2]									1		1	5
12	L320	1		1		1			1			4	13
13	L4	1			1							2	20
15	L14		1	1								2	13
16	L51								1			1	7
17	L203	2		2		1						5	29
18	L311					1						1	9
21	Lapithos	2		2	2	2						8	10
23	Ay. Iak.					1				1		2	6
24	Ay. P.	2									1	3	6
25	Dhali	1							1			2	13
26	Dhenia 6	1		1	1	1						4	12
27	Dhenia	1		2	1							4	8
28	Dhikomo	1		2								3	40
30	Gal.	3			4	1						8	21
31	Kalops.		1									1	3
32	Katyd		1									1	13
33	Klavdhia								1			1	7
34	Kotchati	1	1									2	11
36	Larnaca				1							1	5
38	Livadhia			1								1	13
39	Milia									1		1	10
40	Nicosia	11	12	3		1			1			28	24
41	Palaeal.	1				1						2	22
42	Pol. 4	2				1			1			4	10
43	Politico	5	2	1				2				10	17
46	Yeri	1	1									2	7
47	?Alambra	2	1									3	4
TOTAL		43	25	24	11	19		1	8	4	3	138	10
Percentage of shape		8	40	31	3	19		2	9	4	9	10	

The design has been found at Enkomi(Dikaios 1969-71, pl.54.18; pl.62.1); Aghyrda (a cup, C.M. 1966/X-14/5); near Kyrenia (C.M. 1940/I-11/2); and there are further occurrences at Ayios Iakovos (Åström, 1963, fig.1.1).

MOTIF 52

	Group	jug	jlt	cup	bwl	amp	jar	tnk	flk	btl	oth	total	% of group
1	L2								1			1	4
3	L21							1				1	1
10	L316[1]	1										1	4
11	L316[2]									1		1	5
20	L702							1				1	8
TOTAL		1						2	1	1		5	1
Percentage of shape		1						4	1	1		1	

MOTIF 53

	Group	jug	jlt	cup	bwl	amp	jar	tnk	flk	btl	oth	total	% of group
16	L51								1			1	7
20	L702						1					1	8
30	Gal.	1										1	3
36	Larnaca						1					1	11
44	Myrtou	1										1	13
45	Vounous			1								1	4
TOTAL		2		1			2		1			6	1
Percentage of shape		2		1			10		1			1	

Also note occurrence on two other flasks of unknown provenance, but compare poor quality to the Vounous cup (C.M. A867 and A897).

MOTIF 54

	Group	jug	jlt	cup	bwl	amp	jar	tnk	flk	btl	oth	total	% of group
3	L21		1									1	1
13	L4								1			1	10
24	Ay. P.								1			1	2
34	Kotchati					1						1	5
40	Nicosia	1										1	1
43	Politico								1			1	2
TOTAL		1	1			1			3			6	1
Percentage of shape		1	3			1			3			1	

MOTIF 55

	Group	jug	jlt	cup	bwl	amp	jar	tnk	flk	btl	oth	total	% of group
9	L315 B-C	1										1	8
TOTAL		1										1	1
Percentage of shape		1										1	

This design also occurs on a White Painted III-IV tankard from Dhiorios Aloupotrypes (A.M. 1953.1121) on a bottle and a tankard with no known provenance in the Cyprus Museum (invs A870, A824).

MOTIF 56

	Group	jug	jlt	cup	bwl	amp	jar	tnk	flk	btl	oth	total	% of group
2	L18	1			2							3	5
3	L21	1			2							3	4
4	L29				1							1	3
5	L47				1							1	5
6	L49								1			1	3
7	L50			1								1	1
9	L315 B-C			1							1	2	15
12	L320	1										1	3
16	L51				1							1	7
17	L203				1							1	6
18	L311				1							1	9
19	L313	1										1	10
21	Lapithos	2			5							7	10
23	Ay. Iak.				1							1	3
24	Ay. P.	1										1	2
25	Dhali	1										1	6
26	Dhenia 6	1			1						1	3	9
27	Dhenia				2							2	4
32	Katyd.				2							2	25
34	Kotchati				1							1	5
37	Leondari	1										1	8
38	Livadhia				1							1	13
40	Nicosia	1			4						2	7	6
42	Pol. 4				1							1	2
45	Vounous				1	2						3	13
46	Yeri		1									1	4
TOTAL		11	1	2	28	2			1		4	49	3
Percentage of shape		2	2	3	8	2			1		12	3	

MOTIF 57

	Group	jug	jlt	cup	bwl	amp	jar	tnk	flk	btl	oth	total	% of group
1	L2	1										1	4
2	L18	2										2	2
3	L21								1			1	1
4	L29	1										1	3
5	L47	1										1	5
7	L50	1		1								2	2
10	L316[1]	1										1	4
12	L320			1						1		2	7
19	L313	1										1	10
21	Lapithos	2				1						3	4
23	Ay. Iak.	1										1	3
28	Dhikomo			1								1	10
29	Enkomi								1			1	7
37	Leondari								1			1	8
40	Nicosia	2	2		1				1		1	7	6
42	Pol. 4	2										2	5
43	Politico	2	1					1		1		5	9
TOTAL		17	3	3	1	1		1	4	2	1	33	2
Percentage of shape		3	5	4	1	1		1	5	2	3	2	

MOTIF 58

	Group	jug	jlt	cup	bwl	amp	jar	tnk	flk	btl	oth	total	% of group
1	L2	1										1	4
2	L18	1	1					2				4	9
3	L21	1			1	1		1	1			5	9
6	L49							1	2			3	8
7	L50		1			1	1		2			5	7
8	L315 A					1						1	4
10	L316^{1}					1			2			3	7
11	L316^{2}					1		1	1			3	15
13	L4							1	1			2	20
15	L14					2						2	13
16	L51								1			1	7
19	L313									1		1	10
21	Lapithos					4						4	5
24	Ay. P.	2										2	4
26	Dhenia 6	5			1	1		3				10	29
27	Dhenia				1							1	4
34	Kotchati					1						1	5
35	Kythrea				1							1	7
36	Larnaca							1				1	5
38	Livadhia				1							1	13
39	Milia									1		1	10
40	Nicosia	9	4									13	12
42	Pol. 4	4										4	10
43	Politico	1	1					1				3	5
45	Vounous	1										1	4
46	Yeri		1									1	4
TOTAL		25	8		5	13	1	11	8	2		66	5
Percentage of shape		5	12		2	13	5	24	9	2		5	

MOTIF 59

	Group	jug	jlt	cup	bwl	amp	jar	tnk	flk	btl	oth	total	% of group
1	L2	1										1	4
2	L18					2			1			3	5
3	L21		1		1	1		1	2			6	8
5	L47					2						2	11
6	L49	1						2	1	1		5	14
7	L50					3						3	5
8	L315							1	2			3	12
10	L316^{1}	1	1			1						3	7
12	L320	1				1						2	7
13	L4	1							1			2	20
15	L14					1						1	6
17	L203					1						1	6
18	L311					1						1	9
21	Lapithos				1	4						5	6
24	Ay. P.	2										2	4
25	Dhali							1	1	2		4	25
26	Dhenia 6	3				2						5	15
27	Dhenia	2						1				3	6
28	Dhikomo	2				1						3	30
29	Enkomi							1	1			2	13
30	Gal.	3			3	3			1			10	26
32	Katyd.		1									1	13
33	Klavdhia	1	1									2	14
40	Nicosia	8	8			1			5		2	24	22
42	Pol. 4	3				1		1	1			6	15
43	Politico					1						1	2
44	Myrtou					1		1				2	25
45	Vounous	2		1		1						4	17
46	Yeri		1									1	4
47	?Alambra	1								1		2	4
TOTAL		32	13	1	5	28		9	18	4	2	110	8
Percentage of shape		6	21	1	2	28		19	20	4	6	8	

This motif also appears on a cup from Aghyrda (CM 1966/X-14/5)

MOTIF 60

	Group	jug	jlt	cup	bwl	amp	jar	tnk	flk	btl	oth	total	% of group
42	Pol. 4	1										1	2
43	Politico	1										1	2
TOTAL		2										2	1
Percentage of shape		1										1	

MOTIF 61

	Group	jug	jlt	cup	bwl	amp	jar	tnk	flk	btl	oth	total	% of group
2	L18							1				1	2
3	L21	1										1	1
7	L50									1		1	1
10	L316^{1}					1						1	2
20	L702							1	1			2	15
21	Lapithos				1							1	1
47	?Alambra	1										1	2
TOTAL		2			1	1		2	1	1		8	1
Percentage of shape		1			1	1		5	1	1		1	

MOTIF 62

	Group	jug	jlt	cup	bwl	amp	jar	tnk	flk	btl	oth	total	% of group
2	L18							1	1		1	3	5
3	L21								1			1	1
7	L50	2										2	2
10	L316^{1}								1			1	2
21	Lapithos	1				1						2	2
24	Ay. P.	1										1	2
25	Dhali								1			1	6
27	Dhenia								1			1	2
28	Dhikomo	1										1	10
30	Gal.								1			1	3
37	Leondari	1								1		2	17
39	Milia	1										1	10
40	Nicosia	4			2						1	7	7
42	Pol. 4	1			1							2	5
43	Politico	1	1							1		3	5
TOTAL		13	1		3	1		1	6	2	2	29	2
Percentage of shape		3	2		1	1		2	7	2	6	2	

MOTIF 63

	Group	jug	jlt	cup	bwl	amp	jar	tnk	flk	btl	oth	total	% of group
1	L2	1							2			3	12
3	L21									1		1	1
7	L50									2		2	2
8	L315 A									3		3	12
11	L316^{2}									1		1	5
19	L313	1										1	10
21	Lapithos	1			1	1				1		4	5
26	Dhenia 6								1	1		2	6
27	Dhenia								1	1		2	4
40	Nicosia	1			1					3		5	4
42	Pol. 4				1							1	2
43	Politico	1										1	2
45	Vounous										1	1	4
47	?Alambra	1								1		2	4
TOTAL		6			3	1			4	14	1	29	2
Percentage of shape		1			1	1			5	12	3	2	

The design also appears on a sherd from Dhikomo Onishia (M.C.44) in the Cyprus Survey Collection.

MOTIF 64

	Group	jug	jlt	cup	bwl	amp	jar	tnk	flk	btl	oth	total	% of group
3	L21				1	1			1	1		4	5
4	L29					1						1	3
5	L47									1		1	5
6	L49				1							1	3
8	L315 A					1						1	4
20	L702							1				1	8
21	Lapithos	1				2				1		4	5
24	Ay. P.									1		1	2
25	Dhali	1								1		2	13
26	Dhenia 6	1										1	3
29	Enkomi								1			1	7
30	Gal.				2							2	5
35	Kythrea	1									1	2	13
36	Larnaca	1										1	5
40	Nicosia			1						7	1	9	8
41	Palaeal.	1				2						3	33
42	Pol. 4								2	1		3	7
43	Politico									1		1	2
46	Yeri								1	1		2	7
47	?Alambra								3	2		5	9
TOTAL		6		1	4	7		1	8	17	2	46	3
Percentage of shape		1		1	1	7		2	9	15	6	3	

MOTIF 65

Group	jug	jlt	cup	bwl	amp	jar	tnk	flk	btl	oth	total	% of group
1 L2			1								1	4
2 L18	2	1									3	5
3 L21	2		3								5	6
5 L47	1										1	5
6 L49			1								1	3
7 L50	2		1		1			1			5	6
8 L315 A			1								1	4
9 L315 B-C	1										1	8
13 L4	1										1	10
15 L14	1										1	6
17 L203	2										2	12
18 L311	2										2	18
19 L313	5				1					1	7	70
21 Lapithos	9		1		4						14	17
24 Ay. P.	2										2	6
25 Dhali								1			1	6
27 Dhenia				1							1	2
33 Klavdhia	1								1		2	14
34 Kotchati	1										1	5
35 Kythrea			1								1	7
40 Nicosia	3										3	3
41 Palaeal.	1										1	22
42 Pol. 4	1		1						1		3	7
45 Vounous	2				2					2	6	22
TOTAL	38	2	10	1	8			2	2	3	66	5
Percentage of shape	7	3	12	1	8			2	2	9	5	

MOTIF 67

Group	jug	jlt	cup	bwl	amp	jar	tnk	flk	btl	oth	total	% in group
1 L2	1			2							3	12
2 L18		1		4		1					6	8
3 L21	2			6		1					9	13
4 L29				4							4	17
5 L47			1		1						2	21
6 L49				6							6	16
7 L50	1		1	3	3						8	10
8 L315 A			1	4							5	20
9 L315 B-C	1			1							2	31
10 L316[1]				1	1						2	4
11 L316[2]					2						2	10
12 L320				2							2	7
15 L14	1		1	1	2						5	31
16 L51	1			4				1			6	36
17 L203	1			1							2	6
18 L311				2							2	18
21 Lapithos	1			11	2						14	18
24 Ay. P.	2	1	1	3							7	15
25 Dhali			1	1							2	13
26 Dhenia 6	5			1	2		1				9	26
27 Dhenia	1			4							5	12
29 Enkomi	1										1	7
30 Gal.	3			1	2						6	18
31 Kalops.	2										2	5
33 Klavdhia	3	1									4	29
35 Kythrea				1							1	7
36 Larnaca				1							1	5
37 Leondari	1			1							2	17
38 Livadhia	1										1	13
39 Milia	1										1	10
40 Nicosia	7	6	3	6				1	1	1	25	21
42 Pol. 4	6			4							10	24
43 Politico	2	1		2							5	9
44 Myrtou	1										1	13
45 Vounous	1										1	4
46 Yeri		1		1					1		3	15
47 ?Alambra	3		2								5	9
TOTAL	49	11	11	78	15	2	1	2	2	1	173	13
Percentage of shape	10	18	14	23	15	10	2	2	2	3	13	

This design also occurs on a small jug from Trikomo (MCBA, fig. XIV.15).

MOTIF 66

Group	jug	jlt	cup	bwl	amp	jar	tnk	flk	btl	oth	total	% of group
2 L18		1		2							3	5
3 L21				2							2	3
4 L29	1			1							2	7
6 L49				2							2	8
7 L50	1										1	1
15 L14	1										1	6
17 L203			3								3	18
19 L313	1			1							2	20
20 L702						1					1	8
21 Lapithos				1							1	1
24 Ay. P.		1		2							3	6
27 Dhenia	1										1	2
29 Enkomi						1					1	7
31 Kalops.	1										1	3
32 Katyd.		2									2	25
33 Klavdhia									1		1	7
34 Kotchati	1										1	5
35 Kythrea	2										2	13
38 Livdhia		1									1	13
39 Milia	1										1	10
40 Nicosia		1									1	1
42 Pol. 4	1										1	2
43 Politico	1										1	2
47 ?Alambra	1										1	2
TOTAL	13	6	3	11		2			1		36	3
Percentage of shape	2	10	4	3		10			1		3	

A small jug from Trikomo (MCBA, fig. XVI.15) also has this design.

MOTIF 68

Group	jug	jlt	cup	bwl	amp	jar	tnk	flk	btl	oth	total	% of group
11 L316[2]	1										1	5
19 L313										1	1	10
26 Dhenia 6				1							1	3
29 Enkomi	1										1	7
39 Milia	1										1	10
40 Nicosia	2			1							3	3
42 Pol. 4	1										1	2
TOTAL	6			2						1	9	1
Percentage of shape	1			1						3	1	

MOTIF 69

Group	jug	jlt	cup	bwl	amp	jar	tnk	flk	btl	oth	total	% of group
4 L29	1										1	3
5 L47	1										1	5
7 L50	1										1	1
14 L8			1								1	11
15 L14	1										1	6
19 L313	1										1	10
21 Lapithos	2		1	2							5	6
26 Dhenia 6	1										1	3
27 Dhenia	1										1	2
44 Myrtou	1										1	13
TOTAL	10		2	2							14	1
Percentage of shape	2		3	1							1	

A form of this design is used on a zoomorphic vessel from Livadhia (CM inv 1942/IV-17/2 = MLA 164), and on the handle of a jug from Lapithos (T702.150)

MOTIF 70

Group	jug	jlt	cup	bwl	amp	jar	tnk	flk	btl	oth	total	% of group
7 L50					1						1	1
24 Ay. P.									1		1	2
36 Larnaca								1			1	5
43 Politico									1		1	2
TOTAL					1			1	2		4	1
Percentage of shape					1			1	2		1	

MOTIF 71

Group	jug	jlt	cup	bwl	amp	jar	tnk	flk	btl	oth	total	% of group
13 L4								1			1	10
30 Gal.	1										1	3
TOTAL	1							1			2	1
Percentage of shape	1							1			1	

MOTIF 72

Group	jug	jlt	cup	bwl	amp	jar	tnk	flk	btl	oth	total	% of group
46 Yeri			1								1	3

MOTIF 73

Group	jug	jlt	cup	bwl	amp	jar	tnk	flk	btl	oth	total	% of group
23 Ay. Iak.	1										1	3

MOTIF 74

Group	jug	jlt	cup	bwl	amp	jar	tnk	flk	btl	oth	total	% of group
11							1				1	5
2		1									1	2
TOTAL		1					1				2	

This design also appears on a jug in the Ashmolean Museum (1911.325) of unknown provenance.

MOTIF 75

Group	jug	jlt	cup	bwl	amp	jar	tnk	flk	btl	oth-	total	% of group
4 L29			1								1	3
7 L50								1			1	1
21 Lapithos	1										1	1
24 Ay. P.	2	1									3	6
36 Larnaca							1				1	5
37 Leondari	1							1			2	18
42 Pol. 4		1					1				2	4
45 Vounous				1	2						3	12
47 ?Alambra	1								1		2	4
TOTAL	5	3	1	1	2		2	2	1		16	1
Percentage of shape	1	5	1	1	2		5	2	1		1	

MOTIF 76

Group	jug	jlt	cup	bwl	amp	jar	tnk	flk	btl	oth	total	% of group
26 Dhenia 6					1						1	3

MOTIF 77

Group	jug	jlt	cup	bwl	amp	jar	tnk	flk	btl	oth	total	% of group
2 L18							1				1	2

MOTIF 78

Group	jug	jlt	cup	bwl	amp	jar	tnk	flk	btl	oth	total	% of group
12 L320								1			1	3

MOTIF 79

Group	jug	jlt	cup	bwl	amp	jar	tnk	flk	btl	oth	total	% of group
29 Enkomi						1					1	6
33 Klavdhia	1										1	6
TOTAL	1					1					2	

MOTIF 80

Group	jug	jlt	cup	bwl	amp	jar	tnk	flk	btl	oth	total	% of group
6 L49				1							1	3
24 Ay. P.	1										1	2
27 Dhenia			1								1	2
33 Klavdhia	1										1	6
46 Yeri	1										1	4
TOTAL	3		1	1							5	1
Percentage of shape	1		1	1							1	

This design appears on a zoomorphic vessel from Livadhia Kokkotes (T1.12) in the Larnaca Museum.

MOTIF 81

Group	jug	jlt	cup	bwl	amp	jar	tnk	flk	btl	oth	total	% of group
35 Kythrea	1										1	6
42 Pol. 4	1										1	2
TOTAL	2										2	

Similar designs appear on the White Painted V-VI jug CM A811, and on CM inv 1938/XII-5/2; neither of these have known provenance.

ADDITIONAL NOTE

Since this volume went to press I have been able to examine the collections from the Swedish Cyprus Expedition excavations housed in the Museum of Mediterranean and Near Eastern Antiquities (Medelhavsmuseet) in Stockholm. The following corrections should be made to the lists of pottery, and appropriate alterations made in the lists of motif distribution.

Lapithos T.303B

4	jug	6	28	56	63	65		

Lapithos T.313A

22	jug	6	28	33	63	65	66	
114	amphora	9	16	27	28	33	38	65

Lapithos T.315A

4	bowl	6	9	24	50
20	bowl	9	50		
67	bowl	3	6	17	
74	bowl	5	6	9	17
95	bowl	6	17	67	

Lapithos T.315 B–C

39	jug	6	22	28	65

Lapithos T.316[1]

41	bowl	6	9	50	67
81	amphora	7	10	42	46
127	amphora	6	41	67	
154	bowl	6	9	17	67

Lapithos T.316[2]

33	bowl	3	6	9	50
53	bowl	6	9		
97	bowl	6	17	50	

Lapithos T.319B

41	bowl	6	50

Lapithos T.320

26	bowl	5	6	9	17
29	bowl	7	10	50	
85	bowl	22	56		
89	bowl	17	26		
cbd 3.1	bowl	9	46	50	

Lapithos T.702

81	bowl	3	17	66			
150	tankard	6	20	41	46	61	69

INDEX 1

SITES AND GROUPS

The names in upper case letters refer to the defined Groups to which most reference is made in the text. The numbers printed in italics refer to the listing of all the material in these Groups in Appendix I.

INDEX 2

CONCORDANCE AND INDEX TO MUSEUM INVENTORY NUMBERS

This index allows a cross-reference to vessels identified by a museum inventory number, either to their listing in Appendix I, or to a mention elsewhere in the book.

ASHMOLEAN MUSEUM

1954.1885		84
1968.1155	Magounda	51
1970.874	Krini *Merra*	69

BRITISH MUSEUM

C259 (84.12.10.100)	Yeri	77
C260	Yeri	77
C262 (84.12.10.94)	Yeri	77
C263 (84.12.10.97)	Yeri	77
C264	Yeri	77
C266	Yeri	77
C267 (84.12.10.53)	Yeri	77
C274	Yeri	77
C275 (99.12.29.115)	Klavdhia T. 15	71
C276	Yeri	77
C280 (68.9.5.28)	Dhali	67
C281 (84.12.10.40)	Yeri	77
C283 (84.12.10.193)	Yeri	77
C284	Yeri	77
C286 (84.12.10.41)	Yeri	77
C287	Yeri	77
C289 (68.9.5.15)	Dhali	67
C290 (99.12.29.114)	Klavdhia T. 15	71
C292 (97.4.1.827)	Enkomi	69
C293	Dhali	67
C294 (84.12.10.50)	Yeri	77
C296 (84.12.10.47)	Yeri	77
C297 (84.12.10.48)	Yeri	77
C298 (99.12.29.112)	Klavdhia	71
C299	Yeri	77
C300 (84.12.10.191)	Yeri	77
C301 (68.9.5.4)	Dhali	67
C303	Dhali	67
C306 (68.9.5.30)	Dhali	67
C310 (88.9.27.2)	Ayia Paraskevi	67
C326	Yeri	77
C328 (84.12.10.189)	Yeri	77
C329 (99.12.29.113)	Klavdhia	71
84.12.10.6	Yeri	77
84.12.10.8	Yeri	77
84.12.10.44	Dhali	67
84.12.10.192	Dhali	67
84.12.10.195	Yeri	77
99.12.29.116	Klaudhia	71

CYPRUS MUSEUM

A625	L. Iba	64
A634	*Lambertis* T. 31	76
A636	L. 50. 59	68
A637	*Lambertis* T. 31	76
A649		87
A654	L. 21.105	57
A654a	L. 21.99	57
A657	Kalopsidha T. 17	71
A659	L. 50.203	58
A660	L. 203 A. 26	63
A665	Kalopsidha T. 11	70
A667	Kalopsidha T. 17	71
A671		32 n. 38
A673	L. 14	62
A675	L. 4	61
A677	L. 47.36	57
A678	L. 9	64
A679	L. 13	64
A680	L. 203.18	62
A685	Ayia Paraskevi	67
A686	L. 15	62
A690	*Lambertis* T. 38	76
702	*Lambertis* T. 31	76
A703	*Lambertis* T. 28	76
A704	*Lambertis* T. 9	75
A710	Kythrea T. 1	72
A711	L. 14.25	62
A712	L. 49.74	58
A713a	L. 203.25	63
A714	*Chomazoudhia* T.3	52 n. 30, 76
A715	*Chomazoudhia*	24, 30, 52 n. 30, 76
A717	L. 49.81	68
A718a	Klavdhia	71
A722	Klavdhia	71
A723	*Lambertis* T. 38	76
A726	Hala Sultan Tekke	77
A728	Ayia Paraskevi	67
A729	Kythrea T. 1	72
A733	Ayia Paraskevi	67
A739	Kythrea T. 1	72
A740	Kythrea T. 1	72
A741	Kythrea T. 1	72
A742	L. 50.212	58
A744	Ayia Paraskevi	67
A751	Klavdhia	71
A754	L. 18.145	55
A755	Klavdhia	71
A757	Laxia tou Riou	72

A758	Klavdhia	71
A762	*Lambertis* T. 38	76
A763	*Lambertis* T. 38	76
A765	*Lambertis* T. 38	76
A766	L. 50.269	59
A770	L. 50.268	59
A772	*Lambertis* T. 43	76
A773	L. 29.101	57
A775	Kythrea T. 1	72
A777	Kythrea T. 1	72
A781	L. 203 B. 10	62
A782	Kythrea T. 1	52 n. 28, 72
A783	Kythrea T. 1	72
A787	Kalopsidha T. 11	70
A788	*Lambertis* T. 9	75
A789	Kalopsidha T. 25	71
A791	Kalopsidha T. 11	70
A795	Hala Sultan Tekke	72
A796	Kythrea T. 1.	72
A798	Kalopsidha T. 25	71
A799	*Lambertis* T. 31	76
A801	Kalopsidha T. 11	70
A805	Salamis T. 52	70
A806	Klavdhia.	71
A811		91
A824		88
A827	Ayia Paraskevi 10a.	67
A829	L. 46A. 11.	65
A835	L. 50. 256.	59
A836	L. 18. 178	55
A837	L. 50.260	65
A838	L. 50. 259	65
A839	L. 43B. 11	64
A840	L. 18. 178	55
A841	L. 50. 262	65
A842	Laxia tou Riou T. 2	72
A844	L. 49. 94	58
A849	*Lambertis* T. 8	76
A852	L. 18. 163	55
A856	L. 49. 85.	58
A857	L. 50. 238.	59
A858	L. 21. 75	56
A859	Hala Sultan Tekke	72
A861	*Lambertis* T. 38.	76
A867		88
A870		88
A872	L. 18A. 165	55
A875	*Lambertis* T. 38	76
A876	Klavdhia	71

A877	Klavdhia	71
A879	L. 49. 87	58
A897		88
A898	Klavdhia	71
A901	Kalopsidha T. 11	70
A903	Ayia Paraskevi 23–4,	67
A904		22
A907	L. 21. 107	57
A911	Kythrea	72
A912	Arpera	72
A915		87
A1920	L. 50. 166	58
A1949	Dhenia	69
A1970	L. 51. 27	62
1933/V–22/1	Dhenia *Kafkalla*	69
1933/V–22/6	Dhenia *Kafkalla*	69
1933/XII–18/6	Alaminos	72
1933/XII–18/7	Alaminos	72
1934/II–12/6	Milia	73
1934/II–12/7	Milia	73
1934/II–12/8	Milia	73
1937/III–31/3	Dhenia *Potamos tou Merikas* 52n.28.	69
1937/III–31/5	Dhenia *Potamos tou Merikas* 69	
1938/XI–15/5		47
1938/XII–5/2		91
1939/II–27/3	Alambra	66
1939/III–4/3	Anglisidhes	72
1939/VII–18/1	Enkomi	70
1940/I–11/2		87, 88
1940/VIII–26/1		82
1940/XII–23/1	Politico	76
1941/I–18/1	Politico *Lambertis* 13n.108 76	
1942/IV–17/2	Livadhia	29,50,73
1949/IX–14/2	Nicosia *Ayia Paraskevi* T. 8 73–4	
1950/V–18/1	Kotchati *Ayia Varvara*	71
1950/VI–16/1	Kotchati *Kalamoudhia*	71
1953/II–3/1	Galinoporni	22,70
1953/VII–21/1	Dhikomo *Onishia*	69
1954/XII–2/2	Kalopsidha	71
1956/III–7/6	Galiloporni T. 2	70
1958/I–17/4	Ayia Paraskevi	30, 50, 67
1958/VII–31/1	L. 50. 1	58
1960/IV–19/4	Dhenia *Mali*	68
1963/VI–3/1		80
1963/VII–11/4		87

1963/XI–4/14		52n.28.
1963/XII–20/2	Politico . 4	75
1965/VII–27/1	Pendayia *Mandres*	71
1966/VIII–8/1	Pendayia *Mandres*	71
1966/VIII–8/2	Pendayia *Mandres*	71
1966/X–14/5		87, 88, 89
1967/X–27/4		52n.9
1970/VI–26/4		35
1970/X–7/10	Kotchati	48–9, 72

FAMAGUSTA DISTRICT MUSEUM

MA357	Galinoporni T. 2. 30	70
MA360	Galinoporni T. 2. 63	70
MA363	Galinoporni T. 2. 31	70
MA372	Galinoporni T. 2. 150.	70
1967.1	Kalopsidha	70
1967.5	Kalopsidha	70

LARNACA DISTRICT MUSEUM

MLA123		52n.10
MLA149	Livadhia	73
MLA150	Livadhia	73
MLA151	Livadhia	73
MLA152	Livadhia	73
MLA153	Livadhia	73
MLA154	Livadhia	73
MLA164		29
MLA166	Livadhia	73
MLA168	Livadhia	73

NICHOLSON MUSEUM

51.351 (CM1951/III–14/3)	Dhenia	69
51.353 (CM1951/III–14/3)	Dhenia.	69
51.387	Dhenia.	69
54.36	Dhiorios.	76
58.140	Ayia Paraskevi (Gladstone Street).2.	67
58.141	Ayia Paraskevi (Gladstone Street).3.	67
58.142	Ayia Paraskevi (Gladstone Street).5.	67
58.144	Ayia Paraskevi (Gladstone Street).8.	67
58.148	Ayia Paraskevi (Gladstone Street).6.	67

INDEX 3

INDIVIDUAL VESSELS

This index lists those few vessels (other than those with museum inventery numbers) to which some reference is made in the text. Further details of these vessels is to be found in Appendix I.

BIBLIOGRAPHY

Angel, J.L. 1971, *The People of Lerna*, American School of Classical Studies at Athens.

– 1972, "Ecology and Population in the Eastern Mediterranean", *World Archaeology*, 4.1: 88–105.

Artzy, M., Asaro, F., Perlman, I. 1973, "The Origin of the "Palestinian" Bichrome Ware", *Journal of the American Oriental Society*, 93.4: 446–461.

Ascher, M. and Ascher, R. 1963, "Chronological Ordering by Computer", *American Anthropologist*, 65.5: 1045–52.

Ascher, R. 1961, "Analogy in Archaeological Interpretation", *Southwestern Journal of Anthropology*, 17.4: 317–25.

Åström, L. 1972, "Arts and Crafts of the Late Cypriote Bronze Age" in *The Swedish Cyprus Expedition* Vol. IV 1 D: 473–622. Lund.

Åström, P. 1957, *The Middle Cypriote Bronze Age*, Lund. (reprinted as *The Swedish Cyprus Expedition* Vol. IV 1 B, 1972)

– 1960a, "Cypriote Pottery in the Allen Memorial Art Museum", *Allen Memorial Art Museum Bulletin*, XVII.3: 75–93.

– 1960b, "A Middle Cypriote Tomb from Galinoporni", *Opuscula Atheniensia*, III: 123–34.

– 1961–2, "Remarks on Middle Minoan Chronology", *Kretika Chronika*, 15–16: 137–50.

– 1963, "Supplementary Material from Ayios Iakovos Tomb 8", *Opuscula Atheniensia, IV:* 207–24.

– 1964, "Red–on–Black Ware", *Opuscula Atheniensia*, V: 59–88.

– 1966, *Excavations at Kalopsidha and Ayios Iakovos in Cyprus*, Studies in Mediterranean Archaeology, II, Lund.

– 1967, "New Evidence for Middle Minoan Chronology", *Pepragmena tou B' diethnous Kretologikou Synedriou, B' diethnes Kretologikon Synedrion,* I: 120–127.

– 1968, "Die Antike Kunst und Kultur Zyperns", in J. Thimme, P. Åström, G. Lilliu, J. Wiesner, *Frühe Randkulturen des Mittelmeerraumes*, Baden–Baden.

– 1969, "The Economy of Cyprus and its development in the 2nd Millennium", *Archaeologia Viva*, 3: 73–80.

– 1971, "Pictorial Motifs in the Middle Cypriote Bronze Age", *Alasia* I: 4–14.

– 1972a, "Some Aspects of the Late Cypriote I Period", *Report of the Department of Antiquities, Cyprus*, 1972: 46–57.

– 1972b, "The Late Cypriote Bronze Age – Architecture and Pottery", *The Swedish Cyprus Expedition* Vol IV 1 C, Lund.

– 1972c, "The Late Cypriote Bronze Age – Relative and Absolute Chronology, Foreign Relations, Historical Conclusions", in *The Swedish Cyprus Expedition* Vol. IV 1 D: 674–781, Lund.

Åström, P. and Wright, G.R.H. 1963, "Two Bronze Age Tombs at Dhenia in Cyprus", *Opuscula Atheniensia*, IV: 225–76.

Bellwood, P. 1971, "Fortifications and Economy in Prehistoric New Zealand", *Proceedings of the Prehistoric Society*, XXXVII.1: 56–95.

Binford, L.R. 1962, "Archaeology as Anthropology" *American Antiquity*, 28.2: 217–25.

– 1965, "Archaeological Systematics and the Study of Culture Process", *American Antiquity*, 31.2: 203–10.

– 1968a, "Archaeological Perspectives", in Binford, L.R. and Binford, S.R. (eds.), *New Perspectives in Archaeology*: 5–32.

– 1968b, "Methodological Considerations of the Archaeological Use of Ethnographic Data", in Lee, R. B. and De Vore, I. (eds.), *Man the Hunter*: 268–73.

– 1972, "Contemporary Model Building: Paradigms and the Current state of Palaeolithic Research", in D.L. Clarke (ed.), *Models in Archaeology*, London: 109–166.

Binford, L.R. and Binford, S.R. 1966, "A preliminary analysis of functional variability in the Mousterian of Levallois Facies", in Clark, J.D. and Howell, F.C. (eds.), *Recent studies in Palaeoanthropology, American Anthropologist*, 68.2: 238–295.

Binford, L.R. and Binford, S.R. (eds) 1968, *New Perspectives in Archaeology*, Chicago.

Binford, S.R. 1968, "Variability and Change in the Near Eastern Mousterian of Levallois Facies", in Binford, L.R. and Binford, S.R. (eds.), *New Perspectives in Archaeology*, Chicago: 49–60.

Boardman, J. 1960, "The Multiple Brush", *Antiquity*, XXXIV: 85–89.

Bordes, F. 1973, "Interassemblage variability – the Mousterian and the 'Functional' arguement", in Renfrew, C. (ed), *The Explanation of Culture Change: Models in Prehistory*: 217–226.

Bordes, F. and Sonneville–Bordes 1970. "The significance of variability in Palaeolothic assemblages", *World Archaeology*, 2.1: 61–73.

Bradley, R. 1971a, "Trade Competition and Artifact distribution", *World Archaeology*, 2: 347–52.

– 1971b, "Stock Raising and the origins of the Hill Fort on the Southern Downs", *Antiquaries Journal*, LI. 8–29.

Brainerd, G.W. "The place of chronological ordering in archaeological analysis", *American Antiquity*, 16: 303–13.

Brew, J.O. 1946, "The Use and Abuse of Taxonomy", in *The Archaeology of Alkali Ridge*, Papers of the Peabody Museum, 21: 44–66.

Bucholz, H.–G., and Karageorghis, V. 1971, *Altägäis und Altkypros*, Tübingen.

Bunzel, R.L. 1929, *The Pueblo Potter, A Study in Creative Imagination in Primitive Art*, New York.

Buxton, L.H.D. 1920, "The Anthropology of Cyprus", *Journal of the Royal Anthropological Institute*, 50: 183–235.

Casson, S. 1937, *Ancient Cyprus*, London.

– 1938, "The Modern Pottery Trade in the Aegean", *Antiquity*, XII: 464–473.

Catling, H.W. 1963, "Patterns of Settlement in Bronze Age Cyprus", *Opuscula Atheniensia*, IV: 129–69.

– 1966, *Cypriot Bronzework and the Mycenaean World*. Oxford.

– 1966, *Cyprus in the Neolithic and Bronze Age Periods*, C.A.H. fasicule 43.

– 1969, "The Cypriote Copper Industry", *Archaeologia Viva*, 3: 81–88.

Cattell, R.B. 1965, "Factor Analysis: an introduction to essentials", *Biometrics*, 21: 190–210, 405–35.

Childe, V.G. 1944, "Archaeological Ages as Technological Stages", *Journal of the Royal Anthropological Institute*, LXXIV: 7–24.

Christenson, A.L. 1972, "The requirements of Factor Analysis", *Mankind*, 8: 307–309.

Christodoulou, D. 1959, *The Evolution of the Rural Land Use Pattern in Cyprus*, World Land Use Survey, Monograph 2.

Clarke, D.L. 1968, *Analytical Archaeology*, London.

– 1970, *Beaker Pottery of Great Britain and Ireland*, Cambridge.

Courtois, L. 1970, "Note préliminaire sur l'origine des différents Fabriques de la poterie du Chypriote Récent", *Report of the Department of Antiquities, Cyprus*, 1970: 81–85.

Cowgill, G.L. 1968, "Archaeological Applications of Factor, Cluster, and Proximity Analyses", *American Antiquity"*, 33.3: 367–75.

Daniel, G.E. 1968, *The Origin and growth of Archaeology*, London.

– 1971,, "From Worsaae to Childe: the models of prehistory", *Proceedings of the Prehistoric Society*, XXXVII.2: 140–53.

Deetz, J. 1965, *The dynamics of stylistic change in Arikara Ceramics*, Illinois Studies in Anthropology, No. 4, Illinois.

– 1968, "The inference of Residence and Descent Rules from Archaeological Data", in Binford, L.R. and Binford, S.R. (eds.), *New Perspectives in Archaeology*: 41–48.

Deetz, J. and Dethlefsen, E.S. 1965, "The Doppler Effect and Archaeology – a consideration of the spatial aspects of seriation", *Southwestern Journal of Anthropology*, 21: 196–206.

Delougaz, P. 1952, *Pottery from the Diyala Region*, Chicago.

Dethlefsen, E.S. and Deetz, J. 1966, "Death's Heads, Cherubs and Willow Trees: experimental archaeology in colonial cemeteries", *American Antiquity,* 31.4: 502–10.

di Cesnola, L.P. 1877, *Cyprus: its Ancient Cities, Tombs and Temples*, London.

– 1885–1903, *A Descriptive Atlas of the Cesnola Collection of Cypriote Antiquities in the Metropolitan Museum of Art, New York*, I–III, Boston, New York.

Dikaios, P. 1938, "The Excavations at Vounous–Bellapais in Cyprus, 1931–32", *Archaeologia*, 88: 1–174.

– 1961, *A Guide to the Cyprus Museum*, 3rd edn. Nicosia.

– 1962, "The Stone Age", in *The Swedish Cyprus Expedition*, Vol. IV 1 A: 1–204. Lund.

– 1969–71, *Enkomi, Excavations 1948–1958*, Vols. I–III, Mainz.

Dümmler, F. 1886, "Mittheilungen von den griechischen Inseln. IV: Aelteste Nekropolen auf Cypern", *Mittheilungen des Deutschen Archaeologischen Instituts. Athens*, XI: 209–262.

Dunnell, R.C. 1970, "Seriation Method and its Evaluation", *American Antiquity*, 35.3: 305–19.

– 1971, *Systematics in Prehistory*, New York.

du Plat Taylor, J. 1957, *Myrtou–Pighades: a Late Bronze Age Sanctuary in Cyprus*, Oxford.

Epstein, C. 1965, "Bichrome Vessels in the Cross Line Style", *Palestine Exploration Quarterly*, 97: 42–53.

– 1966, *Palestinian Bichrome Ware*, Leiden.

Eslick, C.M. 1972, *The Early Pottery from Mersin*, 2 Vols. Unpublished M.A. thesis, Department of Archaeology, Sydney University.

Evans, A.J. 1905, "La classification des époques successives de la civilisation minoenne", *Comptes Rendus du Congres International d'Archeologie, Athens 1905*: 209.

– 1921, *The Palace of Minos.* Vol. I, London.

Evans, J.D. 1973, "Islands as laboratories for the study of culture process", in Renfrew, C. (ed.), *The Explanation of Culture Change: Models in Prehistory*: 517–20.

Flannery, K.V. 1967, "Culture History vs Culture Process. A debate in American Archaeology" *Scientific American*, 217: 119–22.

Ford, J.A. 1954, "The type concept revisited", *American Anthropologist*, 56: 42–53.

Foster, G.M. 1965, "The Sociology of Pottery: Questions and hypotheses arising from Contemporary Mexican Work", in Matson, F.R. (ed.), *Ceramics and Man*, Viking Fund Publications in Anthropology No. 41: 43–61.

Frankel, D. and Tamvaki, A. n.d., "Cypriot Shrine Models and Decorated Tombs", *Australian Journal of Biblical Archaeology* (in press).

Freeman, L.G. 1968, "A Theoretical Framework for Interpreting Archaeological Materials", in Lee R.B. and de Vore, I. (eds.), *Man the Hunter*: 262–67.

Friedrich, M.H. 1970, "Design Structure and Social Interaction. Archaeological Implications of an ethnographic analysis, *American Antiquity*, 35.3: 332–43.

Frödin, O. and Persson, A.W. 1938, *Asine*, Stockholm.

Furumark, A. 1940, *The Mycenaean Pottery*, Stockholm.

Gardin, J.C. 1958, "Four codes for the description of Artifacts; an Essay in Archaeological Technique and Theory", *American Anthropologist*, 60.2: 335–57.

– 1967, "Methods for the descriptive analysis of archaeological material", *American Antiquity*, 32.1: 13–20.

Gardner, E.A. *et al.* 1888, *Excavations in Cyprus, 1887", Journal of Hellenic studies*, IX: 1-125.

Gardner, E.A. *et al.* 1889, "Excavations in Cyprus 1888", *Journal of Hellenic Studies*, X: 1–99.

Gardner, E.A. *et al.* 1891, "Excavations in Cyprus, 1890", *Journal of Hellenic Studies*, XI: 59–198.

Gifford, J.C. 1960, "The type–variety method of ceramic classification as an indicator of cultural phenomena", *American Antiquity*, 25.3, 341–47.

Gjerstad, E. 1924, "Topographical Notes", *Kypriaka Chronika*, 2, 246–53.

– 1926, *Studies on Prehistoric Cyprus*, Uppsala.

– 1931, *Cypriot Pottery*, Union Academique Internationale, Classification des Ceramiques Antiques.

Gjerstad, E. *et al.* 1934–7, *The Swedish Cyprus Expedition: Finds and Results of the Excavations in*

Cyprus 1927–1931, Vols. I–III, Stockholm.

Glover, I.C. 1969, "The Use of Factor Analysis for the Discovery of Artefact Types", *Mankind*, 7.1: 36–51.

Grace, V. 1940, "A Cypriote Tomb and Minoan Evidence for its Date", *American Journal of Archaeology*, 44: 10–52.

Hampe, R. and Winter, A. 1962, *Bei Töpfer und Töpferinnen in Kreta, Messenien und Zypern*, Mainz.

Hammond, P.C. 1959, "Pattern Families in Nabatean Painted Ware", *American Journal of Archaeology*, 63: 371–82.

Hennessy, J.B. 1964, *Stephania: A Middle and Late Bronze Age Cemetery in Cyprus*, London.

Herscher, E. 1972, "A Potter's Error: Aspects of Middle Cypriote III", *Report of the Department of Antiquities, Cyprus*, 1972: 22–33.

Hockings, P. 1963, "Ceramic Style in Prehistoric Cyprus", *Man*, 80: 65.

Hodson, F.R. 1969a, "Searching for structure within multivariate archaeological data", *World Archaeology*, 1.1: 90–105.

– 1969b, "Classification by Computer", in Brothwell, D. and Higgs, E. (eds.), *Science in Archaeology*, 2nd edition, London: 649–60.

– 1970, "Cluster Analysis and Archaeology: some new developments and applications", *World Archaeology*, 1.3: 299–320.

Hodson, F.R., Sneath, P.H.A., and Doran, J.E. 1966, "Some experiments in the numerical analysis of archaeological data", *Biometrika*, 53, 3 and 4: 311–24.

Irwin, G.J. 1972, *An archaeological survey in the Shortland Islands*, Unpublished M.A. thesis, University of Auckland.

Johnson, Leroy. 1971, "Interdependent data, cluster analysis, and archaeology", *Proceedings of the Prehistoric Society*, 36: 231–4.

Jones, D.K., Merton, L.F.H., Poore, M.E.D., Harris, D.R. 1958, *Report on Pasture Research, Survey and Development in Cyprus* Government of Cyprus.

Jones, R. 1969, "Fire–stick Farming", *Australian Natural History*, 16: 224–28.

Karageorghis, V. 1958, "Finds from Early Cypriot Cemeteries", *Report of the Department of Antiquities, Cyprus,* 1940–48: 115–52.

– 1962, "Chronique des fouilles et découvertes archéologiques à Chypre en 1961", *Bulletin de Correspondance Hellenique*, 86: 327–414.

– 1963, "Chronique des fouilles et découvertes archeologiques à Chypre en 1962". *Bulletin de Correspondance Hellenique*, 87: 325–87.

– 1965, *Nouveaux Documents pour l'étude du Bronze Recent à Chypre,* Paris.

– 1966, "Chronique des fouilles et découvertes archéologiques à Chypre en 1965", *Bulletin de Correspondance Hellenique*, 90: 297–389.

– 1968, "Chronique des fouilles et découvertes archéologiques à Chypre en 1967", *Bulletin de Correspondance Hellenique*, 92: 261–358.

– 1969a, *Cyprus*, London.

– 1969b, "The Flowering of Cypriote Art", *Archaeologia Viva*, 3: 131–34.

– 1970, "Two Religious Documents of the Early Cypriote Bronze Age", *Report of the Department of Antiquities, Cyprus*, 1970: 10–13.

Kenna, V.E.G. 1971, *Corpus of Cypriote Antiquities, 3. Catalogue of the Cypriote Seals of the Bronze Age in the British Museum*, Studies in Mediterranean Archaeology, XX.3, Lund.

Lamb, W. 1936, *Corpus Vasorum Antiquorum, Great Britain 11, Cambridge 2*, Oxford.

Larsen, L.H. 1972, "Functional Considerations of Warfare in the Southwest during the Mississippi Period", *American Antiquity*, 37.3: 383–92.

Leach, B.F. 1969, *The Concept of Similarity in Prehistoric Studies*, University of Otago, Studies in Prehistoric Anthropology, I, Otago.

Linton, R. 1936, *The Study of Man*, New York.

Longacre, W.A. 1970, *Archaeology as Anthropology,* Anthropological Papers of the University of Arizona, 17, Tuscon.

McKern, W.C. 1939, "The Midwestern Taxonomic Method as an aid to Archaeological Culture Study", *American Antiquity,* 4: 301–13.

McNutt, C.H. 1973, "On the Methodological Validity of Frequency Seriation", *American Antiquity* 38.1: 45–60.

Megaw, J.V.S. 1967, "Art Styles and Analysis", *Mankind,* 6: 393–402.

Merrillees, R.S. 1965, "Reflections on the Late Bronze Age in Cyprus", *Opuscula Atheniensia*, VI: 139–48.

– 1967, "Review of *Excavations at Kalopsidha and*

Ayios Iakovos in Cyprus", Antiquity, XLI: 333–35.

– 1971, "The Early History of Late Cypriote I", *Levant*, III: 56–79.

– 1972a, "Aegean Bronze Age Relations with Egypt", *American Journal of Archaeology*, 76.3: 281–94.

– 1972b, *Introduction to Pottery Corpus of Phlamoudhi, Vounari and Melissa*, typescript.

Murray, A.S., Smith, A.H. and Walters, H.M. 1900, *Excavations in Cyprus*, London.

Myres, J.L. 1897, "Excavations in Cyprus in 1894", *Journal of Hellenic Studies*, XVII: 134–73.

– 1914, *Handbook of the Cesnola Collection of Antiquities from Cyprus*, New York.

– 1926, "Review of *Studies on Prehistoric Cyprus*", *Journal of Hellenic Studies*, XLVI: 289–91.

– 1940–45, "Excavations in Cyprus, 1913", *Annual of the British School at Athens*, 41: 53–98.

Myres, J.L. and Ohnefalsch–Richter, M. 1899, *A Catalogue of the Cyprus Museum*, Oxford.

Nicklin, K. 1971, "Stability and innovation in pottery manufacture", *World Archaeology*, 3.1: 13–48.

Nicolaou, K. 1972, "Archaeological News from Cyprus", *American Journal of Archaeology*, 76.

Ohnefalsch–Richter, M. 1893, *Kypros, die Bibel und Homer*, London.

– 1899, "Neues über die auf Cypern ... angestellten Ausgrabungen", *Verhandlungen der Berliner Gesellschaft für Anthropologie, Ethnologie, und Urgeschichte*, 1899, 29–78; 298–401.

Ohnefalsch–Richter, M.H. 1913, *Griechische Sitten und Gebräuche auf Cypern*, Berlin.

Oren, E.D. 1969, "Cypriot Imports in the Palestinian Late Bronze I Context", *Opuscula Atheniensia*, IX: 127–150.

Overbeck, J.C. and Swiny, S. 1972, *Two Cypriot Bronze Age Sites at Kafkallia (Dhali)*, Studies in Mediterranean Archaeology, XXXIII, Göteborg.

Patterson, T.C. 1963, "Contemporaneity and Cross–Dating in Archaeological Interpretation", *American Antiquity*, 28.3: 289–292.

Petrie, W.M.F. 1899, "Sequences in Prehistoric Remains", *Journal of the Anthropological Institute of Great Britain and Ireland*, 29: 295–301.

– 1901, *Dispolis Parva*, Egyptian Exploration Fund Memoirs 20, London.

Pieridou, A.G. 1960, "Kypriake Laike Techne", *Kypriake Spoudai*, 24: 153–65.

– 1963 and 1964, "Cyprus Folk Pottery", *Cyprus Today*, Vol.1.1: 22–23; reprinted in Vol.II.1: 11–13.

Popham, M.R. 1963a, "Two Cypriot Sherds from Crete", *Annual of the British School at Athens*, 58: 89–93.

– 1963b, "The Proto–White Slip Pottery of Cyprus", *Opuscula Atheniensia*, IV: 187–96.

– 1972, "White Slip Ware" in *The Swedish Cyprus Expedition* Vol. IV 1 C: 431–471, IV 1 D: 699–705.

The Proceedings of a Conference on Land Use in a Mediterranean Environment, held in Nicosia, Cyprus, April 1946, Nicosia, Government Printing Office, 1947.

Rands, R.L. 1961, "Elaboration and Invention in Ceramic Traditions", *American Antiquity*, 26.3: 331–40.

Renfrew, C. 1969, "Trade and Culture Process in European Prehistory", *Current Anthropology*, 10.2: 151–60.

– 1972, *The Emergence of Civilization. The Cyclades and the Aegean in the Third Millenium B.C.*, London.

Renfrew, C. and Sterud, G. 1969, "Close–Proximity Analysis: A Rapid Method for the Ordering of Archaeological Materials", *American Antiquity*, 34.3: 265–77.

Robinson, W.S. 1951, "A Method for Chronologically Ordering Archaeological Deposits", *American Antiquity*, 16: 293–301.

Rouse, I. 1960, "The Classification of Artifacts in Archaeology", *American Antiquity*, 25.3: 313–23.

– 1965, "Caribbean Ceramics: A Study in Method and in Theory", in Matson, F.R. (ed.), *Ceramics and Man*, Viking Fund Publications in Anthropology No.41: 88–103.

– 1970, "Analytical Archaeology – discussion", *Norwegian Archaeological Review*, 3: 4–9.

Rowe, J.H. 1959, "Archaeological Dating and Cultural Process", *Southwestern Journal of Anthropology*, 15.4: 317–24.

– 1961, "Stratigraphy and Seriation", *American Antiquity*, 26.3: 324–30.

– 1962a, "Worsaae's Law and the use of Grave lots

for Archaeological dating", *American Antiquity*, 28.2: 129–37.

– 1962b, "Stages and Periods in Archaeological Interpretation", *Southwestern Journal of Anthropology*, 18.1: 40–51.

Rowlett, R.M. and Pollnac, R.B. 1971, "Multivariate Analysis of Marnian La Tene Cultural Groups", in F.R. Hodson, D.G. Kendall, P. Tautu (eds.), *Mathematics in the Archaeological and Historical Sciences*, Edinburgh: 46–58.

Sabloff, J.A. and Smith, R.E. 1969, "The Importance of both Analytic and Taxanomic Classification in the Type–Variety System", *American Antiquity*, 34.3: 278.

Sackett, J.R. 1969, "Factor Analysis and Artifact Typology", *American Anthropologist*, 71.6: 1125–30.

Sandwith, T.B. 1880, "On the different styles of Pottery found in Ancient Tombs in the Island of Cyprus", *Archaeologia*, XLV: 127–42.

Schaeffer, C.F.A. 1936, *Missions en Chypre*, Paris.

– 1952, *Enkomi–Alasia*, Paris.

Schmidt, E.F. 1928, "Time relations in prehistoric pottery types in Southern Arizona", *Anthropological Papers of the American Museum of Natural History*, XXX.V: 249–302.

Shepard, A.O. 1968, *Ceramics for the Archaeologist*, Washington.

Sjöquist, E. 1940, *Problems of the Late Cypriote Bronze Age*, Stockholm.

– 1940, *Reports on Excavations in Cyprus*, Stockholm.

Smith, A.H. 1925, *Corpus Vasorum Antiquorum, Great Britain 1, British Museum 1* London.

Sokal, R.R. 1966, "Numerical Taxonomy", *Scientific American*, 215.6: 106–16.

Sokal, R.R. and Sneath, P.H. 1963, *Principles of Numerical Taxonomy* San Francisco and London.

Solheim, W.G. 1965, "The Functions of Pottery in Southeast Asia: From the Present to the Past", in Matson, F.R. (ed.), *Ceramics and Man*, Viking Fund Publications in Anthropology No. 41: 254–76.

Spaulding, A.C. 1960, "The Dimensions of Archaeology", in Dole, G.E. and Caniero, R.L. (eds.), *Essays in the Science of Culture in Honor of L.A. White*: 437–56.

Stewart, E. and Stewart J.R. 1950, *Vounous 1937–38*, Lund.

Stewart, J.R. 1960, "Review of *Myrtou–Pighades*" *American Journal of Archaeology*, 64: 240–42.

– 1962, "The Early Bronze Age in Cyprus", in *The Swedish Cyprus Expedition*, Vol. IV 1 A: 205–401, Lund.

– 1963, "The Tomb of the Seafarer at Karmi in Cyprus", *Opuscula Atheniensia*, IV: 197–204.

– 1965, "Notes on Cyprus", *Opuscula Atheniensia*, VI: 157–64.

Stewart, O.C. 1956, "Fire as the first force employed by man", in Thomas, W.L. (ed.), *Man's Role in changing the Face of the Earth*, Chicago.

Stjernquist, B. 1966, *Models of Commercial Diffusion in Prehistoric Times*, Scripta Minora, 1965–1966:2, Lund.

Struever, S. 1971, "Comments on Archaeological Data, Requirements and Research Design", *American Antiquity*, 36.1: 9–19.

Taylor, W.W. 1948, *A Study of Archeology,* American Anthropological Association Memoir 69.

Thomas, D.H. 1971, "On the Use of Cumulative Curves and Numerical Taxonomy", *American Antiquity*, 36.2: 206–09.

– 1972, "The Use and Abuse of Numerical Taxonomy in Archaeology", *Archaeology and Physical Anthropology in Oceania*, VII.1: 31–49.

Thomas, H.L. 1967, *Near Eastern, Mediterranean and European Chronology*, Studies in Mediterranean Archaeology, XVII, Lund.

Thomas, H.L. and Ehrich, R.W. 1969, "Some problems in chronology", *World Archaeology* I.2: 144–56.

Tippett, A.R. 1968, *Fijian Material Culture. A study of cultural context, function and change*, Honolulu.

Trendall, A.D, and Stewart, J.R. 1948, *Handbook to the Nicholson Museum*, 2nd edition, Sydney.

Tugby, D. 1965, "Archaeological Objectives and statistical methods: A Frontier in Archaeology", *American Antiquity*, 31.1: 1–15.

– 1969, "Archaeology and Statistics", in Brothwell, D. and Higgs, E. (eds.), *Science in Archaeology*, 2nd edition, London: 635–648.

Ucko, P. 1969, "Ethnography and archaeological interpretations of funerary remains", *World Archaeology,* 1.2: 262–80.

Veldman, D.J. 1967, *Fortran Programming for the*

Behavioral Sciences, New York.

Villa, P. 1969, *Corpus of Cypriote Antiquities I*, Studies in Mediterranean Archaeology, XX.1, Lund.

von der Osten, H.H. and Schmidt, E.F. 1930, *The Alishar Hüyük, Season of 1927*, Chicago.

Wace, A.J.B. and Blegen, C.W. 1916–18, "The pre-Mycenaean pottery of the Mainland", *Annual of the British School at Athens*, 22: 171–89.

Walters, H.B. 1912, *Catalogue of the Greek and Etruscan Vases in the British Museum, Vol. I, Part II: Cypriote, Italian and Etruscan Pottery*, London.

Ward, J.H. 1963, "Hierarchical Grouping to Optimize an Objective Function", *American Statistical Association Journal*, 58: 236–44.

Weinberg, S. 1956, "Exploring the Early Bronze Age in Cyprus", *Archaeology*, IX: 113–22.

– 1965' "Ceramics and the supernatural", in Matson, F.R. (ed.), *Ceramics and Man*: 187–201.

Weiss, R. 1952, "Kulturgrenzen und ihre Bestimmung durch volkskundliche Karten", *Studium General* V: 363–73, translated and reprinted in Wagner, P.L. and Mikesell, M.W. (eds.), *Readings in Cultural Geography*, Chicago, 1962: 62–74.

Westholm, A. 1939, "Some Late Cypriote tombs at Milia", *Quarterly of the Department of Antiquities of Palestine*, VIII: 1–20.

Whallon, R. 1968, "Investigations of Late Prehistoric Social Organization in New York State", in Binford, L.R. and S.R. (eds.), *New Perspectives in Archaeology*, Chicago, 1968: 223–44.

Wolfe, W.W. 1969, "Social Structural Basis of Art", *Current Anthropology*, 10.1: 3–44.

TABLE 1

NUMBER OF POTS IN EACH GROUP

	Group	jug	jlt	cup	bwl	amp	jar	tnk	flk	btl	oth	total	% of group
1	L2	12		2	7	1	1		1	1	1	26	2
2	L18	22	6		20	7	2	2	4	3		66	4
3	L21	23	3	11	14	5	1	4	7	9	1	78	6
4	L29	10		2	11	1	2	1		2		29	2
5	L47	4		3	3	4			1	4		19	1
6	L49	10		1	11	2	1	2	1	9		37	3
7	L50	28	2	8	11	9	2	5	6	10	1	82	6
8	L315 A	6		2	7	2		1	4	3		25	2
9	L315 B-C	5		1	4	2					1	13	1
10	L316[1]	17	1		15	6		3	2	2		46	3
11	L316[2]	3	1		8	1		2	1	4		20	1
12	L320	7	1	3	10	2			4	3		30	2
13	L4	3		1	2			2	2			10	1
14	L8	3		1	2	1				2		9	1
15	L14	8	1	1	2	3				1		16	1
16	L51	3			7				2	1	1	14	1
17	L203	12		3	1	1						17	1
18	L311	6			4	1						11	1
19	L313	7			1	1					1	10	1
20	L702	5			4		1	2		1		13	1
21	Lapithos	28		5	26	15		2	2	4		82	6
22	Alambra	1			1	3					2	7	1
23	Ay. Iak.	2			27	1		2		1		33	3
24	Ay. P.	19	3	3	9	1			3	4	6	48	3
25	Dhali	5		1					3	6	1	16	1
26	Dhenia 6	15		3	6	3		5	1		1	34	3
27	Dhenia	18	1	4	22	1	1		3	1		51	4
28	Dhikomo	4		3	1	1				1		10	1
29	Enkomi	9			2		1	1	1	1		15	1
30	Galinop.	22			11	5			1			39	3
31	Kalops.	15	1		15	1	1	1		3		37	3
32	Katyd.		3		5							8	1
33	Klavdhia	6	3						1	4		14	1
34	Kotchati	10	1	1	5	1	1					19	1
35	Kythrea	11		1	2						1	15	1
36	Larnaca	9	1		3		1	1	1	2	1	19	1
37	Leondari	7	1		2				1	1		12	1
38	Livadhia	2	1		3				1	1		8	1
39	Milia	4			4					2		10	1
40	Nicosia	42	20	8	18	2			6	15	8	119	8
41	Palaeal.	3				5	1					9	1
42	Pol. 4	23	1	3	7	1		3	2	1		41	3
43	Politico	24	3	1	8		2	3	6	7	4	58	4
44	Myrtou	3			2		1	2				8	1
45	Vounous	9		1	2	8					3	23	2
46	Yeri	6	5	2	6	1			5	2		27	2
47	?Alambra	27	3	2	1	2	1		14	2	1	53	4
TOTAL		518	62	77	332	100	20	44	86	113	34	1386	100
% of total		38	4	6	24	7	1	3	6	8	3	100	

TABLE 2

PERCENTAGE OF EACH GROUP WHICH ARE OF EACH SHAPE

	Group	jug	jlt	cup	bwl	amp	jar	tnk	flk	btl	oth	total
1	L2	46		7	26	4	4		4	4	4	100
2	L18	33	10		30	10	3	3	6	4		99
3	L21	29	3	15	18	6	1	5	9	11	1	99
4	L29	34		6	37	3	6	3		6		95
5	L47	21		15	15	21			6	21		99
6	L49	27		2	29	5	2	5	2	24		96
7	L50	34	2	10	13	11	2	7	7	12	1	99
8	L315 A	24		8	28	8		4	16	12		100
9	L315 B-C	37		8	30	16					8	99
10	L316[1]	36	3		32	13		6	4	4		98
11	L316[2]	15	5		40	5		10	5	20		100
12	L320	23	3	10	33	6			13	10		98
13	L4	30		10	20			20	20			100
14	L8	33		11	22	11			22			99
15	L14	50	6	6	13	18			6			99
16	L51	22			50				14	7	7	100
17	L203	70		17	5	5						97
18	L311	55			36	9						100
19	L313	70			10	10					10	100
20	L702	37			30		8	16		8		99
21	Lapithos	34		7	32	18		2	2	4		99
22	Alambra	14			14	43					28	99
23	Ay. Iak.	6			81	3		6		3		99
24	Ay. P.	39	6	6	18	2			6	8	12	97
25	Dhali	31		6					18	38	6	99
26	Dhenia 6	44		8	17	8		14	2		2	95
27	Dhenia	35	2	8	43	2	2		6	2		100
28	Dhikomo	40		30	10	10				10		100
29	Enkomi	66			14		6	6	6	6		98
30	Gal.	56			29	12			2			99
31	Kalops.	40	2		40	2	2	2		8		96
32	Katyd.		31		62							33
33	Klavdhia	42	21						7	28		98
34	Kotchati	52	6	6	26	6	6					102
35	Kythrea	74		6	14							100
36	Larnaca	48	5		15		5	5	5	10	5	98
37	Leondari	58	8		17				8	8		99
38	Livadhia	25	12		38				12	12		99
39	Milia	40			40					20		100
40	Nicosia	35	17	7	15	2			6	13	7	102
41	Palaeal.	33				55	12					100
42	Pol. 4	56	2	7	17	2		7	4	2		97
43	Politico	41	5	2	13		3	5	10	12	7	98
44	Myrtou	38			25		12	25				100
45	Vounous	39		5	8	34					13	99
46	Yeri	23	18	7	23	3			18	7		99
47	?Alambra	51	5	4	2	4	2		26	4	2	100
TOTAL %		38	4	6	24	7	1	3	6	8	3	100

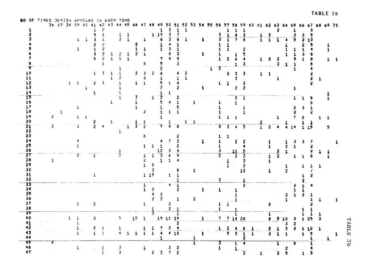

TABLE 3a

NO OF TIMES DESIGN APPEARS IN EACH TOMB

	1	2	3	4	5	6	7	8	9	10	11	12	13	14	15	16	17	18	19	20	21	22	23	24	25	26	27	28	29	30	31	32	33	34	35
1	5		10		3	13		4	6	3				3			6	1		1		1	2					6				1		1	
2	16		25		3	21		11	17	1	1			9			14							3				13	1			1		1	
3	17		26			22	3	10	31	3			3	4	1		14			3	2	6	1	2				22	1					3	1
4	10		15		2	11	1	6	13	1							7					2		2			1	6	1						
5	5		2			6		4	6	2			1	1			1					2		1			1	7						2	1
6	10		10		3	15		6	16	1				3			5					1		7				10	1					1	
7	24		22		3	30		10	28	6			4	7			12			2		7		3			1	21			1	4		3	
8	5		3			11	2	4	7				1				4					1		2				5						2	
9	4		1			4		4	9					2			2					1		1				5							
10	16		8			24	2	17	23				2	7			7					1						15			1	2			
11	7		4		1	11		6	7	3			1	3			6	2				1						4				1			
12	6		3		1	9		4	4					3			7				1	3	1			1	1	6	1					1	
13	1		2			2		2		1					1								1				1	2	1					1	
14	2		5			2		2	3								3											2							
15	5		5		2	2	1	4	5				1	1		1						1						7						1	
16	2		5			4		1	8	2							1					1		1				3							
17	8		2			1		1	11				3	1			1			1								10							
18	5		1		1	5			7	1				1			1				1	1		1				6							
19	2					6			2							1	1										5	6					2	2	3
20	1		8		1	6		1	3		1				1		6			1				1				2							
21	17		21		3	25	3	11	30	7			3	4	2		10			1	2	4	3	2	1		10	29	1	1	1		1	3	1
22	2	1	3	1		3			2					1			1					1					1	2			2	1			
23	4		8		3		6	1	5	19								1		1								1	1		1	2			1
24	2		20		4	16		1	16	3			1	2	1		7		1			1	1	2		1	5	7	1			1	1	2	1
25	2		5			6			5					3						1		3		1			1	4	1			1		2	
26	4		6		1	14	1	3	9	1			6	1			1			1		6						6						1	
27	10		22		2	23	2	6	17				3	2			9				1	4	1	1				16			1	1			
28			3			3			1	1			2	3						1	2	2						1				1		2	
29	4		5	1		3	2							2			2			2								3				1			
30	9		16	1	2	5	13		8	18		1	3	1	1		1							1				1			3	2		1	
31	11	3	15	1		12	2		6		1		1	1														2							
32			2			2			1	1				1			2					1		1				1				1		1	
33	2		8		1	7		1	2	1							2					1	2				1	2				1	2		
34	7		9			6		3	3				1	2			4			1		1		1			1	5						1	1
35	5		7			2		1	4	1	2		1		1		1					1	1	1				4							
36	3		9	1	5	2		1	3					1			2					2		1				2	1				1		1
37			7		1	3	1	1	2	1			1		1		2												1						
38	2	2	3			3			1	1												2						1				1			
39	1	2	3		1	2	1		1				1				1				1														
40	6		25			36	2	8	24	11			5	27	1		5			14	1	29	1	5			3	9	1		2	2		9	1
41	1					1			2			1			1	2					1		1				3	4					1	1	5
42	10		11	1	1	14	5	4	11	9	2	1	2	4			3	2		2		5			2			6		2		1		3	
43	8	2	20	1	1	18	2	2	9	2	2		2	10			3			1	1	5			1		1	4	4	1		1		2	1
44			6			6	1		3			1					3			1								2							
45	1		2			3			5	1			3	3			1			2		1	1				11	8				1		2	
46	3	1	12	1		11			11	1			2	3			2	1			1	2		1	1		1	2		2	1	2		1	
47	8	1	24		2	9	2	1	20		1		1	3			6			1		9		3	2			11	1		1		1	1	

TABLE 3a

TABLE 3b

NO OF TIMES DESIGN APPEARS IN EACH TOMB

	36	37	38	39	40	41	42	43	44	45	46	47	48	49	50	51	52	53	54	55	56	57	58	59	60	61	62	63	64	65	66	67	68	69	70
1						1	2							1	3	1	1					1	1	1				3		1		3			
2						5	1		1	1			1	10	3	7					3	1	6	3		1	3			3	3	5			
3				1	1	3	1		2	1		1		6	3	6	1		1		3	1	7	6		1	1	1	4	5	2	10			
4						2	2				3			1	4	1					1	1							1		2	5		1	
5				1		1	2				1	1		1	3	1					1	1		2					1	1	1	4		1	
6						3	2	1	2	1	2	1			8	3			1		1		1	5					1	1	3	6			
7						5	2	1	5	1				7	4	9					1	2	6	4		1	2	2		5	1	8		1	1
8							1					5		5		3							1	3				3	1	1		5			
9									1					2						1	2									1		4			
10						1	3	1	1		2	3	2	6		4	2					2	3	3		1	1					2			
11								1	2			3		1		1	1						3					1				2	1		
12			1	1		2	3		1		1	1		5	1	4					1	1		3								2			
13					1				1					2		2			1				2	2						1					
14						1			1					1	1																			1	
15									1		3		1	2		2							2	1						1	1	5		1	
16								1			1			5	4	1		1			1		1									5			
17				1							1			1		5					1			1						2	3	1			
18		1										2		1	1	1					1			1						2		2			
19	2			1	1									1							1	1	1					1		7	2		1	1	
20						2		1			1	1			1		1	1								2			1		1	1			
21	2			3		2	4			1	3	2		7	9	8					8	3	4	5		1	2	4	4	14	1	15		5	
22									1																										
23												6				2					1	1													
24				4										4	7	3			1		1		2	2			1		1	3	3	7			1
25				1								1	1	1		2					1			4			1		2	1		2			
26									1					12	3	4					3		10	5				2	1			9	1	1	
27				2		1			2			1	1	3	6	4					2		2	3			1	2		1	1	6		1	
28	1											2		1	1	4						1		3			1								
29												1	5									1		2					1		1	1	1		
30													3			8		1						10			1		2			/			
31						1						1	15		1	1															1	2			
32																1					2			1							2				
33												1			4	1								2						2	1	4			
34												1	2			2			1		1		1							1	1				
35													4	2									1						2	1	2	1			
36													2	2		1		2					1						1			1	1		1
37				1		2						1			2						1	1					2					2			
38													1		2	1					1		1								1	1			
39													3			1							1				1				1	1	1		
40			1	1		3			5		10	1		19	11	29			1		7	7	14	26			8	5	10	3	1	25	3		
41				1												2													3	2					
42				1		2	1		1			1	1	7	3	4					1	2	4	6	1		2	1	3	3	1	10	1		
43				1		1	1		4	1	1	1	1	4	4	10			1			5	3	1	1		3	1	1		1	5			1
44														1				1						2								1		1	
45	4																	1			3		1	4				1		5		1			
46				1			1		3			1			3	2					1		1						2			4			
47							1		3				2	3	7	2								2		1		2	5		1	5			

TABLE 3b

DEGREE OF SAMENESS – PRESENCE-ABSENCE SIMILARITY COEFFICIENT

TABLE 4a

	1	2	3	4	5	6	7	8	9	10	11	12	13	14	15	16	17	18	19	20	21	22	23	24	25
1	1,00	0,58	0,54	0,46	0,51	0,51	0,61	0,52	0,38	0,50	0,58	0,53	0,38	0,33	0,44	0,42	0,42	0,48	0,28	0,34	0,49	0,27	0,35	0,48	0,41
2	0,58	1,00	0,60	0,53	0,54	0,66	0,71	0,42	0,41	0,52	0,40	0,51	0,38	0,33	0,47	0,42	0,42	0,47	0,29	0,38	0,54	0,24	0,32	0,53	0,47
3	0,54	0,60	1,00	0,47	0,61	0,61	0,62	0,51	0,34	0,50	0,40	0,52	0,41	0,25	0,40	0,35	0,41	0,42	0,33	0,38	0,75	0,19	0,30	0,60	0,46
4	0,46	0,53	0,47	1,00	0,68	0,58	0,52	0,45	0,40	0,41	0,35	0,56	0,29	0,41	0,43	0,55	0,41	0,47	0,30	0,44	0,54	0,25	0,38	0,47	0,39
5	0,51	0,54	0,61	0,68	1,00	0,63	0,60	0,56	0,42	0,46	0,38	0,61	0,32	0,34	0,49	0,47	0,56	0,53	0,39	0,38	0,65	0,25	0,29	0,58	0,53
6	0,51	0,66	0,61	0,58	0,63	1,00	0,60	0,51	0,42	0,46	0,45	0,56	0,39	0,30	0,49	0,52	0,43	0,53	0,23	0,46	0,55	0,25	0,29	0,55	0,45
7	0,61	0,71	0,62	0,52	0,60	0,60	1,00	0,46	0,38	0,56	0,48	0,48	0,33	0,32	0,48	0,43	0,43	0,44	0,33	0,36	0,65	0,30	0,30	0,56	0,44
8	0,52	0,42	0,51	0,45	0,56	0,51	0,46	1,00	0,46	0,50	0,48	0,41	0,37	0,31	0,53	0,46	0,46	0,48	0,29	0,32	0,46	0,24	0,25	0,44	0,48
9	0,38	0,41	0,34	0,40	0,42	0,42	0,38	0,46	1,00	0,36	0,43	0,39	0,30	0,47	0,43	0,52	0,52	0,54	0,27	0,30	0,28	0,43	0,21	0,36	0,43
10	0,50	0,52	0,50	0,41	0,46	0,46	0,56	0,50	0,36	1,00	0,56	0,47	0,26	0,32	0,51	0,41	0,41	0,35	0,19	0,37	0,45	0,34	0,31	0,35	0,39
11	0,58	0,40	0,40	0,35	0,38	0,45	0,48	0,48	0,43	0,56	1,00	0,38	0,30	0,33	0,45	0,48	0,39	0,45	0,24	0,34	0,33	0,36	0,35	0,39	0,33
12	0,53	0,51	0,52	0,56	0,61	0,56	0,48	0,41	0,39	0,47	0,38	1,00	0,36	0,35	0,42	0,40	0,44	0,50	0,27	0,32	0,53	0,29	0,30	0,49	0,46
13	0,38	0,38	0,41	0,29	0,32	0,39	0,33	0,37	0,30	0,26	0,30	0,36	1,00	0,29	0,39	0,31	0,31	0,29	0,28	0,17	0,31	0,22	0,23	0,44	0,34
14	0,33	0,33	0,25	0,41	0,34	0,30	0,32	0,31	0,47	0,32	0,33	0,35	0,29	1,00	0,33	0,41	0,35	0,32	0,26	0,35	0,22	0,37	0,20	0,22	0,20
15	0,44	0,47	0,40	0,43	0,49	0,49	0,48	0,53	0,43	0,51	0,45	0,42	0,39	0,33	1,00	0,39	0,54	0,41	0,31	0,27	0,41	0,27	0,26	0,62	0,41
16	0,42	0,42	0,35	0,55	0,47	0,52	0,43	0,46	0,52	0,41	0,48	0,40	0,31	0,41	0,39	1,00	0,46	0,54	0,24	0,45	0,34	0,27	0,28	0,40	0,34
17	0,42	0,42	0,41	0,41	0,56	0,43	0,43	0,46	0,52	0,41	0,39	0,44	0,31	0,35	0,54	0,46	1,00	0,48	0,32	0,35	0,40	0,27	0,28	0,44	0,48
18	0,48	0,47	0,42	0,47	0,53	0,53	0,44	0,48	0,54	0,35	0,45	0,50	0,29	0,32	0,41	0,54	0,48	1,00	0,23	0,33	0,41	0,30	0,30	0,45	0,50
19	0,28	0,29	0,33	0,30	0,39	0,23	0,33	0,29	0,27	0,19	0,24	0,27	0,28	0,26	0,31	0,24	0,32	0,23	1,00	0,15	0,37	0,20	0,18	0,34	0,28
20	0,34	0,38	0,38	0,44	0,38	0,46	0,36	0,32	0,30	0,37	0,34	0,32	0,17	0,35	0,27	0,45	0,35	0,33	0,15	1,00	0,37	0,19	0,24	0,30	0,27
21	0,49	0,54	0,75	0,54	0,65	0,55	0,65	0,46	0,28	0,45	0,33	0,53	0,31	0,22	0,41	0,34	0,40	0,41	0,37	0,37	1,00	0,19	0,32	0,60	0,44
22	0,27	0,24	0,19	0,25	0,25	0,25	0,30	0,24	0,43	0,34	0,36	0,29	0,22	0,37	0,27	0,27	0,27	0,30	0,20	0,19	0,19	1,00	0,23	0,24	0,31
23	0,35	0,32	0,30	0,38	0,29	0,29	0,30	0,25	0,21	0,31	0,35	0,30	0,23	0,20	0,24	0,28	0,28	0,30	0,18	0,24	0,32	0,23	1,00	0,28	0,31
24	0,48	0,53	0,60	0,47	0,58	0,55	0,56	0,44	0,36	0,35	0,39	0,49	0,44	0,22	0,42	0,40	0,44	0,45	0,34	0,30	0,60	0,24	0,28	1,00	0,52
25	0,41	0,47	0,46	0,39	0,53	0,45	0,44	0,48	0,43	0,39	0,33	0,46	0,54	0,20	0,41	0,34	0,48	0,50	0,28	0,27	0,44	0,31	0,31	0,52	1,00
26	0,57	0,47	0,52	0,51	0,53	0,53	0,59	0,58	0,43	0,44	0,59	0,46	0,35	0,39	0,59	0,48	0,48	0,50	0,32	0,32	0,50	0,28	0,32	0,49	0,42
27	0,51	0,57	0,60	0,46	0,55	0,51	0,64	0,51	0,43	0,57	0,49	0,52	0,29	0,35	0,57	0,39	0,47	0,53	0,30	0,33	0,61	0,30	0,30	0,54	0,49
28	0,45	0,37	0,40	0,28	0,42	0,31	0,41	0,35	0,24	0,40	0,38	0,39	0,26	0,23	0,33	0,30	0,34	0,46	0,20	0,19	0,39	0,26	0,31	0,36	0,47
29	0,31	0,32	0,30	0,29	0,32	0,29	0,27	0,33	0,26	0,38	0,31	0,26	0,16	0,20	0,31	0,19	0,37	0,30	0,21	0,32	0,27	0,33	0,29	0,25	0,40
30	0,36	0,43	0,36	0,34	0,37	0,37	0,40	0,42	0,28	0,42	0,36	0,28	0,26	0,19	0,40	0,33	0,33	0,39	0,15	0,33	0,38	0,34	0,30	0,44	0,44
31	0,28	0,35	0,30	0,33	0,36	0,32	0,27	0,33	0,26	0,38	0,31	0,30	0,16	0,30	0,40	0,28	0,37	0,34	0,14	0,37	0,27	0,33	0,24	0,25	0,31
32	0,39	0,42	0,32	0,37	0,44	0,44	0,39	0,37	0,41	0,29	0,34	0,32	0,26	0,23	0,34	0,42	0,42	0,50	0,23	0,23	0,29	0,38	0,27	0,41	0,44
33	0,53	0,43	0,36	0,47	0,49	0,49	0,44	0,43	0,37	0,35	0,45	0,46	0,38	0,32	0,41	0,43	0,43	0,56	0,26	0,38	0,41	0,35	0,34	0,53	0,41
34	0,38	0,41	0,47	0,36	0,54	0,50	0,45	0,50	0,44	0,37	0,38	0,36	0,35	0,25	0,47	0,40	0,50	0,42	0,36	0,31	0,42	0,32	0,32	0,50	0,52
35	0,40	0,43	0,42	0,42	0,44	0,41	0,37	0,54	0,48	0,35	0,41	0,28	0,38	0,32	0,45	0,48	0,43	0,40	0,26	0,42	0,38	0,25	0,18	0,49	0,36
36	0,37	0,40	0,34	0,43	0,38	0,41	0,35	0,44	0,43	0,36	0,45	0,35	0,26	0,29	0,41	0,48	0,34	0,41	0,28	0,34	0,36	0,31	0,27	0,49	0,41
37	0,31	0,38	0,41	0,45	0,39	0,35	0,33	0,26	0,25	0,33	0,30	0,40	0,19	0,29	0,23	0,31	0,31	0,33	0,17	0,35	0,40	0,14	0,37	0,37	0,26
38	0,38	0,41	0,28	0,40	0,34	0,38	0,35	0,31	0,33	0,32	0,38	0,28	0,25	0,27	0,38	0,52	0,35	0,42	0,23	0,26	0,25	0,36	0,31	0,36	0,38
39	0,25	0,32	0,28	0,30	0,23	0,26	0,28	0,34	0,22	0,35	0,37	0,24	0,16	0,21	0,41	0,29	0,33	0,31	0,22	0,25	0,27	0,24	0,21	0,29	0,24
40	0,50	0,52	0,78	0,49	0,63	0,56	0,61	0,47	0,33	0,49	0,42	0,57	0,40	0,24	0,42	0,37	0,43	0,41	0,35	0,34	0,74	0,26	0,35	0,65	0,51
41	0,22	0,17	0,28	0,19	0,30	0,20	0,17	0,26	0,18	0,12	0,14	0,27	0,33	0,16	0,24	0,16	0,24	0,23	0,39	0,18	0,30	0,19	0,17	0,35	0,32
42	0,58	0,60	0,59	0,44	0,54	0,51	0,59	0,48	0,31	0,50	0,49	0,46	0,27	0,25	0,46	0,32	0,41	0,39	0,30	0,32	0,60	0,24	0,38	0,48	0,46
43	0,47	0,55	0,64	0,46	0,53	0,53	0,57	0,41	0,24	0,49	0,39	0,51	0,29	0,23	0,42	0,29	0,35	0,33	0,25	0,32	0,67	0,27	0,30	0,53	0,42
44	0,28	0,22	0,27	0,30	0,26	0,19	0,24	0,35	0,32	0,27	0,23	0,23	0,19	0,39	0,32	0,33	0,39	0,31	0,21	0,29	0,22	0,23	0,19	0,19	0,28
45	0,55	0,38	0,40	0,29	0,42	0,38	0,49	0,45	0,39	0,33	0,42	0,36	0,35	0,21	0,38	0,40	0,45	0,42	0,36	0,24	0,42	0,37	0,24	0,46	0,47
46	0,40	0,40	0,45	0,39	0,51	0,48	0,47	0,43	0,34	0,40	0,45	0,45	0,25	0,23	0,31	0,39	0,32	0,44	0,23	0,26	0,49	0,45	0,20	0,45	0,45
47	0,45	0,55	0,52	0,47	0,45	0,49	0,54	0,53	0,36	0,48	0,39	0,43	0,27	0,29	0,50	0,33	0,41	0,38	0,22	0,40	0,56	0,31	0,28	0,46	0,43

TABLE 4a

DEGREE OF SAMENESS

TABLE 4 b

	26	27	28	29	30	31	32	33	34	35	36	37	38	39	40	41	42	43	44	45	46	47
1	0,57	0,51	0,45	0,31	0,36	0,28	0,39	0,53	0,38	0,40	0,37	0,31	0,38	0,25	0,50	0,22	0,58	0,47	0,28	0,55	0,40	0,45
2	0,47	0,57	0,37	0,32	0,43	0,35	0,42	0,43	0,41	0,43	0,40	0,38	0,41	0,32	0,52	0,17	0,60	0,55	0,22	0,38	0,40	0,55
3	0,52	0,60	0,40	0,30	0,36	0,30	0,32	0,36	0,47	0,42	0,34	0,41	0,28	0,28	0,78	0,28	0,59	0,64	0,22	0,40	0,45	0,52
4	0,51	0,46	0,28	0,29	0,34	0,33	0,37	0,47	0,36	0,42	0,43	0,45	0,40	0,30	0,49	0,19	0,44	0,46	0,30	0,29	0,39	0,47
5	0,53	0,55	0,42	0,32	0,37	0,36	0,44	0,49	0,54	0,44	0,38	0,39	0,54	0,23	0,63	0,30	0,54	0,53	0,26	0,42	0,51	0,45
6	0,53	0,51	0,31	0,29	0,37	0,32	0,44	0,49	0,50	0,41	0,41	0,35	0,58	0,26	0,56	0,20	0,51	0,53	0,19	0,38	0,48	0,49
7	0,59	0,64	0,41	0,27	0,40	0,27	0,39	0,44	0,45	0,37	0,35	0,33	0,35	0,28	0,61	0,17	0,59	0,57	0,24	0,49	0,47	0,54
8	0,58	0,51	0,35	0,33	0,42	0,33	0,37	0,43	0,50	0,54	0,44	0,28	0,31	0,34	0,47	0,26	0,48	0,41	0,35	0,45	0,43	0,53
9	0,43	0,43	0,24	0,26	0,28	0,26	0,41	0,37	0,44	0,48	0,43	0,25	0,33	0,22	0,33	0,18	0,31	0,24	0,32	0,39	0,34	0,36
10	0,44	0,57	0,40	0,38	0,42	0,38	0,29	0,35	0,37	0,35	0,36	0,33	0,32	0,35	0,49	0,12	0,50	0,49	0,27	0,33	0,40	0,48
11	0,59	0,49	0,38	0,31	0,36	0,31	0,34	0,45	0,38	0,41	0,45	0,30	0,38	0,37	0,42	0,14	0,49	0,39	0,23	0,42	0,45	0,39
12	0,46	0,52	0,39	0,26	0,28	0,30	0,32	0,46	0,36	0,28	0,35	0,40	0,28	0,24	0,57	0,27	0,46	0,51	0,23	0,36	0,45	0,43
13	0,35	0,29	0,26	0,16	0,26	0,16	0,26	0,38	0,35	0,38	0,26	0,19	0,25	0,16	0,40	0,33	0,27	0,29	0,19	0,35	0,25	0,27
14	0,39	0,35	0,23	0,20	0,19	0,30	0,23	0,32	0,25	0,32	0,29	0,29	0,27	0,21	0,24	0,16	0,25	0,23	0,39	0,21	0,23	0,29
15	0,59	0,57	0,33	0,31	0,40	0,40	0,34	0,41	0,47	0,45	0,41	0,23	0,38	0,41	0,42	0,24	0,46	0,42	0,32	0,38	0,31	0,50
16	0,48	0,39	0,30	0,19	0,33	0,28	0,42	0,43	0,40	0,48	0,48	0,31	0,52	0,29	0,37	0,16	0,32	0,29	0,33	0,40	0,39	0,33
17	0,48	0,47	0,34	0,37	0,33	0,37	0,42	0,43	0,50	0,43	0,34	0,31	0,35	0,33	0,43	0,24	0,41	0,35	0,39	0,45	0,32	0,41
18	0,50	0,53	0,46	0,30	0,39	0,34	0,50	0,56	0,42	0,40	0,41	0,33	0,42	0,31	0,41	0,23	0,39	0,33	0,31	0,42	0,44	0,38
19	0,32	0,30	0,20	0,21	0,15	0,14	0,23	0,26	0,36	0,26	0,28	0,17	0,23	0,22	0,35	0,39	0,30	0,25	0,21	0,36	0,23	0,22
20	0,32	0,33	0,19	0,32	0,33	0,37	0,23	0,38	0,31	0,42	0,34	0,35	0,26	0,25	0,34	0,18	0,32	0,32	0,29	0,24	0,26	0,40
21	0,50	0,61	0,39	0,27	0,38	0,27	0,29	0,41	0,42	0,38	0,36	0,40	0,25	0,27	0,74	0,30	0,60	0,67	0,22	0,42	0,49	0,56
22	0,28	0,30	0,26	0,33	0,34	0,33	0,38	0,35	0,32	0,25	0,31	0,14	0,36	0,24	0,26	0,19	0,24	0,27	0,23	0,37	0,45	0,31
23	0,32	0,30	0,31	0,29	0,30	0,24	0,27	0,34	0,32	0,18	0,27	0,37	0,31	0,21	0,35	0,17	0,33	0,30	0,19	0,24	0,29	0,28
24	0,49	0,54	0,36	0,25	0,44	0,25	0,41	0,53	0,50	0,49	0,49	0,37	0,36	0,29	0,65	0,35	0,48	0,53	0,19	0,46	0,45	0,46
25	0,42	0,49	0,47	0,40	0,44	0,31	0,44	0,41	0,52	0,36	0,41	0,26	0,38	0,24	0,51	0,32	0,46	0,42	0,28	0,47	0,45	0,43
26	1,00	0,56	0,42	0,36	0,44	0,32	0,40	0,41	0,43	0,41	0,46	0,35	0,59	0,38	0,54	0,19	0,59	0,48	0,38	0,52	0,45	0,58
27	0,56	1,00	0,38	0,33	0,44	0,41	0,36	0,49	0,46	0,45	0,38	0,39	0,39	0,42	0,66	0,21	0,60	0,53	0,27	0,43	0,48	0,52
28	0,42	0,38	1,00	0,31	0,36	0,31	0,46	0,37	0,34	0,24	0,22	0,30	0,33	0,23	0,42	0,19	0,40	0,40	0,27	0,43	0,38	0,32
29	0,36	0,33	0,31	1,00	0,43	0,44	0,32	0,34	0,32	0,30	0,35	0,23	0,31	0,35	0,35	0,13	0,42	0,35	0,35	0,32	0,29	0,34
30	0,44	0,44	0,36	0,43	1,00	0,39	0,43	0,35	0,33	0,39	0,44	0,33	0,52	0,40	0,41	0,27	0,45	0,38	0,36	0,41	0,44	0,45
31	0,32	0,41	0,31	0,44	0,39	1,00	0,27	0,34	0,37	0,34	0,31	0,32	0,48	0,46	0,29	0,17	0,39	0,38	0,24	0,24	0,36	0,42
32	0,40	0,36	0,46	0,32	0,43	0,27	1,00	0,44	0,46	0,33	0,30	0,21	0,48	0,23	0,34	0,19	0,32	0,27	0,27	0,46	0,39	0,33
33	0,41	0,49	0,37	0,34	0,35	0,34	0,44	1,00	0,42	0,45	0,36	0,33	0,48	0,31	0,41	0,31	0,39	0,36	0,26	0,47	0,37	0,38
34	0,43	0,46	0,34	0,32	0,33	0,37	0,46	0,42	1,00	0,47	0,42	0,24	0,59	0,33	0,49	0,29	0,40	0,40	0,20	0,48	0,42	0,40
35	0,41	0,45	0,24	0,30	0,39	0,34	0,33	0,45	0,47	1,00	0,45	0,29	0,42	0,36	0,41	0,27	0,39	0,33	0,26	0,42	0,33	0,42
36	0,46	0,38	0,22	0,35	0,44	0,31	0,30	0,36	0,42	0,45	1,00	0,23	0,33	0,37	0,36	0,24	0,37	0,39	0,28	0,31	0,34	0,46
37	0,35	0,39	0,30	0,23	0,33	0,32	0,21	0,33	0,24	0,29	0,23	1,00	0,25	0,33	0,40	0,13	0,38	0,35	0,23	0,24	0,28	0,27
38	0,39	0,39	0,33	0,31	0,32	0,48	0,48	0,48	0,39	0,42	0,33	0,25	1,00	0,43	0,30	0,18	0,34	0,31	0,21	0,39	0,42	0,32
39	0,38	0,42	0,23	0,35	0,40	0,46	0,23	0,31	0,33	0,36	0,37	0,33	0,43	1,00	0,30	0,17	0,33	0,33	0,25	0,25	0,30	0,35
40	0,54	0,66	0,42	0,35	0,41	0,29	0,34	0,41	0,49	0,41	0,36	0,40	0,30	0,30	1,00	0,30	0,61	0,65	0,21	0,46	0,50	0,48
41	0,19	0,21	0,19	0,13	0,27	0,17	0,19	0,31	0,29	0,27	0,24	0,13	0,18	0,17	0,30	1,00	0,20	0,21	0,15	0,25	0,26	0,19
42	0,59	0,60	0,40	0,42	0,45	0,39	0,32	0,39	0,40	0,39	0,37	0,38	0,34	0,33	0,61	0,20	1,00	0,73	0,24	0,40	0,54	0,55
43	0,48	0,53	0,40	0,35	0,38	0,38	0,27	0,36	0,40	0,33	0,39	0,35	0,31	0,33	0,65	0,21	0,73	1,00	0,20	0,35	0,53	0,57
44	0,38	0,27	0,27	0,35	0,36	0,24	0,27	0,26	0,20	0,26	0,28	0,23	0,21	0,25	0,21	0,15	0,24	0,20	1,00	0,33	0,16	0,28
45	0,52	0,43	0,43	0,32	0,41	0,24	0,46	0,47	0,48	0,42	0,31	0,24	0,39	0,25	0,46	0,25	0,40	0,35	0,33	1,00	0,42	0,33
46	0,45	0,48	0,38	0,29	0,44	0,36	0,39	0,37	0,42	0,33	0,34	0,28	0,42	0,30	0,50	0,26	0,54	0,53	0,16	0,42	1,00	0,45
47	0,58	0,52	0,32	0,34	0,45	0,42	0,33	0,38	0,40	0,42	0,46	0,27	0,32	0,35	0,48	0,19	0,55	0,57	0,28	0,33	0,45	1,00

TABLE 4b

ROTATED FACTOR MATRIX **R-MODE ANALYSIS** TABLE 5

VARIABLE	FACTOR 1	2	3	4	5	6	7	8	9	10
1	-0.10837	0.08250	-0.74740	0.04722	-0.18346	0.09781	0.04145	0.13008	0.05514	0.15750
2	-0.18797	0.19217	0.03107	0.44791	-0.19828	-0.09536	0.01973	0.17936	-0.15480	0.28862
3	-0.28331	0.44646	0.38751	0.13369	0.04465	-0.27948	-0.02098	0.07260	C.25021	-0.26257
4	-0.07494	0.15518	-0.01183	0.75692	0.00519	-0.05242	0.15712	0.08003	-0.10090	-0.10482
5	-0.14143	0.41079	0.19617	-0.18956	-0.11705	-0.05427	-0.00682	0.04708	0.08958	0.05933
6	-0.13586	-0.01355	-0.05751	-0.08927	0.65523	-0.06331	0.10282	-0.19489	0.25950	-0.01698
7	-0.10757	0.05855	0.24430	-0.06258	-0.00453	-0.09773	0.09573	0.55268	-0.14287	-0.29864
8	-0.22798	0.01009	-0.45510	-0.25852	0.03376	0.44832	0.03040	-0.21806	0.27345	-0.14201
9	-0.02201	0.04868	-0.72846	-0.26099	0.13196	-0.28992	0.11199	-0.10130	-0.01701	-0.13076
10	-0.11030	-0.12255	0.14500	-C.04323	-0.16449	0.00294	0.13777	0.28320	-0.08291	-0.11708
11	0.11733	0.10157	0.05714	-0.08672	-0.28962	-0.04638	0.18085	0.20739	0.46770	0.09289
12	0.55769	0.03816	0.06492	-0.01379	0.25334	-0.25507	-0.04928	0.22490	-0.06416	-0.59119
13	-0.14714	-0.45931	0.C8921	-C.22535	-0.08495	0.02183	0.06306	0.31109	-0.17209	0.09152
14	-0.24539	-0.68702	0.01473	0.25681	0.02292	-0.02260	0.15766	-0.28360	-0.03779	0.01049
15	0.58879	0.02811	0.20486	-0.10487	-0.40569	0.23642	-0.13832	0.00764	0.34165	-0.21263
16	0.91023	-0.02212	-0.13026	-0.01832	-0.00691	-0.01169	0.02434	0.07777	-0.03293	-0.00429
17	-0.17794	0.19548	0.03656	0.08378	0.40439	-0.13557	-0.16873	-0.23016	0.63477	-0.13643
18	-0.06542	-0.11741	-0.11481	C.14791	0.13306	0.18289	0.54641	0.15250	C.29651	-0.05875
19	0.04770	0.25460	0.18021	-0.02988	-0.02342	-0.08882	-0.07366	-0.27731	-0.16294	0.00506
20	-0.10849	-0.46378	0.36162	-0.01592	0.30875	-0.16757	-0.12729	0.21807	0.12400	-0.20859
21	0.28486	-0.54946	0.13861	C.0C582	-0.19857	-0.20743	0.00338	0.02410	-0.07429	0.00012
22	-0.26912	-0.33455	0.00214	0.08769	-0.03690	-0.17842	0.16098	-0.21173	-0.33017	0.06451
23	0.49096	0.04758	0.03554	0.00531	-0.16092	0.24962	-0.12399	-0.09201	-0.00407	-0.18196
24	-0.11494	0.02707	-0.25589	-0.20487	-0.19985	-0.27808	-0.15441	-0.28714	0.15112	0.12449
25	0.11364	0.06223	0.02665	0.04941	0.00390	-0.11588	0.83621	-0.00273	-0.06876	-0.07601
26	0.01388	0.10338	0.17126	0.02507	-0.00568	-0.00798	-0.12643	-0.55890	-0.13773	-0.11107
27	0.61563	-0.04038	0.04373	C.16450	0.35242	0.13116	-0.08539	-0.05395	-0.12031	0.27745
28	0.39983	-0.C9903	-0.64455	-0.12424	0.26466	0.03267	-0.18189	-0.05199	-0.06010	0.14777
29	-0.01498	0.16925	0.45070	-0.1C299	-0.29279	0.41532	0.01681	-0.36501	-0.08079	-0.10295
30	0.11444	0.02618	0.01282	0.10598	0.03006	-0.10094	0.81861	-0.02096	-0.06133	-0.07487
31	-0.C5717	0.02383	-0.15470	0.74834	0.03620	-0.02731	0.05069	-0.04407	-0.08434	-0.18551
32	-0.22394	-0.31872	0.10935	C.68343	-0.01463	-0.18752	-0.00196	-0.04674	-0.08903	0.12444
33	0.62086	0.19998	0.08231	0.01164	0.31476	0.01937	0.00097	0.01368	-0.08083	0.32650
34	0.36426	-0.54879	0.23743	-0.06824	0.20018	0.14874	-0.01685	-0.16700	-0.18173	0.22306
35	0.92809	-0.00507	-0.05689	C.02483	0.02520	-0.02138	0.02714	0.03553	-0.02459	0.05164
36	0.21918	-0.26478	0.20023	0.01798	0.49020	0.09267	-0.10005	0.05310	-0.07187	0.47791
37	0.00911	-0.13459	-0.31603	-0.09924	-0.07379	-0.20477	-0.07717	0.01872	-0.05572	0.06789
38	-0.04263	-0.12504	0.12424	0.01590	0.01825	0.05811	-0.09692	-0.48235	-0.08155	-0.14991
39	0.71502	0.05033	0.12449	-0.09830	0.05476	-0.12975	0.16665	-0.26573	-0.14066	0.16363
40	0.24645	0.06766	0.13187	-0.C1350	0.23412	0.68010	-0.13289	-0.01480	-0.05112	0.25395
41	-0.C5546	0.12917	0.26851	-0.18458	-0.04969	-0.09104	0.07274	-0.39334	0.56218	0.02572
42	-0.C3989	-0.03677	-0.13784	-0.09895	0.08333	-0.01293	0.21819	-0.50280	0.09959	-0.05198
43	-0.09261	-0.02014	-0.C8160	-C.15940	0.05409	-0.02363	-0.02366	0.00126	0.69684	-0.01410
44	-0.13450	0.06696	-0.31007	0.45145	0.03343	0.42589	0.29916	-0.25040	0.00625	-0.25647
45	-0.07173	0.05406	0.01017	-0.11574	-0.14077	0.05464	0.16532	-0.32483	0.07298	0.10083
46	-0.07209	0.01001	-0.20418	-0.39274	-0.03983	-0.02658	-0.04651	-0.07897	0.13888	-0.02653
47	-0.12747	-0.52281	0.04011	-0.02392	-0.05778	-0.07787	0.01238	0.06935	0.27136	0.01291
48	-0.13445	0.22073	0.10784	C.15516	-0.35972	-0.02672	-0.12593	0.52185	-0.03165	0.25078
49	-0.18188	-0.01429	-0.13971	-0.51117	0.22184	0.32640	0.06025	-0.00109	-0.23884	-0.24264
50	-0.13989	0.20854	0.08474	-0.25593	-0.01660	-0.31270	0.17596	-0.33716	-0.03328	0.10742
51	0.09526	-0.63236	0.12220	-C.17744	-0.33526	0.10289	-0.03369	-0.03157	-0.27544	-0.12241
52	-0.05622	-0.15525	-0.02156	0.04035	0.11318	0.09248	0.00780	0.01447	0.88876	-0.00315
53	-0.C5071	0.27471	0.26781	-0.12779	0.38660	-0.23892	-0.22886	0.23317	0.17075	-0.36405
54	-0.01341	0.02543	0.12566	-C.01608	-0.24275	0.70594	-0.19601	-0.19191	-0.04307	-0.14556
55	-0.C5831	C.C2069	-0.40463	-0.04191	0.01287	-0.00809	-0.02220	-0.07388	-0.11266	-0.04027
56	-0.10474	-0.12925	-0.15894	-C.10139	0.10569	-0.19810	-0.17682	-0.17389	-0.26008	0.43080
57	0.05922	-0.32064	0.45984	-0.C9470	0.21016	0.04915	0.31910	-0.15920	0.02730	0.31066
58	-0.19912	0.02341	-0.02242	-0.26058	0.05293	0.64786	0.14086	0.22838	-0.12749	0.10560
59	-0.14894	-0.55932	0.30468	-C.16225	0.19024	0.01678	-0.18916	0.02210	-0.27557	-0.35443
60	0.04883	0.02426	0.18701	-0.07194	-0.03046	0.03629	0.72102	-0.00073	-0.04904	-0.01349
61	0.04041	-0.04346	0.12591	-0.05223	-0.01120	-0.11923	-0.09701	-0.03376	0.81473	0.02519
62	-0.C9990	-0.24560	0.57791	-0.17134	-0.18780	-0.09448	0.18743	-0.05366	-0.03314	0.11254
63	0.C2322	-0.11110	-0.C2388	-0.12722	0.48165	0.24739	0.20309	0.06969	0.05265	0.21498
64	0.77870	-0.09122	-0.C3821	-0.02847	-0.30660	-0.21019	0.19015	0.07880	0.08567	-0.24574
65	0.56351	-0.00032	-0.10123	-0.10405	0.39070	0.15637	-0.03692	0.03092	-0.10878	0.47359
66	0.C4781	0.11361	-0.00456	-0.01252	-0.05409	-0.12344	-0.23142	0.07730	0.05052	0.68005
67	-0.22062	0.17030	-0.25385	-C.54946	0.09294	-0.21183	0.27401	0.03223	-0.23638	-0.15186
68	0.00352	0.12678	0.22051	0.02859	0.26923	0.20288	0.06863	0.39521	-0.02230	0.47526
69	0.C9966	0.25433	0.C0423	-0.16220	0.68561	-0.01487	-0.08856	0.10172	-0.09750	-0.10308
70	-0.04443	0.41246	0.29330	-C.00548	-0.05808	-0.00035	0.06074	-0.09502	-0.16521	0.01358

TABLE 5

FACTOR SCORES **R-MODE ANALYSIS** TABLE 6

CASE										
1	-0.43939	-0.08561	-0.07713	C.21586	0.97085	0.61995	0.72662	-0.25817	1.07290	0.02777
2	-0.39260	0.25769	-0.05043	-0.39630	-0.44096	0.10556	-0.10363	-0.93692	0.56473	0.24151
3	-0.02778	-0.18228	-0.30578	-0.29635	-0.17804	0.20025	-0.20486	-0.21301	0.10166	-0.29644
4	-0.33849	0.97086	-0.75838	-0.72523	-0.07985	-0.52519	-0.12178	-0.84661	0.45537	0.15937
5	0.04433	-0.37827	-0.88914	-C.81117	0.33329	-0.43486	0.26205	-0.78260	-0.19240	C.54022
6	-0.47450	0.40031	-0.77611	-0.87302	-0.72876	-0.27939	-0.12267	-1.82770	0.59353	0.37687
7	-0.31075	-0.01136	-0.40821	-0.CC984	-0.08687	0.14701	0.03587	-0.62671	0.05095	-0.10013
8	-0.71933	-0.93746	-0.51684	-0.53757	0.91165	0.28116	0.28595	0.64795	0.17240	0.04323
9	-0.53076	0.04695	-2.99243	-0.35847	0.19198	-0.11719	-0.23381	-0.58854	-0.30715	0.01381
10	-0.57926	-0.61513	-1.09987	0.00581	0.41261	0.62086	0.11582	-0.25711	1.31813	-0.29546
11	-1.04819	-0.63401	-0.84179	0.51307	1.04720	1.88307	1.24589	0.74224	2.05977	-0.16764
12	-0.18925	0.08337	0.55565	0.20410	0.14066	0.22310	-0.62009	-3.01348	-0.09972	-0.69053
13	0.47623	-0.28353	0.82443	0.30676	-0.75055	4.16394	-0.76089	-0.26181	-0.64976	-1.12889
14	-0.15933	1.23838	-0.61757	0.33973	0.70572	0.26631	-0.42696	-0.47979	0.67064	-0.73620
15	-0.10038	0.02146	-1.29272	-1.37491	-0.24698	0.54346	-0.11488	0.61449	-0.69386	-0.40557
16	-0.66504	0.94447	-0.62534	-1.75899	0.62616	-1.04541	-0.11038	0.02641	0.32706	-0.31868
17	0.23832	-0.55907	-1.43172	[illegible]	[illegible]	[illegible]	[illegible]	[illegible]	[illegible]	[illegible]
18	-0.25859	-0.82040	-2.23243	-0.75484	-0.39890	-1.45391	-0.73971	-0.06319	-0.44515	0.55037
19	2.87789	0.39833	0.27884	-0.25581	3.69159	1.60363	-0.38828	0.20006	-0.38105	3.93328
20	0.40733	0.89018	0.67370	-0.90268	0.06925	-0.67470	-1.05152	-0.11836	5.09521	-0.31469
21	0.39633	0.30137	-0.45054	-0.87529	0.37253	-0.16172	0.46948	-0.47450	-0.24856	0.25327
22	-0.21405	0.40942	-1.00659	4.82205	0.31736	0.14597	0.07895	-0.56093	-0.35104	-0.59613
23	-0.13688	-0.11404	0.62164	0.41157	-0.91704	0.27521	-0.18893	1.21547	-0.20751	-0.54993
24	0.32874	1.64932	1.11916	-0.26252	-0.17822	-0.55032	-0.67567	-1.80823	-1.03042	0.19082
25	C.01739	-1.22363	0.57816	0.23994	-0.10361	-0.47973	-0.21813	-0.40029	-0.65814	-0.16458
26	-1.01032	-0.78913	-0.00463	-1.27511	0.88532	0.68075	0.58580	0.97282	-1.09517	-0.07753
27	-0.19069	0.29809	-0.31516	-0.01750	0.24933	-0.14216	-0.14011	-0.16731	-0.12104	-0.15323
28	-1.04463	-4.35501	2.35452	0.27292	0.39911	-0.55274	0.24434	0.65722	-0.94902	0.57349
29	-C.34677	-0.23957	1.00750	1.44933	-0.07822	-0.12869	-0.39777	1.66225	0.30622	0.30860
30	0.03612	-0.18794	0.86752	0.28598	-0.70155	-0.29308	-0.45692	1.85835	-0.84642	-1.71225
31	-C.20634	0.91846	0.13616	C.85005	-1.20379	-0.12317	-0.46412	1.22451	0.12785	0.45789
32	-0.36227	-0.63527	0.26176	0.80217	-0.33886	-1.04507	-1.32081	-0.76409	-0.51536	1.29484
33	0.43483	0.89766	0.26671	0.13347	0.15342	-0.41064	-0.36067	-0.30394	-0.35180	0.01384
34	-0.30642	-0.31318	-0.34036	0.55268	-0.34595	0.37397	-0.77809	0.28692	0.09325	0.19152
35	0.59272	0.63635	-0.63965	-0.16025	-1.86592	0.11418	-0.30315	1.47810	0.80821	0.58690
36	0.00738	2.35387	1.23259	-0.06873	-0.58603	-0.13499	-0.63205	0.23953	-0.49084	-0.33630
37	0.22587	0.99447	2.31984	-1.10353	-1.07381	-0.24591	0.15588	-1.12591	0.62851	0.10577
38	-0.65305	0.38459	0.19394	C.91481	-1.12393	-0.85092	-0.22489	0.01142	-1.10822	1.28176
39	-0.55154	0.64835	1.64956	0.08711	-1.23525	0.04691	-0.31293	1.84609	-0.28866	1.35058
40	-0.73705	-1.85580	1.20555	-0.48592	0.45281	0.11692	0.41527	-0.31020	-0.71316	-0.26695
41	5.72432	-0.33302	-0.48421	0.26312	-1.49691	-0.37907	-0.60362	C.40075	-0.35700	-1.33661
42	-0.32272	-0.39136	0.43911	-0.53634	0.38194	-0.16070	4.23544	1.05998	-0.19738	-0.40463
43	-0.43678	0.22435	1.36924	0.02361	-0.82288	0.43348	2.53290	-0.91690	-0.42732	0.08644
44	-0.06709	0.71072	0.62442	-0.20240	3.30416	-1.40264	-1.18058	1.51516	0.00688	-3.02152
45	0.71523	-1.05532	0.26047	0.35583	0.99291	0.20934	-1.09972	0.36957	-0.78596	0.57518
46	0.16249	0.10938	-0.42343	1.43408	-0.27289	-0.60956	2.87848	-0.42145	-0.37567	-0.59295
47	0.08598	0.52003	-0.26019	0.29019	-0.45272	-0.49776	0.83591	-0.10453	-0.04527	-0.19154

TABLE 6

TABLE 7

ROTATED FACTOR MATRIX **Q - MODE TABLE 7**

VARIABLE	FACTOR 1	FACTOR 2	FACTOR 3
1	0.60050	0.24465	0.27250
2	0.64876	0.30960	0.19952
3	0.54932	0.48022	0.19231
4	0.79812	0.31058	0.00521
5	0.17735	0.68918	0.26484
6	0.48790	0.47123	0.19642
7	0.48903	0.48890	0.25854
8	0.19789	0.49010	0.40867
9	0.24768	0.75209	0.05100
10	0.35588	0.61501	0.15935
11	0.43798	0.42092	0.20607
12	0.22447	0.47463	0.36475
13	-0.03413	0.24691	0.51534
14	0.86301	0.21384	-0.10483
15	0.39718	0.54485	0.06411
16	0.38766	0.33752	0.30069
17	0.22060	0.75125	-0.05589
18	0.22571	0.73826	0.13011
19	-0.06502	0.71893	-0.02157
20	0.86785	-0.01642	-0.00611
21	0.36845	0.63080	0.20829
22	0.63433	0.27293	0.05685
23	0.27937	-0.18498	0.25516
24	0.63282	0.18714	0.27024
25	0.22669	0.31145	0.56676
26	0.04603	0.32051	0.64368
27	0.65135	0.33920	0.21145
28	-0.12340	-0.12444	0.92013
29	0.75969	-0.03207	-0.04794
30	0.39963	-0.19246	0.45099
31	0.91968	-0.05984	-0.10453
32	0.28847	0.01716	0.45275
33	0.61233	0.01535	0.33478
34	0.78045	0.26662	-0.00376
35	0.84518	0.23228	-0.18804
36	0.87689	-0.05446	-0.05404
37	0.80647	-0.27515	0.18069
38	0.57414	-0.02929	0.31197
39	0.82390	-0.26195	-0.01715
40	-0.07103	0.10077	0.93347
41	-0.12391	0.61289	-0.10049
42	0.31228	0.24432	0.57478
43	0.53567	0.00445	0.49690
44	0.64720	0.04382	0.28340
45	-0.13232	0.59774	0.17611
46	0.61919	0.11898	0.31154
47	0.73575	0.21184	0.10319

TABLE 8

FACTOR SCORES **Q-MODE TABLE 8**

CASE			
1	2.16965	2.56691	-0.06059
2	-0.00026	-0.84854	-0.54719
3	5.81052	-0.89175	2.81766
4	-0.27683	-0.50400	-0.64186
5	0.32743	-0.53854	-0.49786
6	3.12296	2.37479	4.22800
7	0.12537	-0.87016	0.10511
8	0.36958	1.51240	0.05757
9	2.44027	4.07637	1.55271
10	0.07762	-0.86008	1.66629
11	-0.21058	-0.50267	-0.67884
12	-0.35573	-0.48799	-0.60142
13	-0.29440	-0.17518	0.29835
14	-0.06945	0.12524	1.55020
15	-0.38412	-0.43332	-0.57692
16	-0.49025	-0.22818	-0.76075
17	1.70847	0.50439	-0.02553
18	-0.33728	-0.53698	-0.49674
19	-0.42522	-0.41304	-0.64448
20	-0.34913	-0.45587	0.12724
21	-0.38464	-0.36707	-0.20680
22	-0.03565	-0.50982	1.56057
23	-0.41633	-0.24415	-0.43232
24	-0.10477	0.01973	-0.31781
25	-0.37969	-0.47172	-0.55342
26	-0.46736	-0.38609	-0.60317
27	-0.67817	1.01180	-0.44324
28	1.05929	4.66025	0.43677
29	-0.31518	-0.48411	-0.27070
30	-0.47372	-0.45020	-0.47540
31	-0.30775	-0.38403	-0.51981
32	-0.19763	-0.59857	0.15037
33	-0.44602	-0.17764	-0.68340
34	-0.63236	0.16064	0.69163
35	-0.54211	0.23507	-0.84859
36	-0.57389	-0.16762	-0.46281
37	-0.43405	-0.35621	-0.69030
38	-0.47818	-0.40320	-0.57251
39	-0.40023	-0.07940	-0.39694
40	-0.45693	-0.31469	-0.57577
41	0.03883	-0.46456	-0.40698
42	-0.39432	0.04636	-0.44048
43	-0.47045	-0.32313	-0.60393
44	-0.21244	-0.17624	-0.25478
45	-0.40621	-0.35075	-0.59448
46	-0.36329	-0.09821	-0.46822
47	-0.23986	-0.33525	0.22089
48	1.18277	-1.06163	-1.21328
49	-0.21049	0.75229	1.36037
50	0.48289	-0.23478	0.66641
51	-0.12735	0.07625	2.41772
52	-0.45756	-0.37848	-0.64260
53	-0.31981	-0.48173	-0.59125
54	-0.52400	-0.33085	-0.47388
55	-0.43442	-0.36633	-0.68887
56	-0.32704	0.12430	0.12906
57	-0.40331	-0.35101	-0.05330
58	-0.16778	0.08093	0.65563
59	-0.45622	-0.03120	2.41492
60	-0.45757	-0.42777	-0.58246
61	-0.26979	-0.36317	-0.71661
62	-0.18303	-0.75712	0.11075
63	-0.36876	-0.24307	-0.29077
64	-0.23309	-0.02720	-0.24072
65	-0.68753	1.54305	-0.51495
66	0.15748	-0.26575	-0.53248
67	0.67412	0.74063	1.55740
68	-0.30119	-0.42478	-0.56810
69	-0.37954	-0.06552	-0.68328
70	-0.41356	-0.40253	-0.62894

CORRELATION MATRIX Q-MODE

TABLE 9a

	1	2	3	4	5	6	7	8	9	10
1	0.97848									
2	0.88564	0.99480								
3	0.84518	0.91784	0.99259							
4	0.86858	0.90271	0.91766	0.99194						
5	0.74120	0.71599	0.82768	0.77495	0.98593					
6	0.83489	0.85447	0.89278	0.90057	0.86803	0.98862				
7	0.89094	0.93078	0.95493	0.89741	0.84791	0.90599	0.99111			
8	0.76072	0.76056	0.80052	0.71918	[illegible]	[illegible]	[illegible]	0.93901		
9	0.64117	0.72751	0.84003	0.74900	[illegible]	[illegible]	[illegible]	0.74741	[illegible]	
10	0.79577	0.84604	0.86524	0.80799	[illegible]	[illegible]	0.70564	0.84058	[illegible]	[illegible]
11	0.85394	0.82831	0.81423	0.78829	0.73274	[illegible]	0.68164	0.81845	[illegible]	[illegible]
12	0.78518	0.82204	0.77023	0.71934	0.75622	0.74168	0.83542	0.81485	0.68180	[illegible]
13	0.46956	0.55618	0.49793	0.36120	0.43349	0.40505	0.51897	0.49578	0.28871	[illegible]
14	0.79119	0.88094	0.85206	0.90033	0.60309	0.75009	0.80762	0.59367	0.62238	0.71021
15	0.61761	0.73218	0.79905	0.74165	0.77375	0.71486	0.77092	0.64368	0.75462	0.72161
16	0.67373	0.73092	0.80304	0.78209	0.72170	0.77413	0.76250	[illegible]	[illegible]	[illegible]
17	0.45754	0.60857	0.75469	0.61607	0.72063	0.67388	0.72836	[illegible]	0.76230	[illegible]
18	0.67730	0.69965	0.82802	0.71509	0.84896	0.83105	0.85116	0.77308	[illegible]	[illegible]
19	0.39125	0.35358	0.40240	0.29514	0.49484	0.36552	0.44590	0.41987	[illegible]	[illegible]
20	0.80079	0.78596	0.72861	0.81477	0.45782	0.68573	0.69020	0.56932	0.42636	0.56776
21	0.81923	0.83622	0.92375	0.85100	0.89172	0.86038	0.90517	0.78230	0.83458	0.81976
22	0.74264	0.73858	0.74660	0.74673	0.58733	0.68368	0.79713	0.56233	0.57405	0.69128
23	0.30413	0.24549	0.28539	0.29984	0.23240	0.21070	0.28465	0.17002	0.13637	[illegible]
24	0.84504	0.83655	0.85299	0.86574	0.66555	0.81798	0.81557	0.66639	[illegible]	[illegible]
25	0.70767	0.73009	0.79858	0.67924	0.72395	0.75522	0.79437	0.71412	0.63403	[illegible]
26	0.63940	0.67980	0.72379	0.58728	0.66010	0.63483	0.73712	0.77293	[illegible]	[illegible]
27	0.92029	0.91811	0.94175	0.92373	0.79337	0.89285	0.93962	0.79787	0.73508	[illegible]
28	0.42688	0.43915	0.41356	0.28863	0.34911	0.37038	0.45506	0.43016	0.16020	[illegible]
29	0.55652	0.59562	0.54321	0.54775	0.40458	0.47508	0.54241	0.43272	0.29757	[illegible]
30	0.47306	0.47575	0.52120	0.50331	0.38904	0.44555	0.50001	0.39076	0.27501	[illegible]
31	0.62101	0.65536	0.60111	0.67655	0.44011	0.57537	0.63005	0.48223	0.38668	[illegible]
32	0.57938	0.60749	0.57118	0.52827	0.43586	0.55002	0.56119	0.44018	[illegible]	[illegible]
33	0.83178	0.73677	0.70732	0.77984	0.61001	0.73584	0.71354	0.61606	0.43571	[illegible]
34	0.81587	0.89193	0.83745	0.84851	0.65619	0.75079	0.85373	0.65132	[illegible]	[illegible]
35	0.61874	0.74350	0.76917	0.75729	0.57655	0.63634	0.71868	0.51010	[illegible]	[illegible]
36	0.64642	0.72422	0.65973	0.72603	0.37402	0.55628	0.63241	0.41197	0.39789	[illegible]
37	0.67755	0.67455	0.60917	0.72737	0.37804	0.56387	0.55341	0.41309	0.31071	0.38709
38	0.66794	0.53276	0.62611	0.67192	0.57024	0.63399	0.67557	0.47739	0.39740	[illegible]
39	0.47556	0.52417	0.46637	0.51290	0.21734	0.39278	0.44888	0.35337	0.21850	[illegible]
40	0.61359	0.63887	0.65528	0.53329	0.59350	0.61146	0.67246	0.63350	[illegible]	[illegible]
41	0.13101	0.14594	0.27648	0.14715	0.35537	0.20142	0.23993	0.19697	0.25773	[illegible]
42	0.79533	0.80237	0.84310	0.76686	0.77763	0.76590	0.86072	0.78576	[illegible]	[illegible]
43	0.80584	0.83571	0.76348	0.77093	0.57992	0.71715	0.81231	0.63811	[illegible]	[illegible]
44	0.82231	0.78212	0.78064	0.77572	0.53329	0.69838	0.74182	0.68184	0.49418	[illegible]
45	0.32615	0.32173	0.43722	0.28601	0.46585	0.35536	0.41289	0.30807	0.41133	0.35482
46	0.79875	0.77988	0.82252	0.83603	0.63174	0.79546	0.81748	0.65201	0.63530	0.68403
47	0.75199	0.80158	0.88554	0.87857	0.66504	0.80184	0.81966	0.60260	0.66887	0.65786

	11	12	13	14	15	16	17	18	19	20
11	0.98039									
12	0.78905	[illegible]								
13	0.43787	0.53394	0.91640							
14	0.70964	0.56747	0.41646	0.98840						
15	0.60960	0.60877	0.50836	0.63892	0.94299					
16	0.59945	0.57758	0.34657	0.67077	0.68822	0.96809				
17	0.52867	0.54607	0.30885	0.52207	0.75442	0.57261	0.94168			
18	0.72919	0.69341	0.32228	0.55327	0.70519	0.70443	0.82493	0.98241		
19	0.35899	0.38249	0.36266	0.23315	0.32522	0.22280	0.41123	0.52930	[illegible]	
20	0.65267	0.58936	0.27085	0.83219	0.42872	0.55401	0.29005	0.43668	[illegible]	[illegible]
21	0.74358	0.74125	0.50544	0.74064	0.80342	0.79788	0.76026	0.86655	[illegible]	[illegible]
22	0.68847	0.61971	0.34196	0.71284	0.54138	0.52739	0.50805	0.63745	[illegible]	[illegible]
23	0.30939	0.06875	0.18108	0.26626	0.20830	0.30293	0.18998	0.25242	[illegible]	[illegible]
24	0.66180	0.61255	0.41994	0.79375	0.60551	0.81753	0.49601	0.64453	[illegible]	[illegible]
25	0.60598	0.66589	0.47718	0.55227	0.61283	0.62282	0.56115	0.71983	[illegible]	[illegible]
26	0.63968	0.66968	0.57158	0.48206	0.64271	0.76211	0.45283	0.60381	[illegible]	[illegible]
27	0.81807	0.78044	0.49611	0.86195	0.73547	0.76856	0.62750	0.77055	[illegible]	[illegible]
28	0.33393	0.45793	0.42025	0.26490	0.26007	0.29742	0.25678	0.32135	[illegible]	[illegible]
29	0.47148	0.47134	0.27905	0.53134	0.48154	0.28575	0.34692	0.40432	[illegible]	[illegible]
30	0.38725	0.28696	0.35588	0.41675	0.43433	0.46265	0.33905	0.36125	[illegible]	[illegible]
31	0.53804	0.43393	0.27143	0.60187	0.49407	0.47062	0.36578	0.46553	[illegible]	[illegible]
32	0.47668	0.52596	0.29687	0.48926	0.28988	0.38311	0.33663	0.40046	[illegible]	[illegible]
33	0.60315	0.57056	0.44237	0.63689	0.53006	0.65949	0.29489	0.51960	[illegible]	[illegible]
34	0.77080	0.71346	0.50613	0.83034	0.68267	0.52424	0.59450	0.63558	[illegible]	[illegible]
35	0.54547	0.48288	0.40448	0.73085	0.70649	0.61499	0.62340	0.59077	[illegible]	[illegible]
36	0.48357	0.46424	0.33341	0.72615	0.60021	0.58717	0.36594	0.41343	[illegible]	[illegible]
37	0.46089	0.37961	0.24090	0.73192	0.38115	0.57809	0.15562	0.28365	[illegible]	[illegible]
38	0.54719	0.48457	0.34676	0.53345	0.48933	0.59684	0.36112	0.50809	[illegible]	[illegible]
39	0.39848	0.29361	0.19146	0.45874	0.38710	0.35193	0.32530	0.25742	[illegible]	[illegible]
40	0.53507	0.63872	0.50654	0.40485	0.52830	0.63311	0.36554	0.40590	[illegible]	[illegible]
41	0.11301	0.19064	0.22208	0.11032	0.26759	0.12735	0.41507	0.36527	[illegible]	[illegible]
42	0.75704	0.70754	0.52228	0.63098	0.69913	0.78215	0.54092	0.71084	[illegible]	[illegible]
43	0.68541	0.67689	0.47902	0.69093	0.57528	0.64720	0.42471	0.54846	[illegible]	[illegible]
44	0.65082	0.63589	0.41173	0.77908	0.48149	0.63635	0.33738	0.52789	[illegible]	[illegible]
45	0.26557	0.31816	0.34320	0.24621	0.36251	0.27273	0.40927	0.47940	[illegible]	[illegible]
46	0.70826	0.55987	0.29689	0.73511	0.54518	0.73593	0.47128	0.64161	[illegible]	[illegible]
47	0.60508	0.57978	0.31217	0.83518	0.68678	0.78494	0.61770	0.67941	[illegible]	[illegible]

TABLE 9a

CORRELATION MATRIX Q-MODE

TABLE 9b

	21	22	23	24	25	26	27	28	29	30
21	0.98991									
22	0.68565	0.92855								
23	0.28899	0.20813	0.94489							
24	0.83163	0.70510	0.29272	0.97922						
25	0.76478	0.69333	0.16811	0.75227	0.97973					
26	0.69676	0.47427	0.09498	0.65018	0.66873	0.97090				
27	0.89052	0.81056	0.23453	0.90090	0.79564	0.71941	0.99508			
28	0.36153	0.35226	0.22201	0.43048	0.66717	0.46449	0.46006	0.95096		
29	0.45565	0.56325	0.21661	0.45789	0.56680	0.30534	0.59529	0.33121	0.91657	
30	0.47455	0.39951	0.76916	0.50780	0.48441	0.36515	0.48796	0.42700	0.48948	0.96856
31	0.52055	0.63503	0.24173	0.60208	0.57589	0.40426	0.68253	0.29432	0.81348	0.50317
32	0.49656	0.50140	0.26226	0.60232	0.61333	0.38957	0.59132	0.50907	0.40183	0.39876
33	0.71530	0.63787	0.25741	0.85900	0.66845	0.57366	0.82874	0.44817	0.53943	0.50846
34	0.75400	0.77286	0.25848	0.72598	0.68584	0.50241	0.86560	0.41638	0.74414	0.46095
35	0.68858	0.62191	0.31475	0.66230	0.60113	0.48951	0.73135	0.21241	0.70972	0.50222
36	0.54732	0.59525	0.29418	0.70380	0.55194	0.44542	0.69218	0.29303	0.58025	0.46281
37	0.52715	0.49421	0.36299	0.78643	0.48207	0.40080	0.70446	0.35580	0.42620	0.51302
38	0.59618	0.66108	0.29998	0.66392	0.60977	0.58708	0.71799	0.41351	0.52873	0.46927
39	0.35977	0.44454	0.17919	0.52841	0.38986	0.38116	0.54079	0.29480	0.64264	0.45733
40	0.61556	0.46644	0.17680	0.62542	0.81276	0.78162	0.63576	0.74204	0.35986	0.48388
41	0.39235	0.20231	-0.01260	0.22181	0.29731	0.09472	0.21168	0.06735	0.05938	0.01996
42	0.81084	[illegible]	[illegible]	[illegible]	[illegible]	0.00073	[illegible]	0.50733	0.51115	0.71139
43	0.68574	0.73415	0.26503	0.80015	0.78028	0.65081	0.83313	0.65364	0.56862	0.52674
44	0.68724	0.69545	0.20654	0.84967	0.71972	0.60354	0.86131	0.44100	0.57212	0.49392
45	0.59840	0.41149	0.05142	0.41903	0.50790	0.30786	0.38493	0.27418	0.21423	0.15190
46	0.74835	0.78901	0.28418	0.89246	0.77459	0.62907	0.86801	0.48617	0.45503	0.50852
47	0.78767	0.75092	0.28688	0.85753	0.76828	0.58712	0.87522	0.40518	0.54303	0.51614

	31	32	33	34	35	36	37	38	39	40
31	0.97627									
32	0.33275	0.91916								
33	0.62098	0.52193	0.95255							
34	0.76410	0.57610	0.69307	0.98353						
35	0.79244	0.40265	0.57915	0.80143	0.96211					
36	0.65426	0.39946	0.62040	0.72652	0.73656	0.92184				
37	0.55396	0.44481	0.76069	0.59010	0.51114	0.64448	0.96165			
38	0.70564	0.55161	0.73801	0.66443	0.61090	0.54010	0.54714	0.95459		
39	0.80159	0.33532	0.50778	0.57136	0.59672	0.59784	0.55112	0.63189	0.92667	
40	0.35514	0.55117	0.58909	0.48931	0.37190	0.41334	0.43554	0.56984	0.31805	0.97408
41	0.03953	0.04805	0.11242	0.23432	0.21787	0.08875	-0.08174	0.04209	-0.05415	0.09385
42	0.58282	0.49335	0.71409	0.67669	0.65230	0.54450	0.57433	0.66467	0.44484	0.78934
43	0.68822	0.54368	0.75715	0.77951	0.60769	0.67367	0.69736	0.72845	0.57055	0.76682
44	0.60405	0.59741	0.78492	0.71293	0.56954	0.63963	0.72337	0.55442	0.52520	0.57170
45	0.13575	0.30726	0.29561	0.35754	0.27679	0.14278	0.09720	0.17300	0.03016	0.31884
46	0.66313	0.54845	0.77573	0.70706	0.62093	0.62534	0.71824	0.70341	0.53446	0.64440
47	0.64481	0.52162	0.71818	0.75870	0.79396	0.77841	0.67726	0.66713	0.49614	0.60046

	41	42	43	44	45	46	47
41	0.77334						
42	0.12040	0.98240					
43	0.09704	0.78481	0.97204				
44	0.09442	0.69337	0.74008	0.97226			
45	0.46029	0.31550	0.22506	0.31339	0.89204		
46	0.13551	0.75764	0.85820	0.79014	0.30962	0.97903	
47	0.19166	0.72733	0.77460	0.74438	0.32754	0.85688	0.98694

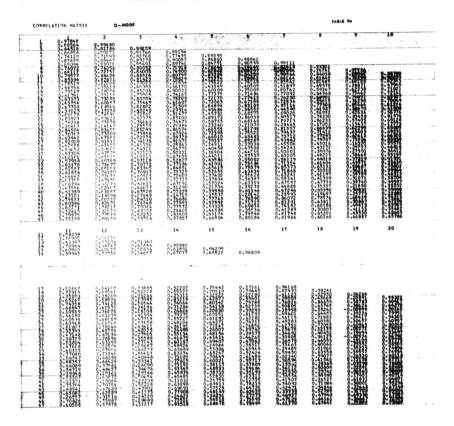

TABLE 9b

Fig. 1a-c

Register No. of Tomb.	2	3	9	6	11	7	14	5	8	4	1	10
Red Ware plain	×	×	×	×	×	×	×	×	×		×	×
relief ornament				×	×			×	×	×	×	×
incised ornament.				×	×	×	×	×		×	×	×
Painted White Ware							×	×	×		×	×
Base-ring Ware										×		×
Black Slip Ware											×	×
Painted White Slip Ware									?			×
Silver											×	×
Bronze								×				×
Porcelain								×				×
Gold, stone bead, figurine, &c.												×

a. MYRES 1897 SERIATION OF TOMB GROUPS (p. 135)

	R. p.	Bl. p.	Bl. sl.	Wh. p. I	Wh. p. II	Wh. p. III	Wh. p. IV	Wh. p. V	R. on bl.	Foreign (Syrian) ware
1st stratum	54	—	210	—	—	6	11	25	4	5
2nd stratum	103	—	172	—	—	30	82	176	5	88
3rd stratum	409	1	385	—	15	164	58	2	22	20
4th stratum	304	4	150	1(?)	26	142	4	—	—	8
5th stratum	180	—	16	1	2	3	—	—	—	—
6th stratum	142	1	3	1	—	—	—	—	—	—
7th stratum	108	—	—	—	—	—	—	—	—	—

b. GJERSTAD 1926 KALOPSIDHA STRATIGRAPHY (SPC p. 296)

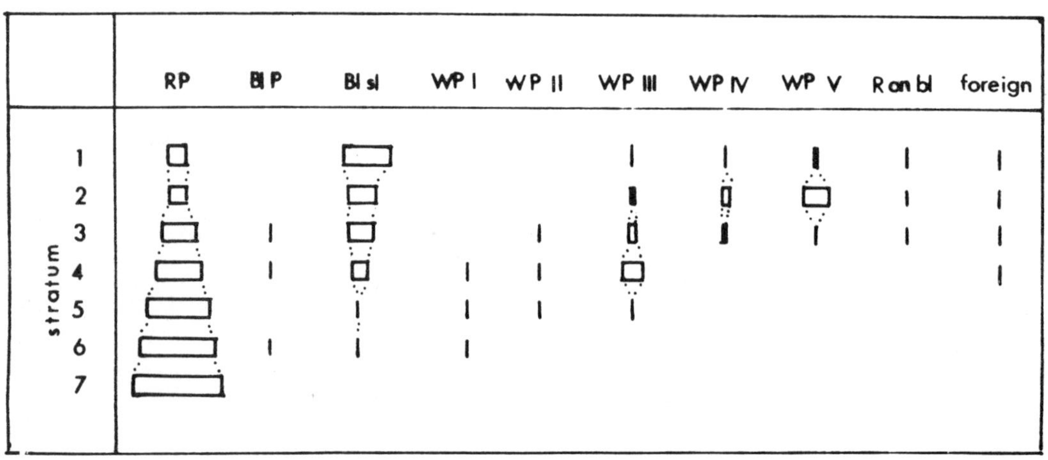

c. Fig 1b AS A HISTOGRAM

Fig. 1d-f

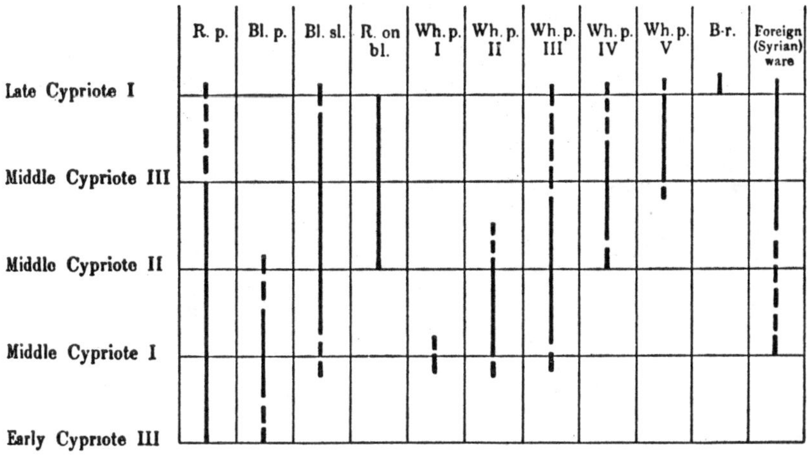

d. GJERSTAD SUMMARY TABLE (SPC p. 273)

Middle Cypriot	White Painted Wares IB	II	III	III-IV WLS	III-IV PLS	III-IV LDS	III-IV SHS	IV	IV-V CLS	V
I		14								
I-II	1	2	3	2				1		
II		4	9	3			2	12		
II-III		5	35	1	1	1	11	76		7
III			4	17	5		3	15	5	34

e. Åström 1957 PART OF SUMMARY TABLE (MCBA p. 198)

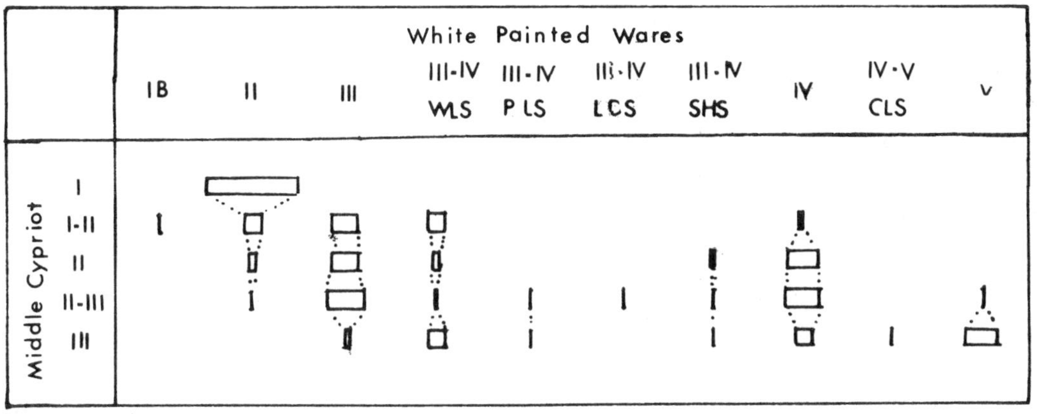

f. Fig 1e AS A HISTOGRAM

KEY TO FIGURE 2

For full composition of the groups see Appendix I.

1-21	Lapithos
22	Alambra
23	Ayios Iakovos
24	Ayia Paraskevi
25	Dhali
26	Dhenia T.6
27	Dhenia
28	Dhikomo
29	Enkomi
30	Galinoporni
31	Kalopsidha
32	Katydata
33	Klavdhia
34	Kotchati
35	Kythrea
36	Larnaca
37	Leondari Vouno
38	Livadhia
39	Milia
40	Nicosia
41	Palaealona
42	Politico T.4
43	Politico
44	Myrtou
45	Vounous
46	Yeri
47	?Alambra

Fig. 2

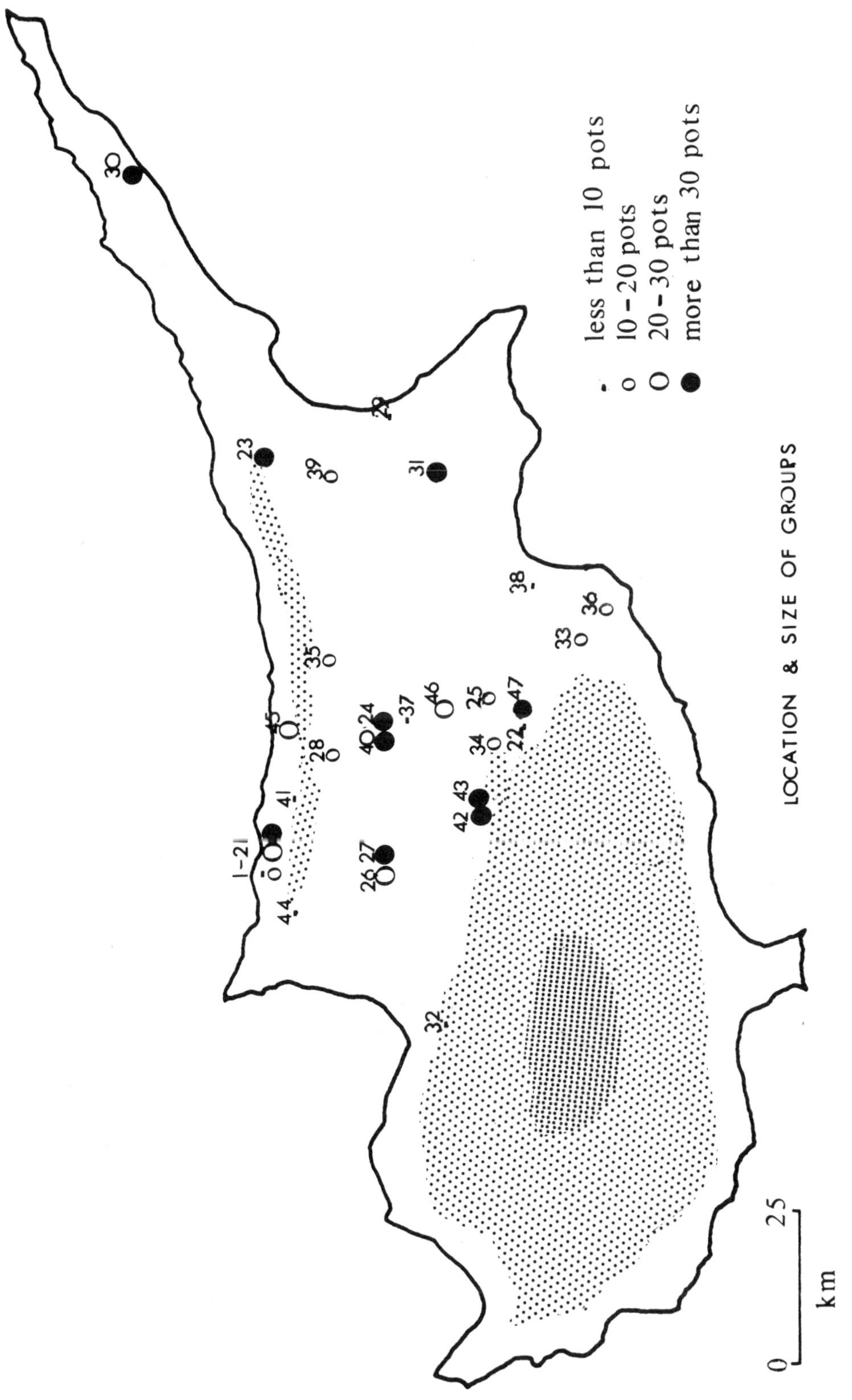
less than 10 pots
10 – 20 pots
20 – 30 pots
more than 30 pots
LOCATION & SIZE OF GROUPS
0
25
km

Fig. 3

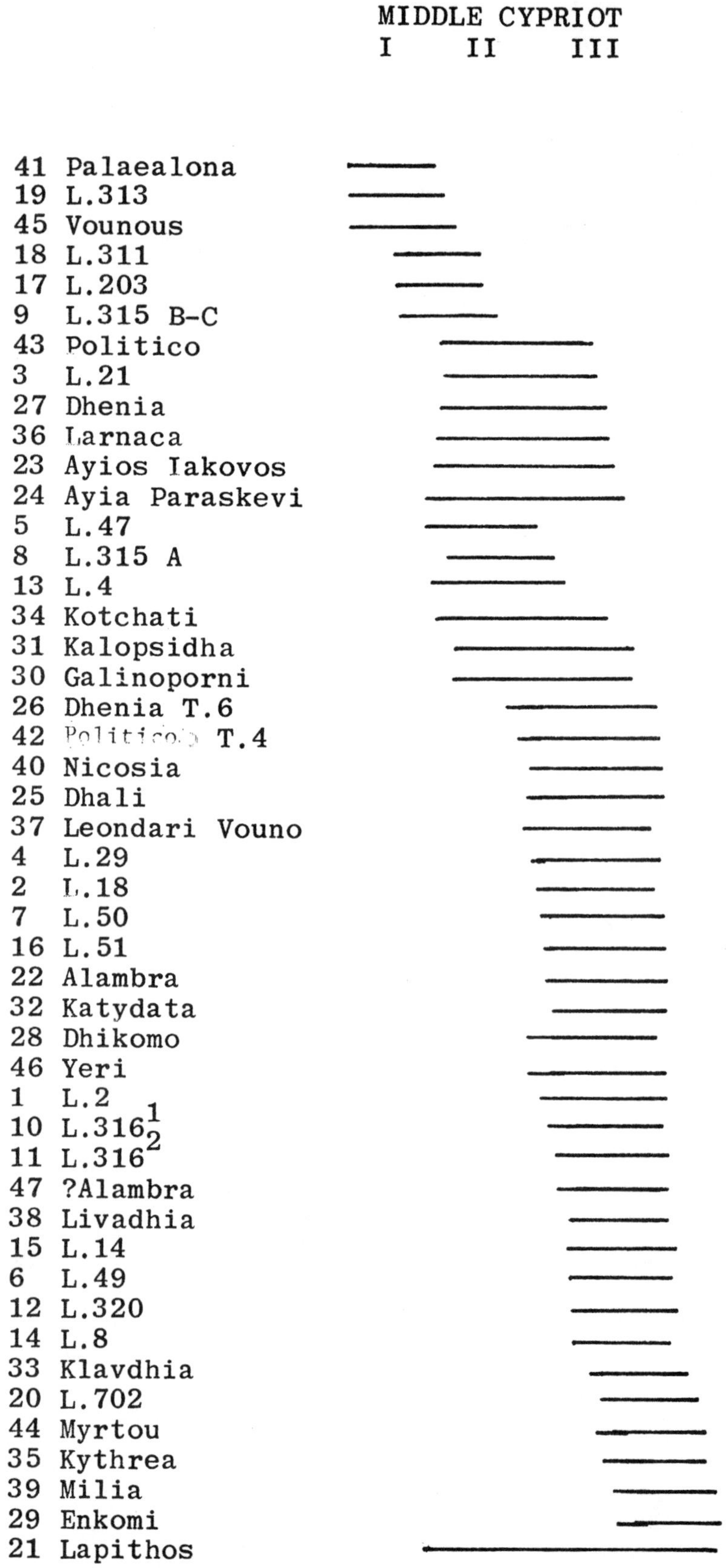
MIDDLE CYPRIOT
I II III
41 Palaealona
19 L.313
45 Vounous
18 L.311
17 L.203
9 L.315 B-C
43 Politico
3 L.21
27 Dhenia
36 Larnaca
23 Ayios Iakovos
24 Ayia Paraskevi
5 L.47
8 L.315 A
13 L.4
34 Kotchati
31 Kalopsidha
30 Galinoporni
26 Dhenia T.6
42 Politico T.4
40 Nicosia
25 Dhali
37 Leondari Vouno
4 L.29
2 L.18
7 L.50
16 L.51
22 Alambra
32 Katydata
28 Dhikomo
46 Yeri
1 L.2
10 L.316 1
11 L.316 2
47 ?Alambra
38 Livadhia
15 L.14
6 L.49
12 L.320
14 L.8
33 Klavdhia
20 L.702
44 Myrtou
35 Kythrea
39 Milia
29 Enkomi
21 Lapithos

APPROXIMATE TIME_SPAN OF THE GROUPS

Fig. 4a

THE MOTIFS

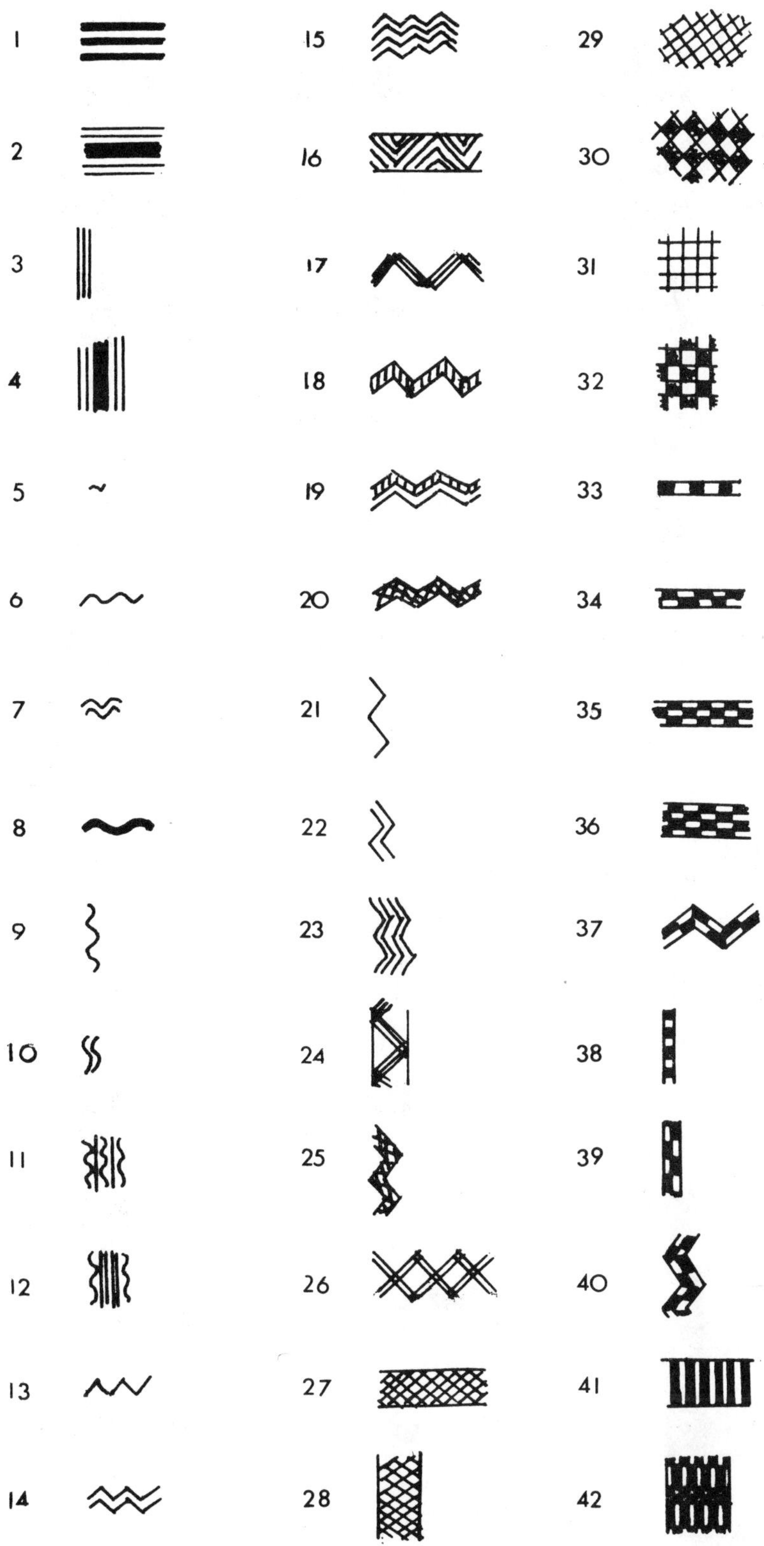

Fig-4b

THE MOTIFS

Fig. 5

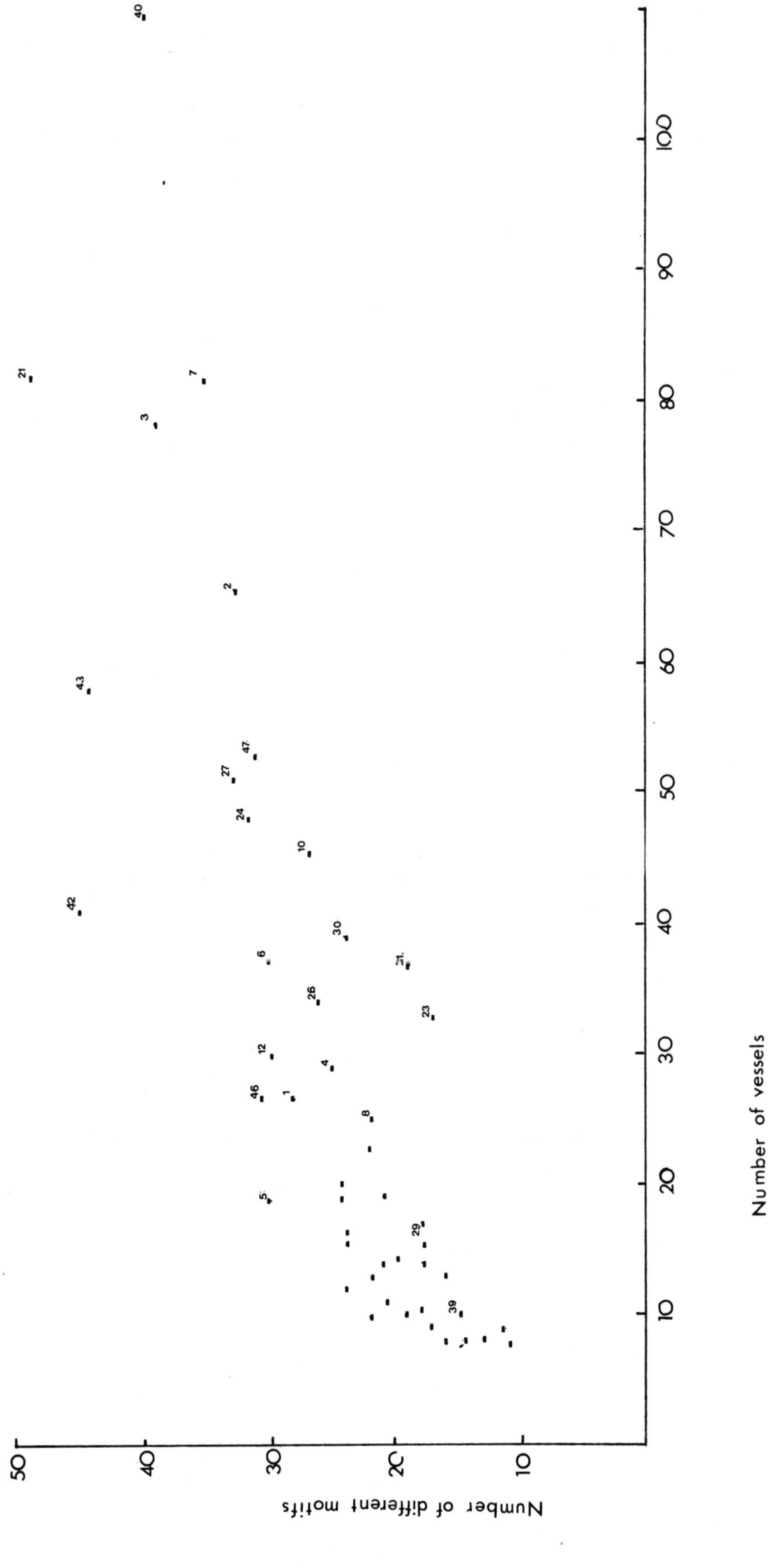
Number of vessels
10
20
30
40
50
60
70
80
90
100
Number of different motifs
10
20
30
40
50

Fig. 6 a-b

a. Proportion of each shape

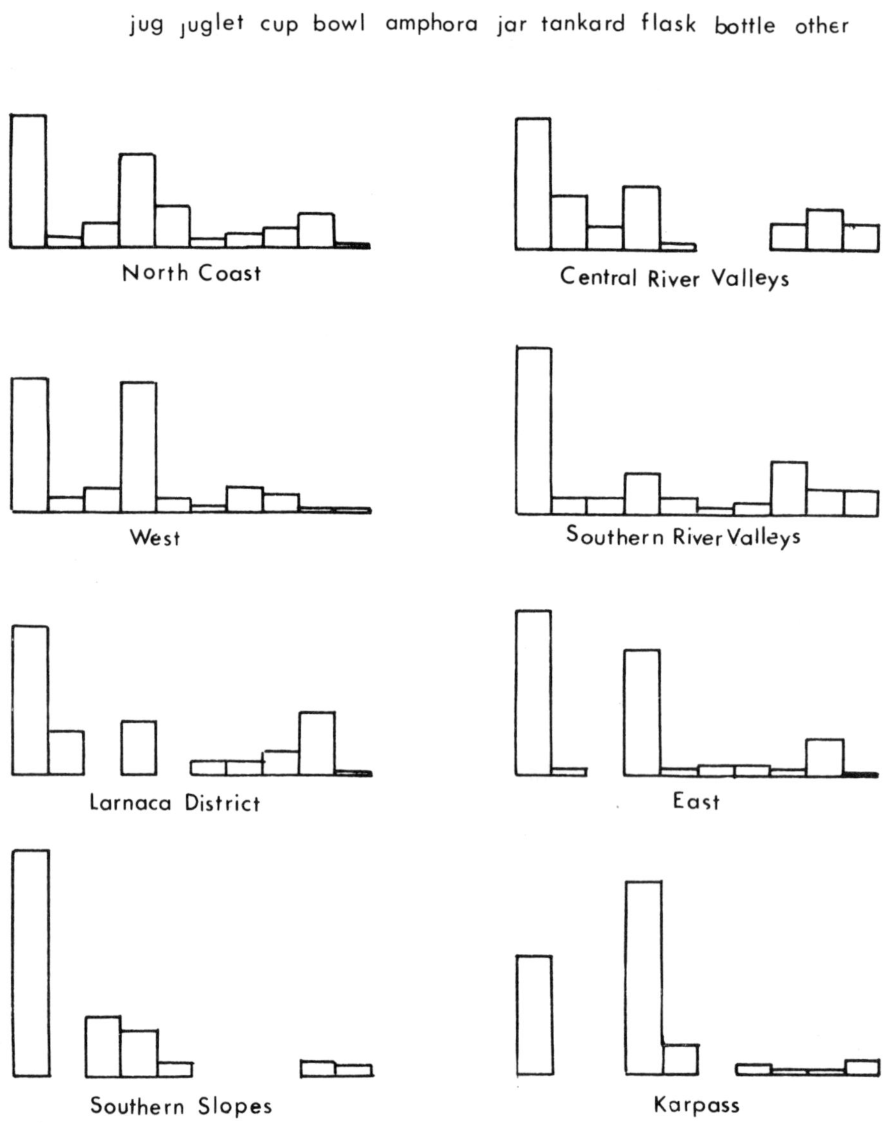

b. Proportion of total sample

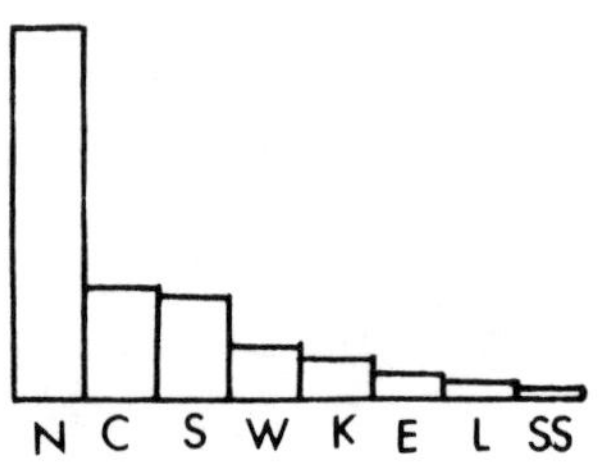

Fig. 7

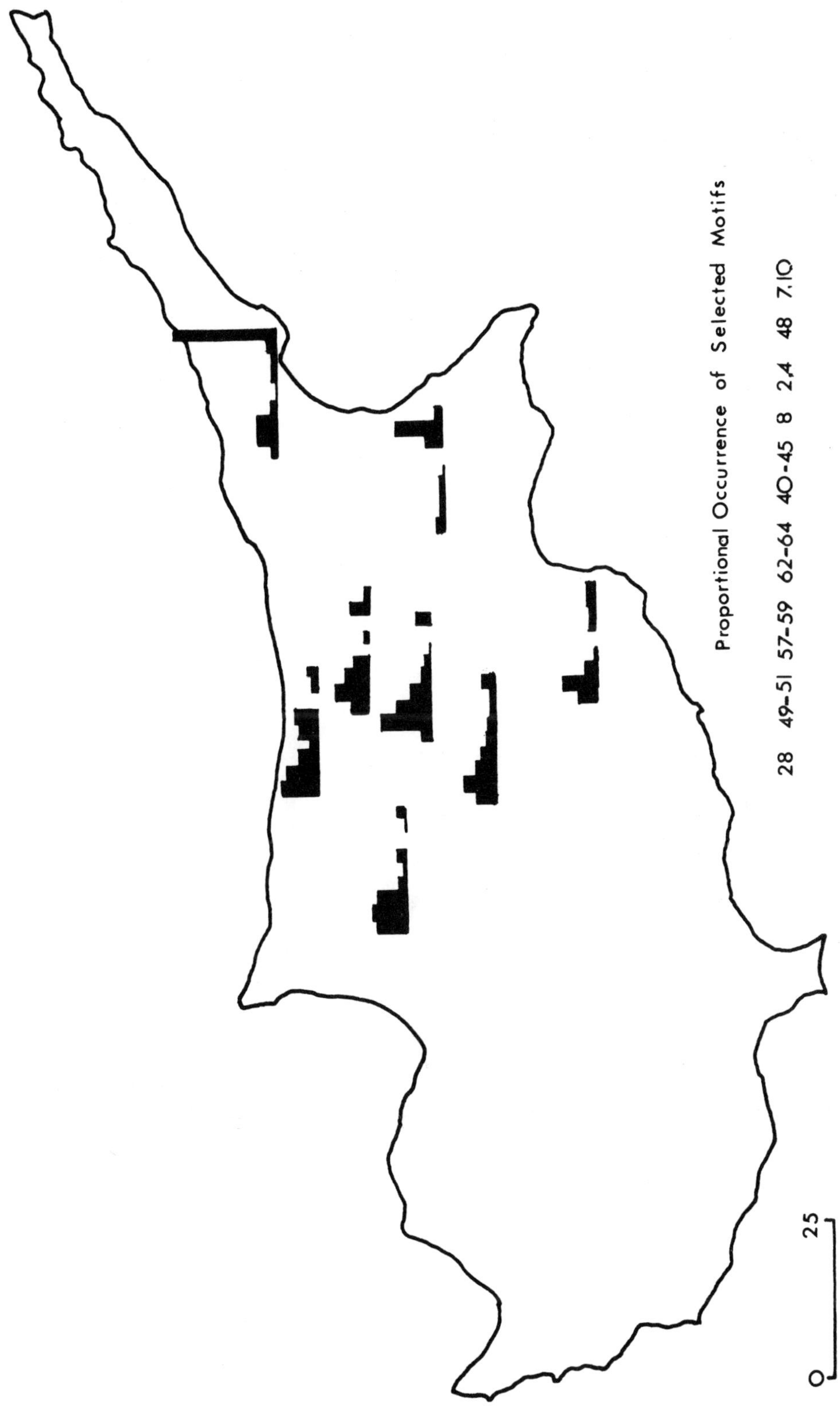
Proportional Occurrence of Selected Motifs
28 49-51 57-59 62-64 40-45 8 2,4 48 7,10
0 km 25

Fig. 8 a–b

a. Factor 1

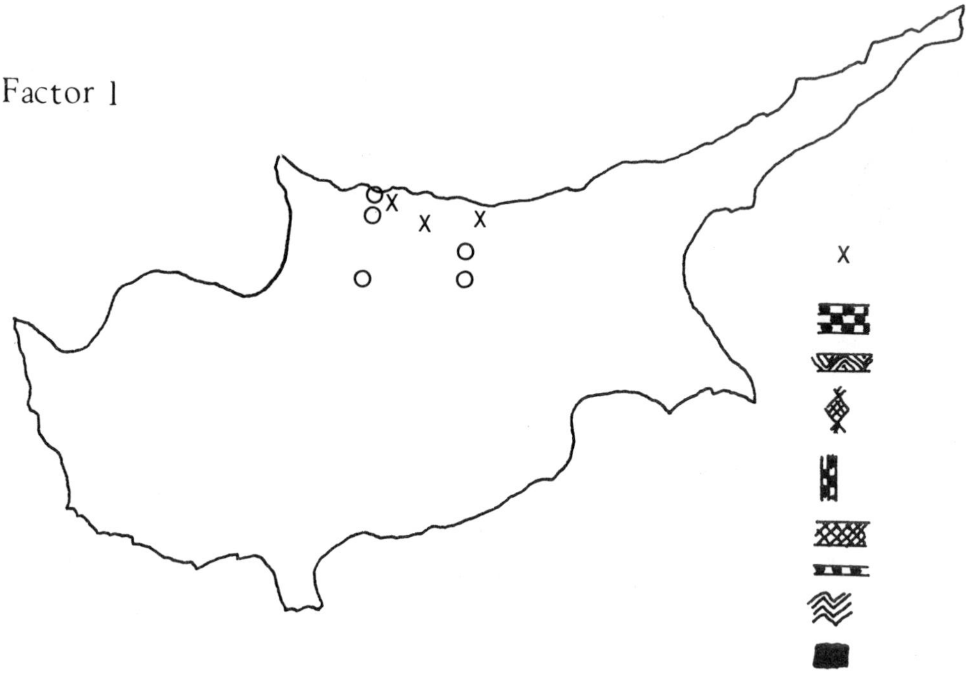

b. Factor 2

Fig. 8 c-d

c. Factor 3

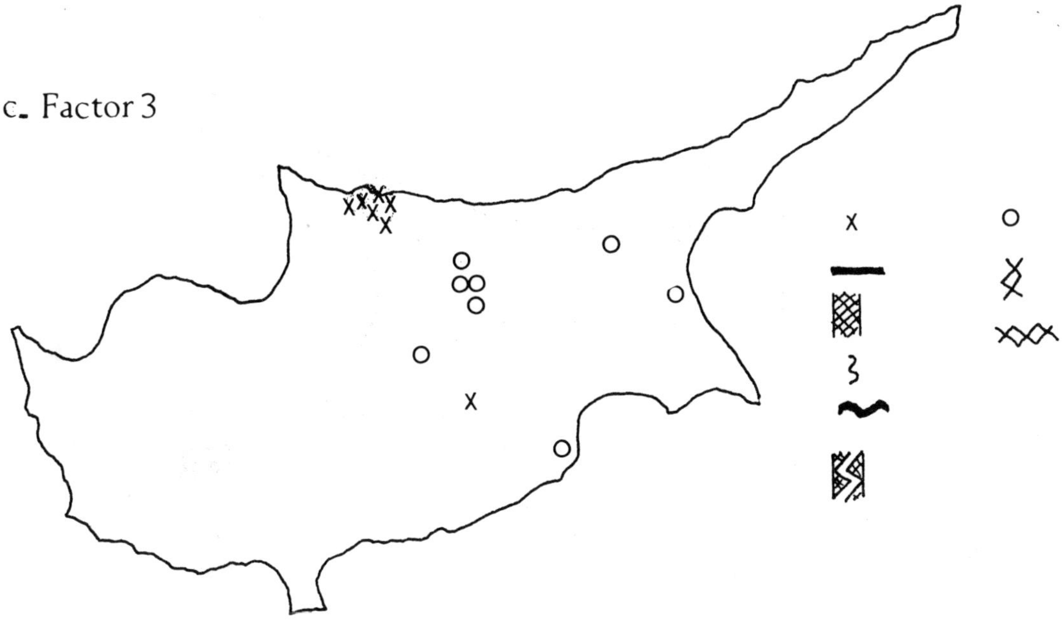

d. Factor 4

Fig. 8 e-f

124

e. Factor 5

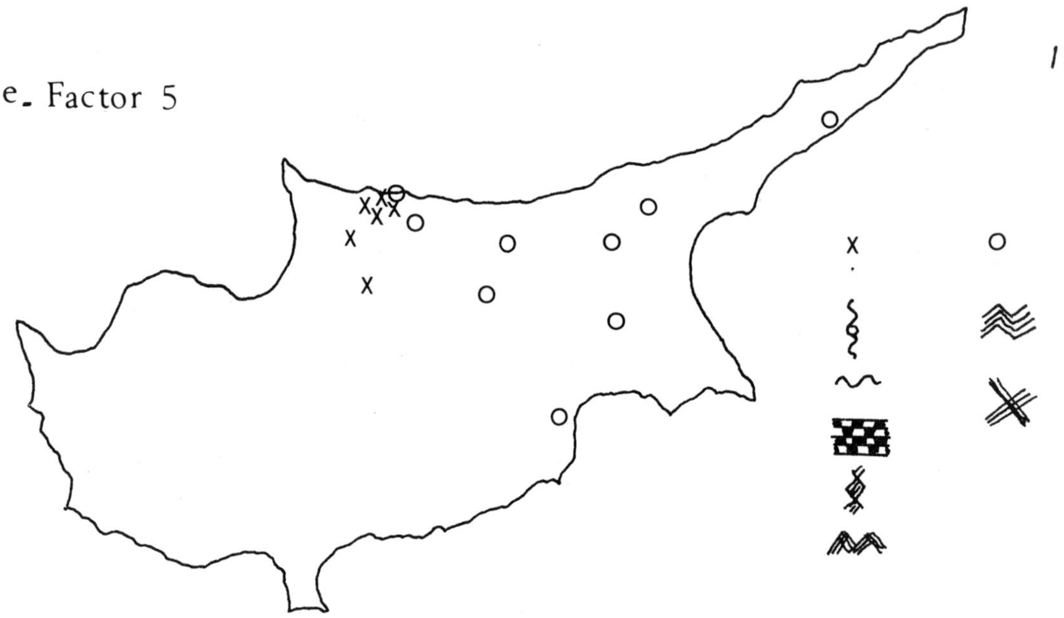

f. Factor 6

Fig. 8 g-h

g. Factor 7

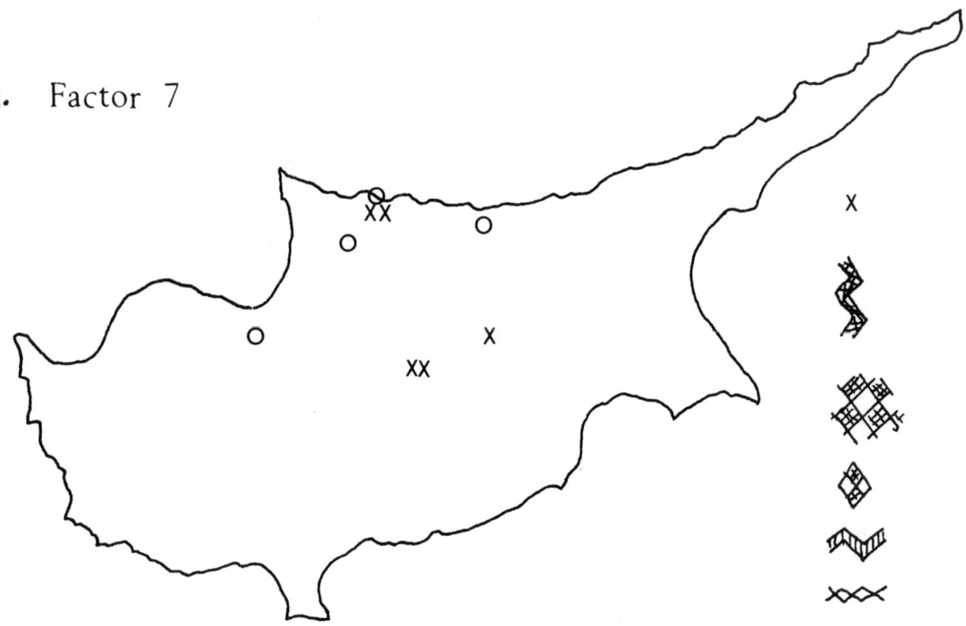

h. Factor 8

Fig. 8 i-j

i. Factor 9

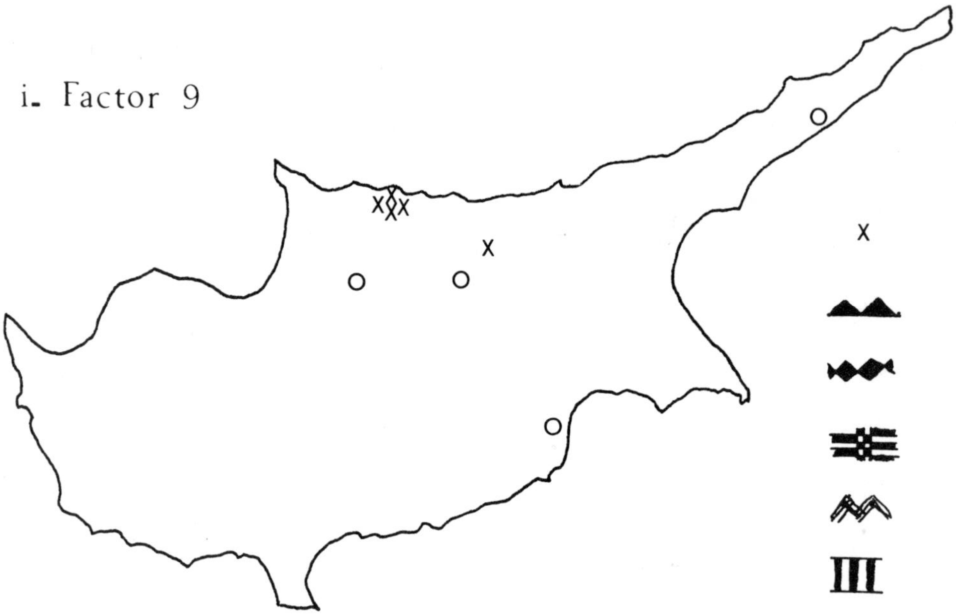

j. Factor 10

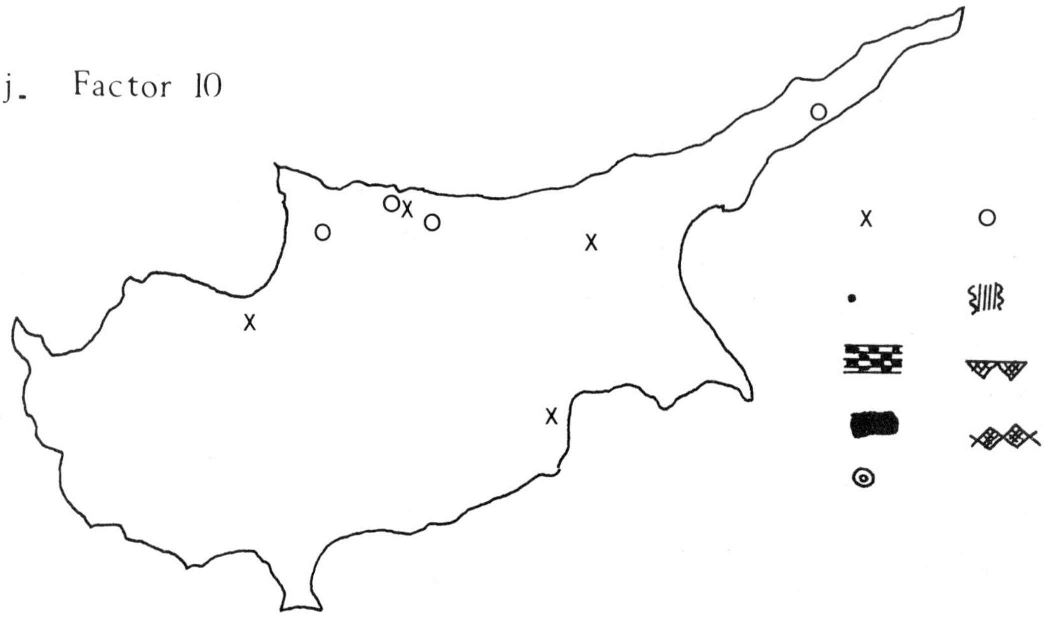

Fig. 9 a-b

a- Factor Q1

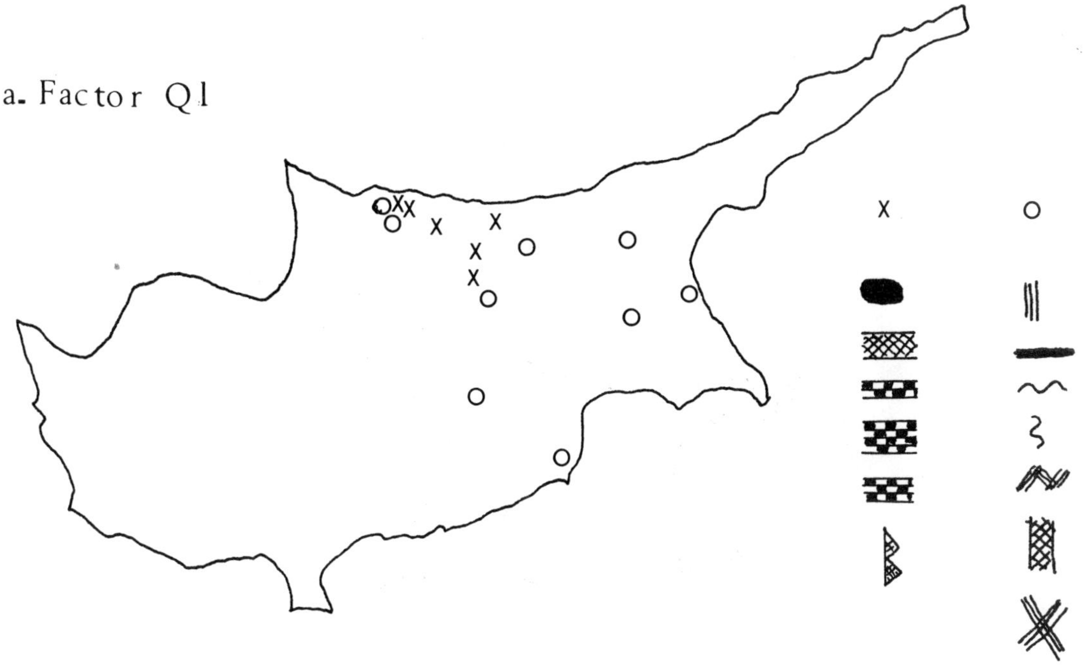

b- Factor Q2

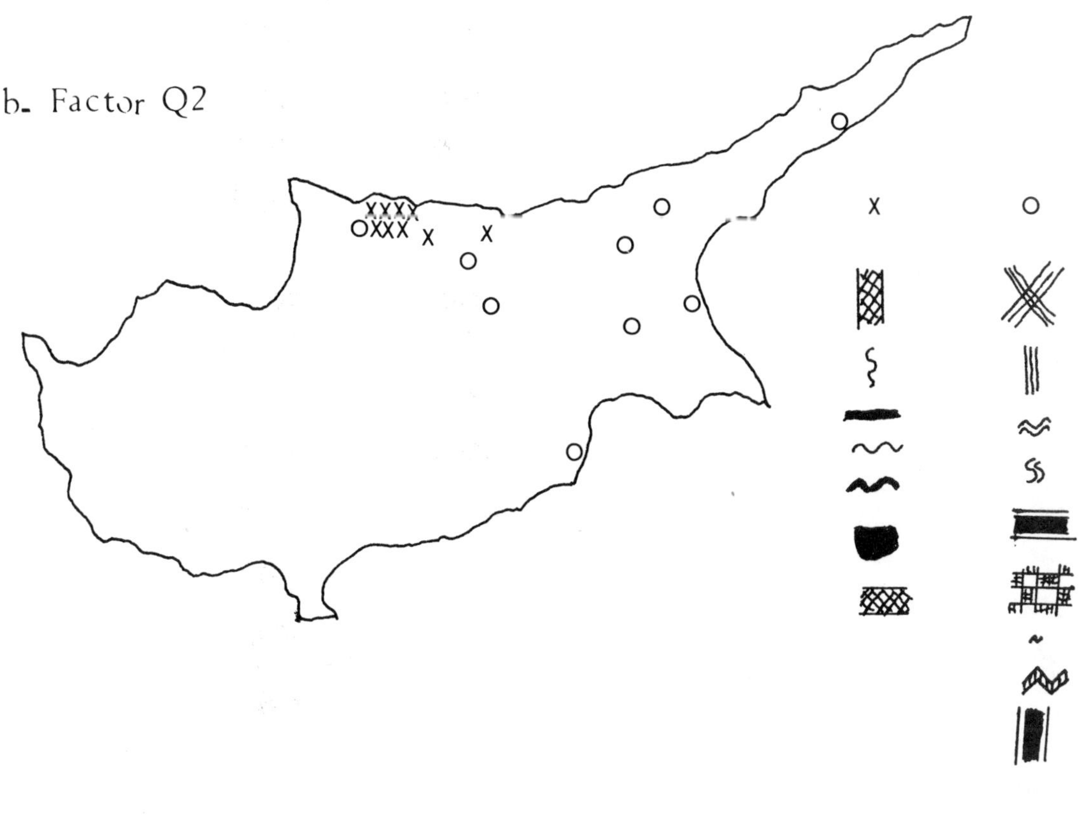

Fig. 9 c

c. Factor Q3

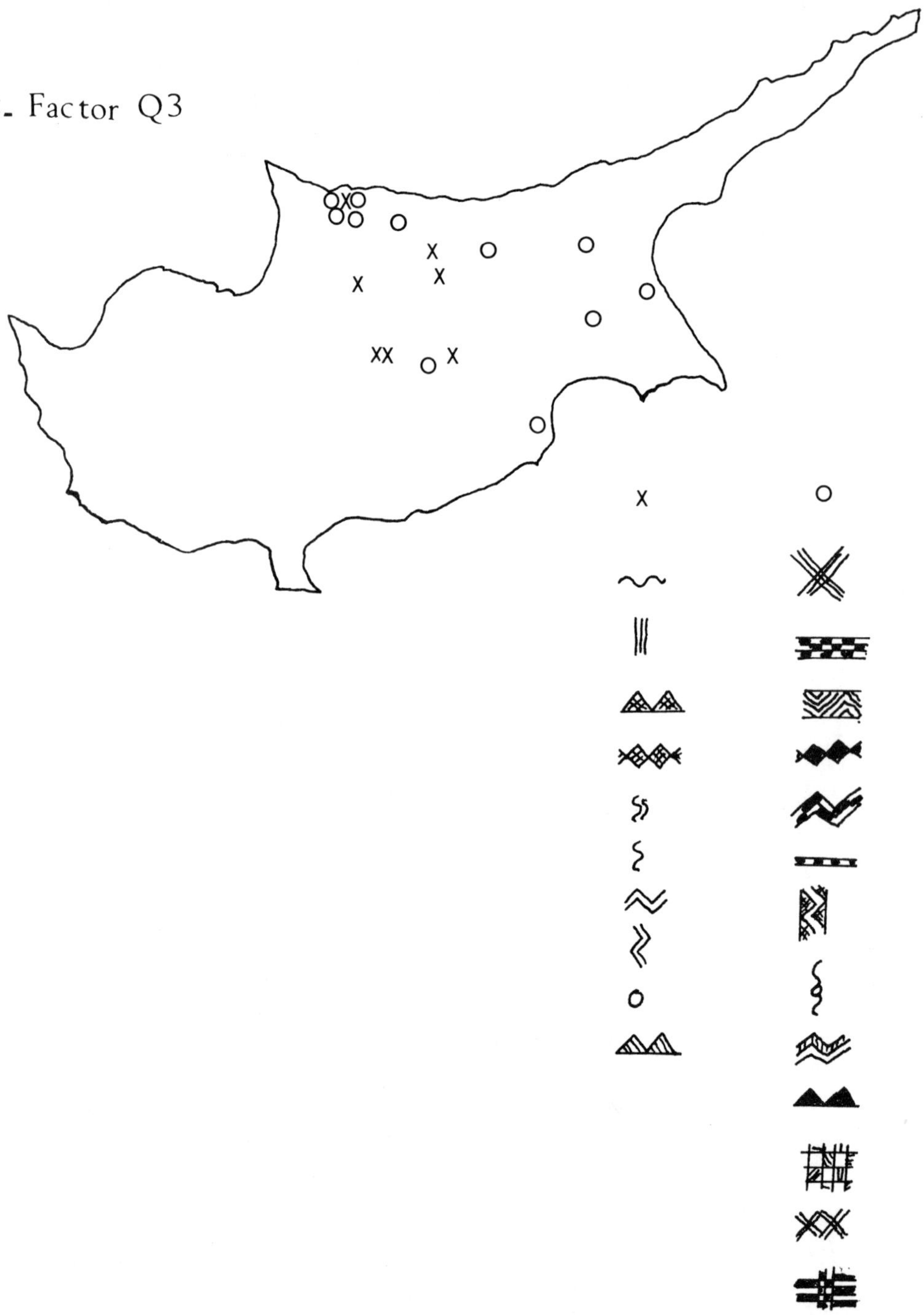

Fig. 10

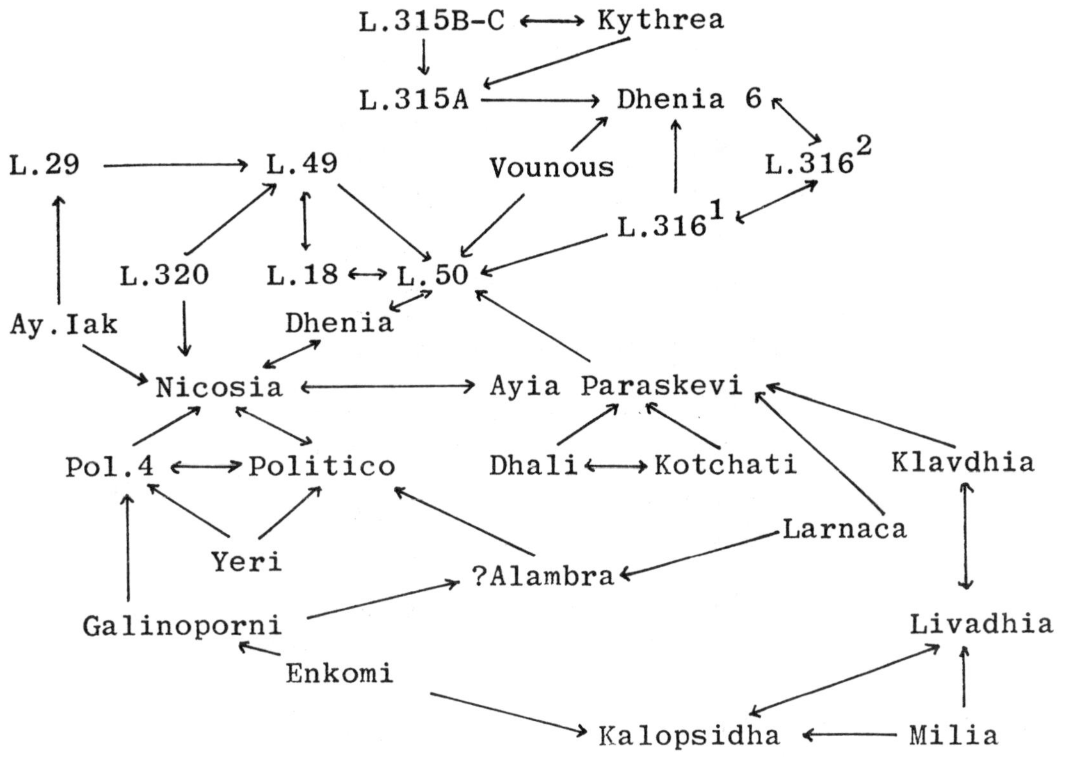

CLOSE PROXIMITY ANALYSIS
SELECTED GROUPS

based on presence-absence
similarity coefficients

Fig. 11

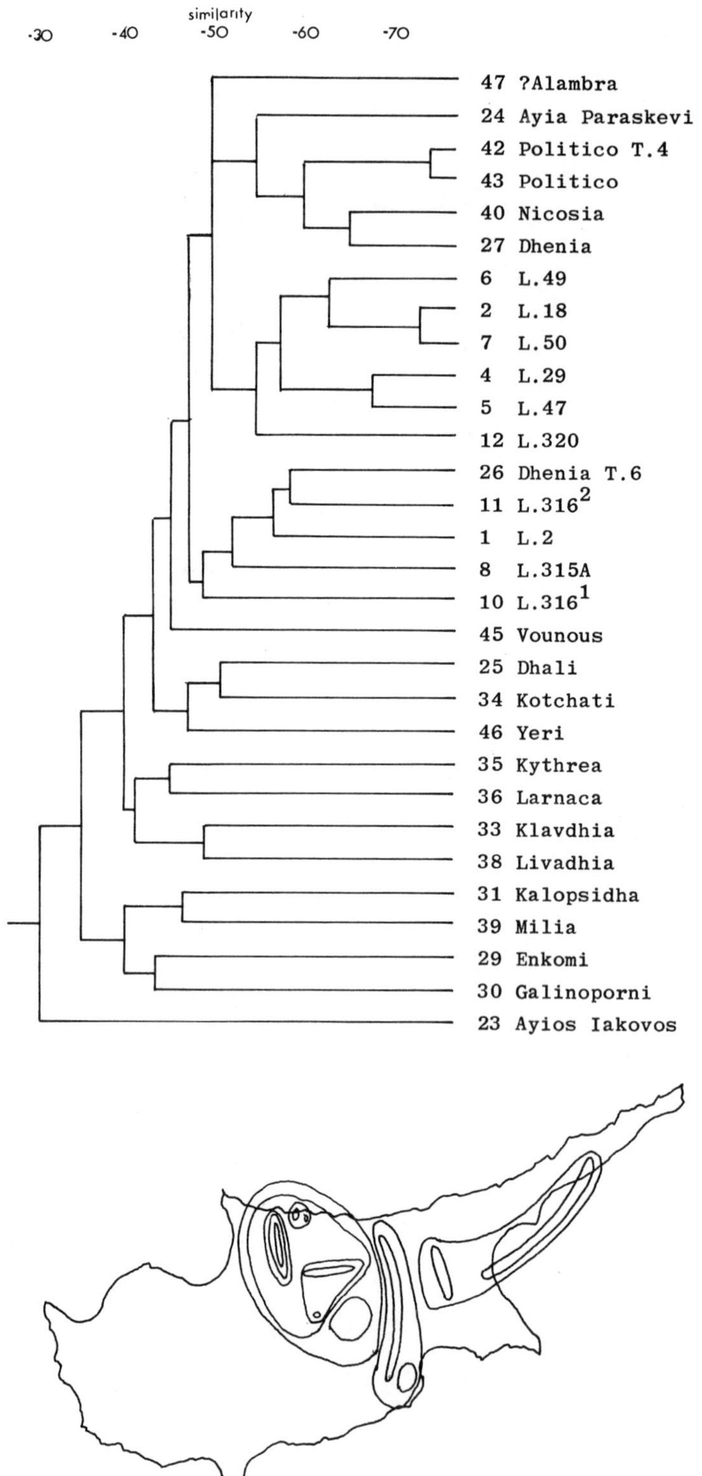

AVERAGE LINKAGE CLUSTER ANALYSIS
SELECTED SITES
Based on Presence-Absence Similarity

Fig. 12

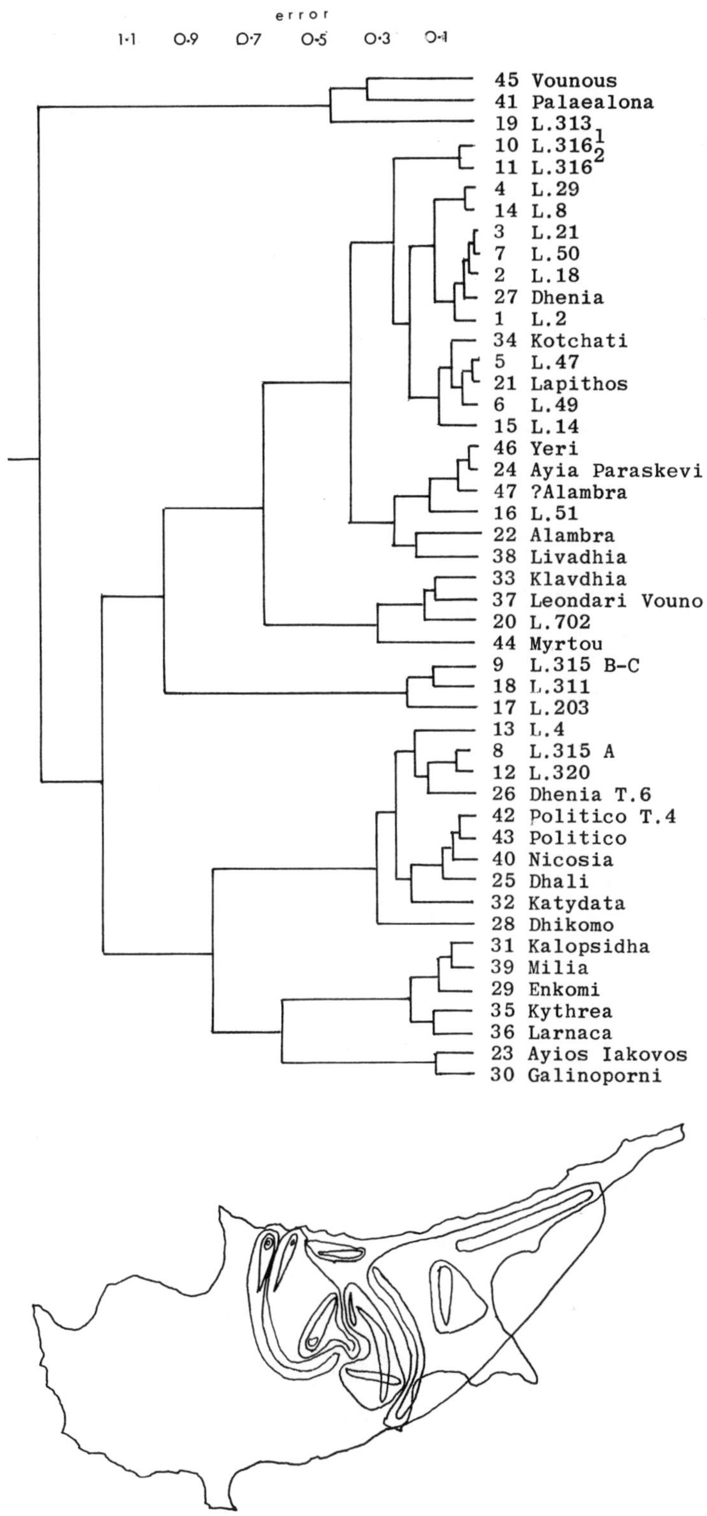

HIERARCHICAL CLUSTER ANALYSIS ALL GROUPS
variables not standardised

Fig. 13

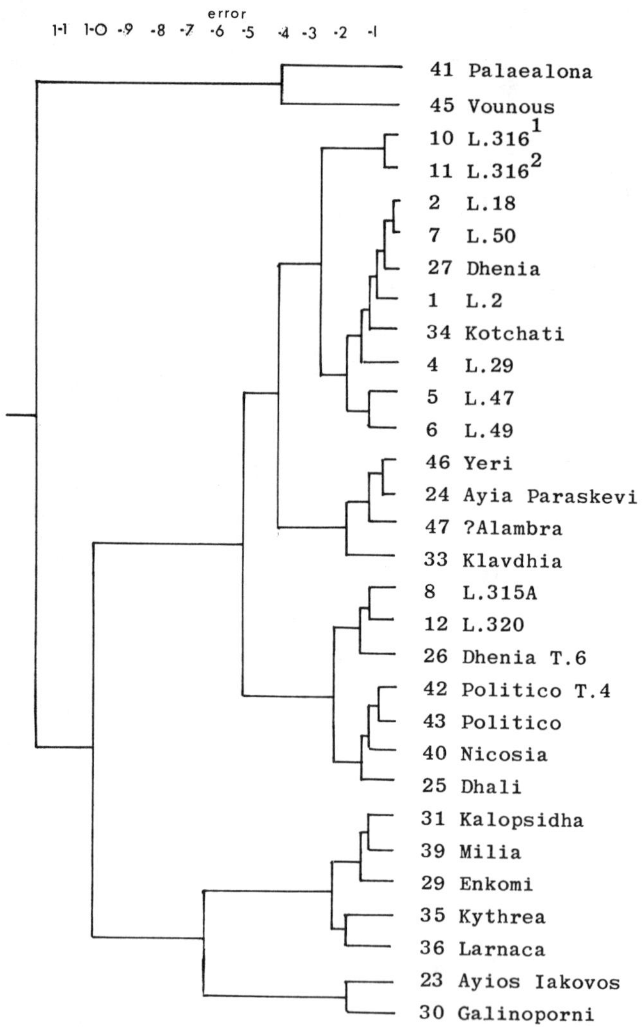

b.

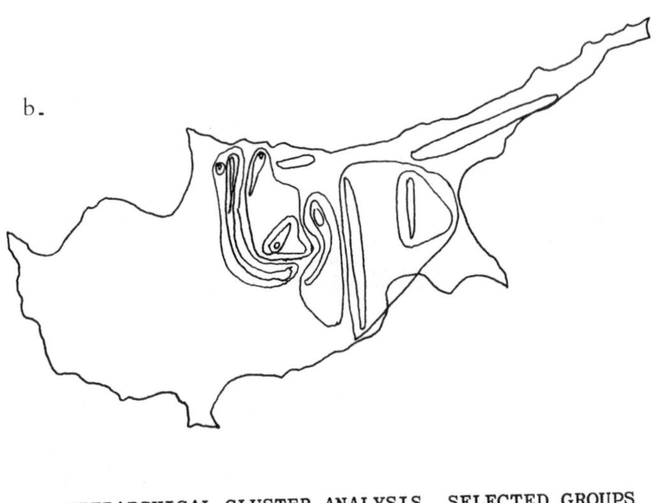

HIERARCHICAL CLUSTER ANALYSIS SELECTED GROUPS
variables not standardised

Fig. 14

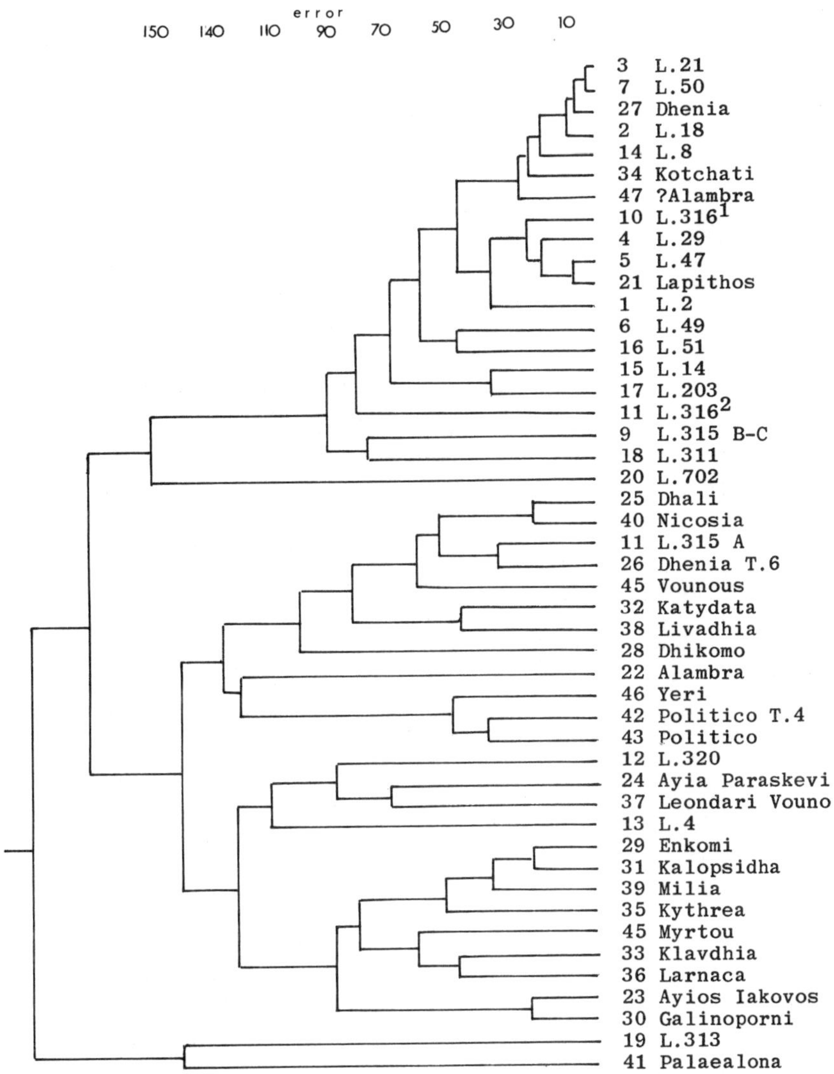

HIERARCHICAL CLUSTER ANALYSIS ALL GROUPS
Standardised Variables

Fig. 15

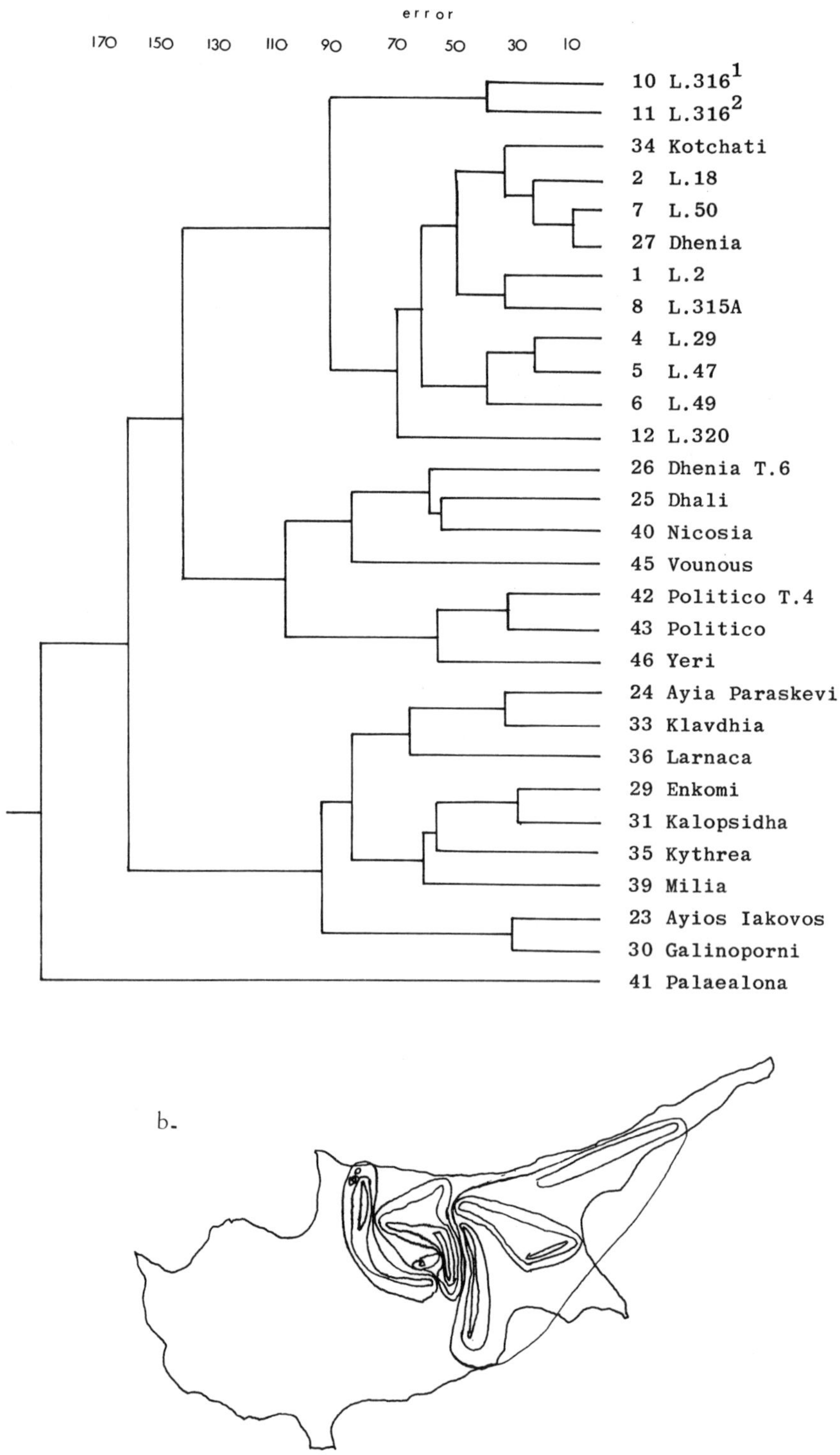

HIERARCHICAL CLUSTER ANALYSIS SELECTED GROUPS
VARIABLES STANDARDISED

Fig. 16

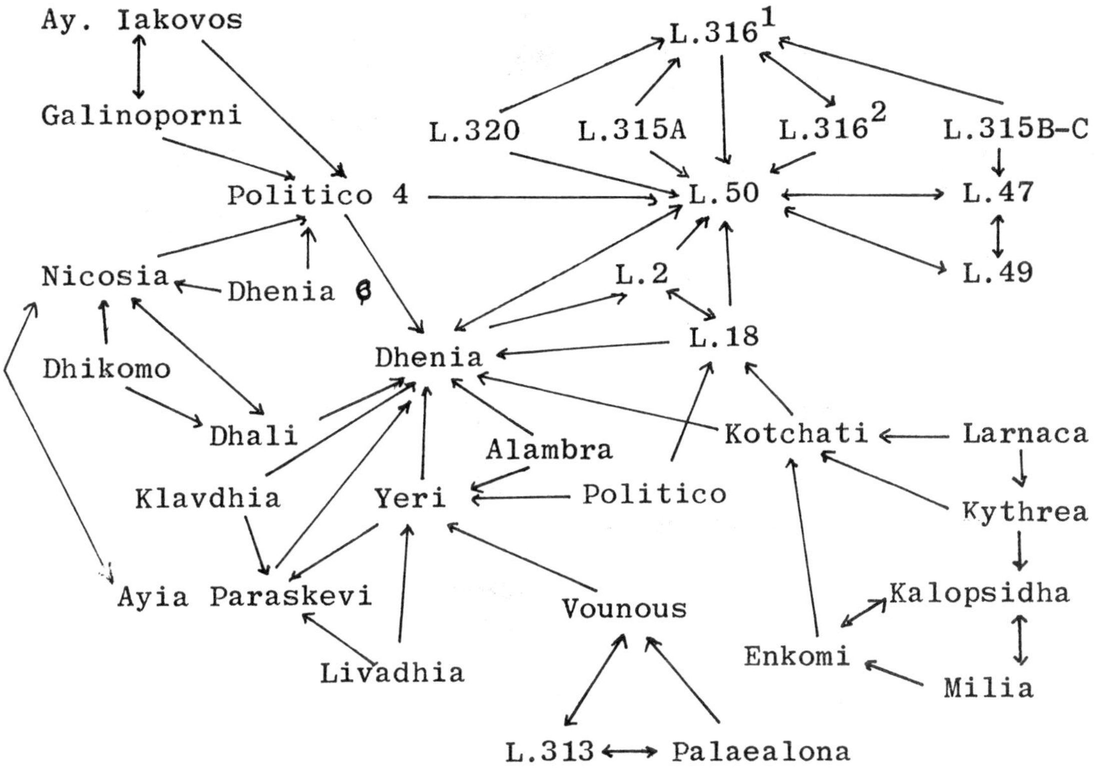

CLOSE PROXIMITY ANALYSIS

SELECTED GROUPS

Fig. 17a

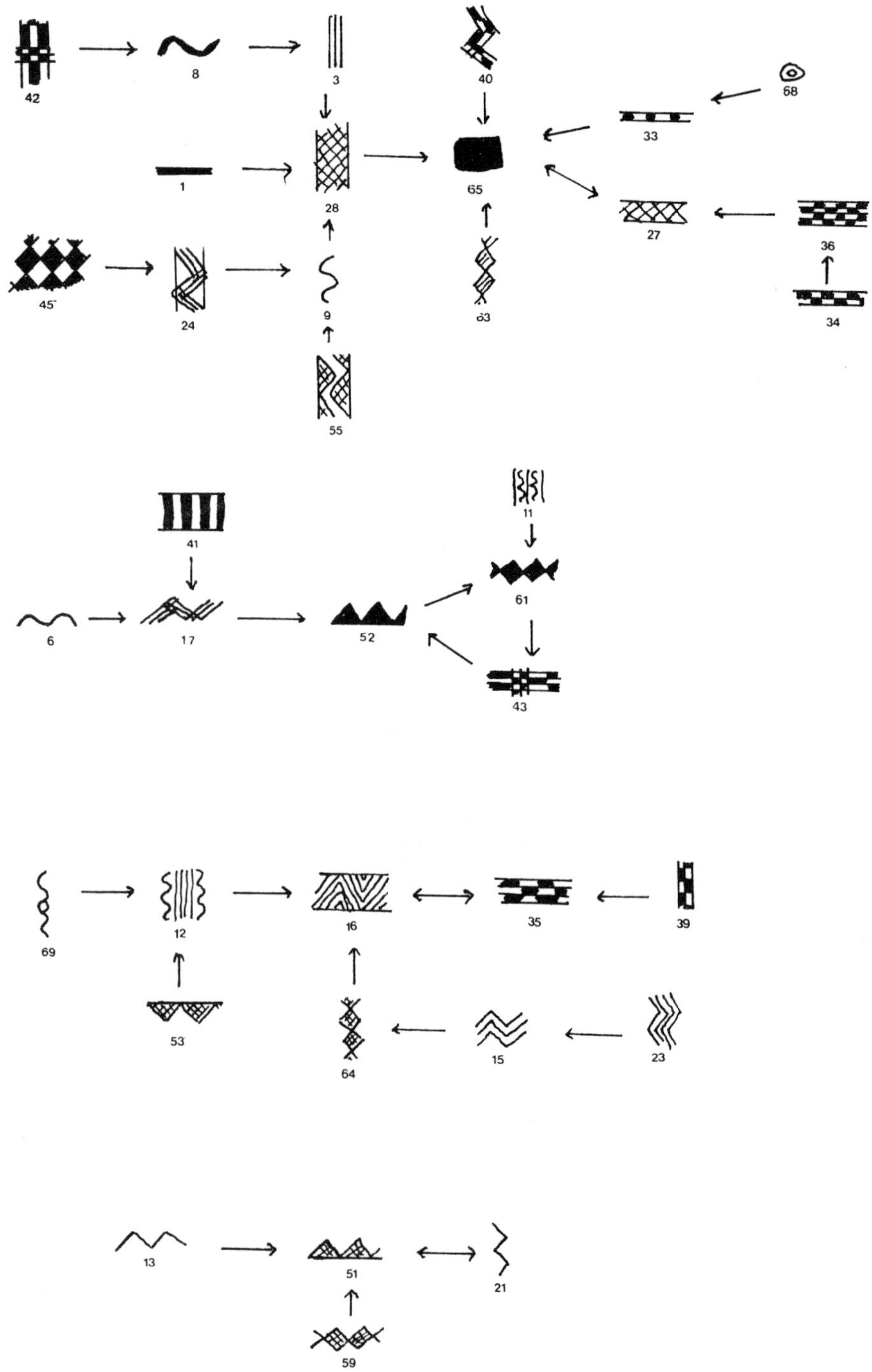

R-MODE HIGHEST CORRELATIONS

Fig. 17b

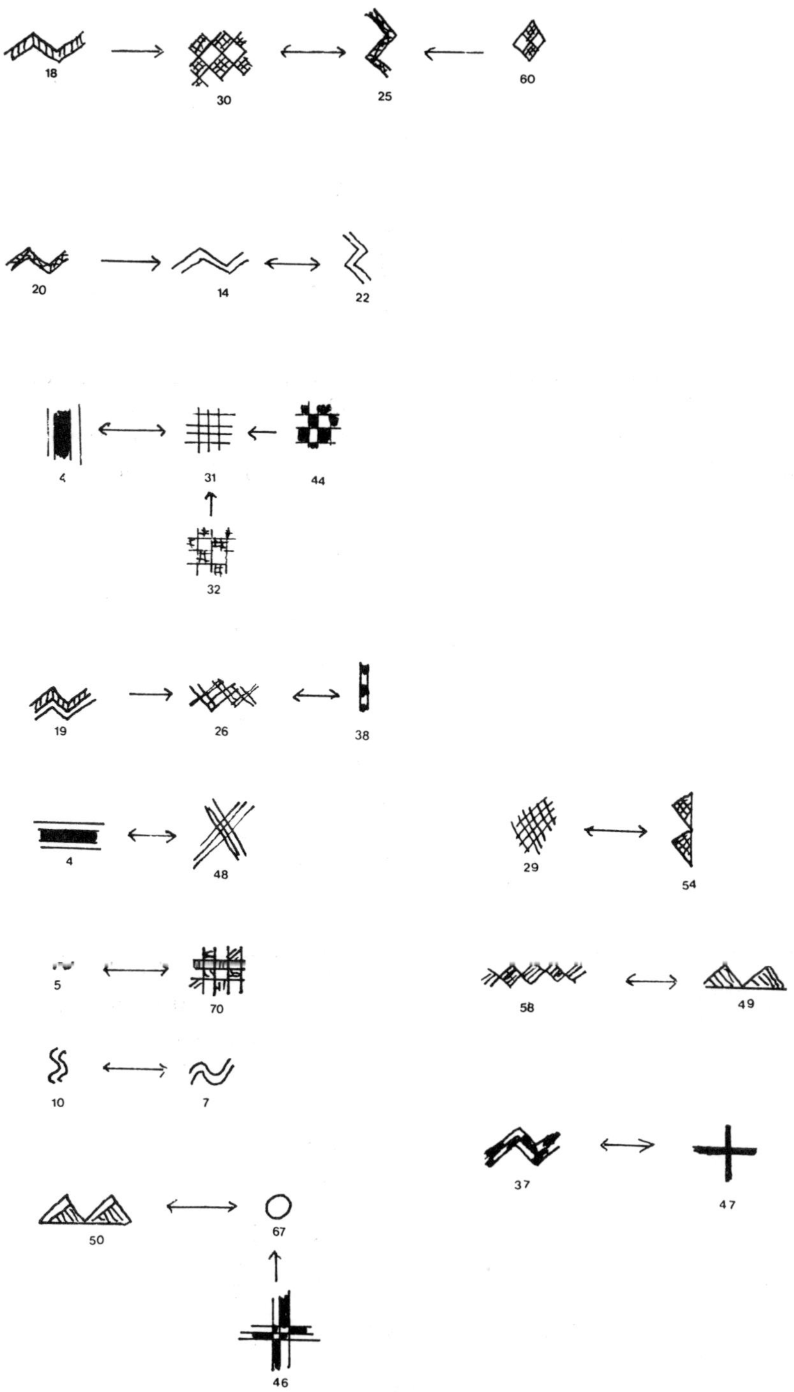

R-MODE HIGHEST CORRELATIONS

Fig. 18 a-f

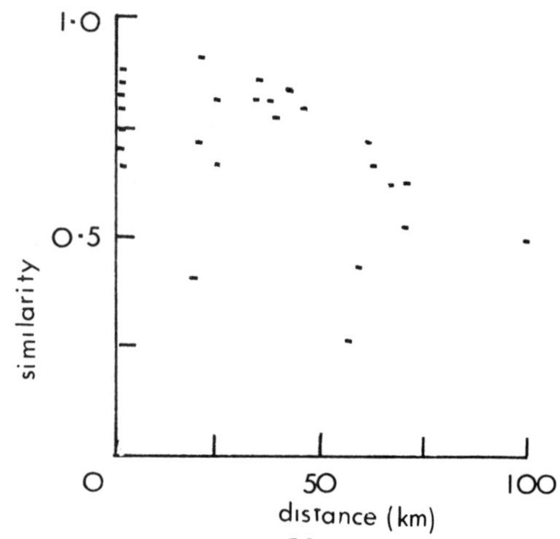

a. L.50

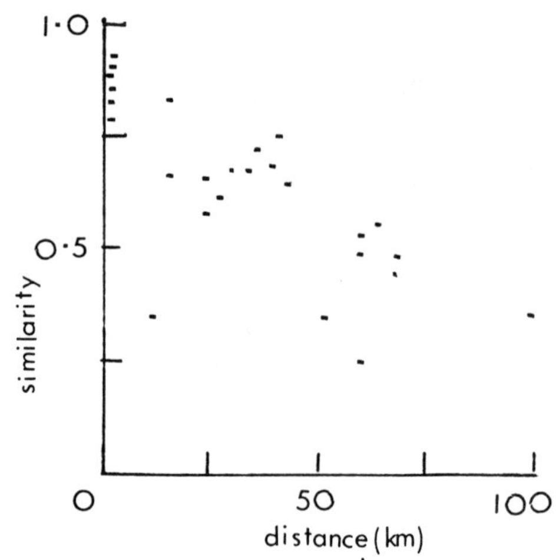

b. L. 316[1]

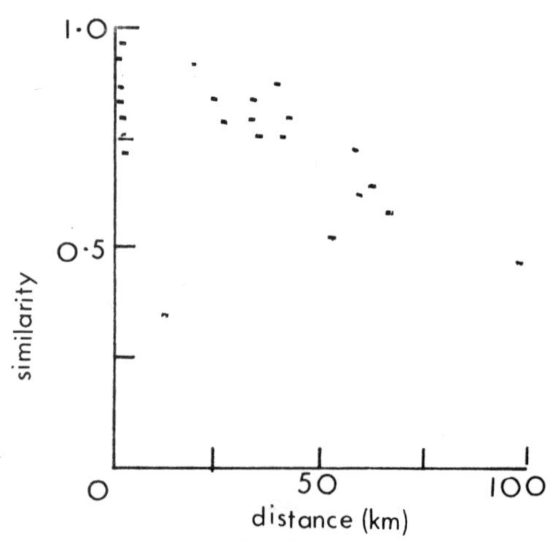

c. L.18

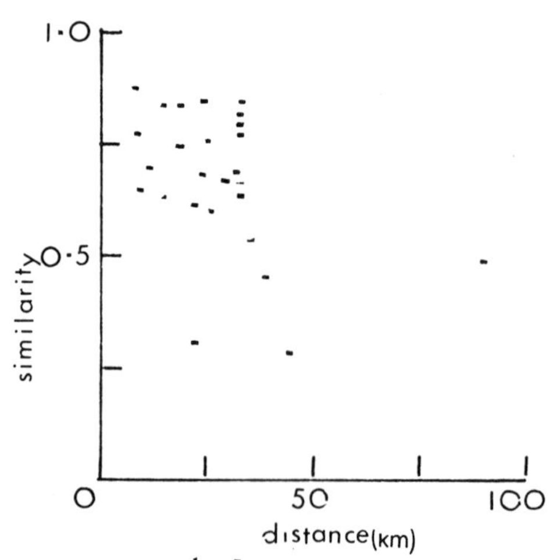

d. Yeri

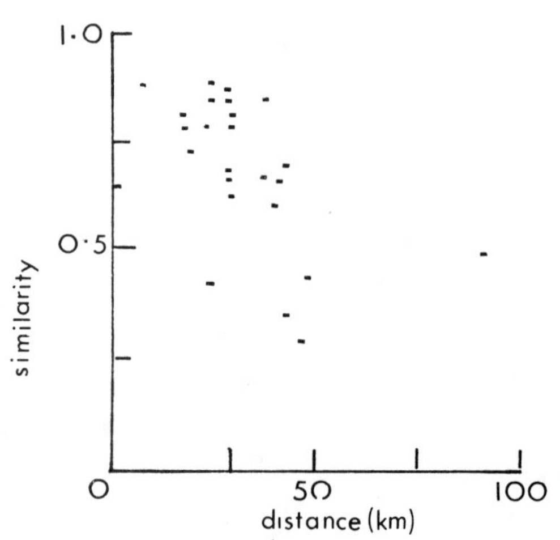

e. Ay. P.

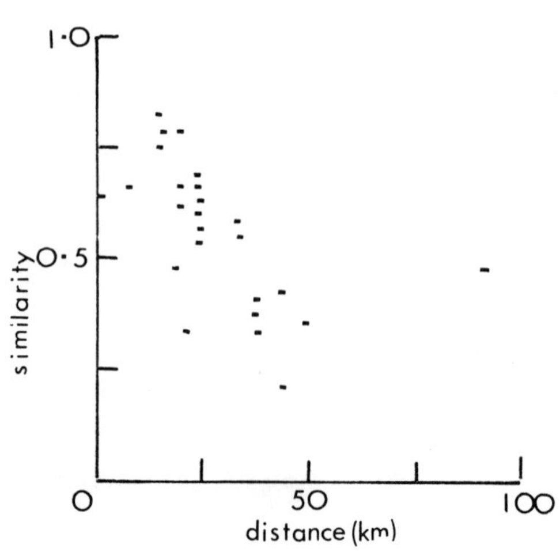

f. Nicosia

Fig. 18 g-l

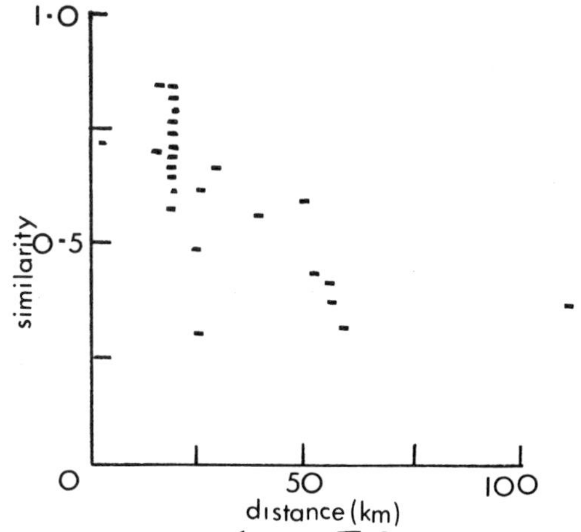

g. Dhenia T.6

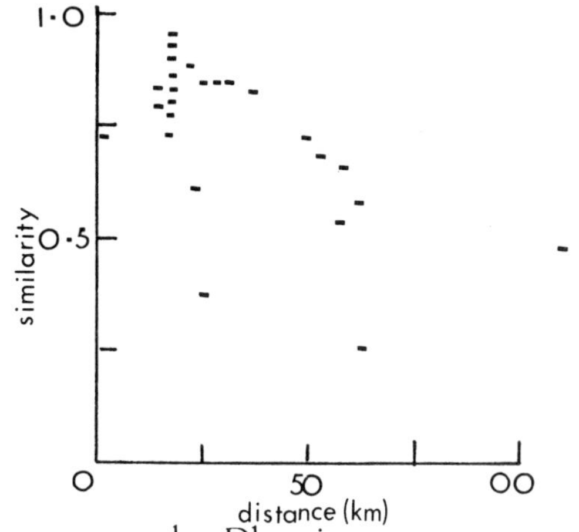

h. Dhenia

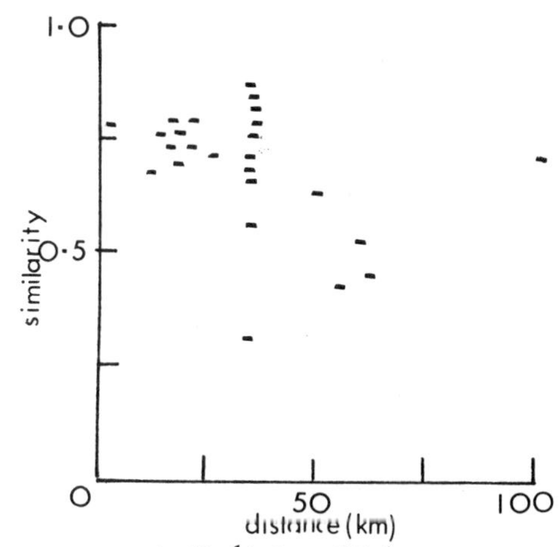

i. Politico T.4

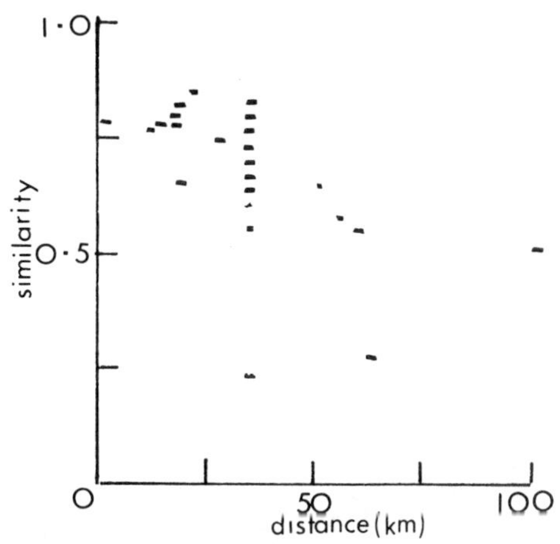

j. Politico

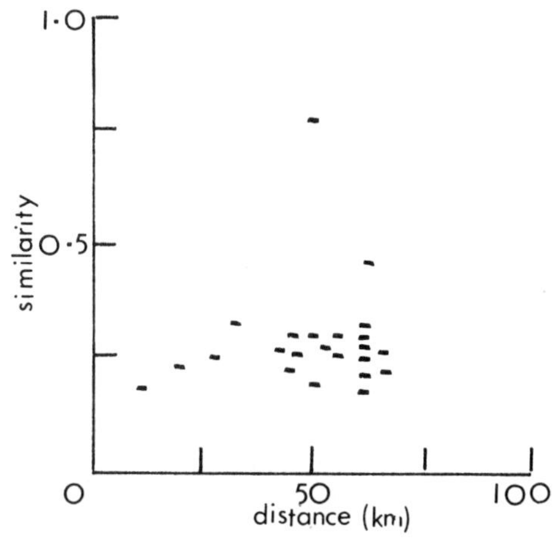

k. Ay. Iak.

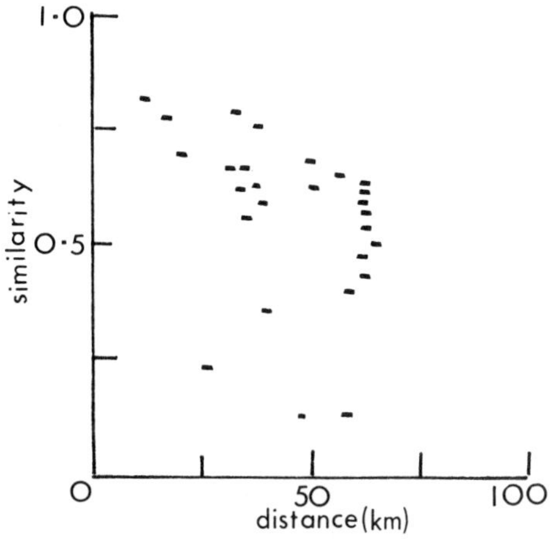

l. Kalopsidha

Fig. 19

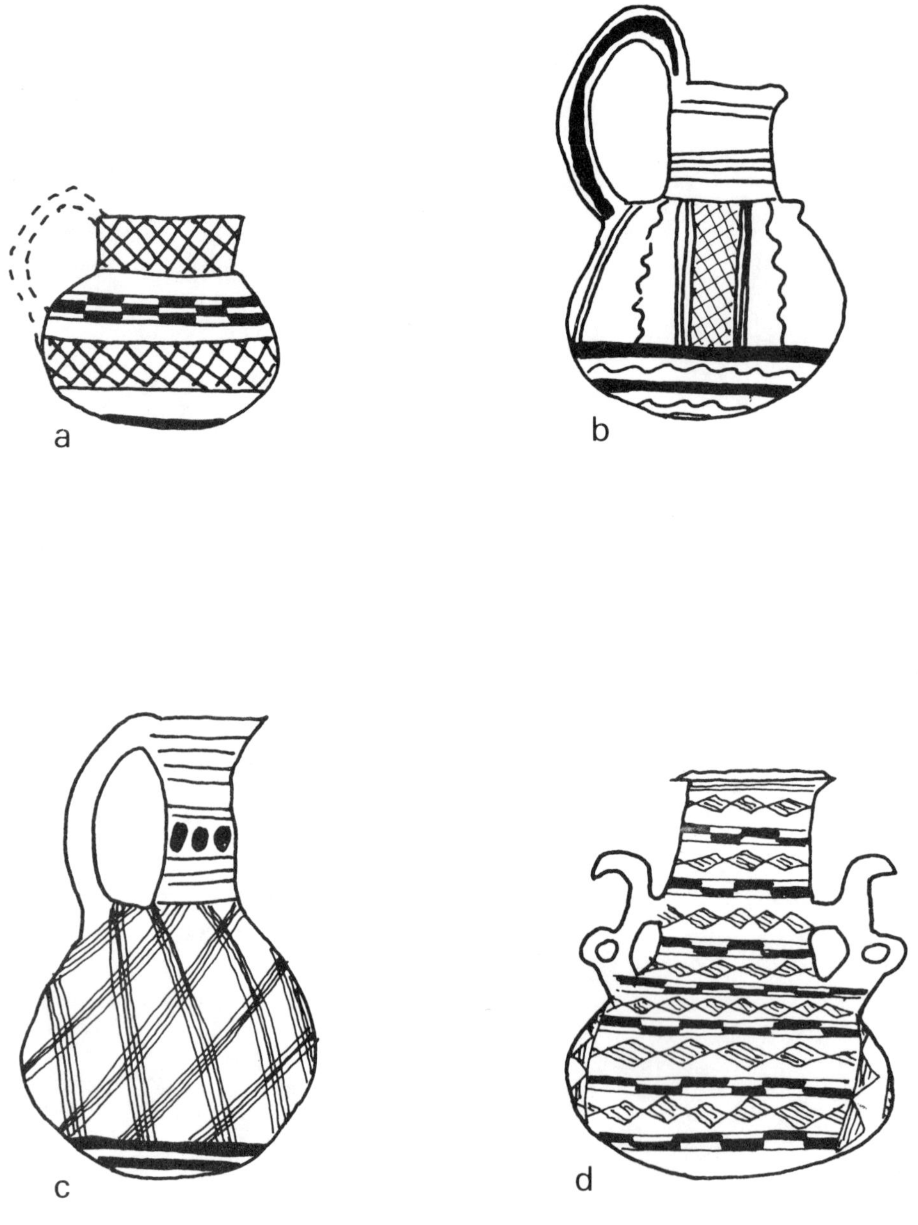

Four vessels from Kotchati (C.M. 1970/X-7/-)
sketch drawings

STUDIES IN MEDITERRANEAN ARCHAEOLOGY

PUBLISHED BY PROFESSOR PAUL ÅSTRÖM, SÖDRA VÄGEN 61, GOTHENBURG S-412 54, SWEDEN

"Studies in Mediterranean Archaeology, published in English and finely illustrated are highly to be recommended." Review Editor, *Greece and Rome*.

"La naissance de cette collection, que dirige M. Paul Åström, est une preuve nouvelle de la vitalité des études d'archéologie mediterranéenne en Suède." Charles Delvoye, *L'Antiquité Classique*.

"La collana di "STUDIES IN MEDITERRANEAN ARCHAEOLOGY" è costituita da eleganti fascicoli in quarto nei quali sono accuratissime la stampa e la fotografia e nei quali i nomi dei collaboratori e la loro competenza si impongono." *Biblos-Press*.

"Each volume gives a succinct treatment of a subject precisely conceived and expressed with clarity. All are well-illustrated and contain excellent bibliographies ... Editor Åström should be congratulated for undertaking this project, and the authors deserve congratulations for their well-ordered, clear presentations. Recommended for archaeological book shelves." E. L. Ochsenschlager, *The Classical World*.

"Questa nuova collana di argomenti archeologici, se continuata, al di là dei 16 numeri sino ad ora annunciati, con un ritmo continuo, si potrebbe rivelare un utilissimo strumento di informazione, di aggiornamento e di messa a punti di molti problemi della storia antica del Mediterraneo." L. Guerrini, *Archeologia Classica*.

Vol. I. Per Ålin, Das Ende der mykenischen Fundstätten auf dem griechischen Festland. 159 S., 1 Karte. Lund 1962. 36 Kr.

... "gehört das Buch von Å' zum Besten, was in den letzten Jahren über die mykenische Zeit geschrieben wurde, schon wegen der ständig von ihm geübten Kritik und der Skepsis, mit der er von anderen allzu gern als gesichert betrachtete Tatbestände unter die Lupe nimmt." E. Bielefeld, *Erasmus*

... "cette documentation magistrale ... fournira désormais la base indispensable de toutes les études d'histoire mycénienne, qu'elles concernent les invasions doriennes ou le rôle de sauvegarde joué par l'Attique dans ce bouleversement." J. Deshayes, *Les Études Grecques*.

"Altogether this is an important piece of work notable for its objectivity and caution." F. H. Stubbings, *The Classical Review*.

"Il libro è in sostanza un completo e perciò utilissimo repertorio topografico, i cui dati sono riassunti in quadri statistici settoriali e generali ... L'interesse del lavoro, per la sua precisione e completezza, va molto al di là della schedatura topografica e stratigrafica e contribuisce notevolmente alla interpretazione storica di un problema gravissimo qual'è quello della formazione stessa della civiltà greca ..." G. A. Mansuelli, *Athenaeum*.

"Serien inleddes lysande med en arkeologisk bestseller, dr Per Ålins viktiga och mycket uppmärksammade avhandling ..., en grundläggande studie över den väldiga kulturkatastrof som under 1200-talet f.Kr. gjorde slut på den mykenska kulturen." C. Nylander, *Svenska Dagbladet*.

"a careful, scholarly and most useful study." *Archaeology*.

Vol. II. Paul Åström, Excavations at Kalopsidha and Ayios Iakovos in Cyprus. With Contributions by Several Scholars. 234 pp., 12 figs. in the text, 51 plates with 213 figs. Lund 1966. 133 Crs.

Publication of the results of excavations at two Bronze Age sites in Cyprus. The chapter on the pottery includes Cypriote, Mycenaean and Syro-Palestinian fabrics. The author also gives a corpus of Cypriote relief bands and pot-marks ("C'est un vrai Corpus, beaucoup plus vaste que je ne le pensais, et il pourrait servir de modèle pour des recherches analogues." O. Masson). There are several appendices written by specialists: H. Helbaek on imprints of grain, N.-G. Gejvall on the osteological material, O. Masson on Cypro-Minoan inscriptions, R. S. Merrillees on an Early Cypriote tomb group, M. R. Popham on White Slip Ware, T. Wieselgren on Iron Age sherds, T. Watkins on the bronzes, S. A. Eriksson on fingerprints, S. Bottema on pollen analyses and H. E. J. Biggs on mollusca.

"Förf.s arbete är substantiellt, det står på en hög vetenskaplig nivå i metodiskt avseende och är rikt på nya synpunkter och uppslag ... Jag kan intyga att det är en fascinerande upplevelse att ta del av de iakttagelser, som förf. har gjort, och av de slutsatser, vartill han har kommit." E. Gjerstad.

"It is a major work ... especially up-to-date in the use of scientific techniques to get the maximum information from the remains." P. Warren.

"I must congratulate you on what must be the most meticulously recorded and published dig ever undertaken in Cyprus." Personal letter from Dr R. S. Merrillees, dated 18th June 1966.

"Cette publication fait grand honneur à son auteur et à la collection qu'il dirige." R. de V., *Revue biblique*.

"Das vorliegende Buch und die ihm zugrundeliegende Ausgrabung dürfen in vieler Hinsicht als vorbildlich gelten." H.-G. Buchholz, *Gnomon*.

"Ce rapport est présenté avec un remarquable souci de précision, poussé jusque dans le détail." P. Amiet, *Syria*.

"P. Åström nous donne un modèle d'étude avec la publication des trouvailles faites à Kalopsidha." M. Yon, *Rev. arch.*

Vol. III. J. R. Stewart, Corpus of Early Cypriote Material. In preparation.

The late Professor J. R. Stewart compiled a corpus of all the Early Cypriote pottery and other arts and crafts which he could trace; he founded his corpus on the excavations of the Swedish Cyprus Expedition and the excavations at Vounous, but included material from other excavations and museums; it also deals with material imported from overseas at the period. This Corpus was originally designed to be part of The Swedish Cyprus Expedition vol. IV: 1, but it proved to be too long. However it is indispensable for anyone using SCE IV: I since it explains the typology of the material; it would be invaluable for anybody who had to sort and classify Cypriote material. The Early Cypriote period was not an isolated phase; the corpus deals with pottery imported from Crete and Syria and the relations with the Aegean, Anatolia, Syria, Palestine and Egypt are dealt with throughout the corpus.

Vol. IV. Paul Åström, The Cuirass Tomb and Other Finds at Dendrá. In preparation.

The finds from the excavations in 1960, 1962 and 1963 at Dendrá in the Argolid will be published in this volume. The unique discovery of a Mycenaean cuirass in tomb 12 at Dendrá focuses particular attention on the circumstances of its finding, the architecture of the tomb and the pottery uncovered in it. A detailed account of the Mycenaean chamber tombs Nos. 13 and 14 and the destruction layer in the Acropolis of Midea will also be given.

Vol. V. Mervyn R. Popham. The Last Days of the Palace at Knossos — Complete Vases of the Late Minoan III B Period. 28 pp., 9 plates, 56 illustrations. Lund 1964. 30 Crs.

"Popham's work is the most important contribution to Knossian archaeology for a long while." J. Boardman, *The Classical Review.*

"Eine ausserordentlich interessante Untersuchung zur sog. reoccupation period von Knossos verdanken wir Mervyn R. Popham." F. Schachermeyr, *Anzeiger für die Altertumswissenschaft.*

"M. Popham nous apporte, avec ce petit volume, une contribution de première importance à l'histoire de Cnossos. En publiant ces vases du M. R. III B qu'Evans avait dédaigné de nous faire connaître, et en localisant dans toute la mesure du possible l'exacte provenance d'après les carnets du fouilleur ou ceux de Mackenzie, l'auteur nous invite à partager sa conviction que cette période correspond bien à une phase de réoccupation consécutive à la destruction du palais proprement dit." J. Deshayes, *Revue des Études Anciennes.*

Vol. VI. Fritz Schachermeyr, Das ägäische Neolithikum. 16 S., 20 Abb. Lund 1964. 15 Kr.

"Die Arbeit F. Schachermeyrs ist eine glänzende kurze Übersicht der Geschichte der Forschung und ihres heutigen Standes aus der Perspektive des Verfassers... Auf wenigen Seiten wird ein meisterhafter Entwurf geboten, der zuerst die Forschungsgeschichte samt allen ihren Versäumnissen drastisch schildert. In weiteren hebt der Verf. mit recht hervor, dass wir es "in Griechenland mit einer Randprovinz der weit überlegenen Neolith- und Chalkolithkultur Anatoliens" — und wir möchten hinzufügen Vorderasiens — zu tun haben." V. Milojčić, *Germania.*

... "une vue d'ensemble très suggestive du néolithique égéen." J. Deshayes, *Revue des Études Grecques.*

"Of special interest in the bibliographical respect is Schachermeyr's *Das ägäische Neolithikum,* which contains a fairly exhaustive bibliography on prehistoric remains in the Aegean area and would be a valuable possession for its bibliography alone." E. L. Ochsenschlager, *The Classical World.*

"Est-il besoin d'ajouter que nul n'était plus qualifié, pour présenter avec maîtrise un tel sujet, que l'éminent spécialiste auquel nous devons tant de fondamentales contributions, livres de synthèse ou *Berichte* chargés de science ?" H. Gallet de Santerre, *Revue des Études Anciennes.*

Vol. VII. George E. Mylonas, Grave Circle B of Mycenae. 10 pp., 10 + 1 figs. Lund 1964. 15 Crs.

"Professor Mylonas' essay on Grave Circle B at Mycenae is a model of conciseness and, incidentally, of modesty." L. B. L., *The Classical Outlook.*

... "a succinct, informative and readable account of the Graves and their contents, followed by a good bibliography." F. H. Stubbings, *The Journal of Hellenic Studies.*

"Les fouilles du cercle de tombes A, à Mycènes, menées à une époque où les méthodes archéologiques étaient encore peu développées, avaient laissé beaucoup de problèmes en suspens. L'auteur, après l'avoir rappelé, signale que la découverte du cercle B, fouillé de 1952 à 1954, permit d'en résoudre quelques-uns. C'est ainsi que, par une étude minutieuse, on a pu reconstituer très exactement les différentes phases de la construction de ces tombes, de même que de l'enterrement des morts: la description de ces opérations occupe la plus grande partie de l'ouvrage. Les offrandes, les armes et les bijoux, trouvés auprès des corps, permettent, par ailleurs, de préciser que ces tombes furent utilisées de 1650 à 1550 environ avant notre ère et que, pour la plupart, elles sont contemporaines de celles du cercle A." R. Vanderivière, *L'Antiquité Classique.*

Vol. VIII. Maurice Pope, Aegean Writing and Linear A. 16 pp., 7 figs. Lund 1964. 15 Crs.

"Professor Maurice Pope gives a useful and sober assessment of the present state of Linear A decipherment with a full bibliography." *The Times Literary Supplement.*

"P.'s kritische Darstellung der Forschungssituation ist ausgezeichnet durch Sachkenntnis, durch den unbestechlichen Blick für das Wichtige und Mögliche und durch die Fähigkeit des Vf.s, ein komplexes und schwieriges Problem klar zu durchleuchten und scharf zu formulieren; wir wünschen die Arbeit den Erfolg, den sie verdient." A. Heubeck, *Bibliotheca Orientalis.*

"Brève et objective mise au point (avec bibliographie, et quatre pages d'illustrations) des problèmes posés par les écritures égéennes du second millénaire (crétois hiéroglyphique; linéaire A; linéaire B; écritures chypriotes; poteries marquées de Lipari et de Lerne; disque de

Phaistos), toutes indéchiffrées sauf le linéaire B. L'accent est mis surtout sur les diverses hypothèses concernant la langue des textes en linéaire A (l'auteur n'y décèle pas, comme fait V. Georgiev, deux langues distinctes); de chacune de ces hypothèses, l'auteur définit le poids, et les faiblesses." M. Lejeune, *Revue des Études Anciennes.*

"eine vortreffliche Übersicht." F. Schachermeyr, *Ägäis und Orient.*

"Pope gives an excellent brief clear judicious statement of the problem and of where our studies stand at the moment... Papers like this are much needed and do a great service... The whole series is excellent." J. L. Caskey.

Vol. IX. Agnes Sakellariou, Die mykenische Siegelglyptik. 11 S., 14 Abb. Lund 1964. 15 Kr.

"The appearance of a monograph dealing with Mycenaean seal glyptic is something of an historic event, since this seems to be the first publication entirely devoted to the subject." V. E. G. Kenna, *The Journal of Hellenic Studies.*

"In her essay on seals and seal impressions, Agnes Sakellariou stresses the importance of these small objects for an understanding of religion and life in prehistoric Crete and Greece... Like other authors in the series, she gives the reader a great deal of information in remarkably brief compass." L. B. L., *The Classical Outlook.*

"Mme Agnès Sakellariou, qui a fait ses preuves en publiant les cachets minoens de la collection Giamalakis à Héraklion, analyse avec finesse les qualités propres de la glyptique mycénienne et en dégage l'originalité par rapport à la glyptique crétoise." H. Gallet de Santerre, *Revue des Études Classiques.*

"Sakellariou... a surtout essayé de nous retracer la genèse et l'évolution de la glyptique mycénienne dans ses rapports avec la Crète. Beaucoup d'aperçus intéressants et judicieux nous sont présentés concernant le parallélisme de ses deux arts et leur opposition tout de même radicale." J. Deshayes, *Revue des Études Grecques.*

Vol. X. Hector W. Catling, Mycenaean Bronzes. In preparation.

Vol. XI. Doro Levi, The Recent Excavations at Phaistos. 40 pp. 59 figs. and plans. Lund 1964. 35 Crs.

"It is a useful summary in English, quite well illustrated." J. Boardman, *The Classical Review.*

"Zeer belangrijk overzicht van de recente onderzoekingen in het Paleis te Phaistos met goede plans en foto's, die nauwkeurig worden toeglicht. Aan het slot is een kleine chronologische tabel toegevoegd en een bibliographie." L. Byvanck-Quarles van Ufford, *Bulletin van de antieke Beschaving.*

"C'est une excellente initiative de P. Åström que la publication en anglais, sous la forme d'un volume indépendant, de l'important article de Doro Levi consacré aux récentes fouilles de Phaistos. Il s'agit en effet, en attendant la publication définitive des remarquables découvertes de l'École italienne, de l'exposé le plus synthétique que nous ait donné jusqu'ici son directeur. De nombreuses figures, accompagnées chacune d'un commentaire, illustrent le texte, dont l'ordre se veut à juste titre essentiellement chronologique." J. Deshayes, *Revue des Études Anciennes.*

"In dankenswerter Weise gibt Doro Levi einen Überblick über *The Recent Excavations at Phaistos.* Es handelt sich dabei nicht nur um eine detaillierte Aufzählung der Grabungsergebnisse, sondern vor allem um einen Abriss der Bau- und Besiedlungsgeschichte von Phaistos, so wie sie der Ausgräber jetzt zu erkennen glaubt." F. Schachermeyr, *Anzeiger für die Altertumswissenschaft.*

Vol. XII. Mervyn Popham, The Destruction of the Palace at Knossos. Pottery of the Late Minoan III A Period. 111 pp., 17 figs., 50 plates. Göteborg 1970. 125 Crs.

Vol. XIII. Manolis Andronicos, Vergina, the Prehistoric Necropolis and the Hellenistic Palace. 11 pp., 15 figs. Lund 1964. 15 Crs.

"In Volume XIII Professor Manolis Andronikos expounds Vergina in Macedonia, some interesting early iron-age tombs with links both to central Europe and to Greece, and a fine Hellenistic palace with a superb floral mosaic." *The Times Literary Supplement.*

"Aus diesem Heftchen erfährt der Leser in kürzester Form, dass bei Vergina in Makedonien Hügelgräber mit 220 Bestattungen (davon zwei Brandbestattungen) untersucht worden sind. Nach den Beigaben (Keramik, bronzene Schmuckgegenstände, eiserne Waffen, ein bronzenes Schwert) schliesst der Verfasser auf die ersten drei Jahrhunderte des ersten Jahrtausends v.Chr. Die grosse Zahl der Bestattungen lässt erwarten, dass ihre, von Andronicos in Aussicht gestellte genaue Veröffentlichung wertvolle archäologische und kulturgeschichtliche Aufschlüsse bringen wird. In dem Heftchen wird auch über die hellenistische Villa bei Vergina berichtet, deren bereits 1861 von L. Heuzey begonnene, seit 1937 fortgesetzte Ausgrabung hoffentlich ebenfalls eine abschliessende Publikation bekommen wird." L. Franz, *Anzeiger für die Altertumswissenschaft.*

Vol. XIV. Photios M. Petsas, Pella. 8 pp., map, 6 figs. Lund 1964. 10 Crs.

Vol. XV. W. Schwabacher, Neue Methoden in der griechischen Münzforschung. 11 S., 10 Abb. Lund 1964. 15 Kr.

"Kurzgefasster Überblick die Entwicklung und die neuesten Methoden in der griechischen Numismatik — der kürzeste, eindringlichste und beste, der mir bisher in die Hand gekommen ist. Jeder Althistoriker, jeder Student der Alten Geschichte under jeder Sammler griechischer Münzen sollte ihn gelesen haben (und womöglich die gewonnene Einsicht — jeder auf seine Weise — auch anwenden)." R. Göbl, *Mitteilungen der Österreichischen Numismatischen Gesellschaft.*

"Cet exposé constitue une excellente initiation aux méthodes actuelles de la recherche numismatique. Une bibliographie choisie l'accompagne." J. Marcadé, *Revue des Études Anciennes.*

Vol. XVI. J. Roger Davis and T. B. L. Webster, Cesnola Terracottas in the Stanford University Museum. 28 pp., 6 plates, 61 illustrations. Lund 1964. 20 Crs.

"In the five thousand duplicates from the Cesnola Collection of Cypriote antiquities which Leland Stanford acquired from the Metropolitan Museum were many hundreds of terracotta figurines. Of these 446 are catalogued briefly here, many of them in groups; sixty-one are fairly well illustrated. However, it is important to know what is where, and such brief publications of large masses of material are welcome." *Archaeology.*

"T. B. L. Webster a, pour ce catalogue, utilisé celui de J. Rogers Davis, qu'il a complété et modifié en certains endroits. Les terres-cuites de la collection Cesnola existant au musée de l'université Stanford y sont décrites avec beaucoup de précision : ces pièces cypriotes remontent, pour les plus anciennes, à la fin de l'âge du bronze ; les plus récentes sont, elles, d'époque romaine. Quant au dernier chapitre, il est consacré à des terres-cuites de facture étrangère, mais importées à Chypre. Les multiples références à des publications récentes, les comparaisons nombreuses avec d'autres terres-cuites, ainsi que les photographies rassemblées à la fin de cet ouvrage en rendent la consultation des plus fructueuses." R. Vanderivière, *L'Antiquité Classique.*

Vol. XVII. Homer L. Thomas, Near Eastern, Mediterranean and European Chronology. The Historical, Archaeological, Radiocarbon, Pollenanalytical and Geochronological Evidence. 1. Text. 175 pp., 2. Charts. (62). Lund 1967. 100 Crs.

An archaeological chronology for southwestern Asia, the Mediterranean, and Europe from the end of the Paleolithic to about 1200 B.C. It is based primarily upon archaeological evidence but utilizes the new methods of dating which have become current during the last decade. Before 3000 B.C., the choice between a high or low chronology when allowed by the archaeological evidence has been determined by radiocarbon determinations, palynological evidence and geological data. After the beginning of the historic civilizations in Egypt and the Near East, the absolute chronologies of cultures in the Mediterranean and Europe have been based upon a high historical chronology. An attempt has been made to include the majority of recently excavated sites important for chronology as well as to include the more important radiocarbon determinations.

"An exceedingly important recent contribution has been made in synthesizing the historical, archaeological, radiocarbon, pollenanalytical and geochronological evidence for the Near East, the Mediterranean and Europe. This work concentrates on the time period between 10,000 to 1200 B.C. and incorporates invaluable charts, which correlate the relative and absolute chronologies for the above areas." C. C. Lamberg-Karlovsky, *Annals of the American Academy of Political and Social Sciences.*

"Thomas's book will be much in demand as a handy, well-organized compendium of up-to-date information from many sources bearing on chronological problems. Students in particular should find it of much interest and value." Merrillees, *Antiquity.*

"Mit einem unwahrscheinlichen Fleiss hat der Verfasser zusammengetragen, was ihm als Zeit-Indiz für die archaeologisch unterschiedenen Kulturen im Raum von Turkestan bis zum atlantischen Ozean dienlich schien . . ." "es ist ein bahnbrechendes Werk." F. Cornelius, *Bibliotheca Orientalis.*

Vol. XVIII. Robert S. Merrillees, The Cypriote Bronze Age Pottery Found in Egypt. XVIII + 217 pp., 37 plates, 4 maps. Lund 1968. 150 Crs.

The book is a valuable addition to our knowledge of Cypriote contacts with other Levantine states in the Bronze Age, and a useful introduction to the relative chronology of the Egyptian XVIIIth Dynasty. While laying some claim to an almost exhaustive compilation of published references to identifiable Cypriote pottery from Egypt, it does not pretend to have done any more than prepare the way for a careful and thorough examination of the small finds, including pottery, of Egyptian origin belonging to the New Kingdom, with a view particularly to establishing valid dating criteria. It has nevertheless broken new ground in its treatment of Cypriote pottery abroad, its approach to the problems of dating objects in Egypt, and in its interpretation of the documents and paintings which supply most of the data of historical reconstruction. The volume is of interest and importance to all who are engaged in studying external relations in the Late Bronze Age Levant.

"une étude telle que le catalogue de R. S. Merrillees mérite d'être largement connue et appréciée par les égyptologues." J. Leclant, Professeur à la Sorbonne.

"Cet ouvrage doit être bien accueilli par tous ceux qu'intéresse l'histoire de la Méditerranée orientale au IIe millénaire av. J.-C." L. Courtois and J. Lagarce, *Syria.*

Vol. XIX. Keith Branigan, Copper and Bronze Working in Early Bronze Age Crete. 122 pp., 4 graphs, 13 figs. Lund 1968. 75 Crs.

The book is a detailed analysis of the development of metallurgy in Crete during the period from E.M. I to M.M. It comprises a comprehensive catalogue of copper and bronze objects and seven chapters of discussion. An introductory chapter is followed by four chapters devoted to the typology, origins and development of the copper and bronze artifacts o fthe Minoan Early Bronze Age. A sixth chapter discusses the metallurgical techniques employed by the Early Minoan metalworkers, and the sources of copper, tin, silver, and lead which they may have utilised. The concluding chapter outlines the main characteristics of Early Minoan metallurgy and attempts to assess its importance to the development of Minoan civilisation. Early Minoan imports and exports of metal objects are considered in an appendix. The catalogue contains about four hundred and fifty entries, classified according to the typology discussed in chapters two to five. The system of classification is designed so as to enable newly discovered artifacts to be entered in their appropriate place in the catalogue. Both the catalogue and the discussion emphasise the richness and inventiveness of Minoan metallurgy in the third millennium B.C., and provide a comprehensive survey and corpus of extant material.

"This monograph is a welcome and valuable contribution to our understanding of the origins of European metallurgy." Renfrew, *Antiquity*.

Vol. XX. Corpus of Cypriote Antiquities. 1. Paola Villa, Early and Middle Bronze Age Pottery of the Cesnola Collection in the Stanford University Museum. With a Foreword by Paul Åström. 53 pp., XIX plates, 260 figs. Lund 1969. 40 Crs.

"I applaud the idea of publishing Cypriote pottery collections in as comprehensive and detailed a way as this, and think that this volume will lay the foundations for a very valuable series of similar publications." Dr R. S. Merrillees.

"Tout est de qualité irréprochable." A. Wankenne, *Les Études Classiques*.

Vol. XX. Corpus of Cypriote Antiquities. 2. In preparation.

Vol. XX. Corpus of Cypriote Antiquities. 3. V. E. G. Kenna, Catalogue of the Cypriote Seals of the Bronze Age in the British Museum. 41 pp., 32 plates. Göteborg 1971. 60 Crs.

Vol. XX. Corpus of Cypriote Antiquities. 4. Haluk Ergüleç, Large-Sized Cypriot Sculpture in the Archaeological Museums of Istanbul. 73 pp., 62 plates. Göteborg 1972. 60 Crs.

Vol. XXI. Elsa Gullberg and Paul Åström, The Thread of Ariadne. A Study of Ancient Greek Dress. 53 pp., 28 figs. Göteborg 1970. 50 Crs.

Observations about ancient Greek dress and textile fibres written by a textile expert and an archaeologist for the layman and specialist.

"I found it quite exciting to have so many of my familiar friends viewed from a novel point of view—i. e. not from their place in the development of Greek art but from how their garments were executed. This is an important contribution to our studies." G. M. A. Richter.

"This small publication is a *must* not only for students of technique and materials but also for critics of sculpture." D. K. Hill, *American Journal of Archaeology*.

Vol. XXII. Niki Scoufopoulos, Mycenaean Citadels. 169 pp., 16 plans, 78 figs., 5 maps. Göteborg 1970. 90 Crs.

Vol. XXIII. Who's Who in Cypriote Archaeology. 88 pp. Göteborg 1971. 65 Crs.

Vol. XXIV. V. E. G. Kenna, The Cretan Talismanic Stone in the Late Minoan Age. 35 pp., 26 plates, 279 figs. Lund 1969. 60 Crs.

The use of the Talismanic stone is an invention peculiar to Ancient Crete and believed to be without precedent in the Ancient World. Too often ignored or believed to be merely a survival of peasant art, here it receives a considered analysis and appreciation, with the result that it throws some light on the complex character of seal use in the Late Minoan Age, reveals a further difference between Crete and Helladic Greece, and by allowing a more detailed estimate of the glyptic of Late Minoan III, also makes its contribution to the chronology of the destruction levels at Knossos.

Vol. XXV. Ora Negbi, The Hoards of Goldwork from Tell el-Ajjul. 55 pp., 5 plates, 35 figs. Göteborg 1970. 50 Crs.

"This is a model publication of an important, and often neglected, subject." R. A. Higgins, *The Journal of Hellenic Studies*.

Vol. XXVI. Leon Pomerance, The Final Collapse of Santorini. 32 pp., 7 + 1 figs. Göteborg 1970. 25 Crs.

Vol. XXVII. Marie-Louise Säflund, The East Pediment of the Temple of Zeus at Olympia. A Reconstruction and Interpretation of Its Composition. 201 pp., 106 figs. Göteborg 1970. 100 Crs.

"Uns scheint es, dass mit der sorgfältigen und reich illustrierten Studie Marie-Louise Säflunds eines der grossen traditionellen Probleme der archäologischen Interpretation gelöst worden ist . . ." H. P. Isler, *Neue Zürcher Zeitung*.

Vol. XXVIII. Sven A. Eriksson and Paul Åström, Fingerprints and Archaeology. In preparation.

Vol. XXIX. Jan Bouzek, Aegean, Anatolia and Europe: cultural interrelations during the second millennium B.C. In preparation.

Vol. XXX. St. Alexiou and P. Warren, The Early Minoan Tombs of Lebena. In preparation.

Vol. XXXI. Studies in the Cypro-Minoan Scripts. 1. Emilia Masson, Étude de vingt-six boules d'argile inscrites trouvées à Enkomi et Hala Sultan Tekke (Chypre). 38 pages, 34 figures, 3 planches. Göteborg 1971. 50 Couronnes.

Vol. XXXII. Gudrun Ahlberg, Prothesis and Ekphora in Greek Geometric Art. Text, 327 pp. Figures, 68 figs. Göteborg 1971. 250 Crs.

Vol. XXXIII. John C. Overbeck and Stuart Swiny, Two Cypriot Bronze Age Sites at Kafkallia (Dhali). 31 pp., 55 figs. Göteborg 1972. 55 Crs.

Vol. XXXIV. Paavo Roos, The Rock-Tombs of Caunus. 1. The Architecture. 124 pp., 6 figs., 62 plates. Göteborg 1972. 100 Crs.
2. The Finds. 61 pp., 17 plates. Göteborg 1974. 40 Crs.

Vol. XXXV. Sarantis Symeonoglou, Kadmeia I. Mycenaean Finds from Thebes, Greece. Excavation at 14 Oedipus St. 106 pp., 274 figs. Göteborg 1973. 100 Crs.

Vol. XXXVI. J. L. Benson, The Necropolis of Kaloriziki. 138 pp., 63 plates. Göteborg 1973. 150 Crs.

This volume, prepared by Professor J. L. Benson, gives a definitive account of a large portion of the necropolis in the coastal plain of Kaloriziki in southwest Cyprus (below the hill of Bamboula on the site of Kourion), which was excavated by J. F. Daniel and others. This necropolis, which includes the famous Sceptre Tomb, was established before the final abandonment of the Late Bronze Age settlement and continued throughout the Iron Age. Its tomb-types and artefacts mirror the process of the blending of settlers from Greece with autochthonous Cypriotes; this assumes a special importance since the main settlement which it served (in the early phases of the Cypro-Geometric Age, at least) has not yet been located. The necropolis thus becomes a valuable source for historical inferences.

The catalogue of finds categorizes over 1100 objects, including pottery, jewelry and glyptics. Professor Edith Porada has contributed a section on glyptics, and Dr H. W. Catling presents a discussion of a unique bronze shield. An important feature of the volume is a critical study of the so-called Proto-White Painted pottery which, taken with White Painted ware, provides the surest framework for understanding how the Bronze Age expired and the Iron Age was born at this site. In effect, the pottery (and pottery studies) pertaining to Bamboula and Kaloriziki interlock in an inextricable way which underlines the fact that there was no interruption in the continuity of civilized life in this important town in Cyprus.

Vol. XXXVII. Philip C. Hammond, The Nabataeans—Their History, Culture and Archaeology. 129 pp., 4 maps. Göteborg 1973. 100 Crs.

Vol. XXXVIII. James R. Stewart, Tell el ʿAjjūl. The Middle Bronze Age Remains. Edited and prepared for publication by Hanna E. Kassis. With appendices by W. F. Albright, K. M. Kenyon and R. S. Merrillees. In preparation.

Vol. XXXIX. R. S. Merrillees, Trade and Transcendence in the Bronze Age Levant. In preparation.

Vol. XL. Gloria S. Merker, The Hellenistic Sculpture of Rhodes. 34 pp., 34 plates, 84 figs. Göteborg 1973. 50 Crs.

Vol. XLI. Charlotte R. Long, The Ayia Triadha Sarcophagus. A Study of Late Minoan and Mycenaean Funerary Practices and Beliefs. In preparation.

Vol. XLII. David Frankel, Middle Cypriot White Painted Pottery. An Analytical Study of the Decoration. VIII + 106 pp., 9 tables, 19 figs. Göteborg 1974. C. 40 Crowns.

Vol. XLIII. Kyriakos Nicolaou, The Historical Topography of Kition. In preparation.

In preparation:

- O. Dickinson, The Origins of Mycenaean Civilisation.
- R. Hope Simpson and O. Dickinson, A Gazetteer of Aegean Civilisation in the Bronze Age. The Mainland and the Islands.
- V. Karageorghis, P. Åström and others, Hala Sultan Tekke I.
- Christoph W. Clairmont, Excavations at Salona, Yugoslavia.
- Ruth Amiran, Early Arad.